MOUNT MARY COLLEGE LIBRARY
Milwaukee, Wisconsin 53222

ISABEL AND THE SEA

George Millar was born in Scotland, and began a career as a journalist in Fleet Street just before the war began. He wrote of his war adventures in two famous books, *Horned Pigeon* and *Maquis*. After the war, he and his wife Isabel sailed their ketch *Truant* through the canals of France, and through the Mediterranean to Greece. The story of this journey is *Isabel and the Sea*, first published by Heinemann in 1948.

Not only were George Millar and his wife completely unqualified to navigate a thirty-one ton ketch through the waterways of Europe, but any unofficial journey into Europe so soon after the war was considered to be something of an adventure and was fraught with hazards. The story of how they achieved it is packed with marvellous anecdotes about the people and adventures they encountered en route.

'A delightful travel book.' *The Daily Mail*

'A long, packed and very readable book and . . . a return to travelling for pleasure.' V. S. Pritchett in the *Bookman*

D0841353

Also available in the Century Travellers series:

A TRAMP ABROAD by Mark Twain*
Introduction by Norman Lewis

EOTHEN by A. W. Kinglake*
Introduction by Jonathan Raban

SOUTHERN CROSS TO POLE STAR by A. F. Tschiffeley*
Introduction by Eric Newby

HOLY RUSSIA by Fitzroy Maclean

THE VALLEYS OF THE ASSASSINS by Freya Stark

THE SOUTHERN GATES OF ARABIA by Freya Stark

FORBIDDEN JOURNEY by Ella Maillart*
Introduction by Dervla Murphy

FULL TILT by Dervla Murphy

A RIDE TO KHIVA by Fred Burnaby*
Introduction by Eric Newby

THE GOLDEN CHERSONESE by Isabella Bird*
Introduction by Robin Hanbury-Tenison

VISITS TO MONASTERIES IN THE LEVANT by Robert Curzon*
Introduction by John Julius Norwich

THE TOMB OF TUTANKHAMEN by Howard Carter
Introduction by John Romer

LORDS OF THE ATLAS by Gavin Maxwell*
Introduction by Geoffrey Moorhouse

SOUTH by Sir Ernest Shackleton*
Introduction by Lord Hunt

ONE MAN'S MEXICO by John Lincoln*
Introduction by Nicolas Cheetham

OLD CALABRIA by Norman Douglas*

* published in association with Gentry Books

MOUNT MARY COLLEGE LIBRARY
Milwaukee, Wisconsin 53222

WITHDRAWN

Isabel and the Sea

GEORGE MILLAR

CENTURY PUBLISHING
LONDON

HIPPOCRENE BOOKS INC.
NEW YORK

84-3266

All rights reserved

First published in Great Britain in 1948 by
William Heinemann Ltd

This edition published 1983 by
Century Publishing Co. Ltd
76 Old Compton Street, London W1V 5PA

Published in the United States of America by
Hippocrene Books Inc.
171 Madison Avenue
New York, NY 10016

ISBN 0 7126 0151 1

*The cover shows a detail of 'Le Canal Saint Martin'
by Alfred Sisley*

Printed in Great Britain by
Richard Clay (The Chaucer Press) Ltd, Bungay, Suffolk

910.4
M61

PREFACE

THIS book is an account of a voyage—I dislike the word cruise—in a thirty-one ton ketch from England to Greece, and I feel it my duty to give warning in the first sentence that the voyage was undertaken by two people one of whom knew little, and the other nothing, about seamanship; those who demand a certain technical soundness from authors who write of the sea should read no further. To spare the feelings of such readers I had thought of sending my manuscript to be corrected by a friend who has designed and sailed yachts for many years; but if I sent such a dressed-up work to the publisher the expert's knowledge would pass off as my own, and I should be guilty of a pretence which, in a book of this type, I should regard as dishonest. Experts will surely notice passages that annoy or amuse them, if only because my nautical terminology is well-intentioned, but self-learned and shaky. At any rate the reader will not be able to say that the author pretends to be anything but a landsman who made a journey by water. Perhaps other landsmen, influenced by our experiences of the simplicity of this form of travel, its excitements, and its advantages, will undertake similar excursions. I like to think so.

Soon after the successful Nazi parachute invasion of Crete a wounded New Zealand soldier escaped from the island in a twenty-foot sailing boat manned by three devoted Cretans. The New Zealander lay on a bed of soft hay arranged on the floorboards. He had never previously been in a sailing boat, and he paid no heed to the mysteries of the boat's progress until, during the second night of their passage, a German aircraft dropped a flare and machine-gunned to such purpose that two of the Cretans were killed and the third mortally wounded. The New Zealander plugged the bullet-holes in the boat's planking, attended to the wounded man, and slid the two corpses into the sea; then he began to experiment with sheet and tiller. Six days later, when he had beached the boat on a North African shore, he was asked by an officer how he had managed so well to sail and to navigate. "I made do," he answered.

Some people maintained that the New Zealander was abnormally lucky, and that he was an exceptionally clever and courageous man; but I feel inclined to believe that in his position most men would have made do.

Isabel and I left England at a time when any unofficial journey into

Europe was considered to be something of an adventure, when the internal conditions of France, Italy, and Greece (to mention only the three countries that we visited) were unstable, and supplies of many commodities—some of them entirely necessary to us—were uncertain. We thought of the Hamble River, a pleasant backwater near Southampton, as the climber's base camp, and of Europe as the mountain looming beyond. The mountain, we were well aware, would test us as well as showing us new aspects of itself. Before departing, then, we sought the help of a wise friend, the Hon. Frank Hopwood, and I should like here to assure him of our grateful recognition of the benefits of his far-seeing and practical advice, which served us well in dealing with scores of matters with which I have seldom dared to strain my readers' patience.

We sailed when any ordinary resident in Britain was allowed to take only £75 out of the country to pay his foreign travelling expenses for a twelvemonth, and although our voyage was astonishingly economical we could not have made it without some additional supply of currency. I should like to acknowledge my debt to the editors of the *Daily Express* of London and *Holiday* of Philadelphia, each of whom published certain accounts of our passage through Europe written by me. Thus qualifying for official recognition as a member of that heterogeneous and ridiculously over-pampered caste, the journalists, I was granted letter-of-credit facilities by the Bank of England.

I must also thank Mr. John Henry Mueller, the Swiss author, who—although we were then strangers—took the photograph of *Truant* appearing as a frontispiece in this book. He took it at Portofino, immediately after our arrival there.

Fordingbridge, 1947.

ISABEL AND THE SEA

1

ENGLAND in the winter cold. The trees hid their patterns against a sky so thick that no man could say where cloud ended and free air began. How romantic the hanging sky, drooping into the outlines of the earth! Although we were at sea level when we walked out of the Swan Hotel and under the railway bridge we had the sensation that climbers know as they near a summit, the sensation of finding a new earth in the sky. A main road led to Southampton behind us and to Portsmouth ahead, the surface shining from soft rain that had but stopped, that soon would fall again. Motor-cars passed filled with men of sombre aspect, the small, box-shaped cars of our dear, impoverished land; silver splashes rose like the wings on Ariel's ankles from their busy wheels. Not two hundred yards from the door of the Swan we came to the Hamble River, still tidal in that part, though far enough from the sea. I leaned on the parapet of the bridge to look down on the mudbanks, tufts of weed and rushes, boats drawn from the water at Deacon's yard, and a white ketch moored fore and aft in midstream. The delight that takes hold of me on arrival at the edge of salt water obliged me to stop there, on the bridge. I looked at the sobbing water of the ebb; at the jersey and seaboots of a man sculling himself in a dinghy to the moored yacht; at the dark, tarry wood of the props holding the boats upright on the oozy land; at the water birds, primeval and impersonal.

Isabel had no wish to loiter on the bridge; to her the water was only water, the boats were only boats. She walked on, tapping her small feet precisely on the footpath that was separated from the roadway by a line of grass. Her compact figure, as I turned to follow, my eyes weeping from the cold, seemed to pass under each figure it encountered, a wren darting nearly beneath the wings of rooks. I overtook her before we turned into Moody's yard and passed with her between the cowled shapes of hibernating yachts to the edge of the water, where the colonel stood.

A tall man, white-skinned, red-haired, his face showed a mixture of *bonhomie* and the wary dignity of the recently demobilised senior officer. Isabel had discovered the colonel, and had a proprietorial regard for him.

1

He was an energetic man, carried from move to move in the game of selling and buying yachts for profit by an energy that seemed to come in hot puffs like the strong, regular exhaust beat of a heavy engine. He was respectably dressed in the tweedy costume of a countryman, with a soft hat pulled hard down over his hair.

"I have been wondering if *Truant* might not suit you," he said. "I know she is on the big side for two of you to manage without help." As he spoke he moved gently off, and then stopped before a line of boats perched up, their keels raised from the earth mixed with sawdust on which we stood.

"You mean that great big black one?" Isabel asked.

"A grand sea-boat," the colonel answered.

"What tonnage?" I asked.

"Thirty-one, yacht measurement, or thereabouts. Of course, this is no great sailer; the fishing boat type. Go round the world in this if you like, but the last one I showed you was a far better sailing machine. You have to decide whether you want speed or safety-with-stamina. In this boat also you get comfort, and that is what you are looking for, isn't it?"

"Yes and no," Isabel said.

"What's that crack?" I asked.

"That's not a crack, it's a shake. The oak becomes dry, you know, and opens up; when it's been in the water for a week or two that oak will be stronger than iron again. She's been laid up since the beginning of the war. Rather sad to see her here," his voice softened, but his eyes flickered over my face.

"Why is she for sale?"

"I was just going to tell you. The former owner died at the beginning of the war. He was devoted to the old boat. His executors wish to sell."

"How old is she?"

"Built in 1919, at Looe, in Cornwall. It was a fishing boat hull, Looe lugger type, you know, and the former owner bought her before she had been completed for fishing and altered her to suit his own ideas. She's done more foreign work than most of them around here. She's been to Norway, Finland, Denmark, Sweden, and cruised a lot in German and Dutch waters. Look, Mrs. Millar, is that not pretty?" He had been edging round the boat as he spoke, but now he stopped under the stern, pointing up at two dolphins, carved and gilded, which were set in the transom.

"I like them," Isabel said.

"She looks very big for two people to handle," I said.

"I know she's a solid lump. But wait till you see how handy she is; the former owner had a game leg and he saw to it that all the engine controls

2

were led to the central wheelhouse;" the colonel climbed up a ladder and began to heave at the tarpaulins that covered the deck.

"Wheelhouse!" I called up to him. "I don't like wheelhouses. I want a cockpit . . ." but he had vanished through a hole in the tarpaulins; his voice boomed: "Come along. Afraid it's a little dark and damp, but you should get a good idea of her roominess." Isabel was already near the top of the ladder. When I followed her up I found them both, crouched under the tarpaulins. The wheelhouse was behind them; I opened a door and stepped inside, striking a match. I saw the spokes of the wheel and two panels of engine controls; the place excited me as though I were not thirty-five, but eight years old.

"Pity about the wheelhouse," I said to the colonel as I came out.

"Well," he answered from the darkness where he was trying to open the hatch leading to the forward living accommodation, "if you don't like the wheelhouse you can always have it cut off . . ."

"And leave a stump?"

"Why not? Leave a nice cockpit amidships. It's merely convention that normally puts the cockpit aft. Drat this lighter! Beastly cheap wartime workmanship." There were three flashes, followed by a wavering light. I followed him into the depths.

"This is the saloon," he said.

"It's very roomy."

"Almost a drawing-room, eh? The former owner was a very tall man, taller than me, and he hated stooping. Here's the galley; many a London kitchen's smaller and less convenient." A few old beer bottles lay on a shelf with a tangle of corroded screw nails and pieces of wire and cardboard. "And there's the bathroom, right for'ard. Good-looking W.C. Yes, by jove, the best made. The old boy had everything of the very best. This boat was the apple of his eye. No expense spared. What a mercy she escaped the bombs! There were plenty around here, you know; she was too close to Southampton and Portsmouth to be a good insurance prospect."

"We could make this boat really comfortable," Isabel said. "If I am going to be sick every time we go on the sea, I think I had better be comfortable in the harbours."

I agreed with her. "What engines has she?" I asked the colonel. "And why are the propellers different sizes?"

"A big American engine and one 'Commodore' are fitted just now, but another new 'Commodore', still in its packing-case as delivered by the makers, goes with the boat; the former owner ordered 'Commodores' for the 1939 season, and one of them had not been fitted when war broke out.

3

You will be able to sell the American engine to pay for the expenses of fitting the new one. From the engine point of view you couldn't buy a better-found sailing yacht in the south of England."

"But do these 'Commodores' burn petrol or paraffin?"

"These are petrol engines, so far as I remember."

"Then that settles it. I shall never buy a boat with petrol engines . . ."

"Oh come," the colonel said. "I'll admit that paraffin has a higher margin of safety, and diesels are very good indeed, but petrol has its advantages, you know, and if you look after engines like these reasonably well there is virtually no danger of fire—I should say about as much danger as there is of being eaten by an octopus or a tiger shark if you bathe off Ryde pier. And after all, travelling very short-handed as you intend to do, two convenient petrol engines like these are the ideal solution. Ever had anything to do with diesels? No; I thought not. Well, they can be tricky. Whereas every ex-soldier knows most of the wrinkles regarding a petrol engine. Then these engines are so up-to-date . . . they're a real joy. When you sail into a harbour you can be on deck doing the heavy work while all Mrs. Millar will have to do is press the starter buttons and then, with the twin screws, she will be able to put you exactly where you want to go. Twin screws and flexible engines will save you the devil of a lot of warping, you know."

"I'll never buy a boat with a petrol engine," I repeated. I knew the sentiment to have a good deal of backing in the yachting world, and I had read it the previous evening in a book written by a man who had sailed round the world.

"Why not?" Isabel asked.

"Danger of fire."

"We can forbid all smoking."

I struggled with my memory. "If any exhaust gases leak, they are heavier than air, they fill the bilges and creep forward invisibly; one day you light the cooking stove and the boat vanishes in a sheet of flame."

"But when was this boat built?"

"In 1919," the colonel answered. "As for the creeping gases, such things may sometimes happen, in fact they do, but never on a boat like this. I fear we can't get to the engine-room with all these covers over the decks, but the for'ard part here is completely cut off from the engines by a bulkhead which goes right through her."

Isabel seemed to be on his side. "If it has been constantly used since 1919 and has spent twenty years going to Norway, Finland, Denmark and Sweden without blowing up, why should it blow up with us?"

4

"What is the price?" I asked.

"I couldn't say, offhand. Let's go to the office and find out."

We all climbed down the ladder, and as we walked past an apparatus for casting lead keels we came upon four carpenters who were working under the instructions of an extremely thin man in a grey suit and a flat grey cap. "Ah! here's the man we want . . . Mr. Bundy," the colonel said to the man in the cap, "these are Mr. and Mrs. Millar, who have been looking over *Truant*."

"Oh yes," answered Mr. Bundy in a noncommittal voice.

"Let's see now," continued the colonel, "what price was being asked for her? Was it two thousand guineas?"

"Something like that," Mr. Bundy said.

"Amazingly cheap, when you compare it with the prices most of them are fetching to-day," the colonel exclaimed enthusiastically.

"Well, yes, as prices go it's not too bad," Mr. Bundy agreed in the manner of the craftsman who believes that perhaps the world would be better if money had never been invented. "I'd say it was about double what you'd have had to pay for her before the war, but in comparison to some others, yes, the price is reasonable."

It was double the sum that we had thought of spending.

"She's a fine old ship," the colonel said.

"Solid," corrected Mr. Bundy.

"But is she in good condition?" I asked.

"Well," answered Mr. Bundy, "she was sound enough when we fitted her out for the last season before the war, but of course we can't say, not until she's been thoroughly examined, what has happened to her since she's been laid up, though there should be nothing *seriously* wrong."

"I'd only advise you to buy subject to survey, of course," the colonel interposed. "And I think that if you agreed to the price I mentioned, the owner would make good any bits of rot that might be found. By jove, I hope you buy her. It would be good to see old *Truant* in decent hands. She used to be a sight for sore eyes, roaring down the river there."

"The old girl can hop along, and the owner was never one to waste time," said Mr. Bundy.

"I wish you could see her rigged," the colonel said.

"Plenty of character," agreed Mr. Bundy.

"How is she rigged?" I asked.

"Gaff ketch," replied Mr. Bundy. "She carried a big squaresail yard. The former owner set great store by that yard. He always had it trimmed, even when she was sitting on the mud here."

5

"Are the spars in good condition?" I asked.

"Capital," he answered. "They're all put by. Where would you be thinking of going in her?"

"Through the French canals to the Mediterranean and on to Greece. Do you think the boat is suitable?"

"Properly handled she should go anywhere . . ."

Isabel had listened to this talk, her head on one side, and fidgeting in the cold. "You don't expect us to buy a boat that we have only seen shrouded under tarpaulins," she pointed out. "Wouldn't it be best for us to decide whether we would like to buy, and then we can talk about all those other things?"

"When can you take the covers off her, Mr. Bundy?" the colonel asked.

"Well, look, it's like this," he replied: "taking the covers off is work, and we're snowed under with work, and not enough men to do it. So many people seem to have nothing better to do than come down and sniff at a boat here and a boat there. I suppose it's interesting enough for them, but for us it's hard work, and I've plenty of real jobs to put the men at . . ."

This prompted the colonel to exclaim: "Yes, indeed! Amazing how people are hunting for yachts these days! Seem to have all the money in the world and nothing to spend it on. Selling boats right and left. If I were you, Millar, I'd lose no time in getting an option on *Truant*."

"Are you really interested?" Mr. Bundy asked me. "If you think she might do you, just name your day and I'll see that the covers are taken off."

While I boggled at such direct speech Isabel answered firmly: "Yes, we are interested. We'll come and see her to-morrow, before lunch."

"Very good. I'll see that she's stripped. Now if you'll excuse me . . ."

"Well, are you pleased?" Isabel asked me on the way back to Southampton, and she added: "I like that man Bundy."

I had liked him too, but in my case the liking was drowned in a respect that amounted to fear. Inside his narrow skull Mr. Bundy carried nearly all that there was to know about boats. I should have felt easier with Mr. Bundy if I had been able to tell him that I knew nothing; that what I needed from him was the expert's advice to the complete novice, and not the craftsman's request for orders from the client. But I believed that Mr. Bundy would scarcely relish so emotional a confession, and the following day when we returned to the yard I again wore the nonchalant, whimsically keen air of the man who knows a lot more than he cares to divulge for fear of appearing boastful. Isabel, whose character is resolute, had no need to dissemble. She was herself. If she wanted to know something she asked a question, and if she thought that the answer was strange or silly, she said so.

It happened to be a sunny day. I stood at the tiller—for there was a tiller right aft, as well as the wheel amidships—as though steering the boat straight over the Southampton-Portsmouth road. The deck surface had a wonderful curve to it, a curve that sloped away from my feet to the middle of the boat, then rose again to the bows. The curve made me dizzy with joy. The wheelhouse, the petrol tanks beneath my feet, the cost, the size of the boat, all ceased to trouble me, and although it was a cold day, and I was wrapped up in an overcoat, I had a picture of myself at the tiller in white sunshine, with the curve carrying us over the sea. Isabel was below, in the main living quarters.

She was standing in the owner's cabin, aft of the saloon. She looked happy, and I knew before she spoke that she was quite reconciled to *Truant*. She wore an ocelot coat and her legs were graceful between the coat and the tan shoes, and seen against the background of yellowish-brown bulkheads, and floorboards that had not been scrubbed for six years. "We must enlarge the big bed and have the small one there taken out to make room for drawers and a hanging-cupboard," she said. "That cupboard there will do splendidly for the linen." She moved to the saloon. "I can't bear this brown colour. We must have all the walls and ceilings and fittings painted off-white, with chintz covers on the seats and a good brown carpet both here and in our bedroom . . ."

"But people don't have carpets on boats."

"Why not?" she asked, looking straight at me with her large eyes. She had taken a pencil from the brown leather handbag that hung from one shoulder, and was making notes on the back of a letter from South America. "What do people usually have?"

"Just linoleum, I think, with mats. Or bare teak floors."

"But neither of us likes linoleum," she said. "It's beastly stuff to live with."

"Personally I had more linoleum than I could stand at my school. But in that book I bought the other day the man wrote about going out sailing in a boat that had chintzes and carpets in the saloon; it began to blow, and soon they were obliged to heave all the wet sails into the saloon; when they went below later they found three inches of water over the carpet, and the covers had to be taken off and dried."

"If they had three inches of water on the floor they'd have been very little better off with linoleum. We won't throw wet sails downstairs. Why should we? There are plenty of other places to throw them. And we won't go sailing when the weather is like that. Besides, I shall have the

7

carpets made with leather edging and press-studs at the corners, so that if we think some disaster is going to happen we can roll them up and put them away." Mr. Bundy now appeared, and she told him about the carpets while I searched his thin face for any scornful reaction. None was apparent.

"It is all according to how you see things," Mr. Bundy said. "Some like to have everything easy to clean and dry—and in our wet climate there's an advantage in it—while others like to have a bit of comfort. I'm afraid carpet's very difficult to get, though. You'll have to find it yourselves if you want it, and then I can get it fitted and laid for you."

"Can we get a refrigerator?"

"Your lighting's only twelve volts, so you'd need a paraffin refrigerator, like the ones the smallest naval craft had fitted before they went to the tropics. Best get the office to write to the makers. I'm afraid they're very hard to get."

"Where's the colonel?" Isabel asked.

"Here," called the colonel. "Here I am. Sorry to be so late. Fellow from Amsterdam wants some speed-boats. Well, what do you think of her?"

"Very nice. Can we see the store?"

An owner who lays his yacht up in some yard usually rents a small room in which he locks away all removable gear, leaving the yacht stripped for the winter. We were led to *Truant's* store by Danny, a small, saturnine, dark man, very sharp-looking and wiry. When Danny unlocked the door the colonel at once boomed behind my ear: "Wonderful gear; nothing but the best; nice outboard there; look at that pile of charts; best-found boat I've seen in ages."

I recoiled, aghast, from the small room with its dusty agglomeration of anchors, chain, sails, rigging, assorted ladders and gangways, mops and brushes, charts, navigational instruments, buckets, flags, spars, a wash-basin in mahogany and porcelain, the outboard engine; but Isabel, moving adroitly into the clear space in the centre, rummaged a little and said: "I thought 'fully-found' meant that everything was provided?"

"Yes indeed," the colonel assured her.

"Well, I can't find any plates, and I can't see any knives and forks, and there are only two enormous saucepans . . ."

"Oh, steady now, Mrs. Millar," the colonel exclaimed. "The war is just over, you know. You would hardly expect to find *household* things still here, would you?"

"Oh well," Isabel said cheerfully. "I would rather bring our own

8

china anyway, and our own linen and silver."

"That's the ticket," the colonel said. He ran his eye around the store-room once more, and remarked that he wished it were still possible to buy such things, but he doubted if the quality would come back for a long, long time, if ever. A faint smell of Harris tweed, fresh and Britannic, mingled with his words and seemed to corroborate them. I felt that I must give him a cheque if only to show him that things were not so bad as they seemed.

"I am sure you will never regret it," he said. He went off to another appointment. Isabel and I picked our way down the little lane that took us from the store-room, past a building shed and the office, to the water's edge. Danny was following along behind us.

"So you're buying *Truant*?" he said.

"Looks like it."

"They must ask a tidy sum for that one."

"Not so much."

"They're all dear now," he said. "At least there's more of her than some of the others, wispy little things. Wish I had some people's money. Don't know where all the money comes from."

"Mine came from a book," I said, snobbishly anxious that Danny should understand that I was a poor man. "I wrote a very bad book, at a time when there were few other distractions and when people's judgments were warped; all the money that I made from that book is going into the boat—if the survey is favourable . . ."

"A book!" Danny said doubtfully. "Go on! First you say the money comes from a book, and then you add that (supposing your first con-tention was the truth) you are of a mind to put the whole boiling into that old black boat. A likely story!"

"Danny," somebody was shouting in the distance. "Danny, Danny."

Danny stopped to light a cigarette. He extinguished the flame of his petrol lighter by allowing the thick-skinned ball of his thumb to fall on it. "We get all sorts here," he said. "We had the wrestling champion of the Empire not so long ago. Only one thing they all has in common, whether they're toffs or parvenoos, they're scratching theirselves in their anxious-ness to fling good money into the sea."

We were about to become the owners of a thirty-one-ton (Y.M.) auxiliary ketch, forty-nine feet long, thirteen feet beam, and five feet draft. Walking down the Southampton-Portsmouth road towards the Swan we passed under *Truant's* black, straight stem. She was beamier and more solid than the yachts on either side of her.

9

"Might she really catch fire, carrying all that petrol?" Isabel said.

"No! Before we saw her I had been reading too many technical books."

"And do you really dislike the wheelhouse so much?"

"Well, I would never have built or ordered a boat with a wheelhouse, but we may find it useful." Her chin was pushed into the collar of her fur coat.

*   *   *   *

Truant was the second boat that I had owned; the first was an undecked fishing boat, twenty feet in length, which I bought for £10 in 1934. It was fitted with a heavy iron centreboard, a stubby mast and a red sail—a balanced lug. I bought that boat and fitted it out with the assistance of Johnny Warren, one of the characters who live and work in and around the former smuggling port of Troon, in Ayrshire. Troon harbour to-day is a gloomy place inside high, wet stone walls, a place where large conger eels may be caught on hooks baited with cheese, where new ships are built, and where ships of many sorts arrive to be repaired or go to the gat-toothed grabbing cranes and the oxy-acetylene flares of the ship-knackers.

Johnny Warren does not smoke, and will only take a nip of whisky on a cold evening when the fish are not biting. He has round, pink cheeks and clever eyes beneath the scoop of a Clydeside cap. He looks after the life-boat in Troon harbour and the flashing light on the Lady Isle, uninhabited except by seals and rabbits, three miles out toward the island of Arran. He gave me my first sailing lesson, and in my own boat. I am afraid that I profited little from it, since the boat was competing for my interest with other means of wasting time; I spent a few pleasant days in the boat and then I wandered away south. A year later I learned that it had perished in a gale, sinking beside its moorings.

My family always lived at the mouth of the river Clyde, but I never heard of any sailors among them. I have felt the sea tugging at me, but clearly in my early youth the tug was more sentimental than real, for had I been an enthusiast I could have spent much of my time on the water. I accepted the rare invitations to sail that came my way; they were just sufficient to show me the sensation of power in a well-found yacht, and the peace and romantic loneliness of quiet anchorages in the West Highlands of Scotland. I learned nothing of any practical value by thus cruising on other people's boats, because if I tried to do any work I was only an encumbrance.

Perhaps my most valuable experience was gained on the pond in Regent's Park not far from the London Zoo where you used to be able to hire punt-shaped boats with balanced lugsails for about one shilling and sixpence an hour. That was where I got some idea of how to handle sheet and tiller. Sudden squalls came tearing through the spectators on the western edge of the pond. This process of learning by experience ended with a minor accident, when one day I took my sister there to give her a "sailing lesson". I was so exasperated by her slovenly manner of sailing the punt to the jetty that I pushed off alone and returned at such speed that close to the edge I capsized and dropped, head first, into four feet of slimy water. I had a long walk, dripping water, and hung with bright tendrils of weed, and had to stop three unhired taxis in Baker Street before I could persuade a driver to take me home.

*　　*　　*　　*

I have confessed how little I knew about sailing before we took *Truant* away from England. I said nothing of it, except privately to Isabel, until we were safely clear of our own island. Fortunately for us, although you must have a licence to drive a motor-car, a motor-cycle, an invalid chair, or an aeroplane, so far as I know you can take your own boat anywhere you like on any sea without any licence. Or, as Isabel used to put it: "You are free to drown yourself," and we both agreed that this was just as it should be.

Isabel's lack of experience more than matched mine. She had twice been in a sailing boat, each time in an undecked boat on a Hawaiian lagoon. She stated that she believed herself, from experience on large ships, to be a "very bad sailor". But to set against this I knew that in spite of her small size and slender bones she had great reserves of physical and nervous strength, that she was a matchless organiser for any kind of life, and the best natural driver of a motor-car whom I had ever met. This last aptitude encouraged me to believe that she would soon be expert at handling *Truant*.

Isabel was confident that we could sail in the European seas without any great difficulty, but she occasionally wondered how we were going to find our way. In response to these doubts I arranged that we should both have lessons in navigation from a retired naval officer. A small, wiry, authoritative man, the commander occupied a fine house on the hill (officially described as "a yachtsman's paradise") overlooking the river and the boat yards. Himself a keen, and of course a most proficient, yachtsman, he was a little mystified by our haphazard approach to the subject. While Isabel knew nothing whatsoever about navigation—and I think was never likely to take with any kind of felicity to the mathematical intricacies of working

11

out Great Circle courses from a series of books of tables—I was able to produce odd scraps of knowledge gleaned from my mass of reading; I also found the simpler types of navigation fairly easy because, during the war, I had learned to navigate a vehicle in the desert with compass, sun-compass or the stars. Our tutor never appeared to realise exactly how little we knew, although it was difficult to gauge the thoughts and reactions behind that politely disciplined naval mask, and the three or four lessons that he gave us were always a long way ahead of the bog of navigational in-expertise in which we were floundering. But I, at any rate, had great benefit from the lessons, for when the navigation was over for the day he would take us down to his garage, where seamanly tidiness and a tarry smell were maintained, and where he showed us the most important knots. I had learned them from Johnny Warren and had forgotten them; the common splice, the bowline, clove hitch, sheet bend, reef knot, and so on, came back to me in the commander's garage. Isabel dislikes knots; while her lovely fingers went through the contortions of splicing soft old rope just to oblige the commander, she willed herself to forget the operation within five minutes of leaving the garage. The commander also showed me the different ways of whipping a rope's end so that the infernal thing is likely to stay whipped (or bound so that the rope does not disintegrate into its separate strands).

I became so maddened by the navigational morass into which our too-advanced instructor led me that I seized a technical book dealing with this subject and devoured it night and day until I felt that to navigate better I should need to have lessons in the use of the sextant and astral observation. On examining charts of the English Channel and the Mediterranean, I saw that our longest trip across the ocean was not likely to be more than three or four hundred miles; so I put the book away on a shelf in *Truant's* wheel-house. And then, thinking the matter over, I realised that I need never have bothered about navigation. I believe that anyone who navigated a tank or a truck in the desert would find it as easy as I did to navigate a small boat on the sea. The essential, I noticed, was to buy the right charts and Admiralty publications for those parts of the world which were to be visited. Isabel had short-circuited those misspent hours. She had decided at our first lesson to leave the navigation and the knots to me.

The commander filled me with the same type of qualms as Mr. Bundy because, like Mr. Bundy, he plainly knew an immense amount about boats and how they should be maintained and handled. After our second lesson in navigation it was agreed that the commander should descend from his flat-staffed eyrie on the hill to "look *Truant* over". He knew Mr. Bundy, of course, and the two greeted each other with business-like respect. They were not unlike in appearance, wiry, energetic men, and about their mouths I thought that I detected a certain lip-pursing similarity. The commander made a few turns right round *Truant*, planting his feet with great precision between the various obstacles that littered the ground, for caulking and scraping of the under-water portion of the hull had achieved a vigorous rhythm. He made a few dry remarks about the boat's sailing qualities, which he did not rate very highly. Then his eye darted to a part of the boat that I had not even considered (although in any future boat I shall give it immediate attention), the chainplates, from which the shrouds mount to support the mast.

"*Hrrrmph!*" he sharply cleared his throat. I climbed on deck and stood looking down at him.

"Anything wrong?" I asked.

"Don't like the look of your chainplates. This one's long enough and strong enough, but the other two seem flimsy to my taste." Now that he mentioned it, they did look a little short. I longed for him to move, but he stood there for an unconscionable time, glaring at the chainplates, which shortened every minute. Then he moved aft. "A fine sea-boat," he barked from somewhere out of sight. "She'll roll, of course, but you could go anywhere in her, *if she's sound*." I had not time to savour this when a sharp exclamation came from under the transom. "Hope you've got some checks on these exhausts. You'll get water in your engine from a following sea unless . . ." But now Mr. Bundy came to my rescue.

"There are two big swan-necks in the pipes just inside the transom," he said. "No water could get through to the engines."

"Hm," observed the commander, who was not prepared to commit himself by saying that anything was right.

A dozen men were working on and in the boat, which smelled excitingly of paint and marine glue and wood shavings. Carpenters were renewing a small square of deck aft of the wheelhouse; others were caulking the deck seams; two men were fitting a new mainmast tabernacle of galvanised iron.

"Your decks are fair," the commander said, "but you'll probably find they leak like the devil after your first experience of real hot weather. Got any awnings?"

"Yes, they're being made at Portsmouth," I said with pride. The awnings had been my own idea.

"You'll need them in the canals. Can't for the life of me understand you taking a solid lump of a boat like this through the canals. *Ditch-crawling!* You'll hate it. Should go round by Gib. myself."

13

"What d'you think of the windlass?" I asked, leading him forward.

"All right," he said. "Low-geared enough. What anchors have you got?"

"We have—six altogether . . ."

"Yes, but what kind?"

"Just . . . ordinary ones," I said weakly, making a large descriptive gesture with both arms and my legs and feet. I was ashamed of myself, for I knew that the different types of anchor had distinguishing names, but I could no more easily pronounce them than ask the way to a post office in the Chinese language.

"Fishermen?" I thought he said. "Well, if I were you I should get a C.Q.R. Can't beat them, in my opinion, either for holding or for general handiness."

"I'll order one," I said. "What size shall we need?"

"You'll need the big one, eighty pounds, not very heavy."

"Eighty pounds? . . . Will I be able to handle that?"

"Should be," he said. "And it's better to have a bit of a struggle getting your anchor than to be nervous of dragging in any blow. Well, let's see what's doing below," and he added himself neatly to the crowd in the saloon. Isabel was explaining with a great deal of gesture to Mr. Bundy and two carpenters that the new hanging cupboard and drawers would have to be altered. Two men were painting in the cabin and one in the saloon.

"White enamel!" The commander whistled. "Nice and light, of course, but it may get dirty. Very . . . dirty . . . indeed . . ."

"It's washable," Mr. Bundy said.

"Very good quality," one of the painters said.

"Where'd you get it?" asked the commander.

"All I know is, there's no more where that came from."

"Hm. Can we have those floorboards up? Cement! She has fitted ballast, I suppose . . ." He began to examine the sides of the cabin. "Far too much boarded-in for my taste," he said sharply. "I like to know what's happening. Might get condensation and rot here without knowing anything about it."

"I don't necessarily agree," Mr. Bundy came to our rescue. "After all, she's just had a survey, and all was said to be sound. There's plenty of provision made to keep the air circulating. I know this isn't the modern practice but it was the fashion when she was built, to board them in like this."

"Hm. Now we know better. Now we know *much* better," countered

14

the commander. "If I were you, Millar, I'd have a good many of those boards off now."

"What!" Isabel exclaimed, "and leave more gaps! Oh no. Those ugly ventilation slits are bad enough."

"I don't expect she'll give any trouble in the way of leaks unless they run her into something sharp and solid," Mr. Bundy said. "After all, she's a heavy-timbered ship."

The commander replied with a half-smile.

Our lessons soon came to a stop because the commander had the misfortune to injure himself severely while helping a friend to repair a circular saw. We visited him in Southampton hospital, where he sat in bed looking like a gun that was about to fire, with one arm covered in plaster and a face from which a good deal of the blood, but none of the character or the spirit, had drained. We corresponded with him from time to time after we had sailed. His replies were infallibly courteous, bland and neat, and we could never read into them any surprise that we had got to the ports we were endeavouring to find, or indeed that we had reached any port at all.

* * * * *

It so happened that we considered making a voyage to Greece in a small boat at a time when the British people, fatigued by the war, the grimness of continuing rationing and emergency laws, and the exhausting process of Britain's inevitable political earthquake speeded and intensified by the war, were suffering from lethargy. We were told in England: "You cannot do that. . . . You must go on a waiting list. . . . It may take two years to get you one. . . . We'll put your name down. . . . Of course we cannot promise. . . . Oh, you won't find a refrigerator anywhere. . . ." Isabel reacted with energy inversely proportional to this lethargy. "I know that one can get *anything* in England if one takes the trouble to look for it. Is it illegal to buy a yacht? No. Well, we are going to buy one. Let's get a list of all the yacht and boat builders in Britain." The list was obtained from the Admiralty; within twenty-four hours of her first sight of it she had written eighty-five postcards; within three days of writing the postcards we had seen *Truant* for the first time.

Isabel has fair hair and large blue eyes which are usually soft and friendly, for just as we are often told that the strongest men are the gentlest and most sentimental creatures so her eyes and mouth reveal a character which can show a rapid contrast of determination with unworldly compassion, tenderness, and generosity. Although she has inherited her father's Nordic colouring and texture of hair and skin, her bone structure, with the fragile-seeming wrists, the long infinitely-graceful hands, the small feet, is purely Latin. Her low-pitched voice comes from the same blood, and so does her habit of gesture, a habit that seems almost exaggerated until she crosses our Channel to warmer skies, spicier food, and a way of life perhaps lazier, but more emotionally tense. She is five feet two inches in height, and therefore small by present English standards. During the inter-war period of the nineteen-twenties and thirties there was general admiration in Britain for tall women with languidly rounded shoulders—denoting equally languid intestines—and this period is now generally admitted to have been one of moral and physical (and even financial!) decadence.

* * * *

Mr. Bundy advised us to have *Truant* put into the water early in the year so that her timbers might have several months to swell and become water-tight before we contemplated using her. Isabel took me down to Southampton through fog and over frost to witness the launching.

"I know the boat will sink," she said to Mr. Bundy.

"Sink!" he answered. "Not her. She'll make a bit of water for a time; that's only natural when she's been six years on dry land, isn't it?"

"No, it will sink."

In the same way, when I had left England for France towards the end of the war she had repeated: "You will be killed; I know you will be killed." On that occasion I had believed her. But by the time of the launching I realised that her vocal pessimism is automatic, and is, in fact, an inverted form of optimism.

Crusts of ice had formed round the edge of the creek into which *Truant* was dragged slowly by three muffled men turning a hand windlass. When the cradle had descended so far that the rounded under-water sections were hidden it was astonishing how the boat changed, as though an elderly countess, lying in a puffy, powdery, unbaked heap on her chaise-longue, had quickly exalted herself with fard, corsets and clothing into an important person. Strangely alive after all those years, the water-borne boat fidgeted in the confines of the cradle, the breeze carrying her now this way, now that. Mr. Bundy had stationed a boy in the bilges, while Danny, dark and more saturnine than ever, stood by the pump, on the starboard side of the deck.

"Making any water, Danny?" Mr. Bundy cried.

16

"Any water yet, Jim?" Danny croaked down the hatch. Then louder, to us: " 'Bout a pint. Wish it was a pint of something else."

They freed *Truant* from the cradle, and towed her away with a motor-boat. I felt strangely useless, standing there with my hands in the pockets of an overcoat; I had read too many books written by men who valeted and floated their own boats to feel entirely at my ease in the role of spectator.

Diagram to show TRUANT's accommodation

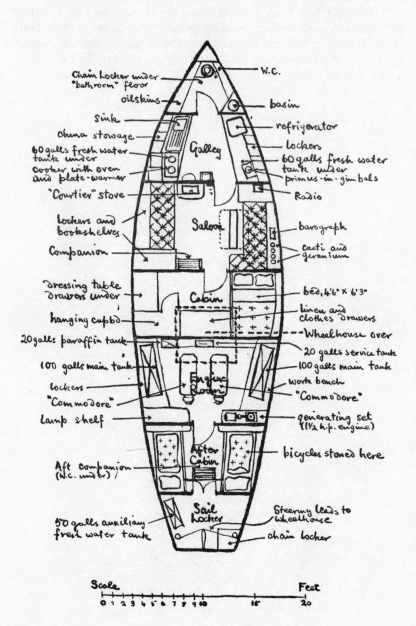

Chain locker under "bathroom" floor
oilskins
sink
china stowage
60 galls fresh water tank under
cooker with oven and plate-warmer
"Courtier" stove
lockers and bookshelves
Companion
dressing table drawers under
hanging cupbd
20 galls paraffin tank
100 galls main tank
lockers
"Commodore"
lamp shelf
Aft companion (W.C. under)
50 galls auxiliary fresh water tank

W.C.
basin
refrigerator
lockers
60 galls fresh water tank under
primus-in-gimbals
Radio
barograph
cacti and geranium
bed, 4'6" X 6'3"
linen and clothes drawers
Wheelhouse over
20 galls service tank
100 galls main tank
work bench
"Commodore"
generating set (1½ h.p. engine)
bicycles stowed here
Steering leads to wheelhouse
chain locker

Galley
Saloon
Cabin
Engine Room
After Cabin
Sail Locker

Scale   Feet
0 1 2 3 4 5 6 7 8 9 10   15   20

MOUNT MARY COLLEGE LIBRARY
Milwaukee, Wisconsin 53222

2

SOME months elapsed while *Truant* lay empty with her stern to the long pier which runs, from Moody's office into the Hamble River like the spine of a filleted sole, the yachts, jutting out from either side, forming the bones. The pier is a spidery structure wide enough to carry a narrow footpath, and although it always seemed to be at least one hundred yards in length, the water was tidal right to the end, where the biggest yachts were moored in the wintertime, and at low tide sat with dignity in the creamy mud.

I disliked the name *Truant*; it seemed to be a little over-romantic, affected and juvenile. But if, during my childhood associations in the west of Scotland, I had learned little enough about boats, I had been taught that you should never take on board a Presbyterian minister, a camera, an umbrella, or a bowler hat, and that it was almost equally unlucky to change a boat's original name. There were other things that irked me about *Truant* in those earlier days: the wheelhouse still rankled; I disliked the tabernacled masts and felt that the spars as a whole were too frail; I envied every man who had a boat with a rounded bow and graceful counter stern as compared to our transom, which I regarded as "cheap", and our straight, old-fashioned stem. In short, I had not become reconciled to having *one* boat, and still longed for a composite of all the pretty ones that I had admired on paper or on the water.

Isabel, who at that time disliked boats generally, suffered from no such cantankerous disadvantages. She was greatly concerned with the colour of *Truant*. There was a good deal of teak work on deck, and this was varnished, but the wheelhouse and the coach roof running forward from it over the saloon and galley and aft of it over the engines were of softwood, and had been painted with graining in a fair imitation of varnished teak. Isabel did not like this at all, and the imitation wood grain was clearly impracticable because when we were aboard we should probably have to repaint it ourselves. Mr. Bundy suggested a teak brown, and we agreed to this rather doubtfully. But the teak brown turned out to be a hot, ugly colour that made the wheelhouse resemble a lump of melting chocolate. Isabel had this painted over with a grey that had a good deal of white and green in it. We liked this colour, which went well with the black hull and white sails, but some inhabitants of the houses clustered around

19

84-3266

that sanctified inlet found the colour too unusual; while we prepared for sea, and they to race or to dawdle around the Isle of Wight on fine week-ends, they shook their heads over us and told each other that no good would come of our undertaking; our white interior, the carpets, our in-experience, and, now, this terrible colour, were advanced as examples of our obvious unfittedness to show the flag abroad. One man described the colour of the wheelhouse as being "half-suitable for a battleship on the China station, half-suitable for an ice-cream barrow on the Bournemouth road".

At the end of April Mr. Bundy had *Truant* hauled out of the water and her bottom was given two coats of the best anti-fouling paint. She could no longer be allowed to sit on the mud, but was moored to two buoys set off the end of the pier. She was there in mid-May, when we arrived to begin our life on board. Mr. Bundy had built us a nice dinghy of silver spruce with a wooden dagger-plate instead of a metal centre-board, a strong mast set right forward to carry a gunter lugsail, and a deep pear-shaped rudder. It was a fairly big dinghy, a ten-footer, and we were glad of its size those first few days, as we dragged trolley-load after trolley-load of belongings down the pier and rowed them off to the yacht. We were glad too of *Truant's* considerable beam and capacious lockers. We took all our clothes and a very large number of books; enough food for six months was stored in the saloon, below the settees and in cupboards and receptacles. Long dresses, a dinner jacket, and other things that we felt we were unlikely to need except perhaps on very odd occasions were packed away in steel trunks beneath our berth.

Truant's interior, with the new carpet, brown-and-beige chintzes on the settees, new fittings and new white enamel, was extremely handsome, but for some days we were very ill-at-ease. Isabel dislikes the smells of paint and tarred rope, and the vessel reeked of both. Our privacy was constantly interrupted by workmen. We had the impression that we were perched in the middle of the river with thousands of curious, deprecatory eyes noting our every movement, our every mistake. Before going to the boat we had been living in a cottage on the edge of the New Forest. We had been obliged to leave the cottage just when the spring was coming in, and the river life seemed dead after that place of living things and earthy, plentiful sounds and smells. The birds flew in clouds around the cottage; two black-birds were nesting in the yew hedge by our bedroom windows, and when we breakfasted in bed we would watch the blackbirds feeding around the rose beds and over the lawn, making traces in the milky dew. The cottage was set in an angle where four lanes met and from morning to evening

20

there was a constant shuffle of Guernsey cows wandering unattended up to the wild grazing in the forest, or picking their way homeward to the milk-maid and the byre, a shuffle sometimes interrupted by the clop of hooves as a band of wild ponies went by, or the tamer horses from Joe Chamberlain's strawberry and mushroom farm or Loder's inn passed, carrying paying equestrians who chose that method of seeing the old trees and history-drenched soil over the hill.

We soon moved from the buoys at the end of Moody's pier to a more isolated anchorage, but although we awoke in the morning with the song of birds from the grounds of the de Selincourts' Georgian house overlooking the river, Isabel continued to find it maddening to be anæsthetised by the wooden walls of our boat and the water outside them, from the full power of spring in the English countryside.

However, we were kept very busy, and we only began to be fitted-out during our last week on the Hamble. Looking around our boat then was a continual satisfaction since there was scarcely a fitting that had not been obtained without effort. We had discovered that different towns had different shortages of manufactured articles, and it was mainly by travelling and searching and questioning that we had managed to buy the things we needed. We had found a second-hand refrigerator in Glasgow; the brown carpet for the saloon and our cabin came from Stirlingshire, and we had discovered a whole selection of Courtier heating stoves while we were motoring through Kilmarnock, although shops in London and the south had told us we should have to wait two years for such a stove; our two-burner enamelled cooker of the primus type with an oven came from Albemarle Street, London, W.1., while the second-hand primus stove that was hung in gimballs for bad-weather cooking came from a farmhouse near Haddington, in East Lothian; we bought a second-hand barograph for a swollen price in Bond Street, and a clock and matching aneroid barometer for the wheelhouse near the Tower of London; our electric fan was found in Portsmouth, the tin bath in Kensington, the searchlight in Glasgow. For six months I hunted through ship chandlers' establishments for ordinary triangular paint scrapers, and three days before we sailed I found two in a small ironmonger's shop in the village of Hamble, down-river from Moody's yard.

Soon after we arrived to live on *Truant* the yard's chief engineer, Harold, came with a tall, khaki-overalled helper to give our engines "a thorough testing out." I was nervous about this, because it meant moving the boat for the first time. When both engines had been run for a little to warm them up, we cast off our mooring, and swept downstream at what

21

seemed to me to be a very fast pace. This assumption was corroborated by the angry shouts of two yacht hands, who appeared on the deck of an immaculate, steel-hulled ketch, and cursed us bitterly for the wash we made. Khaki-overall lay down on the engine-room floor sometimes sniffing at the engines and sometimes tilting his head to listen to them. He had a serious expression, and I at first took this to mean that something was wrong, but such was not the case. The engines were smooth-running, and in the wheelhouse, apart from the ticking of the two rev-counters, there was little to suggest that you were within four feet of seventy horse-power. Clouds of white smoke belched from our exhausts, but Harold said that this was "quite a good sign." I was finding the steering difficult. *Truant* was clumsy on her helm. When we first left the mooring I said to myself: "We shall never get this great brute through the canals." As we neared another boat or any obstacle or mark, such as the spar buoys that indicate the channel of the Hamble, I often had the impression that the boat took it on itself to edge or even lurch sideways towards the danger. At the mouth of the river we saw the wider Southampton Water ahead, and I was glad to leave the wheel to Isabel, pointing out to her that she must get all the practice possible, as steering would be her main part in the actual handling when we set sail. The colonel had said that *Truant* had been designed to accommodate a giant. When I stood on the wheelhouse floor I was just able to see ahead through the bottom of the glass window provided for that purpose, whereas Isabel, standing in the same position, stared into an expanse of varnished teak; she managed to poise herself, however, with her left foot on the port seat of the wheelhouse, her right foot on the coaming of the hatch leading below to our cabin, her left hand gripping the window-ledge, her right turning the wheel. There was no way of altering the wheelhouse to make it more suitable for her; the floor could not be raised or impeded because of the two projecting levers which were used for putting the engines ahead or astern. Later we were to adapt ourselves to sitting on the chart table, Isabel, for some reason, on the port side and I on the starboard, and from there she had a good view. When-ever there was very tricky steering to do, it was she who did it, and then she always adopted that first precarious stance.

Out in Southampton Water, which was dotted with big ships, Harold opened both throttles to their fullest extent while the man lying by the engines listened more assiduously than ever, and sniffed and touched. We circled a freighter from Brazil, and moved back towards the Hamble. Harold, a man given to long silences and short explanations drifting into silence, thought we were doing nine or ten knots. Isabel called to me to take the wheel; she said that she was seasick.

"But there's no sea," I said.

"Oh yes there is."

This was a little disconcerting, but I assured myself that she would soon accustom herself to the movement. When we had returned to our moorings Harold's assistant lingered in the boat to explain some characteristics of the engines to me. While he was showing me the new filters which had been fitted to the cooling-water inlets, I happened to glance into the bilges.

"She made a lot of water on that short trip."

"She did," he answered. "But it didn't come through the stern glands for I was keeping an eye on them all the time."

"Then where did it come through?"

"Probably it was just the vibration of the engines, shaking her up a bit. But if I were you I'd have one of the shafts coupled to a mechanical bilge pump . . ."

"A man was talking to me about such pumps the other day. He said that he was motoring along and suddenly became aware that his boat was on the point of sinking. The bilge pump was pumping water in, not out."

"Be that as it may," said the man in the overall, "I'd have one fitted as soon as they can produce it."

"I'll stick to the hand pump."

The hand pump mechanism was not likely to go wrong. The handle, a T-shaped iron bar, had a small cylinder containing a leather valve fixed to the bottom of the T. You pushed the cylinder into the pump chamber on the starboard side, just aft of the wheelhouse, primed it with a little salt water, and pumped. It was an exhausting apparatus to manipulate, but it gave a fair flow of water; even so, it took me fifteen minutes that evening to pump *Truant* dry. Early next morning I went hunting for Mr. Bundy. I found him in his own little office above a building shed in which a new *Dragon* was nearing completion. He was seated at the drawing board, wearing the tweed suit and flat cap.

"If she continues to make water you'll know that something is seriously wrong," he said. "But I expect you'll find that when she's lying at her moorings she's tight enough."

"But why did she leak so much on so short and calm a trip?"

"Because all these months that she's been soaking her under-water timbers have been taking up, but when you got under way you were pulling other surfaces into the water. I expect when all her topsides have been well slopped around you'll have no more trouble. I don't think you need worry, but she was out of the water for a long time, and if I were

23

you I'd give her a good bit of sailing round before you leave England."

If he thought that I intended to make a fool of myself by going out for "a bit of sailing round" he was greatly mistaken.

* * * *

One of the pleasant aspects of successful marriage is that each party can turn over to the other tasks for which he or she is unfitted. From the day of our marriage I had noticed that Isabel had exceptional talent for achieving neatness in her surroundings. My admiration for this gift was so unstinted that she has done all the packing for both of us ever since. In the same way, since my earliest childhood I have been fond of lighting paraffin stoves of the pressure type fitted in *Truant's* galley, whereas Isabel regarded them with respectful horror. She suggested that since I was so clever with primuses it would be best if I looked after them and lit them whenever necessary.

Isabel took on as her responsibility all of our living quarters, the bathroom, the galley, the saloon and our cabin, and the whole of that accommodation—she called it "my department"—was soon in admirable order. But at the after end of the boat there was disorder, for the engine-room, the after cabin and the sail locker comprised what she referred to as "your department". I believed that my task was less easy than hers. It was true that she had managed to pack a great deal of material and over a ton of food into a surprisingly small space, but she had neater material to deal with than I had. For example, most of the cupboard space in the galley was occupied by fresh-water tanks, but she overcame this difficulty by having the carpenter make special shelves so that all her dishes and utensils occupied compartments which exactly fitted them.

The only easy space in my department was the engine-room. I had bought a great many tools, and these I packed into four canvas bags of the type that carpenters carry when they work; the bags were hung on hooks; four five-gallon drums of engine-oil, a wicker-covered demijohn of distilled water, and various tins of lubricant were lashed against the forward bulkhead and were scarcely in the way, for it was a spacious engine-room; spare parts for the engines were packed under the work bench on the starboard side; the ship's lamps and navigation lights had their own shelf on the port side. No, there was not much wrong with the engine-room. As for the sail locker, which was right aft, and was partly occupied by sixty fathoms of chain, an eighty-gallon fresh-water tank, the metal tiller with its cable attachments leading to the wheelhouse, and the two swan-necked exhaust pipes, wrapped in asbestos and surrounded by metal shields, it was all that

I could do to fit in the spare rope that I carried (sixty fathoms of four-in. grass warp, one coil of two-in. manilla, and one coil of one and a half in. manilla), the sails, and a case of whisky. When I had finished with the sail locker nobody could complain about it because the only way to find out how it was packed was to unpack it. But the after cabin was a different story. Under the former owner's ægis I have no doubt that the after cabin was a habitable place. It was well lit, with its own lavatory and water supply and two excellent bunks. Under my ægis it was never anything but a shambles. I maintained that the untidiness aft was due in part to the exceptional tidiness in the living quarters forward, because Isabel was quick to rid her department of any unwanted object, and space had to be found for it in the after cabin. I argued hotly with her regarding our bicycles. As stoutly as she had demanded carpets, white paint-work and proper space for our clothes, Isabel had insisted that we must carry bicycles. Although I agreed with her that bicycles might well be most useful to us in France and Italy, I loathed the idea of having to pack them into the after cabin, and having to disentangle them from there each time we felt inclined to use them. One sunny afternoon when most of the owners and crews of small yachts were pottering about on their decks with sandpaper and scrapers or paint-pots and brushes, I carried our bicycles down the long pier and loaded the awkward things into the dinghy.

Only one man among the spectators commented, and he said: "I say, are you taking bicycles on *Truant*?"

"Yes."

"Oh!"

I laid the bicycles on deck and began to pack the after cabin. The whole space under the port bunk was filled with sealed tins of paint, varnish, anti-fouling and marine glue. Under the other bunk I packed the awnings in three sailbags with the stanchions and steel wire on which they were to be erected. On the port bunk I built up a solid pile with a foundation of kedge anchors and spare dinghy oars; resting on the anchors were: the patent log and log-line, some instruments in heavy wooden boxes: the pelorus, the station-pointer, the aldis lamp, and a deep-sea depth finder; cleaning gear, odd lengths of rope of different types and sizes, two new deck chairs and a folding table with a white leather top. On the starboard bunk I wedged the bicycles. They were easy enough to pack into the space, but they looked so unseamanlike that I drove screw-eyes into the white paint here and there and lashed the wretched things until they were almost concealed behind my lashings. I was so aware that every object in the boat was to be subjected to violent movements that I went around lashing

25

almost everything that I saw. More than half of these lashings, I subsequently learned, were quite unnecessary, and all of them were stronger than they need have been. But if it was a fault, I suspect that my penchant for lashings was a good fault; Isabel found it most exaggerated, and refused to allow it in her department, where there was one object that really did require lashing; this was a "patent non-spill" tin bucket with a lid to it, which had been beautifully made for us by the tinsmith of Fordingbridge, in Hampshire, and it contained twelve dozen eggs immersed in the preserving fluid known as water-glass. Isabel had placed this bucket in such a way that it could not move laterally, being wedged between a bulkhead and the patent white refuse-bin (for which she had made an ultimately victorious succession of bids at an auction sale in the Fordingbridge drill hall). She forbade the lashing of the egg-bucket so definitely that I resigned myself to a shortage of pickled eggs, but by some trick of balance the bucket never moved during all our periods of bad weather.

Neither of us desired any witnesses of our departure from England, and we had decided that it would be best to slip away from the buoys to which we were attached at such an early hour that no yachtsmen would be awake. For the last ten days of our stay on the Hamble we had to vacate the mooring we had used because the owner had returned to it with his ketch, *Gracie*, and we were moored in a string of yachts further downstream. Immediately astern of us in our new berth was a most handsome cutter. She was no bigger than *Truant*, white, Camper-and-Nicholson-built, and as well kept as the top of a bald organist's head. While we were near her she was only twice visited by her owners, and then she went for a short spin, each time using her engine. A skipper and one hand were always on board, wondering what to do with themselves, rotting with idleness, by the look of them. Immaculate always in blue clothes and white rubber-soled shoes, they watched us throughout the last flurry of our preparations for the sea. We were their favourite pastime. I wonder what they looked at when we had gone. Many a time I could have done with their professional advice; we got to the stage of exchanging views on the weather, but the padded, cat-like certainty of their movements and the infinite disillusionment of their expressions made me regard them—wrongly, in all probability—as soured, rich men's chattels whose favours would be condescending.

Saturday, June the 8th, 1946, was to be a day devoted in Britain to mass celebrations of Victory; we felt that this would be a better day than most on which to leave the country. By Friday morning we had reached that stage when it was impossible to do any more preparing. The river was glassy.

Moisture dripped from the exotic leaves of Chinese shrubs in the de Selincourts' garden. As we rowed ourselves ashore, lazily, for it was warm and the water bubbled thickly beneath the little boat, the smart, blue, ocean-racing yawl, *Amokura*, stole past us, her tall, café-au-lait-coloured sails gently filling in the morning airs, the men on board lighting their first after-breakfast pipes and a woman in the cockpit stretching like a child and breathing deeply. *Amokura* was followed by the white ketch, *Gracie*.

"I should like to have a boat with masts as tall as Salisbury spire," Isabel said. It was a day for masts like that, and it was good to be on the water. Busy dinghies with outboard motors growled round the pierhead. Week-end yachtsmen were pouring into the yard in their cars, dusty from the London road.

We walked up the lane to the post office to send telegrams and to buy English cigarettes to give away in France. Bills were nailed up in the village, advertising a pageant of history, to be held in the de Selincourts' park. The bills announced:

SATURDAY, 8TH JUNE
GRAND SENSATION!
ARREST OF CHARLES I!

We bought a chicken and six pounds of English strawberries. We went to bed very early, with the portholes and the glass doors between our cabin and the wheelhouse uncurtained so that the first light might waken us. Isabel slept calmly, but I awoke in the darkness, remembering that I had forgotten to collect from Harold the two spare propellers which had been specially ordered for us, and which we should be likely to need in the canals. There was nothing to be gained by worrying, since there would be no employee in the yard on the following day, an English holiday. The night was chilly. I could hear the flood-tide pushing upstream past my head.

27

3

River mist entered our cabin with the first daylight. Isabel started the engines while I hoisted the burgee and the ensign. I did that small operation, which was soon to become as natural as brushing a fly from my nose, with breathless care and attention. The hoisting of the ensign was easy enough, but for weeks I had been studying the burgee of every passing yacht, not to determine the yacht club of the owner, for I am inclined to dislike clubs and their symbols, but to ascertain how the small, triangular flag was flown.

The mist lay so thickly on the water that we could see the spars of yachts downriver, but not their hulls. "You can take her away now," I said to Isabel.

"You've undone all the ropes and things?"

"I hope so."

I saw her bend down to pull the levers forward. We moved into mid-stream, mist and dew thick on our decks. We were excited and pleased with ourselves. It was good to surge down the river while the other boats were still asleep, as steady at their moorings as models on a sheet of glass. I had three or four charts of Southampton Water and the Solent, and I began to turn them over as we cleared the mouth of the Hamble. It was the first time in my life that I had been called upon to use a chart. The mist was so thick that I could only steer on a compass course, searching for landmarks when a piece of coast appeared, usually to fade quickly. At the end of Southampton Water the tide came against us. I had known from the Nautical Almanac that this would happen, and that it would persist until we came out of the Solent and settled on our course across the Channel. We pushed on with both engines, and appeared to make good progress. There was no wind; the water looked like thick oil from which tendrils of steam were rising; a swell rocked us evenly, and the white fumes from our exhausts crept forward along the deck until their smell of burned petrol clung to our noses and throats. Isabel disliked this smell as strongly as the movement. She coiled herself on the chart table, and wondered why we had ever left the land.

"Beastly things, boats!" she said.

Warships were anchored off Portsmouth, and nearer to the Isle of Wight

28

were eight big freighters, also anchored. I watched the warships with awe and something approaching fear. I had been told that ships of the Royal Navy usually bothered you with signals if they met you at sea, and although I had all the necessary flags to reply to such signals it would have taken me a little time to do so, as I should first have had to identify their flags with the aid of a very practical book that I had purchased, and then, with the same book (which lists phrases in convenient groups) formulate my reply and hoist the flags. However, they let us pass in peace. When we were a mile beyond them a breeze came off the land. I set the jib, mizzen and staysail while Isabel steered; I had no difficulty with the sails, although I was slow and clumsy at the work. Isabel came forward, leaving *Truant* to steer herself. We soon had the mainsail set and drawing. I was impressed by the sails; the canvas looked a little grey after the years in store, but I thought the loose-footed mainsail a particularly beautiful and well-cut sail—although admitting to myself that I knew nothing about it—and I was relieved that it was so easy to hoist that we had not had to touch the winches mounted on either side of the mainmast. *Truant* was beginning to roll and bounce in the sea that thrust into the sheltered water we were about to leave. I cut down the engines; there was only enough wind to steady her. Near the Nab Tower I streamed the patent log. The wind dropped, the sails flapped and the swell increased. Isabel lay down on the chart table. I was rather busy with my navigation. I had intended to swing the compass some distance off the Nab, but I had not the heart to waste an hour or two in circling on that unpleasant water. I consoled myself by remembering that a young man who had made several voyages with the former owner had told me that our large compass had little or no error. I soon found that we were logging only about six knots, and I had been counting on doing nine or ten, since they had told me in the yard that *Truant* was capable of that speed. We had passed the Nab at 8.11, which gave us about twelve hours of daylight to cover the ninety miles to le Havre.

Truant was making a good deal of water. I was obliged to spend ten out of every ninety minutes pumping her out, and it was stiff work on the jumping, slippery deck. About an hour after we left the Nab we were enveloped in rain clouds. With the shaking up of petrol in the tanks we now began to have fuel trouble. The gravity feed from the main tanks ceased to work. In an attempt to raise the safety factor in the engine-room, I had discarded two electric petrol pumps, leaving one small, hand-operated pump to draw petrol from the main tanks to the service tank and filters. Harold and his associates had assured me that this pump delivered

29

at a good rate of flow, but I found at sea, in the heaving semi-darkness and stench of the engine-room, that either they had miscalculated or the feeds to the pump were also partly obstructed. I took fifteen minutes to pump six gallons. The breeze increased about 10 o'clock, but we continued to press on with the engines.

At midday, although neither of us was hungry, Isabel persuaded me to go below and get some food. I brought tea, biscuits and cake to the wheelhouse, but she could do no more than taste the tea. We had seen no ship or aeroplane since leaving England. The wireless told us, correctly, that the wind would veer from east to west, freshening. There was a gale warning further down Channel; barometer and thermometer were both falling. The sea was darkened by rain squalls.

When the wind came from the west we carried all the sail that we could manage. I shut off the engines, and we continued to log between six and seven knots, often with the lee rail awash. At 5 o'clock I realised that I was beginning to feel the effects of the hard work; my back was throbbing from the continual pumping and for several hours I had been wet in every part of my body, while my hands were sore from adjusting the sheets and other work on deck. I lashed the wheel, leaving Isabel apparently asleep on the chart table, and went below to change my clothes and make myself some tea. The barograph in the saloon showed a ragged downward slope. All was calm and order below decks and each object was in its place. I climbed through the hatch from our cabin to the wheelhouse. My heart stopped beating . . . then I saw Isabel hanging over the rail. I felt the instant whiff of anger that makes a mother strike a child that has nearly been run over. The wind was veering, from the west to the north, and the sea was following, and bigger. Isabel asked if *Truant* was not "leaning over too far" and I tried to reassure her. I had no wish to reduce sail because I perceived only too clearly that taking the wet mainsail off her was going to be heavy work, and also I hoped desperately to see le Havre before dark.

At 7 p.m. we had logged seventy-five miles, and I thought that land could not be distant, but the rainstorms shut us in, and we saw nothing until, at 7.30, two boats appeared ahead of us and roughly on our course; one was a French torpedo-boat of sorts, and the other a small undecked motor-boat with three men in it. I was sure the motor-boat could not be far from land, and at 8.5 I sighted cliffs ahead.

By this time the following sea, according to our belief at any rate, was becoming awkward, and I was obliged to keep a watch on the bigger waves and turn *Truant's* stern to them with a consequent risk of gybing. It was

30

obvious that the mainsail must be taken down. We started the engines, and Isabel took the wheel to head *Truant* into the wind and the black sea. I had been suspicious of the jib halyards before leaving, but had allowed a rigger, who should have known better, to persuade me that they were sound. The moment that I went out on deck those halyards parted, and the jib flapped over the bows. I took some time to get that mess cleared up; then a terrible battle ensued with the mainsail. The heavy canvas was stiff with wetness. I had to fight to get it down, stowed, and tied. The ends of my fingers were split open when it was done, and I was gasping for breath. With only mizzen and staysail drawing, *Truant* was much steadier. It was dark.

Ahead of us we were thankful to see a chaplet of lights so dazzling and numerous that they could only represent le Havre, while out on the sea, between us and the town, there appeared to be other lights. I went to the engine-room, pumped some more petrol, and lit the navigation lights. I could not remember—perhaps because I was worn out with the day's labours—which side should show the red light, and which the green. I asked Isabel, but she did not know, so I had to search for the answer in one of my text-books.

Isabel's hands were cold, damp, and dead white at the ends of the long fingers. I tried to make her drink a little whisky, but she said that whisky would make her iller than the sea. I was very worried about her, and loved her for the sardonic humour that tinged all her remarks although her voice had become so weak that it was difficult to hear it above the boisterous shouting of the wind around the wheelhouse. The sea was shortening and steepening as we approached the land. Skidding, plunging, riding then sliding back, we continued towards le Havre, but the nearer we got the more difficult we found it to distinguish any of the guiding lights described on our charts and in the accompanying literature. We both read and re-read the *Channel Pilot*. At length I decided, much against my will, that it would be criminal folly to approach that dangerous entrance with an onshore wind and with two engines which were beginning to spit and cough and give other unmistakable signs that they were finding their diet unpalatable.

Bitterly disappointed, we put about, switched off the engines, and sailed slowly, though by no means comfortably, seaward with staysail and mizzen. Isabel now had two pillows and three blankets on the chart table.

It happened that I had been reading a good deal about the benefits on such an occasion of a sea anchor, and when I thought we were a safe distance offshore I carried our sea anchor, a strange, bag-like device, from the after cabin, dropped it into the water over the weather bow, and soon had *Truant* riding to it in a manner that gave me infinite satisfaction. I took in the staysail, but left the mizzen, as I thought it would help to keep her head into the wind. It was good to get back into the wheelhouse, although that place had become most squalid, with charts, binoculars, books, pencils, dividers and parallel rulers tumbling everywhere. I squatted on the wet floor, pulled a blanket over my head, and dropped into a sound sleep.

At 3 a.m. I awoke, greatly refreshed, and so chilled that I felt ready for more work, although my hands were smarting badly. Isabel was holding one of them. She had been awake for some time, watching the boat's antics, which were quite terrifying. Our rolling was so violent that she believed that we were going to roll right over, and sometimes I was nearly of the same opinion. We had drifted inshore past a floating red light which had puzzled me since darkness fell. I had another look at the charts—wondering where the devil le Havre Light Vessel could have hidden itself—then I went about the business of getting the boat ready for the run in. When I tried to pump the bilges the pump refused to draw, and I realised from the feel of it that there was some obstruction in the pipe; a good deal of water was visible below the engines, but I had too many other things to do to give more time to the pump. I sat down beside the engines and forced a stream of petrol into the service tank for fifteen minutes. Now that I had rid myself of the chill of sleep, I found that I was both stiff and weak and I did not intend to waste energy on the sails. The mizzen was easy to handle, but I re-opened the ends of my fingers bringing it down. The dinghy—which we were towing—was filled to the gunwale with rain-water and spray; I hauled it under the stern and baled it with a bucket hung on a line. There remained the sea anchor, which caused me great difficulty and discomfort because the night before I had omitted—through laziness or fatigue—to make fast a tripping line so that the bag could be emptied, and then drawn in without a struggle. I took three turns of the warp round the drum of the windlass and, hanging desperately to the windlass during the worst of *Truant's* acrobatics, I painfully hauled the boat up to the sea anchor. When I staggered back to the wheelhouse Isabel asked me if I had been doing anything.

We started both engines and turned to the land, advancing in a series of sliding rushes, each rush ending tipsily as we sagged back from a wave-crest into the trough behind. With no sail on her, *Truant's* movement was nightmarish and unpredictable, but no matter how she rolled and plunged, she kept her decks dry. Soon after we moved the dawn came and showed us, to our chagrin and surprise, that the red light which had so puzzled us all through the night was that of le Havre Light Vessel itself. It had never occurred to me that a light vessel might show a *red* light. Now we could easily distinguish the avenue of buoys leading to the harbour entrance. As we neared the entrance and I saw how thickly the water was sown with wrecks and wreck-buoys, I was thankful that we had waited for daylight. Ships, still grey and still rusty in places from the hard service of the war years, were steaming out, the wind snapping the smoke from their funnels and stretching their flags until they resembled quivering sheets of coloured tin. As we were about to meet an American ship in the fairway marked by buoys both of our engines began to spit, and the starboard one stopped entirely, while the port only turned the propeller enough to give slight steerage way. Had I been more experienced or less tired, I should at once have hoisted sail. But I had lost all stomach for the rain- and wind-swept deck and the discomfort of the ropes in my hands. Isabel asked, pointing at the ship coming towards us: "Do you think he will get out of our way?"

"I think we had better try to get out of his."

I had not been long in the engine-room when the port engine also choked and stopped. Harold's minion had showed me how to clean the carburettors; they were full of dirt. I got one engine going and had the satisfaction of hearing Isabel open the throttle and throw it into gear. The feed to the other carburettor was blocked, and in clearing the pipe I took a full swallow of petrol. This, combined with the smell of hot oil and battery gases and the heat from the engines was too much for me, and when I got to the deck I was sick at sea for the first time.

Immediately inside the harbour entrance, we were confronted by a confusing agglomeration of buoys, a scattered hatching of red eggs. They plainly indicated submerged wrecks, and all the harbour works to be seen above the water showed signs of pounding with high explosive. Ahead of us stretched the different basins of the port, but in a corner, tucked in behind the main mole of the harbour, we saw the masts of sailing vessels. We swung round towards these, and picking a way as we thought best through the wreck buoys, came to the basin, which was small, plainly more than two-thirds tidal, and over-crowded with fishing craft, salvage floats, and a few small one-design yachts.

Our starboard engine seemed to lose thrust as we began to come about in this narrow space, and the reason was soon obvious as a boatload of fishermen yelled at us, pointing at our dinghy, which floated free, with about eight feet of severed rope hanging from its bows; the other end of the painter was wound on our starboard propeller shaft. One of the fishermen sculled to the dinghy and brought it alongside.

"Shall I come aboard and help?" he asked.

"Very kind of you! Where should we put ourselves?"

"Ahead a little bit, and then anchor."

"The notices on the walls say *Défense de Mouiller*."

"Mouillez quand-même. Everybody anchors. Is your anchor ready?"

"No," I said. I had known, of course, that as we approached harbour, all preparations should have been made—the sails properly stowed, the anchor ready to let go, the lead out for taking soundings, the dinghy painter shortened—but I had been unable to summon the energy to leave the wheelhouse.

He heaved the anchor overboard. The sound of the chain was soothing We were connected to earth once more. Painted fishing boats bobbed like Maypole dancers on all sides of us. The fisherman said that if we needed anything we had only to call him.

"That's my boat, *Mireille*, over there."

Isabel made the bed. We drank tea and ate toast, butter and marmalade—she does not feel that she has breakfasted unless there is marmalade—and fell instantly asleep.

*   *   *   *

In the evening we emerged on deck to look around us. Our basin lay in waste ground where only a few landmarks stood out to the mildly inquisitive eye: a small building had a flagstaff and a sign painted on the roof to show that it was a U.S. Naval Station; a few jutting, half-blackened houses; a car-park filled with military vehicles and surrounded by barbed wire; a ship-building yard clustered round the orange-coloured hulls of two small coasters, which had been building for four years. Only a short space in time before our arrival the naval station and what houses we saw would scarcely have been apparent in a mass of building. Here ten houses had survived the war out of five thousand. This had been the prosperous centre of a great seaport, and the prosperity had suddenly turned into dust, rubble and decay.

The fisherman who had helped us that morning was painting the gunwale of his eighteen-feet open boat with the same satisfying blue that enriches most French villages and hoardings. All around us other fishermen were working on their boats, nets, and lines.

"No fishing to-night or to-morrow," our friend said. "Then this blow will probably stop. Where are you going?"

"Greece."

"Through the canals?"

"Yes."

"I wish you could take me, my wife, and three kids, to Marseilles."

"Why Marseilles?"

"It could be no worse than this, and I've relations there. Anyway, in Marseilles you've a soft climate, even if there isn't much to eat, while here you cannot keep yourself warm; and Marseilles is bound to open up again as a great port, whereas this place is finished."

"There was a great port here before. There'll be one again."

"The white men are finishing themselves off," he said surprisingly, rising up in his boat as though to emphasise the importance of his remark. "This port, le Havre, sent ships out across the Atlantic. But all that's finished, or at any rate it'll never be so important again. We have to look to the coloured peoples now, it's nearly their turn to rule the world, and Marseilles is the port for that." He was very earnest. "I'm thinking for my son," he said. "Here we can live because I've the boat; even so we only scratch a living, like half-starved dogs. How long will the boat last? A year, two years; the sea is violent here. Now in Marseilles it might be different."

"Then why don't you take the boat to Marseilles?" Isabel said.

"Eh?"

"Pack all your family on the boat and go through the canals to Marsilles as we are going to do."

"I never heard of a fisherman doing such a thing," he said. "What would we do with our furniture and our house, such as it is?"

"Sell the house, and send the furniture by rail."

"It would never arrive. And the boat is too small for five of us. Where would I find petrol and oil for so long a journey?" He painted in silence for a while. "And how could I leave le Havre? For I was born here."

*   *   *   *

Next day was *lundi de la Pentecôte*, and even the immigration offices were closed. I worked on the boat, straightening the tangle on deck, clearing the bilge pump, which had been obstructed by a piece of rag, and cleaning the petrol system of the two main engines. I made myself so dirty and ill-tempered with the unaccustomed work in the engine-room that Isabel said I must never work there again.

*   *   *   *

We asked several people to direct us to the centre of the town, but their answers were vague. When we had been walking for a time we met a more intelligent pedestrian, an elderly man in a high starched collar.

"Centre of the town?" he said. "There is no centre. This town has been destroyed by war. If we had a centre that would imply that there was a moral force already at work in the town to foster another growth. There is no such moral force. If you want to see where the old centre of the town was, then you are standing within two hundred metres of it. Yes, those ruins over there. But then le Havre was hardly an Athens or a Rome; nobody in his senses would be interested in the ruins of a great commercial city of the twentieth century." He gave us his card, and said that if we needed any assistance we were to call on him. His name looked very stiff and dignified, and the printed card gave the addresses of his home and his office, but these had been scored out with black ink and above them, written in an upright copper-plate, we saw a hotel address and a room number.

It was late when we set out to return to the boat from the place where we had dined. The sea wind, which should have been clean and salty, blew curtains of dust and grit along the roads, curtains that sucked more dust from the rubble on either side as they passed so that far inland the air was thicker and heavier than among the ruins themselves. As we approached the dock area heavy rain began to blow in from the sea. We were passing what I had taken by the light of my torch to be a small hill or a pile of rubble larger than the others, and we were surprised to hear dance music, a French Java issuing from the seemingly featureless mass. On rounding a bend we saw a door with a strong blue light shining out into the rain jets, and over the door the word *Dancing*. We entered, more for shelter, since we were coatless, than in search of entertainment. We stood within what had probably been some large public building. The building had collapsed, and the massive ruins had formed the hummock that I had noticed in the darkness. Owing to some particular strength in the construction of the main door and the staircase landing immediately over it, the collapse had left the doorway intact, and a space inside it. The "walls" of this space appeared to consist of fallen masonry, but a low ceiling had been constructed with stout, unplaned boards. The only issue was offered by a turning staircase, which led below ground. At the bottom we found ourselves in an immensely long room. Our end of the room was lit by a dozen powerful lamps which were fixed to brackets in the low red walls, and which emitted a sizzling noise and a pungent odour, as they burned. Beneath the lamps were red banquettes, red-topped tables with twisted

36

metal legs, and a small dais on which a woman with an accordion and a man at an upright piano were finishing their java. Nobody was dancing, although there appeared at first glance to be a good many people in the room. The strange thing, which at once struck us both, was that the room was unfinished—for at a certain point there were no more lights, no more banquettes, no more tables. The dark, slippery floor continued, the red ceiling and the red walls, and for a space the light stretched into this emptiness; then the darkness softly swallowed the light, the eye searched for a moment in the resulting blur, and returned to the garish room.

We sat at a table and ordered from an elderly waiter, who trembled from some nervous disease, crême-de-menthe frappée, a drink that is popular in such places, since late in the evening it gives a pepperminty and depraved illusion of freshness. We were able then to take stock of the other people. Near us was a couple, plainly French, very young, and carefully dressed. The young man might have been a cadet at Saint Cyr, the girl his fiancée. They were drinking brandy and water, and seemed to have drunk too much of it, and this in itself surprised us, for it is, or was, unusual to see French people of that type in such a condition. They were angry about something, and when I looked about the room I soon picked out the cause of their anger. Eight German prisoners of war were sitting at two tables. They were rough-looking youngsters in old black uniforms, and they were the guests of five American soldiers. That party was only drinking beer. We were not surprised to see the Germans there because we had seen them all over the town strolling unguarded in the streets or even driving themselves about in American trucks and cars marked *PW Driver*. The American soldier, a foreigner on the European scene, felt that it was time to stop punishing the ordinary German soldier. The Americans were openly friendly with their prisoners, more friendly than with the French, whom they could not understand or easily like. Their act of friendliness with the prisoners was known by the stiff word, fraternisation. As for the French, they were under the disadvantage of hating the Germans, and with some reason—were hatred ever reasonable— after defeat followed by years of German occupation. The young Frenchman and his companion hated so fiercely that they were on the way to drunkenness.

"Deux fines à l'eau!"

"Oui, monsieur."

Seated at two tables were six prostitutes who chatted in an apathetic manner and, when a cigarette was lit by one of the party, passed it from mouth to mouth. Near them were two younger women in seedy evening dresses; they belonged to the same trade group as their six neighbours, but they also served the establishment as dancing partners.

I had finished cataloguing the people in the room, and we were discussing the appearance of this person or that, when another client arrived, and a very extraordinary one. He was a soldier too, in uniform soaked by the rain, a tall, cadaverous, negro soldier. He entered swiftly, and we guessed from the way that the resting musicians glanced at him and allowed their interest to sag that they had often seen him before. He sat on a banquette in the emptiest part of the room; he was opposite us, and we were able to study his face without rudeness. The features were regular, even good, but the face was so narrow that it appeared to have been crushed by a press applied to either side. The eyes were far behind the bridge of the straight nose, so that I believed that the man had not man's gift of two-eyed vision, but was obliged to turn his head sideways, like a robin, to see ahead. Frequently nature offsets an exceptionally thin or narrow head by adding to it prominent ears, but in this case the ears were nipped in closely to the skull. The hair was worn exceptionally short, even for a soldier. We both agreed that the negro was very ill. His lips were drawn from his square, ugly teeth and his eyes were swollen and uncommonly bright.

He laid money on the table in front of him, not French but American money, a five-dollar bill. The six prostitutes craned forward at the sight of it, for they attributed an almost supernatural power to the dollar. The waiter brought him a glass of brandy, lifted the dollar bill, put it in his notecase, and counted out the change, several hundred francs. The negro lit a cigarette, and smoked slowly, staring before him, through the smoke. His unconsciousness of the people around him seemed to be quite unforced; it gave me the effect of hallucination: perhaps I was dreaming or imagining the negro, perhaps there was no negro in the dancing place; or perhaps he was detached because he alone was there.

When the music began again everything changed. It was an American tune played without the rhythm of America and therefore as distorted as obscenities written backwards. The young French couple rose to their feet, and danced away from their table with a piston-like forcefulness. Isabel and I followed, and it was she who attracted my attention to the negro as we moved round the floor. He was dancing alone, moving rapidly, and with a curious beat in his step, but portraying all the mannerisms of a man dancing with a woman so faithfully that we did not find his miming at all funny, but rather tragic or terrible. His left arm was stretched out and high, while the right was crooked around his invisible partner. What was

38

more, as he danced he talked to his partner, bending low over her with an ingratiating smile. As he passed us I would catch a deep mumble from him, and even such hackneyed words as: "Honey . . . a long, long time . . ."

Once we danced away into the darkness. The room stretched on, interminably; it seemed that only one-third of it at the most was furnished and lit. As we danced we heard the feet of rats; we returned to the lights. The dancing-place looked quite vivid from the darkness, vivid, with a line around each figure and every piece of furniture. Two of the whores had risen and were dancing together jerkily, the one dancing the male part overplaying masculinity. Was the music never going to stop? We went to our table.

The old waiter had deposited the two fines à l'eau at the next table.

"Is it still raining do you think?" I asked him.

"Yes, monsieur, but surely you are not thinking of going yet?"

Isabel asked him about the negro.

"He comes two or three nights a week," the trembling old man replied; when he spoke of a being even more to be pitied than himself a spiteful scorn came over his face and into his rheumy eye. "It's drugs, you know. That man's killing himself with drugs."

"Has he ever spoken to you?"

"No, but once or twice I've seen him speak to Americans. They say his wife went off with another man, in New York, but that in any case he was always like this. He's a wealthy negro."

"What does he do during the day?"

"He's in the Army. How should I know what he does?"

At last they had stopped playing the *fox*. The negro and the two couples returned to their tables. The orchestra ordered coffee. The French pair had begun to drink their new brandy and water, when I heard the young man exclaim: "Truly, that's too much . . ." Following the direction in which he was glaring, I saw for the first time that the two women in evening clothes were no longer alone at a table. Evidently, while we were dancing, they had been called over by the Americans who were with the party of German prisoners, and the two women were now sitting together, sandwiched between Americans, but nevertheless at the same table as the Germans. The young Frenchman on my left began to make a stupid speech about French womanhood, the stigma of the occupation, and the stigma of seeing the Boches driving around the town while good Frenchmen had to walk, and prisoners gorging themselves on American rations while French children starved. And now Boches in the

39

boîtes, each with his poule. He buried his nose in the brandy and water, but his companion was not content to leave things as they were.

"What are you going to do about it?" she asked coldly.

"Garçon!"

"Monsieur?"

"Deux fines à l'eau."

"Bien, Monsieur."

The trembling old man brought their brandy, smiling a little as he carried away the empty glasses. The negro, since the music stopped, had been sitting as before, staring into the smoke from his cigarette. But now one of the six whores approached him. She was a fat woman, with an agreeable face and an air of great self-composure. She asked him for a cigarette, standing beside his red table and glancing from time to time at her companions while she waited for him to answer her. She had spoken in English, loudly, yet he had not even deflected his eyes to her. She repeated painfully, almost shyly now, for everybody in the room was watching: "'Ave you a cigarette, please, Joe?" She tapped gently on one khaki forearm that rose like a cobra from the elbow planted on the red table, and this time he looked at her. She screwed her face into a smile as his eye came round to it.

"Sure," he said, and held up the packet that lay before him. She took a cigarette, put it to within an inch of her lips, and began to shake it gently to and fro. His eyes swung back to her. "Pardon me," he said, and lit her cigarette with the lighter that also lay on the red table, then he looked ahead again. A titter came from the woman's companions, and perhaps it was this that urged her to sit beside him. Having made up her mind she soused her body down on the red banquette and then with a series of little jerks moved closer to him. The accordion player had forgotten her coffee, the pianist's brownish cigarette was about to burn his lips. But we did not have long to wait. The negro gathered up his brandy, the cigarettes, the lighter, walked across the room, and sat himself at another table. The accordionist let fly with a wailing chord, and slid from it into a tango, the pianist coming in with her. At once the negro jumped to his feet and danced. His feet moved swiftly, in double time to the wheezily sensuous music; he bent his knife-edged head to talk winningly to his invisible partner.

As for the woman, she returned to her companions with the stock shrug of the shoulders.

"She's very, very angry," Isabel said.

"Oh, I don't suppose so. She must be accustomed to that sort of reception."

40

"But it was a most unusual reception," she insisted.

Meanwhile the tango droned on. The two women in evening dress rose to dance. There was a slight argument at their table, in which the women, standing, took part. It seemed to us that while one American wished to dance, the other Americans were persuading one of the women to dance with a German. In the end, with several glances around the place, the woman consented, and the two couples took the floor. Regarded objectively, a healthy-looking young man in a uniform was dancing with a woman in a dirty dress who was almost certainly a harlot; but the man was German, and the woman was French. The young man on our left exclaimed bitterly, while the young woman compressed her mouth and hardened her eyes. Their displeasure would probably have remained no more openly expressed, but the six whores raised an instant hubbub, screaming invective at their dancing compatriot. At first both the woman and her German partner were intimidated, but it only required two or three of the viler remarks to register and the dancer shouted back as obscenely as any of them, glued her body to that of the German, and danced feverishly and with well simulated passion. The young couple on our left began to shout abuse of an unprintable nature.

The band settled down to continue the tango for ever if need be; the woman with the accordion played softly, and leaned her head on one side to hear the better. She remained as unruffled as Isabel, and we thought that perhaps she was not French. The old waiter did not shout, but he fussed round the room, wiping tables with a cloth, and muttering: "A scandal, a scandal, *what* a scandal!"

The German and American party looked sheepish and puzzled. None of them was drunk, and all of them looked quiet men, who wished that they had never caused such a bother. One of the Americans even stood up and offered, as the offending couple passed, to take the German's place, but the woman would have none of that. After a time there were long pauses in the shouting, and it would break out again following a particularly vicious remark from one side or the other.

The one person in the room who appeared to be entirely unconcerned was the dancing negro. Apparently he felt that his partner was happy with him and the indifferent music, since the face that he bent down was radiant, and his smile crinkled the thick skin right up to his eyes.

Isabel had had enough of all this, and so had I. We rose to go; the old waiter stopped us at the bottom of the stairs. He hoped that we would return another night. It was the first time that such a scandal had happened since the *dancing* opened, and he realised what a false impression

41

monsieur and madame were carrying away. But, although he was only doing his duty as a conscientious waiter, by delaying our departure he ensured that we carried away a still worse impression.

During those silences more menacing than the shouts a plot had been hatched, and we saw the culmination of it when one of the whores swept the dancing couple's legs from under them with a chair, and then with a shriek the whole party of six joined battle, kicking, hitting, scratching the woman, and I suppose the man, on the ground. Reinforcements arrived for both sides. The German party stood back, looking most worried, but the Americans waded slowly and good-humouredly into the fight, endeavouring to separate the women, and getting themselves properly clawed and beaten for their pains. At the same time the young French couple hurled themselves across the floor, and while the youth struck and then exchanged blows with an American, the girl lashed repeatedly with her handbag at the head of the woman in evening dress who had been the cause of it all; the blows drew blood and piercing screams, for the handbag had a glittering metal clasp.

The accordionist watched with passionate interest, her head still a little on one side, her arms working tirelessly; she had increased both tempo and volume, perhaps betraying her excitement at the scene so close to her, perhaps in an attempt to conceal the noise of the fight from any passing patrols. Faster and faster she played, and the negro danced around the floor, whirling his imaginary partner almost off her feet, occasionally murmuring a short sentence to her, or laying his thin, wrinkled cheek against hers. But even he was not destined to remain in our memories as a dancing figure, for as he danced past the fight, weaving his body and his feet clear of the arms and legs that swept over the floor, the woman to whom he had given a cigarette walked up behind him, a bottle of synthetic *jus d'ananas* lifted high above her head. The sound of the breaking bottle, clearly audible even in that pandemonium, would not in itself have stopped the fight, but the accordionist faltered and the music softened and died. The negro's head was covered with blood and pharmaceutical pineapple juice but his expression was unchanged. His body maintained the upright for what seemed to be a long time; then it began to buckle at the knees and the hips, and he fell with a terrible sound, as though every bone had been disconnected before his body hit the floor.

The waiter stood forward. "Gentlemen, ladies! I beseech you. . . . The police . . ."

The fat woman was tying her bleeding hand with a piece of pink satin torn from the dress of the German's partner, and she was weeping without restraint. The young Frenchman was stretched out on a banquette. He was moving, but I could not see his face. The Americans, like puzzled sheep-dogs, had herded the Germans and the two dancing partners into a bunch.

"Gentlemen, ladies! Be prudent. . . . Be fair. . . . Be reasonable . . ."

The fat woman and one of her friends began to drag the negro along the floor. His feet were grotesquely large in their rubber-soled boots and the body left a wet trail.

"What are those women doing?" Isabel called to the waiter. "Stop them! What are they doing?"

"Please do not upset yourself, madame. It is better for him that he should recover in the darkness, especially if the military police come."

They had pulled him down the room. The darkness crept along his flaccid legs.

"Is he badly hurt?"

"Not he," answered the trembling old waiter. "Ah! Those abominable women!" he turned from us with a sigh and a gentle good night.

"By the way," I called to him. "What was this place in the old days?"

"It was a shooting range, Monsieur. Gentlemen used to practise here with rifles and revolvers and duelling pistols. I was never here then."

The two women reappeared from the darkness; the fat one had her arm around the other's neck. Both were smoking cigarettes and smiling. The fat one's face was agreeable again.

4

DESPITE our late night, and the thin negroes scented with crême-de-
menthe who pursued Isabel in her dreams, we were already breakfasting in
bed at 6.30, while rain drummed on the deck above us. Our deck—
at this period—was completely waterproof, but to me at any rate the noise
of rain striking a boat is eerie and unpleasant, quite different from the tap
of raindrops on the windows of a house, a sound that seems to enhance
such comforts as may be gathered indoors.

We had been told at the harbour-master's office that we must pass
through the first lock leading to the Tancarville Canal at 8 o'clock.
At 7.30, extremely apprehensive about our chances of extricating
ourselves unscathed from so congested a harbour in a high wind, I began
to get in the anchor chain, finding the windlass extremely hard work until
Isabel gave *Truant* little forward kicks with the engines. Covered with
sticky clay, the chain came in, a glistening and odoriferous grey serpent,
and we allowed much of this filth—many a time we laughed at ourselves
for it later—to pass with the chain through the deck and through the
bathroom to the chain locker, under the bathroom floor. We were too
agitated at that moment about our boat's behaviour in the wind to worry
about dirt. When we had got the anchor, I busied myself with a boat-
hook, pushing *Truant* clear of the solid fishing-boats on either hand. While
darting agitatedly from side to side I frequently fell over, for I was en-
cumbered by oilskins and seaboots, and our pine decks were varnished;
varnish on deck, I learned in these and subsequent moments of stress, can
be very beautiful, but when it is wet it is dangerous. Of course, just as
anyone can learn to frolic on the ice, so anyone can learn to walk, run, and
jump on wet varnished decks.

The fishing-boats had been built to withstand brutal knocks in harbour,
and we were reasonably protected ourselves, since that morning I had hung
over our sides fourteen coir fenders, none of them less than twelve inches in
diameter. But things looked serious when, having eased forward from the
fishing-boats, *Truant* refused to come about into the wind, and we proceeded to run down three flimsy yachts, moored in a row. Somehow, by
our combined efforts, Isabel with the engines and rudder, and I stretched
on our bowsprit, kicking, we extricated ourselves, and moved off into the

outer harbour. Then we detected why *Truant* had been so slow in coming about; the starboard propeller was not functioning properly, and I remembered a little too late that on entering port we had allowed that propeller to sever the dinghy tow-rope, a length of strong two-inch manilla. We congratulated ourselves on two things: the weather was so unpleasant that there had been no witnesses of our departure; and *Truant* seemed to move along quite manageably on the port engine alone.

We passed slowly through several great locks, constructed to lift ships to the higher levels of the port, and at length found ourselves in a long basin with ships of many nationalities towering on either side, and barges packed closely in the shadows, or scuttling about under their own power, or towed in strings by tugs. At the end of this basin we were obliged to stop, and bargees shouted to us that the steel tipping-bridge ahead of us would not lift to permit the passage of water traffic for two hours. The rain of the early morning had given way to a hot sun. We made fast alongside a French boat, a former tank-landing craft. For over an hour we scrubbed and sluiced and mopped at the mess we had made with the anchor chain. Even on deck, it was almost impossible to get rid of the clay, while below Isabel had to wash with soap and hot water every square inch of the bathroom's white paintwork.

When we had eaten a good meal of cold chicken, salad, and the last of our English strawberries we came on deck to sun ourselves and to wait for the bridge to lift. We were both fascinated—although it was not the first time that I had seen them—by the big barges, long, well-painted steel hulls with wheelhouses and living quarters aft. The attractive feature of those craft is the strong impression of travelling domesticity that they give, for since they rarely go to sea, but traverse Europe, or at any rate Germany, Holland, Belgium and France, by river and canal, the movement of the boat is normally as steady as that of a heavy sleigh drawn over smooth ice, and so family life is allowed to spread itself across the decks. Although the self-propelled motor barges can carry 300 tons of cargo in their holds, and are thoroughly workmanlike craft, perfectly suited to the important part they play in the economy of those countries that depend on waterways as we depend on roads and railways, yet they resemble nothing so much as travelling advertisements for the comforts of monogamous happiness.

The barges swarmed with children and small, yapping dogs; they carried hens and rabbits; all of them had little flower gardens in what the people of London would call window-boxes, and many plants in pots which were brought out into the sun during fine weather. Although this was a Wednesday, and we supposed that the usual washing day was Monday,

45

a great many of the barges were hung with wet clothing; on a chocolate-coloured barge called the *Marie Brizard* a large, almost chocolate-coloured woman had her great arms buried in the soapsuds and as she lifted a shirt, a dress or a piece of underclothing as thick and heavy as medieval chain mail to hang it on the cords that were stretched on poles above the black hatches the froth would float from her arms.

At 2 o'clock, with a great many hootings from the boats on either side of it—for the captain of a French barge likes to have a powerful horn, and to use it—the bridge began to lift. This surprised us, for we had paid a special visit to the port office to ask if *Truant* would be able to pass through the canal with her masts in position, and we had been told officially that the bridges, which had all been destroyed by the Germans, had been rebuilt of the swing, instead of the lifting, variety. Furthermore, I could see that there was not much to spare above the top of our mast as we went under, and a second bridge, quarter of a mile further on, looked lower still. We passed under the second one, moving an inch at a time, and I was obliged to lower the burgee; but we passed and there we were—out in the sunny canal.

The Tancarville Canal was cut so that boats mounting from le Havre to the great inland port of Rouen, could save themselves the passage through the shifting and treacherous mouth of the river Seine. Low ground, reclaimed estuary swamps, lay on the starboard hand, while to port gentle hills rose dotted at first with cheap houses and then later, when le Havre lay well astern, chequered with strip cultivation. We formed the second unit of a string of barges hurrying up the canal to catch the lifting tide on the Seine at the far end.

Although I was inclined to fuss about the starboard propeller, and to make fruitless attempts to send the boat along with that engine, even mechanical worry could not rob me of delight in our progress. I steered in the sunshine at the tiller aft, and Isabel sat beside me on a deck chair. We passed a champagne-coloured horse with a lemon-coloured tail; we passed two bourgeois fishermen on the bank, one in a blue town suit and the other in pink overalls, but neither bothered to raise his head to look at us; we passed artillerymen shelling a target down in the swamps, and they abandoned their guns to watch us out of sight; we passed a sleepy village at the water's edge, and a cow raised its face to look unseeingly at us from the grass outside the Restaurant des Pêcheurs. The afternoon sailed by. At six we saw the Tancarville lock ahead, and the barge leading us made for the bank, thrusting its weight against large stakes. The bargee's wife, a handsome gipsy woman, launched their dinghy from a clever, single davit with a chain purchase, sprang down with unbelievable agility, and took a

46

wire hawser ashore. We moved alongside the barge and I asked if we might make fast to them, as the stakes were unsuitably positioned for us.

"Ne vous gênez pas." The man sent two of his brats scuffling along the black iron deck to take our warps. The wife came back to the barge, hauling herself, hand over hand up the falls from the davit. She had brass rings in her ears. One of the children was hers, a wilder, darker, more sluttish child than the others. The husband was a square man with ginger hair and a face wrinkled by years of exposure. We wondered where he had found the dark woman. She told us that she was his fourth wife.

"He kills them off," she said. "When I came on the boat my father foretold that it would be the end of me too."

"Where did you meet?"

"In Belgium," she said. "During the war."

"Did you live in Belgium?"

"Of course not," she said. "I was brought up on a barge. But not such a good one as this. My father was a dirty old . . ." (Isabel had never heard the word she used, and did not forget to ask me later what it meant.) "I always wanted to find a man like this one, though I wish I had found him when he was younger and had fewer children by other wives."

The husband came out of the engine-room. He asked me if we had been going at full speed.

"No, about half speed."

"Ah! I knew you could catch us if you wanted to."

"But your barge goes along well. You were doing about five knots."

Both of them looked at me. "Never talk about knots to us," said the man. "A *marin* talks in knots, a *marinier* talks in kilometres."

"Are you captain of this barge or do you own her?"

He threw back his head and laughed. The woman laid a hand on his forearm and laughed with him. "I struck lucky from the war," he said. "I had a wooden barge with a motor. But it was an old barge. I lost that one in the Canal de la Marne when the Germans machine-gunned us from the air. But after a while the Germans needed captains for barges, and they gave me this one, a good barge, Dutch-built. Well, now the Germans are gone and we own the barge. It's worth more than a million francs. But I wouldn't sell for five million."

They were short of food, and had not seen potatoes for three weeks. Isabel gave the woman potatoes and fresh eggs. They offered to pay. Perhaps they thought that we represented a new type of black-market dealer, coming over from England to sell wares direct from our boat to the river people.

Tancarville lock was a stone cavern, infinitely higher than others through which we had passed. I climbed up a metal ladder let into the masonry, and accompanied the barge captains to the lock-keeper's office. Each captain gave the official twenty francs when his papers had been examined, and I did likewise.

"Do you always tip the lock-keeper?" I asked the ginger captain. (The French canals are run at government expense and there is no charge for passing through them.)

"On the rivers we generally give them ten francs if they're polite, five francs if they're so-so, and sweet Fanny Adam if they're swine, which is rare. We each gave this one twenty because he's supposed to close down at eight, see? but he opened specially to let us catch the tide. Now on the canals we give them nothing at all, because if you tipped on the canals there are so many locks you'd have mortgaged your cargo before you were half-way through."

Some thirty spectators had gathered on the edge of the lock to look down at *Truant's* decks; their feet were level with the burgee. Isabel, her head thrown back to look at them, was answering their questions. Before I could descend the ladder a man caught hold of me; he pointed beyond the lock to the wide river.

"What's this?" he exclaimed. "Madame says that you've no pilot."

"No."

"I wish I could come with you. But keep thirty metres from the right bank and you'll be all right." The others joined in.

"Don't go near the green buoys," one advised.

"Keep the green buoys on your right," another said.

"But he should have a pilot, the river is all dangerous."

"He only draws one metre, fifty-two, I tell you he can go anywhere he likes as far as Rouen, all he has to do is keep thirty metres from the right bank."

"Look here . . ." A man in nautical uniform, who told me that he was the captain of a small coaster anchored in the river, advised me to stay the night at Quilleboeuf. "It is the first town on your right une fois lancé sur la Seine." His expression was apt. No sooner had we left the lock than we were swept upriver by a tide that humped itself over unseen obstacles on the river bottom. The Seine is wide there, with flattish banks. We were mystified by the buoys, which did not conform to what we read in the Sailing Directions; although we had tried to buy a chart of the river, we had not succeeded, since the French were so short of paper at that time that they were not reprinting such publications, and old stocks were exhausted.

We were soon level with Quilleboeuf, and it looked all that the sea captain had promised. We saw the hotel, of which he had spoken, and the restaurants. The only thing that prevented us from tying up there was that the tide was frothing past what was apparently a shoaling beach, and we could see no object to which we might attach ourselves. In a few seconds we had swept past the grey, well-proportioned houses, the boxed privets and geraniums outside the cafés, and were opposite a very different type of place, Port Jérôme, where several tanker barges lay deep in the water after taking cargoes of oil from the refinery. It never entered my head to anchor, and if I intended to make fast to anything the only solution in such tidal water, unless we cared to tend our warps every half hour, was to make use of a buoy or a barge. I chose the latter, and coming about, we put both engines full ahead, and just managed to creep downstream against the flood. Two youths on one of the barges very politely took our warps and we made fast. They said that we would be well advised to turn *Truant* about at slack water, some three hours later, before the ebb tide could arrive "to catch the yacht in the backside". But when we had eaten we felt too lazy to do anything more. I put two four-inch warps over the stern, making them fast to the steel bitts on the barge. Forward there was a new two-inch rope, and although I was going to put a heavy warp there too, the mariniers told me it would more than suffice.

I had not been long asleep when I was wakened by a noise of rushing water so loud that I thought we had been swept downstream and were suspended on the edge of a weir. I hurried out on deck. The ebb had thrust us a good fifteen feet clear of the side of the barge; our two stern warps were rigid, while the thinner bow rope sang, like a violin string; our rudder was jammed hard over, and this was pushing the bow out, away from the barge, but my utmost efforts failed to move it. The tide seemed to be running at about nine knots. I went back to bed, but slept very ill.

Soon after dawn there was a report so sharp that both of us were instantly awake. I ran on deck, to find that the bow rope had parted half-way between the yacht and the barge, but *Truant*, after a preliminary quiver, seemed to ride better without it; she remained some fifteen feet from the barge and parallel to it, with both stern warps bar-taut. A rotund, elderly man in striped trousers and a grey singlet, the father of the youths who had helped us to make fast, inquired if I could spare him some meat. I found two tins of bully beef; when I held them up he expressed great delight and refused to allow me to throw them across the intervening space of rushing water until he had rousted one of his sons out of bed.

49

"Don't throw them to me, monsieur, throw them to the lad, for I am old." I heartily disliked the long quaver he put into the last word, and climbed back into bed, feeling that if I spent many more nights on *Truant* I should be quivering and quavering myself. As I was tumbling off to sleep I again heard the fat man's unctuous voice.

"Monsieur, monsieur!" He was so persistent that finally I pushed my head out of the hatch. "There is my tug," he cried, gesticulating toward a small, distant shape that looked like a black shaving brush walking on the water.

"Oh yes," I began to withdrew my head.

"But you don't understand," he said. "You must cast off."

"Out of the question," I answered. "Look at that tide. We should be carried half-way to the sea . . ." I had to sit arguing with him until the tug was nearly on top of us, and there began to be some truth in his assurances that it was nearly time for slack water. Isabel joined me in the hatchway, and we decided that we must move or risk being sandwiched between the barge and the tug. We found that we were able to make slow headway upstream provided we kept *Truant* away from the main ebb-flow. Quite soon the flood began; we moved to midstream, and with an eight-knot tide below us ran past the banks at some fourteen knots. We could count on the flood-tide all the way to Rouen, a distance of ninety-one kilometres.

Those lower reaches of the Seine are very beautiful. The valley is sumptuously rich with estates, châteaux and woodlands. The river often sharply bends into a wooded hillside and it is in such places that the villages are placed, on the elbow of the river and tucked into the land and the trees. It was a wonderful ride, surging on the back of the unnatural stream. When Isabel went below to cook lunch we entered a wide reach near a hamlet called Duclair; the wind, which a few minutes earlier had been so solidly behind us that I had meditated hoisting a squaresail, was now dead ahead and blowing down the reach in the teeth of the tide to such effect that the tops of the short waves whipped over our bows, flashing spray through the galley hatch. I heard Isabel shout in the stentorian voice that she is able to assume at will: "What's happening?"

A mile further upstream we were again in calm water. She carried the meal aft on trays which were passed through from our cabin to the wheelhouse, and she arranged a "table" between us on the chart-table on which we normally sat, she on the port side. This was the first of many, many meals taken in the wheelhouse. Each of us developed a faculty for steering with a foot and eating at the same time, and sometimes in tricky passages we would quickly alternate at the wheel and still contrive to eat and drink comfortably.

The last stage of our journey was completed in cold wind and rain. In the early evening we came to the factories on the outskirts of Rouen. I had expected to recognise the waterfront in the centre of Rouen because I am familiar with many of Boudin's pictures of the town. I had forgotten le Havre, and the evidence of every half-gutted village that we had passed; the battered façades before the tall wounded cathedral, the temporary bridge ahead, shocked me deeply. We tied up alongside an Alsatian barge. The captain's fat wife told us that the barge would be stopping in Rouen for some days: her daughter was ill with a fallen stomach, and was being treated by a doctor. The tragedy (it could be called nothing less, in France at any rate) of the fallen stomach was our gain, for this was the only barge at the long quay which was not departing with the beginning of the ebb-tide at 4 a.m.

* * * *

Jean Cordelier had fought for General de Gaulle during the war. He told me his real name when he came to see us on *Truant*, but I had forgotten it as soon as I heard it, for I can only think of him by his nom-de-guerre. He is a small man, dark-haired, with an extremely high colour in the cheeks, thick, steel-rimmed spectacles and a mouth that is always as damp as a sea anemone. This dampness affects his speech, which, although it is extremely rapid, is spluttered, rather than articulated. Jean would be the first to admit that he was a very inefficient soldier. He had gone through a part of the war with me, exclaiming at short intervals: "I am badly placed as a soldier; I am a business man, and I will never make a soldier. There is no sense in a soldier's job."

The war was over; he had returned to his business, and he was doing well. The proof of it was that he had a car—a Hotchkiss at that—and he could afford to buy petrol at sixty francs a litre on the black market.

"Don't let's talk about the war," I said when he came on board. "Let's pass a whole day talking about other things."

"I should be only too willing to comply," he said. "But we are going to pick up Marie, and I fear I could not vouch for such discretion on her part." We drove to his villa on the outskirts of the town. The house had been built on the principle that it was cheapest and best to cover a small space of ground and sprout upwards like the beanstalk, and that beauty in architecture consisted of an exotic shape and maximum contrasts in surface decoration.

"There is certainly a touch of the Orient—Japan perhaps—in the roof," Jean said. He adored his house. They had not lived there before the war. Then they had occupied a bigger place, nearer the centre of the town, but that had been flattened by bombs and their only child had been killed in it. Jean took us to the garden while Marie prepared to go out. The garden was small, well-manured, and filled to bursting point with vegetables. The strawberries were huge and succulent; they were dusty, and we washed them in the rain-water barrel before we ate them, then some cress, then more strawberries. It was a pity to dip the strawberries in the water, for this chilled them slightly and spoiled their flavour. Jean was childishly delighted at our pleasure in his fruit. "Is it not good? Are they not delicious? They are best like that, eaten straight from the soil. Do you know what I think, begging madame's pardon? When you kill a bullock his flesh begins to dirty itself, to become tinged with urine from the moment that the life-stream ceases to flow; well, I believe that fruits and vegetables also have their little natural functions, just like us and the beasts, and I believe that the moment *their* life-stream is stopped they begin to go bad." He thought that he had said something very profound. He jumped into the car. "Now it's agreed that to-day we forget about the war, isn't it?" he said as he negotiated the gateway. He drove, very fast indeed, back through the town, for we were going to eat at la Bouille, a handsome village below Rouen, on the left bank. (What is called the left bank of the Seine, by the way, is the bank that is on your left as you descend the river; when going upstream in a boat you are therefore correct in calling the bank on your right hand 'the left bank'.)

Rouen was built on a large elbow of the Seine, and up to the last period of the Second World War it stood on both banks of the river. But as Jean drove us towards la Bouille we saw that little of Rouen remained on the left bank. Both Jean and Marie kept looking about them, at the places that had for years been familiar, and were no longer so. Here the houses had been hit by so many bombs that the streets were no more.

"This is history," Marie said to us eventually, "so in spite of our agreement not to speak of those things, I must tell you that it was in this bend of the Seine that the Allies penned a large part of the retreating German Army, and destroyed it. You should have seen the Germans. They were determined to escape across the river, but the aeroplanes had destroyed all the bridges. They flung themselves into the river. Even those who could not swim—and there were many such—attempted to cross riding horses, riding cows, with the inflated inner tubes of tyres around their bodies, in wash-tubs. But the aeroplanes swept low over the water and machine-gunned them. When it was over half of Rouen was gone, but a German Army had gone too. It is said that ten thousand German bodies had to be removed."

"How were they buried?" I asked.

"They were heaped on lorries and taken up to a big trench on the hill above that château," Jean said. "They spread lime over each layer."

"We went into the shelters," she said. "But when we saw what was going on, and that the aeroplanes were coming very low and only attacking the left bank, we came out to watch. Half of Rouen was destroyed, but it was worth it, well worth it. . . . There, we have told you. I only thought that you would want to know about that. Now let's talk about other things."

Jean began to tell us how they had killed their pig, then we talked about business and rationing, and by that time we had reached the restaurant. There was the usual black-market meal; we drank Normandy cider with the pâté and the fish, Nuits St. Georges with the meat, and calvados with the coffee. Afterwards Jean drove us a little further down the river bank.

"I'm going to show you where Rouen came from," he said. We left the car, and walked up a slippery incline criss-crossed with narrow-gauge railway tracks. We entered a great hole in the hillside, a hole perhaps ninety feet high and sixty wide, and continued to walk under a tremendous natural vault. "Our cathedral and all of the public monuments, as well as the town's finest buildings, came out of this hole," Jean said.

The place was dimly lit, apparently by shafts driven to the surface of the hill. The walls were damp; underfoot was rock on which cinders had been thickly strewn. In the distance I saw a dark, contorted shape.

"I expect you've had enough of this," Jean said.

"How far does it go on?"

"Oh, for a long way." A sailor passed us, walking in the opposite direction, with his girl. I continued to the shape, and found that it was a compressor, of modern German manufacture. Beyond, in the darkness, were lines of other machines; on the cinders, around them I saw small pieces of rag and paper.

"So this was an underground factory?"

"Yes. The Germans planned to manufacture rockets here. They had thousands of Russians to do the work. God knows how many died."

"Did they keep them here all the time? Did they make them sleep in this awful place?"

"No, they marched them away at night, to camps near-by."

Those same cinders had crunched beneath the Russians' feet. The inhumanity of the immense cavern, the sufferings that its walls had witnessed, the damp chill, the smell, were almost enough to turn our stomachs. Almost, but not quite. We had had a good meal; the alcohol still warmed us. Yet the cavern made me feel that perhaps we were wrong to make agreements not to talk about the war; our whims were shallow beside the fate of the slaves and the memory of them.

It was good to get outside, and into the car, where the air was still warm from our late presence. The Russians had been marched nightly from their working place along the road which we now pursued, past a row of bourgeois houses, places with a kitchen, a sitting-room and three or four bedrooms. What must the slaves have thought of those houses and their semi-prosperous inhabitants? The houses were detached from the lane, by small front gardens with wooden palings and fanciful wooden gates. Near the end of the row, we saw a house that was completely burned out.

"Hullo," I said. "That was bad luck. I was just thinking that there was something very strange about this road, and that house made me realise what the strangeness was—no bomb damage."

"That was not done by bombs," Marie said.

"I'll drive you to the top, there's a glorious view," Jean said.

"There's no need to change the subject," she rebuked him sharply. "We have no reason to feel anything but satisfaction about that house."

Jean pursed his damp lips, and drove faster. I wondered at that moment if his marriage, like so many others, had been broken, beneath the surface, by the war. He had been three years at least away from his wife, and he had only returned to her when Rouen was first liberated, because although he had worked in 1943 and 1944 as an agent for the de Gaullists in France, they had been careful to position him in areas far removed from his home, and had forbidden him even to allow Marie to know that he still lived. Marie looked with apparent anger at those pursed lips, and she refused to keep silence.

"The house belonged to a woman who wronged her country infamously," she said loudly.

"Oh come, Marie, the poor creature was only half French, she had a Swiss father, and German-Swiss at that."

"What's the matter with you, Jean? Since the war black is no longer black for you, nor white, white."

"All I know is that the woman was half-German, it's absurd to label her as a Frenchwoman. She should have been left alone. She was a decent enough person. Her house was clean and she paid her rent, asking no favour. It was only natural that she should not have experienced that

54

repugnance for the Germans which most good Frenchwomen felt it their duty to affirm."

"Listen to who's talking," Marie cried.

Jean flushed with that purple tinge often seen in Normandy. "We were all mad in those days of the liberation," he said. "It was good to be home, and so strange. I didn't care where I went so long as I went with you and the others and there was excitement and something to drink."

"So it's all my fault now, is it?"

"I didn't say that."

"Look out!" she cried, as Jean swerved the car to avoid a heavy lorry loaded with gravel, which swung round a bend. It was the last bend of the ascent, and Jean, breathing heavily from the near-accident and probably also from irritation, brought the car to a stop on a high ridge, overlooking the Seine, with Rouen some ten miles away. We expressed our appreciation of the scene in the rather numb fashion that approval must always display itself when it is expected. Marie was not going to let the other matter drop.

"I see that I must tell the Millars about this incendiarism," she said, and without giving anyone time to protest, she hurried on. "The woman, as Jean has remarked in her defence, was a Swiss, in that she was the daughter of a German-Swiss, who had adopted French nationality. She was his only daughter, and although both her parents died when she was young, leaving her in easy circumstances, she worked all her life as governess in one or other of the châteaux you now see before you. Her favourite task was teaching German."

"And why not?" asked Jean.

"Don't interrupt. I forgot to say that she never married, and so far as is known she never had a lover until this war, for she was ugly and the men around here have a wide choice. When the war came, and the Boches settled here, she dropped her work as governess, retiring with her earnings plus all the money her family had left to that small house near la Bouille. In 1944 there began to be whispers among the decent women of the neighbourhood. A German, an elderly man, and one of the swine who were responsible for the poor Russians in the cavern . . ."

" 'Poor Russians!' What did you or your friends ever do for the 'poor Russians' if you pitied them so much? And how d'you know that the German was such a swine? You never even bothered to ask the 'poor Russians'. Possibly they'd have had a good word for him . . ."

"Jean! I'm telling this story . . ."

"I'd like to hear you tell it in a less biased fashion."

"Are you saying that I'm lying?"

"I'm only warning you that there are ways of making the truth sound like lies."

"This German, as I was about to tell you, was seen entering and leaving her house. Naturally, there were suspicions, but if the creature had been less heavy—I suppose the heaviness came from her own German blood—she could have extricated herself. When she was asked why the German went to her house she admitted that he went there at her express invitation. Naturally, from that moment she was banished from all the societies for aiding our prisoners in Germany and not one decent woman ever spoke to her again . . ."

"Naturally!" Jean said.

"And when our great old town was liberated she and her kind were not to be seen in the streets. The first round of celebrations reached its climax, and there was a pause—do you remember, my dear?—when it was suggested that the women who had profited by the presence of the Boches should be made to grieve their departure. A good many common women were caught and had all their hair shaved off. It was late at night when somebody remembered the house by the cave. A crowd drove down there—everybody seemed to have an automobile in those few days—and they shouted at her to open her door and entertain the coiffeur. It would have been well for her had she opened, but she kept the door locked, and she went to an upstairs window to shout at them. She threatened them . . ."

"Did she?" Jean interrupted. "I understood that she only told them that they were tipsy, and that they would regret it later if they did anything violent to an elderly and respectable woman . . ."

"Respectable! Regret! Those words coming from that woman. . . . Well, they gave her five minutes to come out—why should they bother to argue with a creature of her type?—and at the end of the five minutes some of the men set fire to the bushes and creepers that grew round the base of her house. They soaked them in petrol or oil of some sort, and there was a proper conflagration. She never reappeared. She preferred to stay inside and burn to death, rather than face them. Was that the action of an honest, of an innocent, woman . . ."

"Honest! Innocent!" Jean shouted angrily. He threw his cigarette out of the window, and started the engine. "To speak so of a murdered woman who was never charged with any crime! Every time that you and your friends speak of it you convict yourselves. Judge not, that ye be not judged. I tell you, George, it is not even likely that this elderly woman cohabited with her German friend. And if she did, then it will be for the future and for her God to decide whether she committed a crime for which other imperfect mortals were entitled to punish her."

"You and your cohabitation!" Marie said. "A word like that takes all the sin out of what she did, making her crime sound like frogs' spawn in a pond. She was French, was she not, and in the hour of her country's defeat and betrayal by the Germans she took a German into her bed."

"I don't believe that she did, and supposing she did, I admit it would be unsavoury, but what about your friend Gaspard? He had German mistresses during the war, yet that's supposed to be quite decent, for some reason. Can't see any difference myself."

"Gaspard was a prisoner in Germany. It was almost his duty to cuckold German husbands. I know we'll never agree on this; but I'd like to know what you'd have thought had you returned to find that I was one of those who entertained a German. Besides, the Boche was in the house with her, and that was why she never came out to have her head shaved."

"Prove it."

"It makes sense, and my intuition tells me that it was so."

"Your woman's intuition!" Jean spoke so passionately that his glasses misted, and saliva ran down his chin. "Then just tell me how your intuition explains that there was only one body, and that a woman's, found in the burned ruins of her house."

"I don't believe that. It's never been officially confirmed. The police at that time were a queer lot anyway."

He drove to Rouen.

Their conversation had been carried on diagonally, across the car. Isabel, who sat in the back, beside Marie, had not uttered a word. I noticed, however, that when Jean and Marie came on board *Truant* with us to have tea, Isabel sat Marie in the saloon beneath a porthole which was apt to leak. We had arrived on board in a heavy rain shower, and quite soon a succession of drops fell on Marie. Isabel apologised and made her move to another seat, but Marie insisted that they had bored us long enough with their company. Before she was allowed to go Isabel made her presents, and Marie gave us the addresses of some of her friends in Paris, Chalon-sur-Saône, Lyons, and Nice. We walked ashore with them in the rain. Jean paused with his hand on the door of the car.

"I must go straight to the office now," he said.

"But surely you can drive me home first, darling?"

"Very sorry. I'm already late." He drove away.

She opened her umbrella with a snap. She was still a reasonably good-looking woman. "Oh, it's quite all right," she assured me. "There are plenty of buses."

*   *   *   *

He had called himself Dynamo since he had read of the successful Russian football team, the Moscow Dynamos, which made a flashing post-war appearance in the non-Russian zone of Europe. He possessed the square, blunt physique that is more often to be seen in Belgium, Holland and northern France and Germany than in other parts of Europe. I can remember little about him except his self-imposed name, his monumental goodwill and usefulness, and the energy that seemed to hiss from his short, cylindrical fingers as oxygen spurts from a cylinder when a tap is turned. He was the oldest son of the captain of a barge that made fast at night partly to *Truant* and partly to the barge to which *Truant* was secured, so that we woke one morning to find ourselves in the position of the ham in a ham sandwich, all the bread being barge. Although they were not Alsatians but Normans, the new arrivals contrived somehow to be cousins of the Alsatian family, who remained in Rouen because of that obstinately fallen stomach.

The previous evening I had stripped most of the cordage from our masts, and had unshipped the bowsprit. I had attached a label to each separate piece of rigging to assist me in replacing it correctly when it was time to take to the sea again. Yachtsmen in England had advised me to seek the assistance of a large crane for the operation of lowering the masts, but Dynamo said: "What d'you want with a crane when I can ask my family to help? We are accustomed to doing such jobs and cranes cost money." He called his father and two younger brothers and some of the male members of the Alsatian family. We lowered the mainmast first; I held it with a tackle from the stem-head; Dynamo stationed his father and uncle with tackles on the two flanking barges, while he himself directed operations, darting from danger point to danger point. He climbed to the wheelhouse roof to catch the mast in his own short, thick arms. With the mast resting in its tabernacle the peak, they said, would be too high to negotiate the low bridges on the canals; the heel would have to be raised. Dynamo jumped on to his barge for wood and tools, and in a short time he had built a raised wooden pulpit over our mainmast tabernacle. Between this pulpit and the wheelhouse roof we were able to support the masts and booms, as well as the bowsprit, gaff, squaresail yard, dinghy mast and spars and the awning batterns. I gave Dynamo a large quantity of rope, and he lashed all the spars in their new resting place as well as the dinghy, which we set on its side on deck aft. We spread the sail covers over the spars to protect them from the hot sun, and stowed the sails with the rigging in the after cabin. We invited them all below, and offered them whisky and cigarettes. All drank and smoked except Dynamo and his two young brothers. The two brothers accepted chocolate, but Dynamo said that he disliked sweet things. I slipped out on deck with Dynamo and offered him money; he refused it.

"But you could sign my autograph book," he said, producing a thick book wrapped in paper covers which he pulled back to show the scarlet-and-yellow tartan binding. Inside we saw a good many names that were familiar, the names of a tennis player, a French airman, Colonel Lindbergh, Edouard Herriot, General Leclerc, and somebody had signed "Napoleon". Dynamo stood with the pen and the ink-bottle in one strong hand and the book in the other. Isabel had been called away by his mother to have a glass of prunelle on the barge. "Would it be asking too much . . ." he began. "Are you aware of the manner in which Monsieur Churchill . . ."

"Give me the book." In a pugnacious hand I signed "Winston Churchill" and handed him back his book. "It goes like that."

"Admirable!" he said, and we shook hands warmly.

*　　　*　　　*　　　*

At midday we were off. The barges were held apart with the twenty-feet-long, iron-shod barge poles that the mariniers know well how to put to a great number of uses, and we slipped out from between them. That first bridge had to be passed, according to river regulations, against the flow of the tide, and we experienced for the first time the strange things that a stream, compressed between the supports of a bridge can do to an approaching hull, thrusting it now to one side, now, swiftly, to the other. We had passed, like many barges, at the tail end of the ebb-tide, and now ambled up the wide river, waiting for the flood to run up astern and boost us to the first lock on the Seine itself, at Ampréville.

Our friends on the barges at Rouen had warned us that the channels between islands on the Seine were not always deep enough to float *Truant*. Wherever there was a separation of the waters, they told us, we should see a disc one half of which would be red, the other white, and the latter in-dicated the navigable channel. Isabel soon went below to cook. We passed two little islands, each showing a large red-and-white disc; then we came to a third which showed no disc. "Both channels must be navigable," I thought, and I steered on, up the wider stretch of water. A tanker barge was following some two hundred yards astern. When we were well engaged in our channel I looked round, and was a little perturbed to see that the barge had taken the other. Almost immediately there was a most ominous grating noise from our keel. I shut off the engine; Isabel, who had both heard and felt a jar, came quickly to the wheel, and I ran forward to take soundings with the long boat-hook. Isabel kept very calm. But I, envisaging damaged propellers, a strained hull, sandbanks and salvage, ran about issuing wild cries that were neither orders nor imprecations, but rather something in between. I am apt to behave in the way that an Anglo-Saxon likes to believe that a Latin reacts to an emergency, while that less Nordic creature, Isabel, behaves when things go wrong with almost Prussian self-discipline. My pole told me that we were in five feet of water, and surely had barely an inch of it below our heavy oak keel, but we crept on without grounding, into the broad river again.

Wide and peaceful, the Seine wound between foothills. I had never seen France so verdant, and the reason was obvious; surely there had never been so cold, so wet a June. The day was not sufficiently warm for us to steer outside in comfort. Occasional flashes of sunshine alternated with rainstorms. We floated through a whole afternoon of unspoiled country, a little sleepy after lunch, a little dazed by the calm, but complicated, watery world in which we moved, a little surprised by the number of barges that we met or passed and by their movements. The barges did not, as we had anticipated, move sedately up- or down-stream keeping near the middle, and perhaps a shade towards the bank on their starboard hand; in fact they frequently crossed and recrossed the stream. For two kilometres we might follow a barge up the rive gauche and so close to the edge that the small outer branches of the willows would caress our decks, then, although the river stretched ahead apparently unchanging, our leader might turn to port, angle sharply across the stream, and follow the rive droite. They appeared to rate the importance of these movements more highly than any rule of the river, overtaking slowly-moving barges or passing oncoming traffic either to port or to starboard as it pleased them. We had been advised both in England and in Rouen to hire the services of a professional pilot as far as Paris, but neither of us could bear thus to forgo much of the pleasure of so beautiful a journey. In Rouen we had bought a map of the Seine, but it was only an ordinary Michelin road map, which represented a space of 250 miles in some twenty-five inches. Two navigational aids which we had been unprepared to find of use in the narrow waters leading across France were of considerable importance: the compass often showed us exactly where we were on the map, and the binoculars were necessary for distinguishing on-coming traffic, obstacles, red-and-white discs, and lock signals.

I had relieved Isabel at the wheel to allow her to prepare tea when I saw the white line of foam of Ampréville weir. Clusters of fishing-boats were gathered in the soapy-looking water. The lock had just filled with a full quota of barges. I seized the "bulldog" foghorn and extracted from it a succession of loud roars, but the electric signal beside the lock changed from green to red, and we were obliged to stop against the high wooden piles to starboard of the entrance. I made fast to the piles, and we had tea in the wheelhouse while rain streamed down and the barges that we had passed during the afternoon began to gather behind us.

As we entered the lock I was nervously fingering a heaving-line and glaring up at the serge-encased limbs of the lock-attendant, a very long way above my head; but that considerate man, letting down a lengthy pole with a hook on the end, took my bow and stern lines in the hook, a contrivance which I found to be commonly used in the deep locks of the Seine. The barges came pushing in after us. That lock could accommodate nine barges, three abreast. The bargees were remarkably adroit with their hawsers, stopping their craft easily with them on the double steel bitts placed at intervals along the decks. As the water-level rose our lines had to be shortened. I looked after the forward one, taking it through a fairlead to the windlass, and Isabel, aft, was able to use a small winch set there by the former owner. Despite the rain she had a large audience.

First clear of the lock, we moved into a narrow man-made part of the river leading to the main stream above the weir. Now we were in fresh, non-tidal water. We were delighted to be out of reach of salt water, for we had had enough of the sea to last us for a month or two. The fresh water looked wonderfully smooth (smoothness being the finest quality that any watery surface can possess). We travelled between deep pastures which were enjoyed by Norman cows and heifers. Now we searched for a stopping place for the night. The river was shallow at its edges. The banks had a broken appearance and were thickly grown with bushes and trees. Most of the obvious places to make fast, small piers and landing stages, were occupied by fishermen of aspect so single-minded that we dared not place thirty-one tons of living accommodation beneath their earnest rods. As we moved down a thickly-wooded reach we passed a high-diving board, white and spidery against the trees. After Isabel had remarked that there should be five feet of water under a diving board I swung *Truant* round; we edged in, sounding with a boat-hook, and stopped against a wooden ledge stained dark by the oiled bodies of bathers. The willows ceased their swaying and closed over us. Ahead was the structure of the diving board, to starboard a lawn backed by three creosoted huts marked respectively *hommes, dames, garçons,* and astern a great clump of water-lilies. It was the bathing station of St. Pierre-du-Vauvray, but that village was ten minutes walk away, and we could only see one corner of its ruined bridge, the remainder being hidden by the curve of the river. No human habitation was in sight. The faint noises of the wood were around us.

5

No bather destroyed the privacy of our berth. We locked the wheel-house and the hatches, and walked to the village down a grassy path. It was Monday, June 17th, and a crisp, sunny morning. The French shops were shut on Mondays, but, as usually happens in France, there was an exception to the law, and we were able to buy, at legal prices that seemed exorbitant to us, cherries, tomatoes, lettuces and a cucumber. In a market garden we found a large greenhouse, smelling of rich, water-soaked earth, capillaries, and geraniums. We bought three baby cactus plants and a scarlet geranium, and carried them back to the boat, where Isabel painted the flower-pots with white enamel. She stood them in a row near the barograph, above the starboard settee in the saloon. I undressed and went into the river to examine the starboard propeller; this had to be done by touch alone, in the dark brown water; I cleared three feet of rope from it, and felt that the blades were undamaged. Around the blades the waterlily plants raised small clenched fists. We lunched at the Hôtel du Poisson d'Argent. That afternoon we travelled on, upriver, passing one more lock. *Truant* had not been making water since the Channel crossing. It looked as though Mr. Bundy had been right when he said that all that was needed was for the topsides to be "slopped around". We tied up that night at a rickety landing-stage that seemed to have been built to permit cattle to drink from the river without falling in. Shouts and screams woke Isabel at midnight. "The controls are gone! We are drifting!" She sat up in bed. "Turn on the light," she heard. "If you can't find the switch the torch should be on your corner of the chart table. Hurry!" She switched on the light. I was crawling on the cabin floor. This was not the first nightmare that I had suffered since we left England in *Truant*, and we came to believe that, while most men are quick to state that they leave all their cares behind them on taking to the water, with me the usual hearty process was reversed, and my first reaction was to become nervous and harassed.

The next day we passed three locks, and so came to more sophisticated river scenes and an atmosphere that was suburban rather than rural. We were now within easy Saturday afternoon range for the Parisian motorist, and while we saw little of him, we saw plentiful evidence of the way that he amused himself. Here were many *plages*, grander, pinker, more silvery, more expensive, than that to which we had tied *Truant* for her first night in fresh water. Yachts were to be seen, some of them fully-rigged with masts which absolutely precluded their moving under the bridges, and which therefore confined them to a space of river at most a few miles in length. But the French pleb, bless his ugly heart, has no respect for the stamping grounds of those richer than himself, and we were happy to see the common fishing punts clustered thickly around these haunts of artificial gaiety, perhaps on the theory that crumbs thrown from the tables of the rich might attract the fish. War, with the resultant scarcity of food, had increased the desire to fish in France to utterly insane proportions. We saw so many fishermen (and fisherwomen) that the boats, moored by the bank or out in the stream, and their occupants soon merged into the valley as naturally as the river itself. We saw every kind of fisherman, I think. There was a naked one, plump and yellowish, who slid like a maggot into the water as we approached and watched his float with cold, doleful eyes until we were past. Another, near-naked, wore goggles and held a spear. A great band of fishermen with aggressively purple faces and punts well stocked with dark bottles—we thought that they had perhaps been attending a vintners' celebration—reeked of alcohol, tobacco a ad garlic, swayed on their stools, but nevertheless fished solemnly as we passed, although some of the purple faces wore the sly, inverted smiles that come from wine-heated fancies. A man trolled from the back of the mule he was riding along the towpath. An artist sat before his easel, his back to the river; he was painting a green wood, and the hill beyond it, and at his back he had arranged a fan of five fishing rods, each of the reels having a patent bell attachment that would warn him when to desert his canvas. Blessed bell attachments! Many a sleeping fisherman we passed, his rod or rods perched in forked sticks driven into the crumbling river soil, his sleep-drowned ear convenient to the bell that some wild creature in the water might ring. Yet if we saw many, many fishermen, we saw very few fish, and those that were landed before our eyes were anæmic, gentle-looking creatures.

We stopped for the night at a private landing stage marked in Roman lettering on oak signposts *défense d'accoster* and *baignade privée*. The property to which this private landing stage belonged was on the other side of the road that ran beside the river, and the landing stage had been separated by white palings from the road and from the public banks on either side of it. The planner of the estate had placed the landing stage on the general axis, so that from our deck we looked across the road, through the wrought-iron main gates, and down the vista of a straight avenue to what appeared to be a fine mansion. But Isabel pointed out that the house looked either dead or blind, for she disapproves of the French chatelaine's habit of closing her shutters and she said that those "blind" châteaux were symptomatic of the sharp misunderstandings between the different classes of wealth, breeding, and labour which had existed in France before and since the Revolution. A baby goat lay near its mother below the bush to which I attached our bow warp. The stern warp went to an acacia tree.

Walking back into the small town of Tiel the following morning, we saw the burghers push their bedding out over the window-sills to dispel the night's heat in the morning's freshness. A woman, sitting half in the street with a machine to "permanently wave" her hair clamped over her head, was shouting: "Ca me fait mal, tu sais." We were told that there was to be a distribution of milk on the steps of the town hall at 11.30, but we did not care to attend so embarrassing a ceremony, so we called on the milk distributor. The yard gave an impression of subdued prosperity. The laitier came out in overalls, but with a prosperous glint in his sharp black eye. I told him that we were foreigners, and showed him the ration cards we had obtained in Rouen. "You aren't entitled to milk on those cards," he said. "But stop, I'll give you quarter of a litre. And if there's no more, don't blame me but the farmers. They're behind all the miseries of France. It's unnatural that they should wish to make such profits, and should be allowed to turn the hunger of the children to their own advantage. I'm the distributor, and I risk ten times more capital than any farmer round here, yet I'm obliged to take a controlled profit while they sell all their milk on the black market." He charged us the controlled price. This was the last fresh cow's milk that we bought until we returned to England.

We pushed *Truant* away from the clinging weeds with our long boat-hooks. We had not gone far when I thought that I recognised the vulgar piscine on the right bank, and the village on the left bank. It was, it surely was Villennes-sur-Seine, where le beau Simpson had disported himself on summer week-ends before the war. Villennes had been a kind of symbol for me of the pre-war petit-bourgeois elements of France. It was the type of place where the small commerçants of Paris, the people who watched every sou except the sous that they sent down their gullets, week-ended and watched le beau Simpson thrashing the brown waters of the river in aquatic evolutions and padding across the piste to the tango music he loved, pouring into the ears of their daughters stories of the wide world from which he claimed to be a romantic deserter. Villennes is a small part of the fluff on the suburban rind of Paris, but it did not seem so to me as we sailed past because of the Irishman, Simpson, who had translated it for me from social terms and exterior tawdriness into terms of living.

Soon after Villennes we came to a lock, and while we waited there Isabel began to prepare lunch, which we ate passing slowly through the town of Conflans. Whatever it might be on land, Conflans is a cosmopolitan and exciting place from the water. Barges were lined for two miles, bow to stern, three, four and five deep, most of them waiting for orders to proceed into the Parisian area for cargoes. Here the mariniers form a town of their own, with their own shifting population and shifting houses. The decks of the barges were like streets and playgrounds and public gardens. The flags of Belgium, Holland, and hospitable France flew from their bulbous sterns. There were restaurants and cafés run by ex-barge-people for the barge-people, and some of these establishments were themselves afloat, conversions of wooden-hulled barges that had become too old to travel.

On the Seine, only fifteen minutes taxi ride from Paris, is a famous boat-building establishment, the Chantiers Navals de Sartrouville. I suppose that it was an early interest in the French single-handed sailor, Alain Gerbault, that had drawn my attention to this yard.

A small jetty creaked and swayed as it took *Truant's* sideways pull. The Englishman learns in his own country that many of the finest craftsmen work in quiet places. This was true of the Englishmen who made the best shoes, the best men's clothes, the best shotguns, the best yachts, and I hope that it will always be so; when the fine qualities of an article were screamed at the general public through the medium of advertising or a business front, even if such a front only meant handsome shops or offices, then the selective Englishman knew that he might expect little better than a fine second-best. Although the river frontage was inconspicuous, we were a little surprised by the offices of the Sartrouville yard, for our reaction on seeing the polished hardwoods and somewhat theatrical interior was to conclude that although the carpenters had made a damned fine job of the teak staircase, they might do less well with the boat-building in the sheds. But any sport in France is apt to become over-flushed, like the red cheeks of a beautiful consumptive. The French sportsman knows himself to be a rare bird, and he takes himself rather seriously. We were shown into a draughtsman's office where a one-legged man with cropped black hair and a deeply masculine voice made us welcome. The one-legged man soon gathered six or seven around him: he was an ebullient person, a little pompous in his efficiency, for the men working with him knew well what they were about. In a short time they had a cradle in the water, and on it *Truant* was pulled under a small bridge and out of the river into their dry dock. *Truant's* rounded bottom was unspotted in its coat of pale green anti-fouling, and loud was the chorus of Gallic praise as her dripping form was revealed. She was said to be *très marin* (boats being masculine in French). It was 6 o'clock, time for the men to stop work, when they had finished docking *Truant*. Isabel was tired, and went early to bed, while I sat near her in the saloon, writing letters, and feeling remarkably uncomfortable with the boat set, bows up, at a strange angle. The sounds of the neighbourhood came to us very clearly: the rush of traffic on the Paris road, which crossed the Seine on a high bridge four hundred yards upstream, the ticking of a fisherman's reel; the drone of engines running on the test bench of the seaplane factory downstream; the cries of the lads from the racing stables of Maisons-Lafitte, who played football on the other side of the river; the murmurs and subdued exclamations of two lovers who had stolen into the precincts of the yard for some serious privacy.

*   *   *   *

It seemed that there was nothing the matter with our starboard propeller and shaft. Engineers dismounted them, tested, and reassembled. "Very well then," I said, "the trouble must lie in the starboard engine." Two engineers came on board to test the engine. They were soon able to prove that there was nothing the matter with that. The only piece of apparatus that was not functioning perfectly was the rev-counter in the wheelhouse. There had been absolutely no need to stop at the yard, let alone have the boat slipped. I tried to pretend that they had been able to correct some slight fault in the propeller shaft, but it was no use. We howled with laughter.

"At least you can say you were slipped in the place where Alain Gerbault used to practise with his crossbow," the chief engineer said to me. "When he had his last yacht built here they thought there would be no work for me in it, him detesting engines like he did. But he wanted electricity for developing some films he intended to take, so I made him a wind-machine to charge the batteries. I made him different propellers to suit the wind speeds; the smallest would have done for a toy aeroplane. Someone said to him: 'What weapon will you take to the South Seas as well as the bow and arrows?' He didn't like that kind of talk. 'It's here in this pestilential Europe, with the countries that have blast furnaces and power stations and benevolent institutions that I find savages,' he used to say, and according to him those islanders in the Pacific were civilised compared to us. So off he went in the boat we built him to live the rest of his life out among them. But then he reckoned without the Japanese, who took his boat away and killed him because he was a European. Queer, wasn't it? Well, maybe he's better dead. He never could bear an internal

67

combustion engine, let alone an atom pile or such-like."

We moved on upstream. In the late evening a jetty set under a weeping willow appealed to us from a distance, but as we went gliding up to it, ready to go astern and haul *Truant* in with a boat-hook, we found that the jetty was part of the terrace of a restaurant of the rustic type. At fully-appointed tables many puce-faced diners were stuffing themselves with expensive food; the women's tall hats nodded as they chewed. They looked at us with grave surprise, and many an unmasticated écrevisse, radish, or haricot vert, was visible in a gaping mouth, for they were astonished by our silent approach and by our foreign aspect.

"Does one eat well here?" I asked the nearest diner to break the tension.

"Nowhere better," he answered in the same conversational tone. "C'est l'Auberge des Fruits Défendus."

A mile upstream we found a jetty with trees around it to take our warps. I had a nightmare at midnight and awoke on deck, my feet soaked with dew. The illuminations of Paris were reflected in the still rural sky. A man passing swiftly along the road on a bicycle stopped suddenly with a crunch of tyres and said: "Are you a woman or a man?"

"Neither," I answered.

* * * *

An advantage of living on salt water is that, provided large ports are left unvisited, it is surprisingly easy to keep yourself and your boat comparatively clean. We soon found that, while the river had many new delights and varieties to offer, the boat's exterior rapidly lost all pretensions to good looks and cleanliness when it was subjected to land dirts and poisons. This is one reason why, if you intend to go abroad in a lazily enjoyable fashion and without becoming a slave to your yacht or to a paid crew, you should choose a boat that has a comparatively rough exterior, because if you have a smooth one you will be continually worried by the deterioration which it will show when subjected to any extraordinary conditions. We did not leave the landing stage until I had washed down the decks and topsides and Isabel had completed her "housework" below decks. With her developed sense of system she had kept well abreast of such work, while wasting no unnecessary time on it. I was hampered in the deck work by the Seine water, which, there below Paris, was an unnatural cleaning medium, malodorous, oily, and thick with unpleasant refuse. As the Seine leaves Paris it appears to be reluctant to continue its course toward the sea; twisting until it nearly re-enters its own bed, it wastes hours in the ugly region immediately north-west of the capital. At

Satrouville we had been only sixteen kilometres from the centre of Paris by road, but fifty kilometres by river. All morning we moved through a factory belt. This was by no means unpleasant, for there was always something interesting to see, if it was only iron ore being shot into a barge, or the faces of the workmen who turned curiously to the river as we passed. There was a sense of cheating in the journey, the same sense of the unusual that a housewife might experience could she put her kitchen, bathroom, bedroom, and drawing-room, on wheels and drive them through Detroit or Stalingrad.

Being land animals, we are apt—unless we have to fight wars—to take bridges too much for granted. Live as a land animal in Paris, and you can forget that the town exists on two sides of an important river: travel through Paris on a boat and you are amazed at the number and the rich appearance of the bridges which, like Paris as a whole, have little architectural merit but a great deal of charm. *Truant*, having passed the Auteuil Viaduct into Paris proper, negotiated the Pont Mirabeau, the Pont de Grenelle, the Pont de Passy, the Pont d'Iéna (very low, that one), the Passerelle aux Piétons Débilly, the Pont de l'Alma, the Pont des Invalides, and the Pont Alexandre III. Immediately beyond the last-named tumult of contorted iron, painted pale chocolate and lavishly gilded, Isabel made an adroit sweep into a berth on the right bank. We lay astern of a raffish motor cruiser ahead of which there was a large house-boat with a rose garden on its upper storey. The house-boat—I hesitate to commit the name to paper—was called *Le Cran*, and belonged to a wealthy baker, Charles Sander, a man so heavy that he claimed to have increased his weight by one hundred and fifty pounds since leaving the German concentration camp of Buchenwald some two years earlier. Monsieur Sander used *Le Cran* to entertain his friends at large dinner parties, but lived himself in the Avenue Foch. He kept a couple of servants, a man and his wife, on the house-boat, and kindly put them at our disposal. The husband kept a watchful eye on *Truant* when we were not on board, and brought me ice when our refrigerator could not keep pace with the demand.

We quickly dressed ourselves and went into the streets. The afternoon was dark, blustery, and threatening rain. Women who were too exotically dressed for such weather glared at themselves in shop windows which were skilfully gay after those of London yet did not present many objects worth buying, since they seemed to show monopolies of women's shoes—made of rope or straw—women's handbags—white, puffed-up, and over-decorated with yellow tin—and beautiful bottles filled with coloured liquid masquerading as scent. The bottles were not for sale.

69

6

ON our third morning in Paris the weather reverted to normal and the streets were no longer cold, glum, and taxi-less; the June sun burned so hotly that pedestrians could not lean for long over the iron parapet of the bridge to stare at us; refuse, including the corpses of dogs, cats, and fish, that the stream deposited in the narrow space between *Truant's* hull and the quay wall had to be cleared twice daily with a prodding boat-hook. One hot evening as I returned on foot I heard a great noise of voices from the river. I went cautiously to the bridge and peered over the parapet. This was the disadvantage of living on a boat in Paris: eighty minutes earlier I had left Isabel reading *Swann's Way* in the saloon; now I saw her moving about the boat, giving people drinks. A house usually has a back door through which the owner may escape as unwanted visitors enter the front, and it has a façade behind which he can keep his privacy without rudeness. Life on a boat is unprotected by such civilised devices for privacy. Who were all those people? Their presence was violently annoying to me because on the previous day my feet had been attacked by such fits of itching as nearly to drive me mad. I tore my shoes off, there on the bridge, and stood in my socks on the hot flags of the pavement, rubbing one foot angrily against the other. Who were they? After a time I put on my shoes and went down to *Truant*.

*　　　*　　　*　　　*

When the last visitor had departed, with a dinner engagement looming ahead of us, surrounded by mouldering ash-trays and sticky glasses, we decided that we could not spend another day near the Pont Alexandre III. We washed and changed into clean clothes and mounted our bicycles. Down the quay, across the throat of the Place de la Concorde, with the Chambre des Députés seen across the bridge, then the Tuileries gardens, the leaves dusty and tired after a long, hot day with the traffic rushing past them, the Louvre on our left, the bird shops with the canaries and larks locked up in their cages, shut away for the night over the frogs and tadpoles in glass tanks. We turned over the bridge to the Île de la Cité, down, past the bird market, past Nôtre Dame, and over to the Île Saint Louis. Four or five people were bathing off that island, where a ramp descends the bastion and a tree hangs over the river. That would have been a pleasant place to put *Truant*, we thought, but we saw that the water near the edge was studded with rocks, and we decided that it would be more prudent to lie away from the island, on the left bank. We sat for a little in the café at the apex of the Place Dauphine. We rode through the markets, closed down for the early part of the night, the streets littered with the outside leaves of cabbages and lettuces and wooden cases that had contained butter and cheeses.

* * * *

Sander's man, standing among the rose bushes on the deck of the house-boat, *Le Cran*, and clutching in his left hand the English cigarettes that I had given him, waved us an energetic good-bye with his right. Where the low, triangular garden splits the river at the end of the Île de la Cité, we took the left-hand channel. Fortunately I had bought a map in St. James's Street which in some manner described the navigable possibilities of the Seine from Paris to the confluence with the River Yonne; the map at least showed under which archway of each bridge the traffic was supposed to pass. This was more important than might be supposed, for the barges travel at a surprising speed, and, if there are two arches through which traffic may pass, one is usually set aside for mounting and one for descending traffic, yet these are seldom indicated for the benefit of strangers on the river. Nearing the Nôtre-Dame end of the Île de la Cité we swung sharply to starboard to take the right-hand channel past the Île Saint Louis. Isabel edged into the left bank while I sounded with the long boat-hook, a task at which I was becoming proficient. Fishermen, all elderly men, were seated on the low quay against which we set *Truant*, but eight or nine of them moved uncomplainingly to make way for us, while the whole line of seated men contracted a little as each man adjusted himself like a section of the bellows of a concertina. When I had seen to the bow and stern lines, I went below to work in the saloon, the fan agitating my papers. At mid-day we walked across the bridge to the island. It was a hot day, and the smells were enough to give a saint carnal appetites, for even the pavements of Paris seem to reek of good living.

When we returned in the evening the fishermen were still squeezed around *Truant*, and a pair of lovers were behaving with scientific shameless-ness in the shadowed place where the metal sinews of the Pont Sully crossed our quay.

Unable to sleep because my feet were again attacked by the mysterious itching, I worked late into the night, while Isabel slept, undisturbed by the typewriter. The water round us gave up large bubbles which broke with an eerie noise against our hull. Above us shone the beacon-like windows of the Tour d'Argent, a restaurant set on the top of a building—a Parisian lighthouse.

7

DRAB human streams—hatless women dressed in grey or black or a mixture of the two—trickled through the channels of the streets to the nearest market, which was set in the tilted and irregular space of the Place Marbeuf. The women looked at us with sharp attention, because few societies are more conservative in their habits than the poorer strata of the Parisian population, and we carried shopping bags made of netted cord, while their bags were of black oil-cloth. It was a spirited market; the stalls showed a great variety of food and cheap merchandise, and hundreds of vociferous buyers struggled around them. Plunging in with gusto, Isabel bought French beans, celery, spring carrots, artichokes, tomatoes, radishes, mushrooms, lettuces, parsley, chervil, cherries, pears, straw-berries, peaches, bread, and our cheese ration for the week. She stood for a long time in a queue leading to a splendid charcuterie stall on which sausages, pâté, and smoked ham were displayed. When her turn came she was told that the ration cards—cartes d'isolés—which we had obtained from the mayor of Rouen did not entitle us to charcuterie, but only to ordinary butcher's meat. We had already visited several butchers' shops; each of them showed approximately the same notice: "Meat next week—perhaps."

*　　　*　　　*　　　*

When we began to move out of Paris we had a busy time making our way up the stretch of the river immediately above and below the Pont d'Austerlitz. Tugs were gathering strings of cement-carrying barges, and the tugmen were in no mood to make way for a yacht or to waste time in showing any degree of consideration.

"Où allez-vous comme ça?" asked the first lock-keeper.

"À Marseille."

"I hope you're in no hurry to get there," he said, and told us that a chômage which would stop all traffic was about to begin on the Seine locks above Paris. The locks had been in need of repairs for many years, and the work had been postponed during the war years.

"How long will the chômage last?"

"At least fifteen days," he answered.

Isabel climbed ashore and read the notice pinned to the wall of his cabin. "It says that the locks as far as the River Yonne will close on July 1st, which is Monday. To-day is only Saturday, and one day will be enough to take us out of the river and into the canals."

"And what about the lock-keepers?" the man asked angrily. "Madame doesn't consider us. All the traffic disregards us. This is the machine age, granted; but remember the human factor. The locks begin their chômage on Monday; true enough. To-day is Saturday; equally true. You say: 'That still leaves us two days to travel.' But I say: 'My lock must be dry for the workmen to begin on Monday morning at seven. All the other lock-keepers above us will be letting their water go, so I'll have a lot to deal with. Therefore I must begin to empty my bit *now*, even if it is only Saturday.'"

"Does all that mean that the locks will close to-night?"

"Most likely, my friends. You had better put on the sauce if you want to get much further."

Afraid that the chômage might confine us in the factory area surrounding Paris, we followed his advice, and opened both throttles. *Truant's* engines roared throatily. As she charged up the middle of the river waves followed us; and the fishermen yelled at us from either side when their punts rocked and plunged in our wash and the coloured umbrellas tipsily swayed; and the waves climbed silently over the edges of the rushy banks to swamp men settled comfortably in the tall rushes, with rods, sandwiches, omelettes-à-l'espagnol, cherries, beer, and tins of maggots. We were greatly delayed in the locks because the nerves of the lock-keepers were frayed by all the complications of the impending chômage. It was early evening when we passed Corbeil, a small, semi-rural town less than forty kilometres from Paris. If we could negotiate le Coudray lock beyond Corbeil we knew that we would be nearing the fringes of the Forest of Fontainebleau, and wilder country; but these hopes were soon quashed, for when we arrived at the lock we found that one gate was about to be lifted from its hinges by two cranes, and masons were striking ghoulish echoes as they attacked the stonework.

We could get no sense out of the lock-keeper, a thin, excitable fellow who, judging by the breath that mingled with his words, had been fortifying himself for the occasion with the scented alcohol of cherries. Neither of us felt inclined to return to Paris. We allowed *Truant* to drift downstream while we looked about us for a suitable place to stop. Since it was a hot Saturday, the river was at its busiest. Young women, office workers and factory girls from the Paris area, enjoyed an all-too-brief dose of open

74

air, and competed for the attentions of young men who wore nets against the misshaping effect on hair of the river water, and whose masculinities were emphasised rather than concealed by the latest mode for male bathers in France, which consisted of a small bag in front and a string behind. We dropped anchor near a stony bank, half-covered with prickly shrubs and therefore free of bathers. The bank protected the entrance to an artificial lake used for loading into barges the sand obtained from quarries in the vicinity. Three hundred yards upstream was le Coudray lock, with a cobbled quay, a row of pollarded trees, and two restaurants, Au Rendez-Vous des Mariniers and the Hôtel du Barrage. Down our side of the river as far as we could see were wheat fields and pasture; twin sticks, used by fishermen for mooring their boats, pricked out from the water near the rushy banks. On the far bank, a road was backed by a wooded hill round which a branch railway threaded its way. Opposite us, standing by the roadside, were three houses, each house surrounded by its livestock, hot hens, ducks, geese, mangy dogs and plump, castrated tom-cats. Beneath each house a boat prodded its blunt nose into the bank. The water that evening was foaming because the lock-keepers above were letting all their surplus run through. *Truant* swung a great deal to her single anchor, so I let out chain, dropped a kedge anchor and then hauled in on the bow chain. Anchored fore and aft, we were so much more comfortable than lying to a dusty quay that I wondered why I had not thought of it before. We were not depressed by the prospect of two stationary weeks, although we should have preferred to have been halted in more countrified surroundings.

We had continued to have some trouble with *Truant's* engines, entirely petrol trouble caused by dirt from the tanks clogging the feed system. I passed the whole of our first morning at anchor working in the hot engine-room, getting myself covered with oil and petrol, and gradually pricking myself into ill-humour; I suspect that the reason for this reaction, apart from the discomfort of such work, was the feeling that I did not fully understand what I was doing. The most maddening of my mechanical responsibilities was an elderly one-horse-power petrol engine that charged our lighting batteries. This had first given trouble at le Havre, and now, although I took it to pieces and put it together again, it would do no better than run for a few minutes and then stop. Isabel had a look at me when I emerged at midday, and advised me not to go back to the engine-room.

The thermometer, set in the shade inside our well-ventilated wheel-house, registered eighty-five (Fahrenheit) and we decided that we must erect the awnings. This operation took all afternoon, because I had to

75

remove a lot of gear to get at the awnings and their battens. We brought upon deck our geranium plant, the cacti, and the folding table and chairs.

The light beneath the awnings, cool, soft and flattering, reminded me of my grandmother's tea-tent, a magnificent affair with six poles and medieval fringes that used to be erected on her lawn every summer. Hot from the afternoon's exertions, we children would rest on linen-covered chairs round the table that was reserved for us, away from the grown-ups' stuffy grandeur. Near the canopied section of the tent was the small, straw-lined house of Benny, the tortoise, who usually pottered about among the lettuce leaves and other damp green food with which he strewed the playground contained by a wire fence six inches high; Shem, the snuffly black pug, lay in the corner of a wallflower bed, one bulbous, disgruntled eye on the old-fashioned delicacies of the tea-tables. Such tents have disappeared, I think, from middle-class British gardens, since the women now prefer to burn their skins.

My feet were attacked by the itch, which now had spread to my hands. I stood the discomfort in silence for a time, wondering dismally if it could be leprosy, and what would happen to us if this proved to be the case. But Isabel noticed my restlessness, and had the good sense to connect my ailment with the engine-room. "It must be caused by petrol," she said. We then recalled that the first attack had come on the day that we had filled the fuel tanks in Paris, when, barefooted, I had washed petrol from the decks. As soon as this explanation was found the disease vanished, and never reappeared. We did not move from *Truant* that first day because the crowds were again thick on and near the river. Paddle canoes came past, so close that they often scraped our side, while the occupants of both sexes stared their fill at us. When darkness fell we rigged a mosquito net and slept under it on two mattresses stretched upon the cabin top.

* * * *

Our black paint was beginning to show large blisters. (*Truant* would have looked less well with her topsides painted any other colour but black, although white would have been a more practical colour for so hot a voyage. Mr. Bundy had suggested when we began to fit *Truant* out that all the paintwork should be burned off before repainting, and I now wished that we had accepted his advice, which had been rejected because we believed that no paint would survive the trip through the canals and because the colonel had said—as we remembered bitterly afterwards: "In England materials are cheap and labour is dear whereas on the Continent labour is cheap and materials are non-existent. If I were you I should take a good quantity of paint with you, and once you're through the canals you can have her repainted on the Riviera for a mere song.") The river water turned to steam as I washed down the hot deck and topsides. Isabel was fighting the flies which had multiplied horribly in our living quarters That evening we pushed the dinghy over the side, piled the two bicycles in the stern, and ferried ourselves across the river. Sixty men were working hard on the lock in day and night shifts. Their overflow filled the tables of the two small restaurants. We rode up the towpath to a wood called the Bois de la Guiche. Inside the wood we met an extraordinary conveyance, a kind of low dogcart, pale blue, mounted on motor-car wheels; a powerful young horse needed all his muscle to drag the trap over the ruts and through the bushes encroaching on the narrow track. Three hugely fat men sat squeezed into a single seat. Their rumps overflowed and melted into each other like candles that stand before a roasting fire. Their fat arms, strong, and dark with hairs, were interlaced along the back of the seat. Their great, purple faces shone with sweat. Where had they been? What had they been doing in that deserted and impoverished wood?

It seemed ridiculous to take the bicycles back on board, so I entered the back yard of the small house nearest *Truant*. A woman came out through the open kitchen door, a frying-pan filled with browning potatoes in one hand. She was feeling the heat, and wore some kind of woollen shift above khaki shorts, tight on her muscular thighs. She helped me to put the bicycles in her cellar, half below ground and with a large bed of hay spread in one corner. She talked loudly at us, scarcely pausing for breath until we were in the dinghy and crossing the water.

"Ai, ai, ai, the heat! It saps you; but there; the men must be fed. I used to be in a factory. That was the life. A factory girl is responsible for herself, and factory life suits me. I only left the factory when the Germans took it into their heads to ship me off to Berlin, and now I can't go back because I've three big Poles to look after. Of course every woman wants a man, and if she's poor how can she have man and freedom too? I like my husband and I like work. It's a question of balancing the two. So now I just take casual jobs. For instance, I'd be glad to do any laundry for you if you can spare me some soap. To-morrow I'm off to pick green peas. You couldn't call that important work, now, could you? But it's surprising how they reimburse pea-pickers to-day, and also they give you some peas for the pot. It's because I'm away to-morrow that I'm cooking this evening. These potatoes are for to-morrow's dinner for the three of them. Have you any German prisoners in England? Well, I only hope you find them a bit more civil than the ones around here. A few days ago I was working with some of them at the farm on top of the hill there, and do you know what they were saying? 'C'est nous, les maîtres,' they said."

*   *   *   *

The road to Corbeil was cushioned with warm dust. Near the town a crop of ugly villas had sprouted among the market gardens. From the river the town had looked attractive, but inside the dark streets it was ordinary. We rode on slowly until we came to the market, a big rectangle surrounded by commercial cafés. The rectangle was covered with stalls selling cheap clothing, pots and pans, lavender "from the mountains" in paper bags at two francs the bag, quack medicines, combs and buttons, fried potatoes and fritters. A butcher's shop was inlaid like a wound in a blank wall, but we recoiled from the yellow-ochre fat of the horsemeat on the marble shelf. We left our bicycles at the *velo-garage*, paying three francs to the woman attendant, and plunged into the food market, a steel-and-glass building. It was an excellent market.

The thermometer was rising. At certain times of day when the shifts were changing at the loading chutes boatloads of rough sandy men came out of the creek astern. Nobody rowed on the river; each boat was propelled by one man sculling, bending his trunk, legs and arms in curves almost as sinuous as those made in the water by the long, narrow oar-blade. Those working men passed us like pirates, looking with sardonic intentness at the strange world that we represented. Sometimes they would exclaim at the sight of a teapot, a cup or a saucer. They probably told their families that we always had our noses in the trough. We spent many days without touching land, sometimes sailing or pottering round in the dinghy—which I taught myself to scull in the Seine fashion through the groove in the transom—sometimes swimming in the dark, cool water. Isabel cut a Japanese mosquito-net into suitable shapes and sizes to make the portholes and hatches fly- and mosquito-proof. (Before leaving we should have been wise to have had every porthole fitted with a screen of fine, rust-proof, wire mesh.)

*   *   *   *

Travelling in a boat is very different from travelling by land conveyance and staying in houses or hotels. When we arrived in France we both had a feeling that we had cheated, that we were still in our own country. We could not convince ourselves that we were "abroad". We had not been twenty-four hours in the Corbeil-le Coudray reach when we considered ourselves to be a part of the landscape. We were saddened and shocked, like our neighbours, by an accident in the lock.

A wooden dam had been erected at the upper end of the lock to keep the Seine out of the space where ten men were cementing and adjusting the lower hinges for the gates. The authorities had few skilled workers with whom to put the inland waterways to rights, and the task was being hurried. The men were working fifteen feet below the surface of the river; the wooden dam vibrated to the tapping of their tools and bent before the pressure of the river until it cracked and split into three parts, allowing the water to boil into the lock. Nine men came to the surface and were fished out, some of them cut and bruised, but all alive. The tenth, an Algerian, did not appear. His friends stood around the lock, swearing in a dazed manner and stupidly calling his name until suddenly his black hair broke surface, and his body stiffly shot half clear of the water and then fell back. They soon had him out. The local doctor was away on holiday, so they telephoned the fire brigade at Corbeil. The sapeurs pompiers full of pride in themselves, their uniforms and their service, did not take long to arrive. Two of them flung themselves upon the Algerian while the others stood round, gravely motioning back the crowds of children who were curious to see how impermanent life can be, and what death looks like. For a long time the firemen were there in their hot, serge uniforms, their shining helmets catching the sun. But even they could only work the man's poor lungs like a bellows; they could not call his heart to life. It was generally agreed that the Algerian must have been killed by a blow on the head when the dam broke.

The accident was still in my mind that evening, and the following day, a Saturday, when a cold strong wind blew down our reach, a wind from Paris, from the Cheviot Hills, from the Faroes, from Iceland. It blew away all the week-enders and all the flies, and once it nearly blew us away too. I happened to look up from my work, and saw the bank moving past the porthole. We put out a second anchor aft and took down our awnings. Waves sweeping up the reach from Corbeil, smacked at our sides and stern.

In the afternoon a small blue British yacht came up the reach from Corbeil. This was the last sight that we had expected to see, and we were not altogether pleased. However, we shouted to the man and woman who were visible, the man steering at the wheel in the cockpit, the woman standing forward by the anchor. We invited them to tea.

They made fast their yacht to *Truant*. She was named *Elpis*, the Greek for "hope", and was only a third of *Truant's* size, a ten-ton yawl with a long counter and a spoon bow. We noticed at once that we were in

79

contact with experts. The manner in which this husband and wife were dressed two hundred miles up-river gave notice of seamanship many gradations more advanced than anything we could offer. They wore identical windbreaker jerkins over flannel shirts, linen trousers, canvas shoes with rope soles. They introduced themselves as Douglas and Gwenda Hawkes. Douglas is a neat, small man, grey-haired, with a deeply-lined face and a fetching, innocent expression. He has a deep, rather husky voice that is a little hard to understand as he likes to rush at the beginnings of his sentences and then slur and slash the ends of them. He gives an impression of reflective abstraction, while Gwenda, his wife, offers a complete foil with her brisk, matter-of-fact manner, incisive voice, and literate way of speaking, but I suspected then, as later, that Gwenda was the more romantically-minded, and Douglas the more practical. Gwenda is taller than her husband, very slender, with a face that is saved from asperity by an impertinent nose and a lively intelligence of expression. Both had lived much in France; both had been drivers of racing motor-cars. They worked in England during the war, and began as early as 1942 to plan their voyage. Their planning had been so thorough that it showed us up as the flimsiest of amateurs. In 1942, while bombs were falling on the boat-yards in the south of England, Douglas bought *Elpis*. He knew the full history of the boat. The planking was all teak. Over a period of three years, he had a new teak deck put on her, fitted her out with more patent deck winches than you find in any normal racing yacht and had her copper-sheated for the warm waters of the Ægean. His sixteen-horse-power auxiliary engine was much more than something to provide motive power when required; it pumped the bilges, it ran an auxiliary plant which worked a hydraulic windlass for the anchor chain, it operated a hose for washing down the ship. Douglas's engine, like ours, consumed petrol. He had filled up most of the available space which would not interfere with the accommodation with tanks for petrol and fresh water, and his bilges were packed with tins of food. As a result of all this ballast *Elpis* was deeper in the water than she should have been, particularly when we first saw her, for all boats built for the sea sink down on their marks when they enter fresh water. Gwenda cooked on bottled gas, a system that we had eschewed—wisely as it turned out—because we believed that the gas might be easy enough to obtain in France, the country of its early exploitation, but that it would be unobtainable in Italy and Greece. Their refrigerator also worked on gas instead of paraffin. Although the interior of *Elpis* had been meticulously planned by this ingenious and skilful couple, it seemed like a beehive when compared with the spacious and airy cabins of *Truant*.

Gwenda, who was obliged to cook in a small cupboard at the after end of their saloon, and who had not even room there for an oven, exclaimed in wonder and envy when she saw Isabel's galley.

"Of course," Gwenda said, "when we reach the Mediterranean we shall score, as *Elpis* undoubtedly sails a great deal better than *Truant*." From the depths of our inexperience, we wondered. We remembered her remark.

We were leaving England only for a voyage, and had every intention of returning there, but the Hawkes were sailing to the Ægean with the idea of finding some place with more sunshine than England in which to settle. To us, then, who are attached to our own land by such ties that we are never likely voluntarily to contemplate leaving it for more than a year or so, there was something both spectacular and sad in our meeting. We dined with them on the terrace of the Vieux Garçon, a riverside restaurant about a mile above the lock, dined so copiously—Douglas was an impelling host —that I awoke poor Isabel at four the next morning as I clambered out of bed to write a long letter to a friend in Washington.

It was a stifling morning on the river. We re-erected our awnings, and Gwenda slung a kind of tent over their cockpit. Douglas was early afloat in their pram dinghy, a mahogany shell just large enough to carry two people. He had a brush and a pot of blue paint, and he was giving their topsides a new coat, although they looked perfect enough to us in all conscience. At midday we walked up the hill to the Pacha. We were able to eat outside surrounded by the village, even if it was only a village on a route nationale forty kilometres from Paris. Douglas and Gwenda were amused to be there, for they had frequently driven their fast motor-cars past the restaurant, which they had never noticed, although they both recalled that the corner on which it stood was particularly dangerous if you were travelling over a certain speed. The meal cost 2,750 francs. Two horses passed while we were eating the tournedos, puissant, round-footed stallions, their quarters shivering like bags of jelly. They were followed by two slow, steady oxen, male Wagnerian sopranos with ruminatively bad-tempered eyes. Douglas spent all the afternoon doctoring our charging motor. He did to it all the things that I had done myself, and I never had such a useful lesson in mechanics. He put on his spectacles and a slightly clerical expression. He became neither heated nor dirty, for he held his spanners as surely as a draughtsman holds his inking pen, and after each little operation he wiped his hands on a pad of cotton waste. While he worked, he smoked innumerable cigarettes, and when I reminded him gently—I would not for worlds have disturbed him at his work—that there were 280 gallons of highly inflammable spirit within a few feet of our heads, he told me that there was no risk whatsoever. I was not sure that I believed him, but I bowed to his long experience.

* * * *

All three Poles were there when Isabel and I arrived with our water-cans. The woman was cooking.

"I brought you some corned beef," Isabel said to her. (Since the war you could say "corned beef" in French; the foodstuff had won a—surely temporary—place in the language, although it was generally pronounced corn-*edd*.) "And some tinned milk and cooking fat."

"What do you want in return?" the husband answered.

"Why, nothing. We have more of those things than we know what to do with. We don't eat very much meat."

"We shall eat it at midday," he answered. "Potatoes begin to pall, and the bread is bad these days, sour and bad."

"Ah, pour bouffer les patates il n'y a rien comme les Polonais!" exclaimed his wife. "Four times a day, they have to eat potatoes, and they never wish to eat them twice cooked in the same fashion. Thank God, I can make them peel the things themselves since they find no other employment. At least I'm in a position to repay your generosity. My brother in the north has just sent me some farm butter. It was no present, for in return we have to find him petrol coupons on the black market."

She kept her butter in a wire cage hung on a string down the well-shaft. It came up out of the darkness like a pale worm with some green moss lying over it. She gave us nearly a kilo, and it was as good as butter can be.

* * * *

A hint of thunder muttered early on the hot morning of the July 14th holiday, when cyclists from Paris came sweating up the river banks in their thousands, and every panting train disgorged a load of families at the small station above the lock. Any piece of bank that could imaginatively be considered a plage was early covered with squatters and their scrappy belongings. The men often retired behind bushes to modify their clothing, but the women, wisely mistrusting the shelter of the bushes, preferred to use a different system, at the same time more decent and more suggestive. Each party of women brought some large, opaque garment which was handed round from individual to individual, and beneath its folds the change from land to water clothing was wrought.

The lock-keeper presented to us a face grossly swollen and coloured a deep puce after the early celebrations of the 14th, but he was capable of reasoned speech, and he told us that his lock would open the following morning.

Many tents had been erected by the holiday-makers along the banks, while others, who did not possess tents but who were not going to allow that to deter them from staking out their little areas of riverside space, had already made up double and single beds by laying blankets and pillows on the dry ground. The sky was beginning to show a congestion of oily cloud, and our barograph had drawn a sudden descent. I worked all afternoon on deck, shaded by the awnings yet still panting in the heat. At 4 o'clock Isabel called me below to light the stove for tea, and no sooner had I entered the galley than the storm struck with so sudden an onslaught that one instant there was stillness and heat, the next pandemonium, with cold wind, rain and, worst of all, the grinding of stones under our keel and bilges. Isabel was first on deck. She rescued two hundred pages of manuscript. The flower-pots had spilled the cacti and the geranium over the deck. She had to put off in the dinghy to retrieve from the river a book which Gwenda had lent her. Meanwhile I was endeavouring with the boat-hooks to get *Truant* clear of the shore. She had dragged two of her anchors and was listing severely as she grounded near the stony bank. We saw that the first thing was to deal with the awnings. While we fought with them I noticed the pathetic tents and bedding of the trippers, blowing everywhere and frequently landing in the water, and the *Elpis*, swinging madly to her single anchor. When we had spilled the wind out of the awnings I was able to haul off-shore. Isabel reported that a jet of water was finding its way through the deck and directing itself at our bunk. The commander's forecast that the decks would open up in the heat had thus been realised after just over one month's cruising plus the traffic of Parisian visitors in heavy shoes. We slept with oilskins over the sheets; the lightning and rain did not stop until dawn.

I had been disturbed several times during the night by the thudding of the diesel engines of barges passing upstream to form a queue in front of the lock. At seven o'clock I put my head outside and counted thirty barges where the evening before there had been but two, and I was astonished to see another yacht, well forward in the queue. When I examined the yacht through binoculars I saw that she was a French-built motor-cruiser of about *Truant's* size, a boat of the river type, with a great deal of top-hamper; she was lashed to a barge, and therefore was not proceeding under her own power. It was obvious that if we were obliged to wait our turn for the lock we should not get through it that morning. Downstream I could see two slowly-advancing columns of black smoke, which indicated tugs towing strings of barges. We hoisted our dinghy in the davits aft, where we judged that it would be handy in case of need, but well out of the way for the locks; the best alternative position was the coach-roof, but there it interfered too much with the already limited field of vision from the wheelhouse. After ten minutes hard work we retrieved our three anchors, and moved across the stream to the last barge in the queue, a slatternly oil-tanker registered at Marseilles. The crew, husband, wife and five children, appeared to regard us with distaste, but two of the youngest children took our warps. We were surprised to see that *Elpis* had made no move; Gwenda was scrubbing the deck, her trousers rolled up to her knees. I pointed aft to the two advancing smoke columns while I hailed her. "Better take your place in the queue before they arrive."

"I know, I know," she answered with a tinge of wrath. "Our engine has chosen this of all mornings to give trouble. Douglas says it's a broken magneto spring, and he has no spare."

"What's he going to do?"

"Make another." She went on scrubbing, putting a great deal of vigour into her strokes. (She and Douglas were anxious to get through the canals as quickly as possible, for although *Elpis* was much smaller than *Truant* she drew six feet of water as compared with *Truant's* five feet. Gwenda had been corresponding with experts at Lyons, who had told her that the sooner *Elpis* reached the Rhône the better, for the effect on that river of the spring snows melting in the Alps would not last much beyond the end of July.)

I crossed the steel deck of the barge, landed, and walked to the lock-keeper's office. "You know we were the first boat here," I said to him. "We've been waiting for fifteen days."

"True enough," he answered, his vinous breath most heavy in that confined space. "But you'll just have to wait your turn and go through when I tell you . . ."

"Naturally," I said. "We're entirely in your hands." I walked back to *Truant*. When the lock gates opened and the leading barges started their engines with puffs of bright blue smoke he came running down the towpath, his face glistening beneath his blue cap.

"Eh, Churchill!" he yelled. "What are you waiting for? In you go, in you go." We moved into the dark lock and the gates closed behind us.

84

8

WE were the last boat to leave the lock. I wrapped a twenty-franc note round a two-franc piece, and threw it to the lock-keeper, who yelled: "Vive l'Angleterre!" an expression which was already so unusual as to sound farcical, although it had been common enough when it was clandestine a year or so earlier, while there were still German troops on French soil.

Isabel dislikes processions. She thrust old *Truant* past barge after barge. Steering presented hair-raising problems because we had long waits at all the locks, and to further complicate the press of traffic there was a fierce cross wind. The seven locks between le Coudray and the point where we left the Seine had sloping, instead of vertical, sides, and we should have been in difficulties with our rounded wooden hull had we not been mothered by a Belgian barge, which offered its comfortable flank to us. Every lock-keeper, surly at being back at work after the fortnight of chômage, allowed the water to boil in at its maximum speed. The Belgians travelled in an unladen and powerfully-engined barge, *Étoile de Verviers*, which easily outstripped all craft but *Truant* on the river; when we were through our last lock on the Seine Isabel opened the throttle and we moved past them. The *Étoile's* propeller flailed at the water aft; she thrust a mattress of foaming water before her bows; amidships maman was hanging up the washing. I threw eggs to the youngest Belgian, who adroitly caught all but one of a dozen, and this, splashing yellow on the black metal deck, was pounced on by a dog resembling a liver sausage.

In the late evening we left the river, swinging to starboard into the water *garage* at the entrance to the Canal du Loing. We had travelled 452 kilometres on the Seine, which we left with deep regret, and in agreement with those writers, artists and travellers who have placed its beauties above those of the Rhine, the Thames, the Volga, the Euphrates, the Mississipi, the Nile, the Yang-tsze Kiang, the Ganges and the Amazon.

*   *   *   *

There are three main routes by rivers and canals from Paris to the Mediterranean.

I shall name the most easterly first: this is generally called the Marne

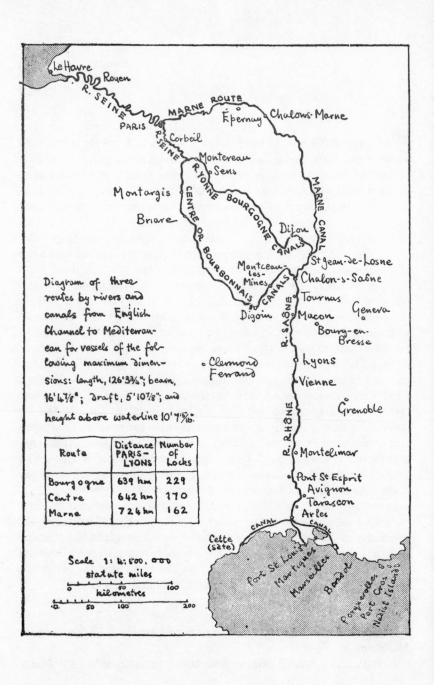

Le Havre
Rouen
R. SEINE
PARIS
MARNE ROUTE
Épernay
Chalons-Marne
Corbeil
R. SEINE
Montereau
R. YONNE
Sens
Montargis
Briare
CENTRE OR BOURBONNAIS
YONNE
BOURGOGNE CANALS
MARNE CANAL
Dijon
St Jean-de-Losne
Montceau-les-Mines
Chalon-s-Saône
CANALS
Tournus
Geneva
Digoin
Macon
Bourg-en-Bresse
R. SAÔNE

Diagram of three
routes by rivers and
canals from English
Channel to Mediterran-
ean for vessels of the following maximum dimen-
sions: length, 126'3¾"; beam,
16'4⅛"; draft, 5'10⅞"; and
height above waterline 10'7¹⁵⁄₁₆".

Clermond Ferrand

Lyons
Vienne
Grenoble
R. RHÔNE
Montelimar
Pont St Esprit
Avignon
Tarascon
Arles

Route	Distance PARIS-LYONS	Number of Locks
Bourgogne	639 km	229
Centre	642 km	170
Marne	724 km	162

Cette (Sète)
CANAL
CANAL
Port St Louis
Martigues
Marseilles
Bandol
Porquerolles
Port Cros
Nudist Islands

Scale 1: 4,500,000
statute miles
0   50   100
kilometres
0   50   100   200

route. Instead of continuing up the Seine from Paris, the traveller turns to port up the River Marne, and reaches the River Saône via the Canal Latéral à la Marne, and the Canal de la Marne à la Saône.

The middle of the three main routes is called the Bourgogne route. It follows the Seine, the River Yonne, a tributary of the Seine, and the Canal de Bourgogne which drops down through the Côte d'Or country past Dijon to the Saône.

The third, called the Centre route—or the Bourbonnais route—turns southward from the Seine a few kilometres below the big river's confluence with the Yonne and follows the Canal du Loing, the Canal de Briare, the Canal Latéral à la Loire, and the Canal du Centre to the Saône.

All three routes join the Saône at or near Chalon-sur-Saône, and from Chalon the traveller descends the Saône to Lyons. In that great town he passes through the last lock, and trusts his vessel to the violent Rhône, which roars down its savage valley to the Mediterranean.

Comparing the three routes: The Marne route is the least beautiful, the longest (724 km.), the most modern, and has the smallest number of locks (162). The Centre route carries the heaviest barge traffic, is 642 kilometres in length and has 170 locks in it. The Bourgogne route is the shortest of the three (639 km.), but has the largest number of locks (229). To compensate for this, it is the quietest route because it is avoided by much of the heavy traffic, and it is generally considered to be the most beautiful of the three. As a further attraction it passes through the finest wine country in France.

In England we had made up our minds, then, to travel by the Bourgogne route. But the chômage which had stopped us at Corbeil spread from the Seine up the Yonne and into the Canal de Bourgogne, so, as we had begun to feel that time was pressing, and we were already late for certain appointments in the Mediterranean, we decided to take the Centre route.

The *garage* at the entrance to the canal was a place where barges loaded and unloaded and waited for cargoes. These were smaller barges than the *automoteurs* to which we had become accustomed, and although a few of them were driven by engines, most of them were drawn by mules, horses, donkeys or a combination of two or three of those hard-worked animals. The small barges unloaded their cargoes into the aristocratic river barges, which gathered at the entrance to the *garage*, although not infrequently the big barges carried cargo themselves through the canals to Chalon-sur-Saône, Lyons, or Marseilles.

We had to sound our foghorn several times before a man came slowly from a café near the first canal lock, and began to open the gates. The opening thus presented to our bows appeared to be so narrow that even Isabel blinked as she looked at it. The Seine lock can take at least nine barges in one load, while the canal lock only holds a single barge, and then if the barge is of the bigger dimensions, it occupies almost every inch of available space. The stretches of water between locks on the French rivers and canals are known to the lock-keepers and to the barge traffic as *biefs*, a word which sometimes appeared to be pronounced to correspond with the English "beef", and sometimes with "B.F." The first bief on the canal was a short one, but when we had reached the end of it 8 o'clock was striking, and the locks were closing for the night. We pulled in at a grassy bank. To our right was a mere, showing great clusters of water-lilies. Occasionally a large fish or a number of small ones broke surface between the juicy plants over which dragonflies passed, rudely joined in pairs, and the midges and mosquitoes hung in misty clouds illuminated redly by the dying sun. We had a drink at the Bar de l'Écluse and then strolled back to bed.

When I jumped ashore next morning my legs were wet to the knees by the dew in the long grass. We were soon through the lock, which opened at six; the canal beyond it presented a strange sight. Four or five of the small barges sprawled over the water, strange pencil-shaped things, with about half *Truant's* beam, about twice her over-all length, and huge twin rudders emerging from the outer edges of the square sterns. These barges were disposing themselves to pass through the lock after the night's sleep, and the crews pushed them from our path with long barge poles which men, women and children employed with admirable skill. Amidships on each barge was the stable, low and square, with unglazed windows for ventilation; as we approached, horses, donkeys, and even the more blasé mules pushed their heads out of the stable windows to regard us. Owing to the design of the barges, only the best accommodation amidships offers sufficient headroom for the animals, and the human crew are obliged to live aft, where they camp beneath tarpaulins. The cooking is done there, and often as we overtook or met one of them we would see a woman dividing her attention between the cooking pots on the wood stove and the twin tillers with which she was supposed to keep the vessel on its course. Under such conditions the general standard of steering was erratic. As we passed those first barges we were so interested in them, and particularly in the mules' faces looking out of the windows, like old men peeping from the cubicles of a Turkish bath, that it took us a little time to notice that while our engine was still turning we no longer advanced. We had run aground;

but concerted pushing with two boat-hooks freed *Truant* (and clouds of swirling mud) from the bottom.

Many mariniers dislike the Canal du Loing because of the sinuous course it pursues, but the curves did not worry us unduly, and we were disposed to find the early, well-wooded stretches most beautiful, although, soon after the start, rain began to fall. We were obliged to shut ourselves in the wheel-house and it was a penance to emerge at the locks dressed in oilskins and sou'westers. At 1 o'clock we tied up rather awkwardly to a flimsy bridge, and cooked ourselves a fine meal, which we were consuming when *Elpis* appeared. The Hawkes, pinched with cold, damp and exasperation— for *Elpis* had been aground several times—wore oilskins and had tied towels around their necks to keep the water from penetrating. They sat in their cockpit eating damp sandwiches and drinking red wine; they told us how envious our wheelhouse made them feel. Douglas had mended his magneto by cutting off part of a hacksaw blade, drilling it, and tempering it. When they moved on we followed them, and both boats ran aground in front of the entrance to a lock. It was only after hard work with the poles and both engines racing astern, that we managed to get *Truant* off the mud. We were scandalised by the canal, for *Truant* drew ten inches less than the maximum depth allowed there, yet it seemed that we were liable to run aground when we were almost in the middle, while when we went to the side to pass another craft we were in the gravest danger. *Elpis* moved into the lock, and we followed. *Elpis* remained nicely alongside the wall with her bow and stern lines made fast to one bollard above, but *Truant*, with her great beam, was much more unruly, and as the water rushed in she surged forward until her stem was pushing at *Elpis's* flag-pole, which bent under so unusual a strain.

The canal lock-keepers were all mutilated veterans of the 1914–18 war. Their employment carried with it a very small salary, but a reasonable house and garden set often in lovely country, and they were apt to be more friendly than the river men. Douglas and I complained to this one— who although he had a wooden leg had just come back from the forest with a shot-gun hanging on a leather sling from one shoulder—about the state of the canal.

"It isn't so much lack of water as excess of mud," he answered. "I don't believe my bief has been dredged for thirty years."

A few hundred yards above the lock our port engine petered out, and when we put the starboard engine into gear the propeller turned but might as well have remained stationary, for all the propulsive effect that it had on the boat. The explanation was clear. Mud was not the only failing of the

Canal du Loing; the waters were thick with weed of different varieties. The rushes did not cling to any part of *Truant* and much of the weed was innocuous; but one species which grew in floating clumps, with green flowers and horny tendrils as strong as blackthorn, had gathered around both propellers. We had been brought to a halt opposite a village; the men of the village were returning from their work in a cement factory. They stood looking at us in wonder, their faces and clothes so covered with powder that they looked like exceedingly bad sculptures. We hauled *Truant* to the bank, took ropes across the tow-path and tied them to trees. *Elpis* was no more than a speck in the distance. I descended to the engine-room, very annoyed with the port engine, since I had overhauled it at Corbeil. I soon traced the trouble to one of the filters; when this had been dismantled, cleaned, and replaced, petrol flowed again, but it was useless to think of proceeding without clearing the propellers. I was hot from my labours in the engine-room and steam rose from my skin when I appeared on deck, ready for swimming. My appearance caused a sensation in the village. The water was cold at first, then it seemed to be warm and thick. I could see nothing under water, and I had to dive again and again to clear the starboard propeller; the port one presented an easier task because I was able to stand with my toes on the rushy bottom and duck head and shoulders to tear away the weed. The water was a strange grey-green colour, and I did my utmost to convince myself that it was unlikely that sewage was allowed to enter the canal. I was about to leave the water when a Peugeot stopped beside me on the tow-path and an agitated young man climbed out, shouting that he was official of the Ponts et Chaussées. "Who is the owner?" he cried.

"I am."

"Eh?" He looked all over *Truant* and I had to speak again before he dropped his eyes to the water; the moment he saw me he snapped: "Forbidden to bathe in the canals."

"I am not bathing, monsieur, I am disengaging my propellers from the weeds that flourish in your canal."

"You are breaking the law when you bathe, monsieur, and as for the weeds, they will be better when we get more boats with motors and propellers through the canal. In the old days we had so many automoteurs that the weeds were kept very low indeed; but the Germans took a lot of the automoteurs for their intended invasion of the British Isles. It will take time to rebuild, and in the meantime you at least have the knowledge that your propellers are helping to clear the water for the more fortunate boats that will follow you. Another point," he said, indicating our rope, "I must inform you that you are liable to a fine for obstructing the chemin de halage with your ropes. However, permit me to wish you bon voyage . . ." The villagers had not taken their eyes off us, and they were still standing there like inferior statues when we swept away.

The canal's biggest initial surprise for us was the amount of traffic on it. The small, pencil-shaped barges proceeded down the biefs at a speed of only one mile per hour, but they were in a greater hurry than ourselves to get in and out of the locks. While the barge was in the lock the animals grazed by the edge of the tow-path, and when the gates opened they were driven forward with blows and shouts until they had their weight fully on the long tow-rope and the pencil bumped its way clear of the stone walls. The animals were usually driven by the bargees' youngest sons, who shouted at them, just like French peasants at the plough.

"Why do you always shout 'Yee! Yee!' when you want the beasts to move?" I asked one boy.

"What else would I shout? Everybody shouts: 'Yee! Yee!' "

"In English books for children people say: 'Gee up!' to make a horse move, but the horses in England are now so intelligent that they need no instructions except for an occasional slight click of the tongue, or perhaps the words: 'All right,' spoken in a conversational tone."

He kept his beady eyes on me for an instant. "Funny the *horses* should have made all that progress," he said. "Yee! Yee!"

As we moved along the canals we could watch the water apparently running downhill from the banks on either side of us because the propeller in driving the boat forward also sucked water from the canal ahead. Each meeting with an automoteur, or even with one of the larger horse-drawn barges, called for most careful steering and for a reduction in speed. As the boats approached both were raised on a hump of water and then, when the bows crossed, the level descended so abruptly that sometimes our keel would strike bottom.

The second day in the canals brought equally bad weather, wet, with the wind bending the tall rushes on either side. Rushes on the rivers are one of the characteristics of rural France, but on the canals I had thought to see trim banks. In France, however (and who am I to grumble?) all assumes a Gallic tone, and the canals are rush-banked, a little unpractical, lovely. We had a difficult day, travelling from Souppes to near Montargis from 8 a.m. to 8 p.m., with two stops to clear weed from the propellers. The first stop came after we met an automoteur on a sharp bend, and I had the choice of steering into the approaching barge or through a thick clump of the weed that I knew to be dangerous. Almost instantly both propellers were stifled. We steered to the bank and I went sadly below to undress for bathing. I was in the water for over thirty minutes; the weed on the propeller shafts and blades was so resistant that I had to ask Isabel to hand me down a clasp knife on a lanyard. When I emerged, shivering, and in no mood for conversation, a man whom I assumed to be a village schoolmaster took me to task from the bank where he had been standing watching me.

"You may not bathe in this canal, monsieur," he said.

"I had no desire to bathe in this canal, monsieur."

"But you were bathing, monsieur."

"No, I was clearing weed from my propellers, monsieur."

"I have not made myself clear, monsieur. You may not bathe in the canal. Seven people died yesterday; they are believed to have contracted a malady through bathing in this canal. You will see notices to that effect at every lock."

"Excuse me, monsieur, but why did you not think fit to deliver this message before I entered the water?"

"Excuse *me*. . . . When you first entered the water I was startled. . . . And then, when I heard you talking to madame from the water—you remember that she brought you a knife—I realised that you were American or British, and it never entered my head that you might speak our language. I was trying to form a phrase in English; please believe me, monsieur, but I could not remember the word for water—I have no talent for languages—and every time I tried to think of it the word for sauce, *gravy*, came into my mind—'you know how words do intrude on these occasions—and I could hardly speak to you of sauces." At the next lock his gloomy words were confirmed. Notices headed *Danger of Death!* forbade all bathing.

"All were dead of the same illness within twenty-four hours," the lock-keeper told us. "It was a malady, the name of which we could not catch, and the symptoms were fever and vomiting with paralysis of certain parts of the body, and other extremes of physical misery." I went down to the saloon and had a strong drink of whisky. We had not gone a mile past the lock when both propellers again fouled. Isabel had no intention of allowing me to re-enter the water, and she encouraged me to devise a tool capable of tearing off the weeds. The tool was made by securing a four-inch nail at the end of a long piece of mahogany which Harold the engineer had given me to serve as a dipstick for the petrol tanks. We succeeded in ridding ourselves of the weed by fishing from the dinghy with the new tool, but it was a long job. I was visited by the depressing thought that we might have to do this every kilometre or so for the rest of our trip; but I was over-pessimistic; no later waterway was so badly clogged with weed as the Canal du Loing, and I got into the habit of clearing any weed while *Truant* was high up in the lock, when it was easy to crouch at the edge and fish around the propellers.

The lock-keepers had good crops of fruit and vegetables in their gardens, and they laid the surpluses out in baskets to tempt mariniers to buy. At one lock the elderly woman who opened the gates for us begged so eloquently for a little petrol to enable her "to visit her sick son" that I siphoned ten litres from a tank and gave it to her. Isabel was already ashore, buying vegetables and butter, and to her purchases the grateful recipient of the petrol added a kilo of fresh butter and a litre of fine eau-de-vie. Our food on board could not have been better, and we were thriving on the hard work. Even Isabel was eating as much as a normal person, and she insisted angrily that she was putting on too much weight, singing one of her improvised songs which began:

"Great slabs of fat

"Run off my hips . . ."

The wind became fierce but we stopped for the evening sheltered by a wooded hill, with immensely tall poplars along the edge of the dark water. We landed and walked a little in woods where the dripping moisture made a haze of golden steam and snails were out on almost every leaf. There was a field of Indian corn on the opposite bank. In these idyllic surroundings I had another nightmare, and awoke on deck, with the conviction that *Truant* had sunk in a current of such strength that she was bumping along the bottom towards the edge of a weir.

We were off next morning at seven, and passed early through the old town of Montargis where the canal narrows, and runs like a winding street lined with pavements and houses; the inhabitants were rising and coming out to look at the sky. I inquired of each bunch of women that we passed: "Excuse me, mesdames, but can you tell me where I can find Mme. Duval?"

"Which Mme. Duval?"

"The blanchisseuse who has a hosepipe with which she fills boats' tanks with drinking water."

"There is no such Mme. Duval."

We had read of Mme. Duval in Captain C. E. A. L. Rumbold's book, *Yacht Cruising in Inland Waterways*, and the captain almost over-protests his generosity in divulging the name and address of this "queen of washer-women" in Montargis. We remembered when we had not found Mme. Duval in the whole length of Montargis that after all the French "Duval" is an equivalent of the English "Smith", and it was possible that at the last moment the captain had changed his mind and given the queen a false name so that she might serve him unencumbered by too many other commitments if he again passed Montargis. I contented myself with taking two loads in four four-gallon water-cans, at the lock which is placed on a corner at the end of the town. This was a particularly high lock, and in the canals the lock-keepers did not bother to take our ropes or even to make them fast. We were obliged to develop a technique for dealing with all locks unaided. In very high ones there was always a steel ladder let into one wall, and when she had *Truant's* nose inside the lock gates, Isabel would try to edge over so that I could climb the ladder, carrying up the ends of our bow and stern warps; I would throw the loops over the bollards on shore and then return on board. When the lock was low, or even of medium height I could usually climb ashore from our high bows, without the help of a ladder.

I was pouring in my last load of water when I noticed that it was bubbling out of the funnel. I had worried that morning, thinking that we were running out of water, whereas the tanks must have been nearly full. From then on I kept a mental note of when the tanks were filled, and how much was put into them. We used about six gallons of fresh water a day, and full water-tanks lasted us for a month.

Two locks were passed after Montargis, and then we came on *Elpis*, hauled to the bank under some overhanging trees. "Just more trouble," Gwenda shouted, while Douglas raised his face from the engine to smile at us. We passed on, but a couple of locks later, though we blew our fog-horn a hundred times, the lock-keeper stood looking at us, and refused to let us in until *Elpis* arrived. We went into that lock together, but this time with *Truant* ahead of *Elpis*, a better arrangement, for, strangely enough, the water is least disturbed at the end into which it rushes. The Hawkes were dismayed by the amount of mud that *Truant* stirred up as she travelled along. They had good opportunity of judging this, as they followed us for the rest of the morning. We had a long wait in a village which was situated under a small hill, which we had to climb on a staircase of six locks. *Truant* and *Elpis* both ran aground while we waited; then *Truant* fouled a fishing-rod set on a tripod to catch pike, and I had long explanations—amicable, as it turned out—with a white-capped fisherman. Finally we got tired of the endeavour to keep our boats afloat; Douglas made *Elpis* fast to a small bridge and we went alongside *Elpis*. A crowd of hooligans, loafers, peasants, tinkers, young women on holiday, and shop-keepers gathered to exclaim at the temerity of people—and women too!—who ventured across the seas and the canals in such frail embarcations. An official of the Ponts et Chaussées arrived to state formally that we must not tie up to that bridge, but his expostulations were partly drowned in the general clamour, and since they were unnourished by dissent they gradually died away, and then he was as agreeable as any man. Gwenda said that his behaviour was another example of laisser-aller, the curse and the blessing of twentieth-century France. We had a rough passage up the staircase of locks. In one of them the lock-keeper's wife (who was either disgruntled over some domestic mishap or was an anglophobe) sent the water in so violently that *Truant's* bow and stern lines both jumped from the bitts; this happened when I was in the engine-room, and Isabel was alone on deck. *Truant* was leaping from side to side of the lock, and was overlapping *Elpis* when we got her under control. We saw how near a thing it had been when we looked at the blanched faces of Douglas and Gwenda, whose voices, raised in monitory clamour, had been audible above the inrush of the waters, Isabel's shouts and mine, and the offended cries of the lock-keeper's wife. In the ten-kilometre bief at the top of the staircase we waved the *Elpis* past, and pulled in to the side to have our lunch, which Isabel had begun to cook while we were in the locks. Our system of eating differed from that of the Hawkes: our breakfasts were similar, and just about as light as breakfasts can be, but they normally ate only sandwiches, fruit and wine at midday, and Gwenda prepared a large meal in the evening; we preferred to eat well in the middle of the day, then have tea in the late afternoon, and eat very lightly in the evening, if at all. Each crew thought, to the end of our journeying together, that its own system was the best; I should, however, remark that it was easy for us to cook in our airy galley while we were under way, but Gwenda would have had to perform within a few feet of their engine and in conditions of considerable discomfort.

When we moved to the end of the bief we looked downhill—an extra-ordinary sensation, for we had been climbing all the way from the English Channel to that point, 557 kilometres from le Havre—into the wide and rich valley of the Loire. Each lock, from above, looked like a sheet of glass ending in a precipice. For some reason, that afternoon I was feeling tired and out-of-sorts, and I worked myself into a rage when, at the second lock of the descent, the lock-keeper made me push *Truant's* bows against the forward gates so that he could fit in astern of us a metal barge which contained German prisoners and was towed by other German prisoners, tugging with leaden persistence at a frayed old rope. The bows of the barge were rubbing against our dinghy, hanging in its davits, and I was concerned about *Truant's* safety, but these were poor excuses indeed for my display of temper. The lock-keeper was in no kinder frame of mind than myself, and invective jumped from *Truant* to the quay and back again. I regret to admit that in one heated sally I upbraided him for putting Germans in the same lock as our boat. I could have bitten my tongue off the moment the words were spoken, for undoubtedly some of the prisoners understood French. In sharp contrast to my boorishness, the Germans were being most helpful, doing their utmost to save our dinghy from being scratched, and smiling with wistful amiability at seeing something that they could understand, two Aryans more fortunate than themselves travelling through foreign lands. One hundred yards of smooth water separated that lock from the next, and situated on the bank was a prison camp. Shame rose in me as I looked at the familiar sight; when I had been among similar squalid huts, mud paths strewn with cinders, rubbish bins and rickety latrines, I had always had victory to look forward to, or dreams of escape to an undefeated homeland. In le Havre we had seen the Americans with their ready sentimental kindness pampering their German prisoners. Those that we saw in French hands on the canals, and they were numerous, were not well-treated. I watched the prisoners carefully after the first meeting in the lock. France will pay one day, I suppose, for any needless bitterness that was directed against the broad, slouching figures with expressions so wooden that they betrayed the will to banish expression from faces and bodies that showed the signs of malnutrition: swollen bellies, patches of Chinese white at the nostrils, bony joints, scaly lips.

We passed the last lock of that staircase with a few minutes to spare before the evening closing hour and a twenty-three kilometre bief ahead. We had now entered the Canal Latéral à la Loire set in the Loire valley, parallel to that wide, shallow river, which journalists always regard as being strategical, although throughout much of its length any oaf can wade across it without getting his knees wet. The Loire canal has few locks, and it runs through unspoiled country, well-wooded and green. At 9 o'clock we came to the great aqueduct which carries the canal across the valley, a distance of four kilometres. This engineering accomplishment, which is constructed in a floridly Haussmannesque manner, is regarded with pride by French mariniers as an example of what Frenchmen can really do if they set their minds to a thing; pictures of it, frequently to be seen in the saloons of the barges, are painted on sections cut from large trees, the bark being left in place to form a kind of frame, and the painting being executed faithfully and glossily in thick oils. The bridge is a one-way affair just wide enough to take the biggest barge, and it offered us two or three spare inches on either side. The waterway is lined with wooden boards, and there are wide stone pavements on either side of it, then ornate railings mounting electric standard lights. The barges are often allowed to steer themselves across at slow speed, while their crews walk beside them, admiring the magnificent prospects up and down the valley, and the unusual sight of rivers, roads, trees, houses and even birds, beneath the hulls of their own vessels. The water on the bridge was as smooth as a gutter in a modern city. *Truant* required careful steering. I sighted her bows on the twin memorials at the far end of the straight perspective. Isabel stood on deck near the wheelhouse, warning me if we strayed an inch or two from the course, and exclaiming in the same breath at the beauty of the evening and the splendour of the valley.

There were days of travel in the canals when we felt so tired as to be thankful when 8 p.m. arrived and the locks closed down, and other days when the locks were not too frequent, and when the ceremony of tea at 4 p.m. and the beverage itself so invigorated us that no more fatigue was felt until we were in bed; this day and evening were in the latter category and we travelled in the darkness, with the stars reflected in the canal, that was visible because it shone blacker than the night under which it slid along. At length we settled beneath what seemed to be a wood, and it was only when we turned out our lights that we saw that the wood was in fact a village set on an eminence.

Next day we swept on, along the most agreeable of canals. At midday we went through a lock which was worked for us by a sophisticated woman of middle age. As we left the lock I had an impulse to ask her if there was any good restaurant at hand, and she directed us to the Pension Beauregard, which proved to be a somewhat flamboyant edifice, much of its frontage covered by lettering advertising the comfort of its beds, the number of its bedrooms, its modern plumbing, and the excellence of its chef. It was not one of the most pleasant parts of that canal. The pension had been built near a corner of the waterway where there had been much flooding, and the ground was sedgy and intersected by deep ditches. Our arrival caused something of a sensation among the aperitif-drinkers on the terrace, vociferous men and women, some genuinely young and others aping youth, and even among the quieter guests, who were already at table in the dining-room, but who stood up, deserting their plates for a grudging half minute, to look at our boat through the open windows. Most of them were attacking their second course when we entered the dining-room. Each guest paid 250 francs a day, and most of them were decent bourgeois people. A few had children; all were painstakingly dressed for the seaside, although the swollen costs of living had driven them to the canal-side instead. They had come from Paris, or even farther, to bathe in water which we were too fastidious to touch with our hands. When we left the dining-room we were approached by a man of about my age with the hard-soft face of a woman's hairdresser—though that was not his profession—and wispy red-gold hair, thinning on the crown of a domed head. He wore Austrian-type shorts, cut out of white leather in Paris, and slit at the sides, the slits being tied up with fetching leather thongs. His legs were self-consciously shapely and garlanded with red-gold curls. He asked me without needless preamble if he and the wet-chinned little girl clinging to his hand might make a journey in our boat. I told him that we should be honoured if they would care to join us as far as the next lock. Vastly excited by my acquiescence, which perhaps he had hardly expected, he whirled round on one heel and sprang into the Pension Beauregard, whence his voice sounded clearly, shouting: "My camera! my raincoat! my pump! My comb, the yellow comb! Where is my pump?" Every occupant of the pension was excited by Ginger's success, which he trumpeted from the first storey. "The Englishman invited us. Natalie! are you not ready yet? Don't move, Monsieur, we come, we come!" In an instant he appeared on the terrace, threading his way impatiently past the orange-painted tin tables, pushing a bicycle cluttered with every conceivable type of gadget and cycling club badge. He was followed by a young woman, blushing and plump, who also pushed a bicycle; the wet-chinned child kept pace by clinging to the back fork of the woman's bicycle. They handed their machines over the rail to me, and I put them on deck, aft of the wheel-house. I suspected that many more of the pensionnaires, excited by the success of Ginger, intended to ask us for a ride, but we were spared their presence on board by an unfortunate occurrence. At the head of the procession which streamed from the Pension Beauregard towards us was a robust young woman, plainly, from her energetic bearing and general advertisement of almost fruit-salty good health, the natural leader of that holiday group. In her excitement she forgot to look where she was going; one instant she was there, and the next all that remained of her was a robust scream, which ascended from a ditch filled with nettles and brambles In the consequent turmoil, and while the leader of a moment before was herself led blubbering back to the pension, Isabel and I made haste to cast off. Most of the pensionnaires had turned away, choosing to succour the woman in distress.

"She's severely stung on the tail," one cynic cried to our red-haired passenger.

"It surely isn't the first time," he replied. We had the impression that he

98

was annoyed that the accident should have divided the attention which would otherwise have gone entirely to his own venture. He set himself in a pose on the forward part of the boat, staring down the canal with an intent expression, the muscles braced in his right leg, which was becomingly raised on the bowsprit mounting. But when the pension was out of sight he turned briskly to get all the information he could before we arrived at the lock, a journey of some eight kilometres. I never met such a man for questions. He poked his long nose—it had chrome-yellow freckles on it and red-gold tassels hanging from the nostrils—into every corner of every cabin. He asked me where I had bought my watch, how old my wife was, and how much I had paid for the boat, our lunch at the pension, my shirt, my linen trousers, and the foghorn. Soon I was fencing every question with something approximating to the armament manufacturer's standard answer to journalists: "I can neither confirm nor deny . . ." And finally I became so maddened that I ruthlessly questioned him, considering my next question while he was answering the last. I learned that he was called Salvador Mondino, and was an immigrant to France from Catalonia. His work was in Paris; he made women's handbags: "Mais seulement les plus chics, les plus jolis." The wet-chinned girl, he said, was not his daughter, but his niece. He was newly married. "My wife loves me so much that she could eat me," he said. "She is twelve years my junior, and this marriage has opened new horizons for her. How does she strike you?"

"Charming."

They had been in the Pension Beauregard for one week, and it had rained every day. "Wet weather and no sun—pénible pour moi," Salvador explained, "parce que je suis très sportif. Mais quandmême, pour les nouveaux mariés le temps n'a pas tellement d'importance, vous comprenez?" We were not sorry to say good-bye to them at the lock, where Salvador, although he thanked us gracefully with words, did not offer to assist with our warps. He set his niece on a small seat over the back wheel of his bicycle and they rode off, his legs glinting in the sun; the young wife turned her head away from nature and towards her red-gold man.

We stopped for the night under beeches that languidly dropped leaves and insects on our decks. A caterpillar came sensuously down through the skylight, as though it enjoyed every movement on the smooth white-enamelled surfaces. Isabel made me carry it ashore and lay it in the green forests of the grass. Some larger animal, a rat or a snake, was active all night in the waterweeds beside the boat, and this noise was sufficient to waken me at intervals, so that, long before 6 a.m. on a fine, summer morning, we had breakfasted and were under way. We were obliged to wait for several hours behind a queue of pencil barges at a hump-backed double lock which led to another canal bridge. We tied up to one of the small barges, and crossed its decks to land, using the large gangway equipped with a derrick across which the two mules had come to their stable to have a bite of food and a siesta. The whole barge smelled most pungently of mule, and although both of us greatly admired the animals, and enjoyed seeing them in action, we thought that for our own use we preferred the internal combustion engine. (For the benefit of those interested in such matters, I must say that we never had any suspicion of engine smell in our living quarters, in the wheelhouse, or on deck. The reason for this was that the engine-room was aft of the living accommodation, and separated from it by an airtight bulkhead.) We walked into the village near the locks and Isabel bought a handsome sausage, a thousand grams of bread, a litre of red wine, and half a kilo of tomatoes, since we thought that for once we would have a simple picnic as we travelled instead of eating our usual, more formal meal.

It was obvious when we entered the first of the big locks that the water was going to be extremely turbulent, but since nobody ashore would take my warps I had to climb up a fifty-foot ladder to attach them to the bollards, leaving Isabel alone on board, and once I was up there the ladder, which was against the entrance gates, was useless for returning to the boat, far below. The water was already beginning to seethe, foam and bubble, with Isabel darting from one end of *Truant* to the other, when I decided that extreme measures were necessary, and managed to reach the deck by descending the stern warp, hand over hand, an unpleasant experience with the warp apparently eager to jerk me off, and vicious water below in which no swimmer could have considered himself safe. The experience was dramatised by the spectators and the lock-keeper, who all yelled curses at me and called me every kind of fool until I reached the deck, when they sent down loud bravos and compliments which I was too busy to accept with becoming modesty and graciousness. I hate such acts, since my arms are the weakest part of my body, and are never to be depended on, having been strained by the different games, sports, and pastimes to which my type of British youth was constantly exposed when it would have been better employed in learning to play the piano or to paint in oils. On the end of the bridge (I was steering) we had a slight collision with a barge; no damage was done to either party, but for the first time I indulged in recrimination with a mariner, and got better—or worse—than I gave. Isabel suggested that being captain of a ship was making me irascible.

A bief twenty kilometres in length lay ahead of us. The sun beat down. I set the engine at a steady throb, pushing us on at about four knots, and we ate and drank on deck while Isabel steered with the tiller. We had the impression of sailing through the jungle. In places the tall rushes bent across the water until they nearly met above us. Beyond the Loire valley, to port, we saw forests and rugged hill country, while to starboard the fields fought to keep back the encroachment of the forest. Now and then a hunter, with his gun and his fierce, hairy dog, allowed us to distract him for a few seconds from his study of the wood. There were many birds, kingfishers darting before us like azure bullets along the narrow waterway, terns, strangely foreign so far from the sea, hawks of many breeds and great buzzards—which at first we took for eagles—planing on steady, delicately-adjusted wings over the trees. The place set an enchantment on us; we could not bear to leave it, and at the first lock we fell into conversation with the lock-keeper. He was a dark-visaged man, powerful in all his reactions, with the narrow, intense, wrinkle-set eyes of a man at home with nature and even with violence. Beside the lock was a kennel, and although the lock-keeper was more eager to talk of his favourite politician, Mr. Winston Churchill, he was willing to tell us about the two dogs which leaped strongly at the wired-in run of the kennel set in the shade of a contorted fig tree. One of them was a beagle, with fifty-per-cent of English blood in his veins, while the other was a cross between an old French breed, the griffon nivernais, and an English otterhound. They were used as a pair for tracking down and settling with the lock-keeper's favourite quarry, the fierce wild boar. He claimed to have shot a large number of boars in the winter that was past, and there were signs of them all over his house, which was set back a little from the lock, and below it; a row of yellowing tusks showed along one window-sill and bristling skins were drying, nailed to the front door. The sanglier paid a hunter handsome dividends in those days of scarce food, for the flesh is justly prized, and the dead animal provides a good quantity of fats which are among the best obtainable for cooking, greasing leather, and—some say—for the treatment of rheumatism, skin inflammations, and sexual sterility or weakness. We turned from admiration of his lusty dogs to tactful appreciation of the fowls, Leghorns, Rhode Island Reds, and bantams, which strolled at will through the open door of the house in search of morsels around the cooking stove and the square dining table covered with a rusty-red cloth as thick as a carpet and tasselled round the edges. He shouted to his wife, a handsome and dignified woman, telling her to leave the three goats she was herding, and to fetch us goat cheeses and eggs. We decided to stop

101

there, and made *Truant* fast to some bollards 300 yards above the lock. It was the night of July 20th, and we were told that on August 1st the whole canal was to be drained for dredging and repairs. Otherwise we might well have spent a month in that place.

After breakfast I extracted the bicycles from the after cabin and we rode off into the forest. We spent the whole morning riding and walking along woodcutters' paths, and saw no man until we came to a village in a clearing where we drank red wine in a sombre room surrounded by scrubbed wooden tables at which perhaps a dozen rich peasants, singly and in small groups, were getting a little drunk on the same sour beverage. We returned to the canal through a more cultivated area. It was nearly midday, and the farms looked so prosperous that I chose the largest of them, which was also a mill, and therefore very rich, and called to ask if there was any place in the neighbourhood where we might eat. Having frequently experienced the hospitality of such people, I had expected an invitation, but we were unlucky, since there was only an old crone in the kitchen, and no great quantity of food in preparation, and she advised us to go to the bistro in the small village of Avril-sur-Loire, near the lock.

A man was gutting fresh-water fish by the back door. The drinking place was a dark kitchen. We sat at a table and ordered glasses of white Burgundy as apéritifs. "Yes," the woman said, "you can eat here in half-an-hour if you don't mind taking the luck of the pot." This proved to be the cheapest (350 francs) and by far the best of our restaurant meals in France. It was not what we ate—hors d'œuvres with pâté de lapin, roasted veal, fried potatoes, haricots verts, pissenlit salad, fruits, and angel-cake made with coffee cream—so much as the manner of its preparation. The woman and her family group of six ate and drank what we did at a separate table. I don't know her name, but she is a great cook. The village where this genius practises her art consists of little more than this and another even smaller and more rustic bistro, and a church. When I told the lock-keeper of our meal he said: "Ah, you should have given her warning and it would have been better." He took us into his garden, for he had half-a-dozen gooseberry bushes hanging with fruit almost as big as pigeons' eggs which he said would only rot, since neither he nor his wife could eat gooseberries. "The stomach is my weak spot," he said. "You see, only the grands mutilés could get the jobs on the locks, and I am a grand mutilé because I was hit in the stomach. But the bullet in my guts has turned out to be something of a blessing after all for it was the means of putting me on a régime which makes me healthy above most men of my age. What age would you give me?"

102

"Forty."

"Fifty-one," he said with a scowl, not because he was displeased at looking ten years younger than his age, but because fifty-one is always too old for some men. "The doctors told me I wouldn't live long after my stomach wound, but they were calculating for an ordinary Frenchman, who will put his appetite first and his life second. I gave up drink, except for a glass when I feel like it, and I drink milk with my food. As for smoking, I stopped that altogether, for, as I said to myself: 'Why clog your innards with sticky, stinking tobacco juice?' Then, I have another rule for health; I rarely eat beef, but at least once a week we kill a fowl; the white meat of chicken is the best meat of all. When I shoot partridges and pigeons I give them away, for I feel that they are not for me, and anyway I prefer a good chicken cooked gently in the oven, and eaten either hot with a salad, preferably of cress, or cold with a good sauce mayonnaise. I'm an easy man to please; my tastes are all simple. My work here suits me for it gives me that freedom which is necessary to me. My hunting is a help to us: I breed clever dogs and sometimes I sell them profitably, and I also sell most of the game, including the sangliers. I've been able to make a study of the breeding of goats, and I find that if the nannies are not kept beyond the age of six the milk and the cheese have no goaty taste and are superior to cow produce. Our goats are like children to us; they're very beautiful, for you will have remarked that they're of the Alpine breed, with the dark streak down the spine and the deer-like head. At night here the mosquitoes are terrible; next winter I intend to build a mosquito-proof house for the goats, because there's no way of protecting them in their present place; however, if the torments of the insects become unbearable the goats cry to me and I get out of my bed and go out in the dark to spray them and their place with insecticide. Before the war we kept cows, but the Germans killed one, and at a bad period we were obliged to kill the other. Necessity drove us to keeping goats, and I doubt now if we would ever go back to cows. The goats make the devil of a lot of work, for they must be watched while they feed, and if they are to be kept to a good standard they must have plenty of sweet green food. D'you like plums? Then come out to the garden and you'll taste something."

When we had eaten his plums he took us into the house and we drank Dubonnet, which had been brought to him by barge. He did a great deal of trading with the mariniers as they passed, for they were quick to assess the shortages in some districts and the surpluses in others. The lock-keeper did not give them money for the Dubonnet and wine and the grain for his fowls that they brought him, but cheese, vegetables, fruit, home-grown tobacco, and his tobacco ration from the shops. He showed us technical books on the breeding of goats and gun-dogs, and laid out his shotgun and two rifles for my inspection. We both had the impression that this resourceful and energetic man was full of some suppressed excitement which he shared only with his wife—for it showed in the meaningful looks that they occasionally exchanged—and we formed the opinion that despite the isolation of the place where they lived and worked, they were deep in some political game. They came aboard *Truant* in the evening. The talk, in the brightly-lit saloon, was exclusively political. The pair of them took the understandable line of unlearned people, that France had once produced great men, but did so no longer, and perhaps never would again. Mr. Churchill had recently been discarded as a peace-time leader by the electorate of his country, but the lock-keeper maintained that Churchill could quickly have saved France, since all that France needed was a powerful, and not necessarily an idealistic, leader. They believed that the defeated Germany would make a speedy recovery and would soon again be a major power while France was in danger of sinking for ever into representing a tawdry fun-fair for more wealthy nations. When I suggested that it was necessary for the partitions separating the nations of the world to be first made transparent and then blown away altogether, the lock-keeper asked in some astonishment: "But are you then a communist?" He believed himself that stronger nationalism was the first thing to be achieved. After two hours of hot talk across the cabin we went on deck and as they climbed down into the long grass on the bank the lock-keeper said to us: "Well, write now and then to let us know how you get on. You know our name. Or don't you?"

"Yes," Isabel said, and she spoke their name.

"Ssh!" The lock-keeper, vaguely illuminated by the light from the portholes, looked uneasily at the dark woods around us. "Ne criez pas si fort, ne criez pas si fort, madame," he said testily. So although we had enjoyed their company, our last impression of the lock-keeper and his wife was one of fear and conspiracy.

We moved at 7 o'clock the following morning. We were greatly surprised to see fresh steak on sale at a lock, but the woman said: "You are now in the Charollais and here we eat beef twice daily."

"Unrationed?"

"Our country produces beef. We have eaten meat twice daily all through the war, and since the war." I was reminded by this of the difference between Britain and France, for my mother lives in Ayrshire, a county that produces vast quantities of milk, yet milk, cheese and butter products were even more strictly rationed there than in other parts of Britain. The women, when we had bought their beef-steaks, produced two roses and a carnation for Isabel, whose bearing while we were entering the lock they had loudly admired, crying: "One can see that she knows what she is at, that one."

A little later, as we were passing an uncouth barge one of the men on it shouted to the other about Isabel, who was steering *Truant*, and to my— perhaps stupid—annoyance, he referred to her as a *gonzesse*. Immediately after this incident we came to a lock where, although we were the only mounting traffic, there was a string of small barges waiting to descend. We were slow to leave the lock when we had been raised to the higher level because three of the barges ahead of us were slewed across the river. We waited for the barges to straighten themselves, while they, forgetting that we needed much more water than they did, and could not squeeze right up to the bank of the canal to pass them, waited for us to approach. Our caution drew shouts of protest. The first such remonstrances came from a small boy goading the mules that drew the leading barge: "Eh!" he shouted at me as I stood coiling our forward warp, "this is not the sea, bloody idiot."

Surprised by such direct language, I disdained to reply.

"Out of our way, capitalists!" shouted a woman whom I took to be the muleteer's mother. She was tall, thin, and hag-like.

"Get out of our way; and it will be a pleasure to pass such an unsavoury barge as yours," I replied.

"Nous, c'est pour manger," she shouted, jabbing the water viciously with her long barge-pole.

"It astonishes me that you earn enough to buy food if you manage your barge so incompetently."

"With us it is not the life of the château."

"Obviously not."

"I defecate upon you," she said as we approached still nearer, but, apparently changing her mind, she spat on our deck, and described me as a crapule of inverted sexual habits. In my reply I referred to her as a putain who slept on her face. Isabel, who has been very carefully brought up, had found much of the French used in these exchanges to be outside her vocabulary, and believed that I had been too gentle with my repartee. She became very excited in the cool of the evening when the birds were active, and she saw beside the canal a small owl, a great many jays, and some tree-creepers. I was more interested in the cattle in the fields on either hand, resplendent animals. The Charollaise is large, magnificently muscled

105

and pure white with a pink tinge of flesh, a cow sculpted by Michelangelo, painted by Rubens. She appears to be as lazy as she is beautiful and she likes to lay her spotless flanks in the cool grass. Those white splashes of muscle on the fields reminded me of bull-terriers, seeking out the only patch of sunlight on the carpet and basking in it. Some of the bullocks were five feet wide. When the locks had closed we found a deserted reach with no houses, roads, or telephone wires, in view, and settled for the night opposite a row of eighteen chestnut trees. I lit the cooking stove and went up to sluice the decks. A black cat was delicately hunting in the woods, apparently as taken with his own movements as with his carnivorous anticipations of the kill and moving with set pauses, as though a million eyes regarded him. We sat up late with a light on deck. The night was quiet and hot. Isabel wrote letters and I read Balzac's *Village Curé*. That day we had passed fifteen locks and covered seventy kilometres; very good going in the canals.

Next day we entered the Canal du Centre, which we dreaded because many people had described to us the density of its traffic and the frequency of its locks. We saw at once that this canal was less well maintained than the fine Canal Latéral à la Loire, and that the lock-keepers were more surly. We ate lunch moored comfortably to the overhanging branches of a large plane tree, and went so far as to take a short siesta after the meal, but we cursed the siesta for the rest of the day, for it permitted two motor-driven barges to slip past us, and we were obliged to follow them for most of the afternoon and evening, since the biefs were so short that we were unable to take advantage of our superior speed and pass them. In the evening we traversed the extravagantly picturesque village of Paray-le-Monial, and came to the lock beyond it with almost an hour to spare before closing time. But the white yacht which I had seen back at Corbeil was in the lock, while an excessively dirty barge, which seemed to contain a platoon of gypsies of all ages between seventy and six, was waiting to go through. The white yacht was being towed by a tractor, and had passed *Truant* while we were exploring the forest near Avril-sur-Loire. Although about the same size as *Truant*, she was of a very different quality, with almost the whole of her interior devoted to an immense saloon with a cocktail bar. She had been sunk by the Germans and had spent several of the war years submerged at le Havre. A Seine boatman and his wife were seeing her through to Marseilles, where she was to be taken over by a new owner. They did not even bother to steer the boat through the locks, allowing her steel hull to crash from side to side as the tractor dragged her along.

The gypsies on the barge ahead set up a great chorus of shouts at us, thinking mistakenly that we would try to push through in front of them. But the old lock-keeper took so long to pass first the yacht and then the barge that it was five minutes to eight when the lock was once more clear, and he limped away to his house. I stood on deck sounding the foghorn. A young couple came from the house on the left bank.

"No use blowing any more, he won't open again," the young man said. "He's old and tired. You'll have to excuse him." On the façade of the speaker's house was a notice board painted in chocolate and gold with the words, Aristide Pernod, *Sculpteur*, and behind the house was a yard filled with marble crosses and small tombstones. "Where are you going?" he asked.

"Greece."

"But you'll change boats at Marseilles."

"No."

"My God!" he said.

"Now be sensible," his wife said to him. "I'll have a time with you after this, well I know it." And turning to me she explained. "He reads too much of that Pierre Loti, and while living by a canal is good for business, since it makes possible the cheap delivery of stone for my husband's work, it's also infernal since he sees boats from foreign countries, and it reminds him that others, whom he is unchristian enough to envy, have work that encourages them to travel."

"Silence!" the husband said, and he asked a great many questions about the boat.

"He's very fortunate to have a good job, especially now," the wife said. "Soon there'll be war memorials again, as there were from 1920 to 1930. I'm trying to get him started on some war memorials but he won't do it for he says that this time there won't be memorials . . ."

"The memorials for the war that ended in 1918 became a mockery to the human race when war broke out again in 1939," cried her husband.

"Such words are dictated by laziness. You're disinclined to work, so you invent nonsensical moralities. Your tools rust in the shed while you argue that there'll be no memorials. But other sculpteurs," she wielded an imaginary mallet, "are at work, and when the call for memorials comes we shall remain poor."

"The trouble with women is that they have no souls," the sculpteur said to me. "It's women who make wars, for they tie down their men to the daily needs."

"Listen to him. All he has to do is chip and rub at a little clean stone,

107

and I wonder how much of that he'd do if he hadn't got me tied down to attending to his daily needs . . ." The telephone bell sounded in their house and the woman ran in. We heard her talking loudly into the apparatus, and then the tinkle of the bell, and she came out very excited, her previous bad temper forgotten. "It's the pink stone," she said. "They're despatching it to-morrow."

"Ah, good!"

"I adore the colour, pink," she said. "It makes a lovely tombstone for it takes on a beautiful shine."

"Supper's ready," Isabel said.

At 5.15. a.m. we breakfasted, and at 5.45 we cast off, ready to slide *Truant* into the open lock. But we could not move. While we had slept the lock-keeper below had lowered the water level in our bief, and *Truant* was firmly aground. I dropped the dinghy into the water, took a four-inch warp across the canal and made it fast to an oak tree; then both of us worked hard on the windlass until we had hauled her free. When we entered the lock, I was disposed to forget the lock-keeper's wooden limb and to remember that he had been unhelpful the previous evening. His opening remark did nothing to soothe my temper.

"Were you aground?" he asked.

I said something about "ce sacré Canal du Centre," which so offended his canallic pride that he asked me why I used the canal if I considered it to be so offensive.

At the next lock we again found ourselves behind the gypsy barge, and while we waited we again ran aground. The gypsies were determined to keep ahead of us, and they were a sound combination. Three of the younger children were set to yell: "Yee! Yee!" at the two fairly powerful horses which only had the smallest type of barge with nothing in it beyond the family's household effects—and these were few—to pull, and they travelled at such a pace that we could not overtake them even in a three-kilometre bief. Had we overtaken them we thought it extremely doubtful that they would vacate the centre of the canal to let us pass. Before the end of the morning I was feeling muscular fatigue. At each lock I had to jump or climb ashore, and make fast our warps while Isabel stopped *Truant* with the engine and looked after the stern warp; then I was usually expected to help the lock-keeper by closing one of the lower gates while he closed the other, and when that was done I had to jump either to *Truant's* deck, or if that were too low, to the roof of the wheelhouse. While the water rushed in I kept the warps both taut by tightening on the windlass, a procedure which, with constant repetition, was more exhausting than it sounds. When the water had risen to its upper level I went ashore again, opened one of the gates, freed the warps from the bollards, and climbed aboard as Isabel began to take *Truant* out. Many of the lock gates on that canal had been destroyed during the war with twenty-lbs. high-explosive charges, and had been only roughly repaired to the Germans' orders; as a result almost every gate was twisted out of true, and was very hard to move with its ungreased gearing mechanism. When *Truant* was clear of the lock I coiled the warps in preparation for the next lock, which, on that canal, was often only a few minutes distant. Although I had been advised to use light rope in the canals I persisted with the four-in. manilla, partly because at times a very severe strain was put upon the bow warp, while the same might have happened to the stern warp had the engine at any time failed to stop *Truant* as we entered a lock, and partly because I felt that the thicker, softer rope was less liable to damage Isabel's lovely hands.

The canal climbed hard all morning, and the gypsies flogged and screamed on, just managing to keep ahead of us until the dark town of Montceau-les-Mines, where with howls of triumph they swung their barge up the inlet leading to the colliery where they were to receive a cargo. We looked with favour upon Montceau—an important mining town, judging by the number of pit shafts to be guessed at, the number of slag heaps, and the number of barges carrying coal—because there we passed the white motor yacht as well as the gypsies. The white yacht had to stop while the tractor driver went to a restaurant for his midday meal. Isabel had begun to cook as we passed the gypsies, and we ate as we travelled, not daring to stop in that swiftly-climbing canal while the way was clear ahead. We had barely finished eating when we reached the summit of the Canal du Centre, 1,000 feet above sea level on the watershed between the valleys of two great rivers, the Loire and the Saône. The canal descends to the latter river down the wooded valley of the River Dheune. At 8 p.m. we were stopped by a lock which was forty kilometres and twenty-seven locks from Chalon-sur-Saône, the end of the canal. It was a pretty lock, but there was no place provided for boats to moor, and the lock-keeper forebade us at first to attach our ropes to his handsome pear trees. However, he came from the Midi, and when we had given him a drink on board he himself attached the ropes in a manner calculated not to reduce the fruit yield of the trees. There was a large main road running up the opposite bank and all kinds of traffic, cars, agricultural wagons, a binder with a three-horse team, pedestrians, cyclists and a bus, stopped to have a good look at us. My legs were so tired from all the jumping that I had done—we had passed twenty-five locks that day—that I could not sleep easily.

Isabel wakened me at 4.45 a.m. We breakfasted and washed down the boat, and all was ready for our start at 6. I was dressed in shorts and tennis shoes, the best clothes for jumping; we well knew that twenty-seven locks would take a lot of doing in the working day of fourteen hours. However, all of them were descending locks, and we had realised that there is much less work going downhill by canal than going up; in that respect a boat navigating inland waterways resembles a bicycle on the roads. The main difference is that going upstream the water rushes violently into the locks, throwing the boat about, but going down, the water in the lock remains as calm as the surface in an emptying bath-tub, and all the commotion is outside the lower gates. We found that one warp was sufficient in the descending locks, and altered our procedure accordingly. As we entered the lock I lassoed a bollard on the quay with the spliced end of a four-in. warp, leaving the warp lying on deck for Isabel to make fast when she had stopped *Truant* with the engine. Meanwhile I went to close one lock gate while the lock-keeper closed the other, then I went to the other end and opened the sluices. When the water was nearly out, I cast off the warp and Isabel coiled it on deck while I opened one gate and the lock-keeper the other. If the lock was a shallow one I took a running jump to the deck or to the roof of the wheelhouse as Isabel steered out, but more often I was obliged to climb down the ladder sunk into the damp masonry while Isabel steered carefully towards me—a delicate business, for if she came too close too soon the boat would hit my wall and bounce away from me and we both knew that it would be risky if I fell into the water in front of the advancing monster—and at the right moment I jumped from the ladder to the deck. On one occasion I failed to jump and had to run after *Truant* along the bank of the canal until we found a suitable place for boarding. We made good progress although we were not favoured by fortune, for every one of the locks was closed against the descending traffic, and we had to sound our foghorn and wait endlessly, frequently running aground. It was a stifling afternoon with a hint of thunder in the syrupy air and the lock-keepers were surly. We learned that we were fast overtaking the Hawkes's boat, and the canal people, unused to seeing British yachts, could not believe that there was not some family connection between *Truant* and *Elpis*. They repeatedly asked me to admit that Douglas was my papa.

Tea at 4 o'clock revived us somewhat, but the last part of the canal contains some dangerous bends and at one of these I nearly ran us into trouble; we were travelling too fast on the port engine, and it was necessary to turn suddenly to port; I threw the engine into neutral, then astern, and swung the helm hard over. Even so we were careering at some six knots into a bank of ominously solid appearance, when Isabel, whose reaction had been quicker than mine, started the starboard engine and gave a tremendous kick with it which carried our bows round and clear, our starboard fenders grazing the bank. We were anxious to push through to the river that evening, but 8 o'clock was striking as *Truant* entered Chalon-sur-Saône, and we were obliged to stop for the night before the first of the three locks in that town. The first lock is situated in what may easily be the most sordid part of Chalon. It was certainly the most unpleasant place in which we had spent a night on *Truant*, but we were so tired that we cared little. We were surrounded by the windows of tenements, all open, some black, some yellow with light which seemed to pulse in the hot darkness; twenty yards astern was a factory. We slept heavily.

We negotiated the lock at 6.15 the following morning. The walls when I went down the iron ladder to do my spectacular leap to *Truant's* deck, smelled abominably of urine. Between the second lock and the third and last, there was a long basin where many barges lay, and among them was the delicate, blue shape of *Elpis*. It was still too early for Douglas to be awake, so we slipped past them with the engine throttled down, but an individual of greasily-pompous aspect who stood on the cobbled quay above the yacht shouted to us in French: "Stop! Stop, Monsieur Millar! Here are your friends." We paid no attention beyond a few vague gestures of understanding, and put *Truant* alongside the same quay, but some two hundred yards nearer the gates of the final lock. While I was attending to the warps the greasy man came up at a smart trot. Although his words had to compete with breathlessness consequent upon his hurry to join us, he explained that he was what he described as 'the finest pilot who ever took a boat up or down the Saône.' I gathered from the rest of his talk that he had arranged to pilot *Elpis* and would like also to pilot *Truant*.

"But if you're piloting *Elpis* you won't be able to pilot us," I said.

"Ah, yes. But I think that Monsieur and Madame Hawkes may be able to get another pilot, and I should greatly prefer to pilot you, for I have taken a great fancy to you and your ship."

"But we have no intention of taking a pilot," Isabel said. "We have a map of the Saône, and anyway, it's a nice placid river."

"Placid!" he exclaimed. "The Saône has killed men, yes, and women too! As for your map, madame, I doubt if your map will greatly assist you for the simple reason that there are no maps of recent date . . ."

"Ours is recent, and it was made in London."

"Then the map-makers of London must be holy men or water-divinersat-a-distance, for the channel of the Saône is constantly changing."

Later, when we strolled up the quay to call upon the Hawkes, the pilot followed three yards behind us. He had an unpleasant habit—he appeared to be of a nervous disposition—which consisted of scratching at his behind and the tops of his legs while he talked. When he was trying to impress us his scratching became feverish. He had a face like a speckled toadstool and a voice that was half-strangled or partially lost through some wrong turning of the vocal pipes. We preferred to have him in the rear of our advance. Gwenda was up, and busily at work on their teak decks, looking very neat and active with her linen trousers of the Breton fishermen's rusty colour rolled up to the knee, and when we approached we found that Douglas also was awake, but his delightful face wore the surprised and almost aggrieved look of a late sleeper who has been disturbed before his usual hour. Dressed in silk pyjamas, Douglas was tinkering with his engine, and the cockpit was neatly dotted with little piles of sparking plugs, washers, tools. The pilot coughed suggestively at my shoulder.

"Are you employing this man as a pilot?" I asked.

"Certainly not!" answered Gwenda, always the more aggressive of the Hawkes ménage. "It's all right, he doesn't understand a word of English. We don't like his face, and we've been warned that there are a good many bogus pilots on this river. Have you seen his papers?"

"He showed us a printed card."

"Exactly, anybody could have such a card printed. No, we've engaged a proper Saône pilot who was recommended to us by the captain of a barge."

"I don't want to have a pilot," Isabel said. "We have our map."

"We've no map," Gwenda said, "and we draw six feet, which is a lot too much for this river, they say."

"Pilots always magnify the difficulties and dangers," Isabel said.

"I should get rid of the chap behind you," Douglas said to me. "As a matter of fact the only way that we could do so yesterday was by telling him that he could pilot you."

Turning round, I told the pilot that we had been most impressed by his appearance and his qualifications and that if we decided to engage the services of a pilot we would surely remember him. He retired, doubtfully, for a short distance, and remained by a lamp-post, watching us. Douglas invited us on board, and gave us a drink. Gwenda laid down her deck-scrubber and came aft to reveal their programme. They intended to leave Chalon the following day, Saturday, and travel slowly down the Saône to Mâcon, where the pilot could find a bed, and his patrons food and drink in the hotel in that town which is renowned for the excellence of its table;

they planned to visit on the Sunday the Yacht Club Gilbert Dumas, twenty-three kilometres north of Lyons. She showed us a letter from René Salagnac, a Lyons architect and a well-known cartographer of the Rhône, with whom she had been corresponding for some time in order to ascertain that it would be possible for *Elpis* to descend the Rhône. Salagnac invited the Hawkes and ourselves to be the guests of the Yacht Club Gilbert Dumas, of which he is a prominent member.

"I wrote to him, saying that we'd all arrive on Sunday evening," Gwenda told us calmly. "Sorry to have let you in for this, as I remember you both said that you didn't care for yacht clubs. As for the pilot situation, we'd be delighted if you'd like to follow us. After all, we draw more than you do, and where we pass you can follow."

We retired to hold council in *Truant's* saloon. We agreed that, despite all advice to the contrary, we were not going to take a pilot on the Saône, and Isabel suggested that we leave Chalon at once and "get out into the country". I wrote an unctuous letter to Salagnac, complimenting him on his map of the Rhône and on his courtesy towards visiting foreigners and explaining that, after the passage through the canals, our boat was really too dirty to visit so distinguished a club, and that we preferred to leave the representation of our country in the infinitely superior hands of M. and Mme. Hawkes. I handed this letter to Gwenda and said that we should see them in Lyons. We moved *Truant* through the last lock, and out of the canal to the livelier water of the river. We had taken eleven days to pass through the canals by the Centre route.

9

AFTER the narrow, sluggish canals the Saône felt like the sea, limitless and buoyant. A few kilometres outside Chalon we were struck by a wind from the south, a wind so strong that it slashed us fiercely if we offered our faces to it, and at the same time so hot, so *airless*, that it suffocated. We were obliged to shut ourseves in the wheelhouse; it became impossible to stand on deck. The wind battered at the wheelhouse, and the thermometer inside registered a shade temperature of ninety-five (F.) The reaches of the Saône are long and straight; little shelter is offered by the surrounding country. Since we were heading into the wind, we had to use both engines as we passed down the wide, foam-flecked river with dykes on either side and great herds of dun-coloured cows which slid and slithered down the dykes to stand in the tawny, snapping water, their udders submerged and their bodies, like the hull of our boat, faced into the wind and the waves. Sometimes there were goats mingled in the herds. Buzzards and pink hawks crossed a sky in which the sun showed through a glaze. We had not accustomed ourselves to these unusual sights and conditions when we approached a dredger in the middle of the river. The dredger showed a signal indicating the side that was supposed to be free for river traffic, but the gale had slewed the square vessel to the other side and had so tautened the hawser to the shore on the "navigable" side that I doubted if we could pass. We hove to, both engines turning over, and sounded the foghorn. Immediately the dredger, which we had thought to be deserted, spouted men from every black corner. The captain, in a crushed blue cap with a gold badge, appeared on the bridge. "Continue, continue!" he bellowed through his megaphone. "You have a good six metres of water right to the shore." When I opened my mouth to answer the hot wind filled it, and I could not speak. Two members of the crew, who had seen where the trouble lay, began to slack off the hawser, while the captain, apparently unaware of their actions, upbraided us for our indecision. *Truant*, meanwhile, had insufficient way on her to give control, and was rolling wildly in the troughs. Slowly, we got her head into the wind, and pushed her over the submerged hawser. When we were well past I looked astern, and saw that the dredger had run ashore, while the captain was dancing on the deck, shaking his fists at us and at his crew. Our next difficulty was at a lock (the biefs are lengthy on the Saône, and this was the first of the eight locks between Chalon and Lyons, a distance of 141 kilometres), where we had a struggle with the cross-currents of wind and water to take *Truant* alongside. The Saône locks are constructed on a different principle from those on the Seine, being wider and shorter, and we did not like them so well, since the gates are very large and take a long time to open or close. I asked at the first lock if there was any place that might offer us shelter. "Keep going," the lock-keeper said. "This is the vent du Midi, and it should ease a lot this evening. You wouldn't be safe at anchor around here, and it's against regulations to keep you in the lock. Try to get as far as Mâcon to-night, there's a bit of shelter there." We struggled on. The pounding was so severe that I feared for the spars, and for the tabernacle supporting them. Neither of us could leave the wheelhouse to prepare food, since one had to steer while the other worked out the course from the map which we had bought in St. James's; it was a diagrammatic map, made in 1935, and showing the river running straight down the middle of a long sheet of paper with measured instructions regarding courses and obstacles. The cartographer had tried to make the navigator conscious of the hazards he incurred on that section of the Saône with expressions such as: *Passage très délicat, Ralentir*, and, *Très peu d'eau, digues sousmarines, graviers, rochers*. Occasionally we would distinguish such hidden dangers by the foam that capped them. The work made us hungry, and we decided that we would make a great effort to stop in the small town of Tournus, which we hoped to reach at one-thirty; an hour earlier than that we came upon a small boat in which two men were desperately rowing against the wind. They made exaggerated gestures for assistance, gestures which seemed calm and ordinary in those tempestuous surroundings. Isabel took the wheel and slowed down to the minimum speed that would give steerage way, while I threw them a line. The younger man came on board, the water from his rough clothes cascading to the deck. He was a fine specimen, about forty years old but showing glistening teeth in healthy gums as he panted from his exertions. I handed down my dinghy pump, and the older man, a wizened monkey with the signs and balance of an open-air life on him, pumped out the water that more than half-filled their boat. When the bottom boards began to appear the monkey took a steering oar and settled himself in the stern, the pump clutched in his left hand. Isabel set *Truant* gently ahead, and we towed the boat on a long line. The other man came into the wheelhouse, exclaiming in astonishment at the silence of the engines, and at the sight of a woman at the wheel.

"We had made a big catch of gudgeon when the wind struck us," he said. "The wind came at nine, and we had been fishing since four. We were quite near Tournus then. All that we could do was row against it. The submerged dykes are dangerous for a small boat with this wind. The fish market in Tournus closes at three in the afternoon. Thanks to you, we shall be there in time." His clothes steamed in the heat, filling the wheel-house with a smell of fish, sweat and damp wool. He showed us the channel, and very often his local knowledge differed from our map. He said that they would get "a great price" for their gudgeon because the bad weather would prevent rival fishermen from taking supplies. The gudgeon, an insignificant fish, is greatly prized in that and other regions of France for making *la friture*, which is considered a delicacy, but which has always been no more than fried fish to me for I was reared in Scotland, where fish are fish.

They showed us where we might set *Truant* alongside the quay at Tournus. There was barely enough water, but the place was well-sheltered by a sunken barge and a high quay-wall. I used our two long boat-hooks, barge fashion, to hold *Truant* out from the wall. The old man gave us a bowl filled with gudgeon, while the younger one, André Marceau, asked us to go to his farm that evening to get milk and eggs. I gutted the fish with scissors, on deck, and we made la friture for lunch. When we had eaten we went to bed. The hot wind, exhausting and maddening, still flogged at us. . . . After tea, we washed the boat and ourselves, got out the bicycles, and rode to Lacros, the village where Marceau had his farm. As we approached the village—laboriously, because although the wind had dropped it was still strong by ordinary standards—we rode into the centre of a herd of dairy cows.

A long, two-storeyed building with byres, stables, workshops, and grain-stores underneath, living quarters on the upper floor, and fine space for storage in the attics provided by the steep, tiled roof, was occupied—on the semi-detached English suburban principle—by two farming families, one of them that of our fishing friend, Marceau. The walls were made of rough blocks of stone of that damp colour that must chill the heart of any who have seen Wormwood Scrubbs prison, in London. When we arrived Madame Marceau knew nothing of us, for she had not seen her husband since he had rolled from their feather bed at 3.30 that morning to go fishing, and in that part of the world country people seldom encumber their lives with the telephone. She was waiting for the cows to arrive, she said, and in the meantime she set two clean chairs for us in the yard beside the chair of her old mother-in-law, who shot piercing questions at us and

116

still more piercing glances while her gnarled mahogany hands clacked away at the crochet-work she was doing for somebody's baby. The yard was dirty, and was prowled by three hungry gun-dogs of the pointer class as well as by fowls and cats of many species; the skins of sangliers were nailed to all the doors on Marceau's side of the building. Two immense cows of more than usually ruminative appearance walked side by side into the yard, changed their formation to Indian file, and entered the byre, where each went to her stall and began to pull at the hay mixed with green-pea plants which filled the mangers. The grandmother adjusted the halters while Madame Marceau began to milk. In Lacros the cows leave their byres unattended by men or dogs after the early morning milking, and they all meet at the memorial in the centre of the village, whence they walk out in a herd to pasture on the banks of the Saône. In the evening they return as a herd to the memorial, where they split into their small units and so return to their byres. I should have liked Kipling to have seen them. The cows did not give a great quantity of milk, it seemed to us, considerably less than the yield of Jerseys or Ayrshires, but they were very attractive beasts, solid, yet active crosses of the Bresse breed. We were now on the Bresse side of the Saône, in that part of France which is famous for its dairy produce and its table fowls; across the river are the Charollais beef pastures and, saving the landscape from flatness and the people from thirst, the Beaujolais hills rise beyond. Small wonder that the people round Tournus are rosy, good-humoured (notwithstanding their tendency to liver disorders), and fertile.

Madame Marceau was forty-three years old; she had three children and two grandchildren. Much worn with work she was still a handsome woman with plenty of life in her. Her auburn-haired daughter fetched a bottle of white wine, and we all went into the house. While we were there Marceau himself arrived. He looked around him with hard eyes, and his mother hastily drained her glass and left the room, permitting herself one beseeching look at him. He kissed his wife fiercely, with a surprising amount of passion for an embrace so public and so perfunctory, and sat at the table between his two foreign guests.

"Red wine!" he said. "That white piss is no use to me." The auburn-haired girl scuttled to the cellar and when she came back he laid a hard hand affectionately across her buttocks with a noise like a wooden surface striking butter. She yelped and wriggled herself down on a chair. The red wine was full-bodied, fourteen degrees in strength. "Ham!" he shouted. "Butter!" The ham was home-grown, and had been hung in the wide chimney so that the smoke from the oak logs might cure it. It was a bluish-red colour and he cut it with a long knife that bent sideways unless it was truly drawn. "Bread!" We ate largely. "More wine!" The girl brought two more bottles, and received another smack. "Do you like sausage, madame? Sausage, girl!" A little later he cried: "Tart! Surely there's a good tart somewhere?" And later still: "Cheese!" and then: "Coffee!" When the coffee was set on the table he himself rose, and with a wink at me set two bottles on the table. "La Goutte," he said. A horned devil carved from wood climbed up a ladder inside one of the bottles, his body submerged to the throat in the pale yellow alcohol which our host now poured into the glasses and into the coffee. Then we tried the other bottle. A son-in-law came in, a mason from Tournus with a cadaverous face and thin, strong arms fully revealed, since his shirt sleeves scarcely reached below the armpits. He carried his baby son, the Marceaus' elder grandson, a lusty, froth-blowing baby, whom every person in the room except Isabel and me greeted with those insanitary, sucking, prehensile kisses that most French elders reserve—in public—for the very young. The yellow alcohol reached only to the devil's ankles, when I put my hand out to cover the aperture of Isabel's glass as Marceau was about to pour again. My gesture greatly amused our hosts, although I was only thinking of the bicycle ride home and the somewhat difficult access to the boat. Isabel swore later that when I rose from that over-hospitable table I reeled in two directions before finding the upright. Our bicycles were fitted with powerful German lamps, and the small dynamos sang out lustily as, with the wind behind us and the hill in our favour, we raced back to Tournus. A motor barge had moored beside us; the family were eating on deck, quite near our cabin, and were discussing pig-breeding in the moonlight.

Eager to take advantage of the clean water of the Saône, we were up very early, and while Isabel did her housework I dropped into the river and washed the topsides, which had been badly marked by the swinging pressure of the coir fenders in the 164 locks through which we had passed. The paintwork was blistered, the grey paint on cabin top and wheel-house as well as the black on the topsides. Generally speaking, from a distance *Truant* did not look bad when I had finished washing her, and when I had thrown some of the dirtier fenders overboard and replaced them with clean ones, but I was aware that a more pernickety yachtsman would have felt it necessary to do about a week's hard work on the paint-work and on the decks. By 9.30 we were in the Tournus market, a picturesque affair which is held up and down one long, narrow street. André Marceau's wife and daughter met us in the market and they came aboard *Truant*, where they both drank whisky and ate chocolate biscuits.

118

They were less positive on the boat in their stiff, town clothes than they had been at the farm the night before. Madame Marceau recommended us to eat Chez Muzeau, and she did well. We had an excellent meal in that workers' bistro, and it only cost us 375 francs with plenty of wine. Isabel was surprised at the antics of the clientèle, chiefly butchers and flushed farmers, who laid hold of the two maids whenever these approached with loaded hands, and were quick to subject the women to unresented indignities before the bottles and plates could be laid down. As we returned from the restaurant we saw *Elpis* passing quickly downstream. Gwenda's sharp eye at once distinguished us from the other figures in the town and she raised a thin bare arm to us. Douglas was sitting by the wheel, but I saw no sign of their pilot. We were soon under way ourselves, and travelling steadily with the current, which flowed at a rate varying from one to three kilometres per hour. In the evening we passed through the middle of a regatta which was being held in the reach above Mâcon, through boatloads of spectators, speed-boats, and large punts manned by crews of paddlers, jousters armed with long lances standing on raised platforms in the bows. We saw *Elpis*, at the quayside in Mâcon; Douglas and Gwenda were coiling ropes on deck. We continued downstream for another two hours; then I dropped the C.Q.R. anchor in the middle of a long, wide reach. A dignified country house looked through a vista of trees at our anchorage, a poised façade of pale lemon-colour, buff stone facings around doors and windows. We noted in the Saône valley a certain number of these exceptionally beautiful châteaux, resembling somewhat the Georgian country houses of England, and infinitely finer than the monstrously heavy, ugly, and vulgar places which draw uneducated sightseers to the Loire valley. I passed a night of violent dreams, and twice Isabel had to hold me in bed to prevent my rushing on deck to beat off the attacks of pirates and river-monsters.

Although we had anchored the previous night in an empty stretch of river, we awoke to find ourselves surrounded by fishing punts, each with its grave crew of two. It was a Sunday, and evidently that section of the Saône was especially poissoneuse. I retrieved the C.Q.R. without any difficulty, which greatly pleased me for it showed that I had gained in strength and marine expertise, since at Bursledon I had handled its eighty lbs. with dangerous clumsiness.

It was a day of hazy distances. In places the fascinating wildness of the banks of the Saône, a tawny, dusty wildness with an impression of space and age in it, would give way where civilisation had laid a turd in the form of a bathing station or a *cercle nautique* with strutting townees and small boats fit for nothing but play. Even in the wilder stretches there were many ferries, and a notice board on the ferryman's cottage usually offered some such invitation as: *Auguste! Sa Friture!*

We viewed the Yacht Club Gilbert Dumas at one o'clock, and hoped that all the members of so imposing a club would be at table, and that we might slip by unobserved. Isabel started the second engine; we were nearly level with the club, and going at speed, when a man in a white coat came running out of the building with a Union Jack which he hoisted on the flagstaff and slowly lowered and raised in salute. Now all the members, dressed up in their Sunday finery, a blue-and-white array, came trooping to the dining-room balconies to look and wave and applaud. A man who appeared high on the roof discharged several starting-guns. Grateful though we were for those extraordinarily polite attentions, they were more likely—so peculiarly ungregarious are we—to hurry us past than to persuade us to stay. Isabel remained at the wheel, but I managed to thrust myself out on deck and waved self-conscious acknowledgments, very much aware of my tousled hair, and rough old clothes, which contrasted poorly with those of the smart yachtsmen on the balconies. Isabel in her anxiety to pass, had been edging the throttles open notch by notch, with the result that we drew behind us a wash which made all the little boats moored before the club plunge their bows madly under and rear up on their rudders. A mile or two downstream, still trembling, we anchored and ate lunch, congratulating ourselves on our peaceful surroundings, and imagining with awe the speeches, the toilettes, the champagne, the yachty, technical conversation from which we had been preserved by our own timorous rudeness. Douglas and Gwenda, we told ourselves, would worthily show the flag at the twenty-third kilometre post.

The Lyonnais is a rough customer, and the lower reaches of the Saône on that hot Sunday afternoon were thickly clustered with young Lyonnais and Lyonnaises at their roughest. Parisian bathers had watched us pass with respect, almost with awe. The Lyonnais flung themselves at us, clinging dangerously to our fenders, "raced" us in skiffs and paddle canoes, shouted to us that we might well give them rides and a host of other suggestions. Unfortunately the word "truant", for which I never cared in English, has a French translation, truand, which is even more silly and which can be excruciatingly ugly when pronounced by a coarse fellow with a boiled-lobster-coloured face and torso above shrunken bathing shorts. Those lower reaches of the Saône are full of rocks and shoals, and they would have been difficult enough to navigate without the constant fear of dismembering bathers or smashing pleasure boats. Some of these nuisances, however, probably gave us excellent advice, because frequently men in boats warned us of rocks ahead, and ordered us to alter course, which we invariably did, being humble navigators. Is it a peculiarity of the French character that those who were kind enough to gratuitously issue such warnings did so in a disagreeable manner, as though it were wrong of us to put them to the trouble of doing us a favour?

It was tea-time when we began to pass through Lyons, a town that I had known exceptionally well during the war, and a town which, because of its many bridges, suffered greatly from the German retreat and consequent demolitions. The destruction of the bridges had ruined most of the quays, and we went right through the town without finding a suitable resting-place. At length we decided to make fast to a barge near the Gare de Perrache. It was a night of tropical heat. Thanks to our netting and other more scientific aids which were brought to bear on this special occasion, my old enemies the Lyons mosquitoes were unable to renew battle, although I heard them intoning dreadful tribal hymns in the darkness beyond our defences.

We found that we had chosen a disagreeable position; the barges in our vicinity were tankers which had brought Algerian wine from Marseilles, and although that wine can be most fortifying as a beverage, its acid smell was far from pleasant. We had decided to take 950 litres of petrol in Lyons, and going on foot to the offices of the oil company we noticed how clean and prosperous the town was looking, and how many good things at almost reasonable prices were in the shops. Isabel, for some reason, had expected to find a dark, terrifying city, a Sheffield or a Glasgow, and she was able, like me, to see the charm of Lyons and the very special character of its inhabitants and its streets and restaurants. When our business in the town was finished we felt that we must visit the architect, René Salagnac, to apologise for our failure to stop at the yacht club. The brothers Salagnac are noted athletes, ski-ing and yachting being only two of their accomplishments. The younger brother, a tall man, with fair hair worn en brosse, was inclined to be suspicious of us, and at once referred somewhat sourly to the salutations with flag and gun which we had chosen to ignore. The elder, René, broader and dark, was more immediately friendly. Soon the talk was flowing on all manner of subjects, including food. René Salagnac described himself as a wolf, because he said that he invariably ate meat twice daily, and claimed that during the war when such carnivorous habits became an impossible luxury he pined away and nearly died. I thought that I noticed an almost Dracula-like pointedness in his teeth and a wolfish set to his lower jaw. The two brothers were anxious to visit

121

England to study housing there, but we told the wolf that he would be well-advised to stay away from a country impoverished by war in which for the first time in history, all men had meat, and so no meat-eater had enough. The younger brother told us that had we stopped we, and not Douglas and Gwenda Hawkes, would have been invited as guests of honour to a dinner to be given that night by the president of the Syndicat d'Initiative of Lyons for the crew of the first British yacht to arrive since the war. We learned from Gwenda that *Elpis* had approached the Yacht Club Gilbert Dumas in silence. No British flag had been dipped for them, no cannon sounded from the roof. "You can't blame them" Gwenda said. "They weren't going to be caught a second time." They had thoroughly enjoyed their evening at the club, but the pilot had left them there; and as they were making for Lyons they ran aground so firmly that Douglas was obliged to take an anchor out ahead in the dinghy and they winched the boat free with their powerful hydraulic windlass. "It means that we shall have to haul her out of the water when we get to the Mediterranean," Douglas said.

"Is she making any water?" I asked.

"None at all. That's to say, I forget when she was last pumped out, but I looked in the bilges to-day and there was barely a cupful. Is *Truant* making any water?"

"No," I answered with a reasonable approximation to the truth.

* * * *

At 8 o'clock, on the evening of our second day in Lyons, Gwenda called us and we set off, following *Elpis* to la Mulatière, the last lock on the Saône. Salagnac knows the Rhône from scores of journeys up and down it in all types of boat, and from his own mapping of the river from Lyons to the sea, a remarkable piece of work which began as a sketch map for the use of those friends in the yacht club who might wish to take their boats to the Côte d'Azur for the summer. He also knows the professional pilots on the Rhône, and he had been insistent from the first that boats drawing as much as *Truant* and *Elpis* must have pilots, pointing out that a boat going downstream travelled at such a speed that any kind of mistake was likely to be disastrous. We felt strongly that the Rhône valley was going to constitute one of the most interesting parts of our whole journey, and that it would be a pity to have a third party, unused to our ways, on board. At length Salagnac had given in to the extent of agreeing that it would be safe enough for us to follow *Elpis*, provided we kept within fifty metres of her counter all the way, but *Elpis* must have a pilot on board, and the finest on the river. Gwenda said that she did not in the least mind having a pilot. From the housekeeping point of view when pilots had to be carried she bought cold food and prepared lunch the previous evening, leaving it in the refrigerator. They gave the pilot an apéritif before his meal, wine with it, and brandy with his coffee. She told us this as we sat inside the lock, where we were to spend the night; soon we had to climb to the land, where René Salagnac wished to introduce us to our Rhône pilot, whom we could not see in the dark, but who had the interesting name of Pépé Male and very beautiful manners. The lock-keeper also had good manners—but we learned later that Gwenda had given him 100 francs to encourage him to open the lock punctually at 6 in the morning—and our conversation by the lock swooned in a flood of politesses, although at one moment Isabel had referred to "the Hawkes" and Gwenda had barked at her: "Don't call us 'the Hawkes'." We slept with the deep note of the Rhône in our ears, and I had a nightmare or two.

10

It was 6.30; the morning mist allowed swirling eddies of clear air to touch the surface of the water, and the lock gates had been open to the Rhône for some time when Pépé Male, the pilot, arrived with the appearance, the heated eyes and the relaxed face, of a man who has been making love all night. He was a magnificent specimen, a forceful, physical man, not very tall, but built in the manner of the north of France, square, sturdy and sure, with black hair and protuberant eyes widely set. He wore a white shirt with the initials *P.M.* worked in blue over the left pap, grey trousers tightly belted on a large but firm stomach, leather sandals over clean white socks. He carried an attaché case and a pale tweed coat. Only twenty-seven years old, he had already achieved the status of a fully qualified captain on the Rhône, and he had an astonishing aura of dignified authority.

"You understand that it's necessary to stay awake on the Rhône?" he said to me. "Watch my tail, because sometimes I'll go as slow as the boat will allow me, and sometimes as fast. If we go aground with the small boat you'd best anchor near us, for you've a big reserve of power, and you may be able to get us clear. Very good. Are we ready?" He laid his attaché case on the coaming of Douglas's cockpit, folded his coat and arranged it on the case, took his seat by the wheel and said to Douglas: "Marche avant, s'il vous plaît." There was a bubble of foam under *Elpis's* counter, and she moved gracefully out. Isabel put both engines into gear, and we followed.

Any small boy who enjoys tobogganing, ski-ing, or descending water chutes would be enthralled by the descent of the Rhône, for the river is a wild tormented thing racing down from Lyons as far as Arles, a distance of 283 kilometres, at a speed which is said to approach eight knots. We felt *Truant* kick and bounce in that water; we watched the banks fly past while both our engines were throttled down; we followed the *Elpis* in the twisting channel which sometimes ran so close to the rocky shore that we could spit, if so inclined, on dry land and sometimes in apparently aimless zigzags across the breast of a wide, grey-green torrent. When we passed between the supports of a bridge the water was piled up in hillocks against the buttresses and there was a hollow in the centre; we took these places at

124

a faster speed than normal, to increase the effect of our rudder, because as the boat emerged from the hollow it would achieve such amazing skids that an impression of some force as mysterious and as all-embracing as gravity took me by the throat, the heart and the stomach; often then we would see the lighter *Elpis* slewed broadside to us, and apparently heading for the bank. *Elpis* was not, as Male had warned us, easy to follow because at times he would slow right down without any signal to us—twice we saw him taking soundings with a long pole—and at times he would push the little boat to her fullest speed in order to keep her in the channel. Male steered throughout the day, and we saw Douglas, robbed of his usual work, wandering about the deck like a stranger on his own boat, looking now at the bank through field-glasses, now staring into the rushing waters, wondering no doubt how his lead keel was faring among the mysteries that they concealed. At midday, when Isabel had cooked food, which we ate side by side in the wheelhouse, we saw Male refuse an apéritif and a few minutes later he bolted a few mouthfuls of meat and salad, watching the river all the time. Twice in the long day's run we met paddle tugs, great brutes with low, ugly snouts, dragging convoys of motor-barges into the current. On these occasions Male steered very close to the tug and with hand signals as inexplicable to the outsider as those of tictac men on a race-course inquired what depth of water lay ahead of us.

We passed four young men in two canoes. They wore wide peasant hats, made from grasses, to protect their heads and shoulders against the white sun, and their uncovered torsos were burned black. Steering close to them, we learned that they were Swiss. They had put their canoes on the Rhône near Geneva and were paddling down with the current to Marseilles, where they intended to entrain themselves and the canoes for Switzerland. Both canoes had waterproof covers, ringing the bodies of the paddlers to save their gear in the event of an upset. They carried tents, mosquito nets and stoves. Although they looked tired and thirsty, we half envied the young men because a thirty-ton boat is too much of a responsibility on such a spirited river, and the Rhône valley is a fascinating place for any traveller who does not require his scenery to be bottled, tamed, and technicoloured. (Another interesting journey with a canoe might be to join the Saône in the hills of the Vosges, follow that river to Lyons and then the Rhône to the sea.) The Seine valley is green, civilised, varied and rich. The Saône valley is wider, wilder and rich. The Rhône valley is savage; it is the birthplace of winds; it is a wound baking under the same sun that blistered a message of genius into the pale eyes of Van Gogh, struggling in the desperate scenery. In that valley there are no bathing stations. The occasional men and women whom we saw were as dried and stringy as the goats; fishermen did not sit in cushioned punts, covered with parasols and surrounded by such amenities as beer, omelettes, and fly switches; instead they crouched by strange, roughly constructed nets which could be lowered into the river and suddenly lifted as the fisherman threw his weight against the counterpoising mechanism. In the narrower passages, where the river had cut a deep incision through the rock, each building, an isolated farm or monastery, seemed to be an outpost crouching on a slippery surface, striving to retain its position against the forces of the winds. The majority of the bridges and the small towns were in ruins from the recent war. Ruins on the Seine had offended us bitterly; but in the Rhône valley ruins were somehow more at home, less extraordinary. Perhaps ruins on the face of the moon would seem ordinary. I had frequently travelled south by road to Avignon and Arles and beyond, but on those hurried journeys I had little impression of the valley or of the great river. A road represents civilisation so completely that country can no longer be savage when a road runs through it. A river can be part of the landscape, and the Rhône does not belong to men whatever it may do to make electricity for the Swiss and the French; it is the escape route to the sea of the Alpine snows; it is the colon of the Alps.

At 5 p.m. Gwenda waved signals to us which made it obvious that they intended to stop for the night at Pont St. Esprit, a small town 191 kilometres from Lyons and 132 kilometres from Port St. Louis, at the mouth of the Rhône. *Elpis* turned in the centre of the river, well above the place where we were to secure ourselves against the side of a barge, and drifted astern downstream with her engine still going full ahead to give steerage way. Isabel brought *Truant* round further downstream, and with both engines was just able to stem the current. We moored securely to the barge and *Elpis* came alongside us.

It was very hot. A great many boys were bathing. They dived in upstream and their wet heads, blowing and trumpeting, came floating swiftly past us. The pilot said the best restaurant was Aux Trois Pigeons. The town had been damaged, but not too severely, by American bombers striking at the German rearguard. My sandalled feet sank into the streets, and I felt dust warm between my toes. Several men attached themselves to us, and we bought them drinks—pastisses of course—in a seedy but agreeable bar in a small square. Pétain had made Pernod and other drinks of the pastisse type illegal during the war, and this was the first that I had tasted on that journey. Still technically illegal, pastisse was sold openly in every one of the many bars we visited in Pont St. Esprit, but it was always poured from an unlabelled bottle, and it varied a good deal in colour before the water was added, and in taste. The opinion of those with whom we drank was: "The government would legalise pastisse if it had any sense; for this would save much blindness." Gwenda and Isabel drank one or two Cap Corses, but Douglas and I were thirsty, and Male was buying round after round of drinks. He was so polite and so generous that it was impossible to refuse him, and difficult to resist repaying him with more and yet more alcohol. Anybody who would like to see the Midi without casinos, tourists, and international hotels might visit Pont St. Esprit and spend a night in its million bars. Wherever we turned there was the broad, humorous flood of southern accent, the clicking of the crickets in the dusty plane trees and of the games of bowls beneath the trees, and the laughter and song and argument of the bars. The Rhône had lifted us from Lyons, that stodgy industrious place, to this town of heat and debauchery which was in another world, a worse one and a better one. Aux Trois Pigeons was a bar like all the rest, but in the depths of it there were several long, narrow, marble-topped, bronze-legged tables. Male sat next to me, slightly bored, I was sure, with his foreign employers, but concealing his boredom, and showing little sign of the pastisses he had drunk. We had rough food and plenty of wine. Two men began an interminable quarrel at the bar, but suddenly, when they had protested for the hundredth time that only blood could settle their scores, they kissed each other, wept and laughed with and at each other, and began to get drunk together. It was the Midi. Pépé Male was a figure there. Men and women came to fawn over him. He accepted their tributes without shyness. He was a pilot. The men wanted jobs on the river and the women wanted his money or his body; there was nothing surprising in that; he was well accustomed to it, he was a pilot. He did not come from the south, himself, and while he accepted the southerners' toadying ways as normal and as his due, he did not condescend to adopt them himself. He was from the Pas de Calais, and until he was nineteen he had worked on his father's barges on the Seine. He qualified as a Seine pilot before changing to tanker barges on the Rhône. "I wouldn't return to the Seine after this river," he said. "It would be too easy."

"Is it true that the Rhône channel shifts daily?"

"Yes, it's true."

"Then how d'you tell where the channel lies?"

"By watching the surface of the water."

"And when there's a wind?"

"Still by watching the surface of the water, but then it's more difficult,

127

and I must account for two things at the same time and the effect of each on the other, the effect of the bottom of the river on the surface that's already moved by the wind." During the war the barge he commanded had been destroyed, but the company had retained him as a spare captain to replace men who were sick, and to act as pilot for strange vessels. He lived with his wife in Lyons, and had no children. He wanted, he said, to continue in that employment until he died.

Douglas had left the electric fans going in his cabin, but the heat of the engine and the heat of the day were still in it. I heard Gwenda tell him that she was going to sleep on deck. "Go ahead," he replied.

She was sleeping there, with the dew pearly on her blanket and on her hair, when I went on deck at 5 next morning. I knew that it would be an uncomfortable day for I felt the mistral, the wind that is born in the Rhône valley and that blows down, often with sudden force, across the Côte d'Azur, bringing metallic skies and headaches and crops of murder and arson to the cities of Marseilles, Toulon and Nice. I had risen early because I was unaccustomed to carrying such a cargo of alcohol as the town had offered, and because I had a good deal of work to do in the engine-room. Sweat poured from me as I bent over the engines and batteries. I had been putting on weight, as well as strength, since the hard days on the Hamble river when loading the boat had made me lean. When the engines were ready for the day I let a rope trail into the river, dived in, and pulled myself back to the transom (which had a couple of small iron steps let into it most conveniently for the bather who wished to return to the ship). The Hawkes ménage was coming to life. Douglas likes his morning sleep, and finds early starts disagreeable. "Stinking day," he observed, pushing his body dressed in silk pyjamas out of the hatch. "Stinking day. Beastly wind. Filthy hot. Coffee ready yet?"

"No," Gwenda said.

"I wonder if we've got enough petrol to get to Marseilles," Douglas said. "What do you think about the masts?"

"Let's stick them in at Arles and be done with it," Gwenda said. "What are you going to do, George? Where are you going to fit out?"

"At Marseilles," I answered. "To tell the truth I've hardly thought about it. I've been putting off the evil day. It's been so pleasant in the rivers that I'm not looking forward to reaching the sea."

This was received in silence. Then Douglas said that they intended to drop the pilot at Arles, have lunch there, and see whether there was a crane capable of setting his masts in place. Isabel and I thought that our best plan would be to take the Roman canal that leads from Arles to

Marseilles and to have the masts stepped in the latter port. Male had spent the night in a hotel. He had not taken his attaché case ashore, for it was empty, and was carried only from a desire to appease the conventions. We travelled extremely slowly when we cast off, since Male was of the opinion that *Elpis* would only clear the river bottom in that first stretch by one or two centimetres. She had twice touched bottom the day before. The morning was a repetition of the previous day, except that the valley gradually flattened as we travelled south. We ate an early lunch and were at the coffee stage when we passed the Pont d'Avignon, sadly damaged by the war and surrounded by wild eddies and whirlpools. At 1 o'clock we reached Arles and *Elpis*, slim and graceful in profile, swung round ahead of us and sidled to a quay. We followed them. The Hawkes were ashore in a flash, eager for the restaurant. Pépé Male led us through streets only wide enough to take a man and woman walking abreast or one donkey with laden panniers. Arles had been bombed, and Gwenda said that it would sadden her too much to stay there. Male took us to a big, empty restaurant. We drank beer with them to quench our thirst and then Douglas, Male, and I had pastisses to make the quenching more permanent.

Isabel and I almost ran through the streets, a little relieved to be on our own again, although we liked the Hawkes. We had given them 500 francs, our share of the pilot's expenses and pourboire. The bill for his services would come to us later, when the company's managing director returned from England, where he was trying to arrange for the construction of new barges. We soon got *Truant* out into the stream, and when we swung her bow down-river we saw that there was no chance of passing through the Arles-Marseilles canal as there were workmen and scaffolding at the entrance to the first lock and a large notice saying that the canal was *en état de reconstruction*. The alternative route lay straight down the Rhône to Port St. Louis, and so to Marseilles.

We saw from Salagnac's map that the Rhône changes character below Arles and, except for one short difficult passage—caused it is said by the submerged ruins of a Roman village—is deeper and slower-moving. We were astonished to feel *Truant* touch bottom, with a most unpleasant jar, only a few hundred yards below Arles, and in the middle of the river. Otherwise the journey was uneventful. The river banks became lower and huge horse-flies and mosquitoes flew into our wheelhouse, coming out of the swamps of the Camargue, to starboard. A British pilot who flew repeatedly over the Camargue during the war told me that he thought it must be the most beautiful place on earth. We saw inlets, running from the river into the swamp, inlets edged by rushes and low, sap-laden bushes. I

129

pictured the interior of the Camargue with great bulls standing knee-deep in water, snakes and frogs hissing and croaking on the tufts of the higher ground, and egrets floating in the air.

Port St. Louis smelled very strongly of oil. The river traffic turns there, through a large lock, to avoid the shoaling Bouches du Rhône, and we found ourselves in difficulties in the lock, for we had not realised as we entered that much of the river's current was also entering. I was in something of a fluster when we got *Truant* secured, and was not inclined to be receptive when scrofulous customs officials in khaki American trousers and operatic caps, boarded us in an inquisitive stream. They obliged us to do a lot of senseless manœuvring—dangerous on account of the current—in the basin beyond the lock. They held us in useless conversation while they poked about the boat and stared uncomprehendingly at our papers. But although they had the energy to pour out observations and questions and to tramp coal dust into our decks they had no energy to spare for the task of visaing our papers. At length their chief came along, a man whose high, shaven head did not belie his intelligence, for he gave the following instructions: "Just stamp their papers and write on them: 'Yacht *Truant* seen when she passed Port St. Louis on such and such a day'—work out the date yourselves for I'm on holiday—and then they will be able to go through all the formalities with the customs at Marseilles, while from our point of view we'll be cleared . . ." We thanked him with bitter politeness, for who, in the modern world, would dare to be rude to a customs official? Many of those who would do nothing for us had drunk my whisky, for I had followed (in vain) the Scottish horse-doctor's prescription for customs men—'drench them'. We proceeded down the length of straight canal that leads from Port St. Louis and joined the sea at the Gulf of Fos. The mistral had died, but although the water was smooth and clear a swell set across the two-mile width of the gulf.

Approaches to Marseilles: it was strange to work to a chart again, and to peer into the compass in order to pick out our destination, Port Bouc, on the other side of the gulf. *Truant* rolled badly, and I feared for our spars. Many wrecks protruded from the sea.

"I thought you said that the Mediterranean was always flat calm," Isabel said.

"She'll roll less when we get the masts up and a bit of sail on her."

The entrance to Port Bouc was partly blocked by sunken ships and we were shown the way in by a stream of small white boats with blue prows which were bouncing out for the evening's fishing. Inside the big harbour most of the buoys marked on our chart seemed to have gone, but our combined flair for direction gave us the route into the ship canal that leads to Martigues. The canal was lined with shacks where families were disposing themselves for the night in conditions of ultimate squalor, and with American ships called by those names which seem to verge on the prosaic, names like Joseph P. Mulvaney or Henry Hobart Hodgson. We were stopped in the darkness by the large swing bridge at Martigues, that feminine and slatternly French town which is known as the Venice of Provence. I can never hear its name without associating it with a certain bearded British painter and a song which goes, unless memory betrays me: *Adieu Venise provençale, adieu pay-ee-ee de mon amour. . . . Adieu, cigalons et cigales, qui dans les prés chantent toujours. . . .* We edged *Truant* against a bomb-shattered quay, the stones white and powdery in the moonlight, and walked across to the Bar de la Marine. The barman recommended a blue restaurant. He said that it was a very good restaurant, and the flies certainly were of the same opinion for they accorded it their almost undivided patronage. I am fond of dirt, and I like smells, but there are times when even my type of dirt and smell-lover feels a longing for something as simple and clean as the inside of a fresh white shirt, as a grilled sole, as a dentist's hands. After our experience of the customs at Port St. Louis we were not in the mood for the blue restaurant filled with sweating diners, and with a menu offering little but the spicy delights of bouillabaisse and cous-cous, both excellent when desired. We asked for omelette and the chef obligingly made one of yellow leather, at twice the cost of the bouillabaisse and the cous-cous. There was plenty of wine in the restaurant, at an exorbitant price, for wine was scarce at that time in the country where it was made and near Marseilles, the port receiving much of the alcohol produced by North Africa. In the hot street outside the blue door the people jostled softly, like fishes in a pool. The night was stickily sweet, with bats feeding over the heads of sailors, pimps, bargees, and soldiers. A very strong current from the Étang de Berre set in under *Truant's* bow, and clamped the boat against the quay.

A crowd of fishermen in white jerseys with thin, azure, horizontal stripes were examining *Truant* from the quay when I first went on deck in the morning. The C.Q.R. anchor caused a lot of hilarity; the pattern had been developed in Britain during the war, and it was the first of its kind that they had seen; they called it *la charrue de la mer*. The swing bridge opened soon after 6; we cast off from the quay and advanced towards the opening; but when the man who controlled the bridge saw us approaching he turned a lever and slammed it shut in our faces. I deduced from this that I should have tipped him, and remembered, too late, certain remarks to that effect from the scrofulous officials of Port St. Louis. But his rudeness had so incensed me that I would have turned round and sought another route to Marseilles rather than bribe him. We struggled in the current for a considerable time, sounding our foghorn, keeping the engines ahead and seeking to avoid approaching the sides of the waterway with their sharp prongs of broken masonry, while all manner of leisurely traffic dawdled across the bridge, an old-clothes man, a child with a broken doll in a three-wheeled perambulator, a policeman. At 6.30 two fishing boats came up behind us and the bridge grudgingly opened to let us through. We turned to starboard out of the current and into the canal, which is really at that point the southern rim of a lake, the Étang de Berre. The canal is separated from the Étang by a solid wall of granite blocks, standing up five or six feet above the level of the water; we moved in water that was only choppy, but the Étang was greatly disturbed by the mistral sweeping across it, and spray flying over the breakwater soaked our decks. At times the canal revealed a disconcerting shallowness where the points of reeds stood out from the water. To starboard was a strangely dead piece of land, smelling of fuel oil, crossed by pipelines and dotted comparatively inconspicuously with oil-storage tanks. As we passed this oily region I looked for and found in the after cabin the searchlight I had bought in England; I screwed it to the holder provided for it in the bows. The flex was led aft through the galley hatch. We were approaching the Rove Tunnel. There were German prisoners working near that part of the canal, and I was explaining to Isabel that an insufficient diet bloats a man's stomach but sags the pouches below his eyes when we saw a sign saying *HALTE!* Thinking that this had been erected for the benefit of the prisoners, I did not slow down, but as we passed the sign a little man in uniform sprang from a hut. He shrilled on a whistle gripped between his teeth, with the part holding the pea pushing up into his grey moustache; his face, purple with whistling or with rage at our speedy passage, threw us into such convulsions of laughter that we were quite unable to stop. We were a long way past, and in the stony gulch leading to the tunnel, when the official took the whistle from his teeth and yelled: *"Votre nom? nom de dieu?"*

"Truand!" Isabel shouted, with a Spanish accent.

"Troublante?"

We were beyond shouting distance before she could reply, and the black mouth of the tunnel swallowed us. The Rove Tunnel is 4 miles 900 yards in length and is high enough and wide enough to take a small ship. When we entered it we moved in a fuzz of light from the entrance, and

132

could just make out the bright pinhead of light that was the far end; as we moved in, the fumes from our engine gathered around us. The searchlight drew yellow gleams from the wet vault, and the infinitely small semi-circle of sunlight ahead grew momentarily in candle-power until it dazzled and hypnotised. I found that the only way to steer without drunken weaving was to keep low down in the wheelhouse and steer on the sunlight by masking it with the outlines forward of the windlass, the anchors, the searchlight. The latter was useful in that it showed me when I began to make a mistake and approach or leave the starboard side of the tunnel on which we had trained it. Cold drips from the roof of the tunnel fell on the boat. We were through it in forty minutes, and were thankful to be out, blinking; Marseilles lay ahead.

11

THE prospect of entering the great port of Marseilles filled me with understandable qualms. There I should be obliged to raise my boat from the official status of "autobus" to the more dignified and responsible status of "sea-going vessel", and there the masts, with their complicated (and I feared forgotten) appendages, would have to be erected. However, when you actually perform any task it is easier than it seems in anticipation or even in retrospect, because the different problems offer themselves little by little and in simplified form until no major and complex problem remains. The first decision to be made on leaving the tunnel was the choice of route to the Vieux Port, our destination in Marseilles, which was still a few miles distant, for we were at the western end of the bay, and the main mole of the port and the island holding the Château d'If appeared to form pincers at the eastern end. We could either follow the ship canal, which runs round the northern rim, and is protected from the sea in the same way as the canal round the edge of the Étang de Berre, or we could take *Truant* boldly out across the bay. Had the weather been docile, I should have chosen the second alternative; as it was, we looked upon the sea whipped by the mistral that whistled from the rocky eminence under which we had just travelled, and we thought of our spars perched over the deck on their gimcrack tabernacle. The prudent course was to follow the canal. Isabel went below to find sandwiches and wine. I steered *Truant* carefully past a few wrecks and then set her going at six knots as the wide canal opened ahead. We were moving past the outer suburbs of Marseilles. Isabel had just re-appeared on deck with the sandwiches when there was a shuddering jar. The engine went on turning normally but the boat assumed a slight list to starboard. We were aground. I set both engines pulling astern. The bow rose a little and the stern went down; the list to starboard increased. We were some 20 yards from the sea wall while to our left 100 yards of water whipped by the mistral stretched to the shore, where there was a small sporting club, a *cercle nautique*. Vessels which drew more water than *Truant* were passing between us and the sea wall. Taking soundings with a boat-hook, I learned that *Truant* had perched herself on a very shallow bank of mud reinforced with rocks. I launched the dinghy—which instantly began to make water, since it had been hanging for some days from its davits, exposed to a hot sun—and rowed away with our largest kedge to the full extent of one of the big warps. I dropped the anchor off the starboard quarter; the list increased a little when I hauled on the warp; I worked harder and the anchor began to drag. Pausing to allow my breathing to become normal, I looked at the rudder and saw that running into the mud had put such a strain on it that it had cracked right across the blade; like most shallow-draft boats, *Truant* had a rudder of weak shape. I took out another anchor forward, then another. I could see quite clearly now that had I steered six feet more to starboard we should never have run aground. We both worked hard on the windlass. At this point a gorilla-like man in blue swimming shorts with a curly mat of brown hair over his chest and straighter fringes across his shoulder-blades, paddled himself out from the *cercle nautique* in a white canoe. Although his body was forbidding, he had an agreeable face, resembling that of my grandmother's black pug, Shem.

"You're by no means the first that I've seen on that bank," he said. "Such accidents were common when the Americans had just liberated the town and there were many naval craft in these waters."

"And did those who ran aground here get clear?"

"Very few of them by their own endeavours. Tugs came from the Entreprises Navarro."

"*Tugs!*" The word was enough to send us flying to the windlass again.

"You will never move the boat like that," he said; however, he obligingly came aboard and lent a hand. The three of us managed to increase *Truant's* list to starboard, but the keel had not moved one quarter of an inch, and in my heart I knew that the tug was inevitable. Hundreds of yachtsmen's stories relating to the fees demanded for salvage floated biliously in my mind. The gorilla-like man had too much logic to over-exert himself in a lost cause: "Faut un remorqueur," he kept repeating.

"Je ne peux pas me payer le luxe d'un remorqueur."

"Mais écoutez, monsieur, why don't you telephone the Entreprises Navarro? I'm sure that they'll make you a most reasonable price."

"What type of firm is the Entreprises Navarro."

"A salvage firm. They undertake to raise sunken ships with divers and so on, and they have tugs . . ."

"*Tugs!*"

"I assure you, they will be very kind to you when they see your predicament."

"I cannot imagine that the salvage firms of Marseilles would be more altruistic than the salvage firms of other places . . ."

135

"But we'll never move your boat like this."

"No. We won't move her."

"And you say that the rudder is broken?"

"Yes."

"So that. even if you moved you could not proceed to the Vieux Port, you would have to stop in this vicinity?"

"Yes."

"Then you will have to stop with the Entreprises Navarro in any case, for they have virtually a monopoly around here."

"Ask him if he is a shareholder," Isabel said in English. My resistance to the Entreprises Navarro had been beaten down, and I agreed to go ashore and telephone them. When I jumped into the dinghy the water-logged little boat began to sink beneath my weight. I baled with a canvas bucket. The hairy man had put on a shirt, white linen trousers and a white cap when I reached the *cercle nautique*. We went to the nearest bar to telephone. The man at the other end of the line told me that to discuss such matters over the telephone was against the business rules of the firm; surely the reasons must be plain to me. I must call in person. My companion took me to the tramway terminus. A car would leave in ten minutes, and this would deposit me at the door of the Entreprises Navarro. He left me, giving me his telephone number in case we found ourselves in further or continued difficulties. I was already inside the tramcar, when I looked out to sea and noticed that Isabel was having truck with the crew of a beamy, workmanlike boat of the type called a chalutier. I leaped from the tram, ran down the beach, jumped into the dinghy, and rowed as quickly as I could to the stranded *Queen of the Seas*. When I reached her ominously-sloping deck I found Isabel in converse with seven extremely dirty men and one extremely clean one, who introduced himself to me as "Chief ngineer of the Entreprises Navarro". He spoke with a delightful Marseilles accent, and wore a high, soft, brown hat, a white shirt, and those trousers so popular with Frenchmen of the south, made from a small-check tweed, brown in this case, cut low in the waist and tight over belly and buttocks. He was a good-looking fellow in the late thirties. dark, with a thin, smooth face that was just a little bit too certain of its own enticing potentialities. I hastily inquired of Isabel if fees had been mentioned.

"He asked me if we were insured, and I said that we were, so he said that it wouldn't cost us a penny . . ."

"We aren't millionaires," I told the engineer.

"I know, I know," he answered softly. "This operation will only cost a few thousand francs, and your insurance will pay that. The quicker we get your boat off, the less it will cost. The main thing is not to get flustered (énervés) and to take the whole operation calmly." He repeated this good advice to his men, for the men of the Midi have to fight their own temperamental excitability as well as other difficulties.

They tried to pull us off stern first, but my stout four-in. manilla began to part in the middle under the weight of the tow. They took two warps to the forward end. The chalutier drew more water than *Truant*, and the men on board said that the channel was narrow at that point; they feared that the warps would break and that their boat, suddenly released from the dead weight astern would fly across the channel and hurl itself against the sea wall. "There would be no means of stopping such a disaster," they said, watching the tow-ropes anxiously.

"Il ne faut pas s'énerver, les gars," the engineer kept repeating. But finally they disobeyed this injunction, and, beginning to feel very énervés indeed as the midday period for repose and eating approached, they backed towards us until there was a good deal of slack in the tow-ropes, and then hurled forward fifty tons of oak, diesel engine, men, and dirt. *Truant* moved a little.

"Are your propellers clear?" the engineer asked me.

"Yes."

"Then I beseech you to give us the maximum assistance with them."

I started the engines as the chalutier came astern. Again it charged forward. There was a tremendous jerk which tore away *Truant's* fairleads and parts of her forward bulwarks, and we slowly moved clear. They towed us to their yard, a most filthy place, with a quay one-inch deep in coal dust. Employers and employees made us welcome. They were too anxious to help. The chief engineer offered to send down a diver to examine the underwater portions of the hull.

"No thank you," I said. "The boat's making no water, I'm sure that there's no serious damage."

"But . . ."

"It is very good of you, but I must see my insurance agent in the town before authorising any such expense."

"I would dive myself," the chief engineer said. "Eh, Robert, fetch the suit and the pumps. It won't cost you a centime, Monsieur Millar."

"No, thank you."

"I think that you're making a mistake, if I may say so without offence."

"You may say so; but, no thank you." There were two directors. The one who was introduced as the managing director was round, fat and very hot in a gaberdine suit of café-au-lait colour. "How much will the assistance given to us by the chalutier cost?" I asked him.

"Extremely little. Probably only some 2,000 or 3,000 francs." I thought his price very reasonable, but I never heard of it again, nor did I again meet that director. The other director was thin, with white hair and a ewe neck; he wore a suit of cream-coloured linen and a bright blue necktie. I arranged with him for carpentering repairs to our bulwarks, fairleads and one cat-davit and for major repairs to the rudder, which was to be strengthened, we agreed, with a metal harness. At this stage of agreement there is nobody to rival a Frenchman, except perhaps an American, for those are the races that can attack a job with maximum impetus—although the American tends to have greater staying power. Within five minutes the ewe-necked director had had a derrick fitted and had taken our rudder away to the machine shops, and three carpenters were making their way forward along our decks with measuring rules and small saws in their hands.

"Lock everything," the chief engineer said to us. "Our men are honest, but there is a limit to honesty. I will show you a place where you can eat like an emperor and his empress. And to-night you must eat at my house." He drove us in his car to a restaurant where we tried, without success, to eat our sorrows away with 800 francs worth of hors d'œuvres, fried red mullet, steak, salad and so on. When we returned to the boat the engineer asked if our meal had been costly in the French idiom of the day: "Was it a sledge-hammer blow (un coup de masse) between the eyes?" The firm provided a car in which we drove to Marseilles to see the insurance agents. It was suffocatingly hot and the air was dirty, for the mistral had stirred the dust from the ruins left by the German Army. I tried to calculate how much explosive the Germans must have used on the docks in the three days before they left Marseilles; I wondered if the wreckers had cursed the heat, the toil, the insanity of their task. We were both tired, and went back to the boat early. I was about to confess to the engineer that we should be obliged to postpone our engagement with him for the evening, when he conveniently told me that his wife had not been able to find any food. He and the ewe-necked director came down to the saloon and drank whisky. Ewe-neck drank avidly, and at a great speed. The engineer was thirsty too. "That's a thing we can all do in Marseilles—drink," he said. When they had gone we had each to make out statements for the insurance company. About 10 o'clock, hot and exhausted, we tumbled into bed.

We were up at 5.30. There were all the promises of a day of scorching heat. The water around us was covered with patches of oil and fine coal dust, which looked all the dirtier because the water itself was clear, and through the surface streakiness it was possible to see the bottom with its litter of battered objects. These included a ship's binnacle and a very old tug-boat, sitting on the bottom with small fish hanging under the rails and beside the stump of the funnel, which had been broken off near the deck. The water smelled badly, but our deck was so filthy from the boots of workmen stepping directly to it from the coal dust of the quay that I washed it. The car that had taken us to Marseilles the previous day had had a puncture and was hors-de-combat, since there was no spare wheel; but the firm provided a van with an all-metal body which absorbed the heat and stored it so efficiently that when we opened the door a blast of burning air came out. The driver, sensible young man, was shirtless at the wheel of this pulsing inferno. I squeezed in next to him and Isabel sat on my right. The world shimmered around us through a haze of heat and petrol fumes. The driver was obsessed with the story of a man called Joey-le-Noir.

"Who is this Joey-le-Noir?"

"He's been in all the newspapers."

"We haven't read newspapers for over a month."

"Joey was a coloured American soldier, a truck driver. He formed a gang here in Marseilles, using French people to help him and to guard him, people from the underworld. Joey-le-Noir murdered many people. They caught him only when he had killed eight of his fellow Americans, all drivers of trucks. He sold their trucks, their money, their wallets, their clothing, the gold from their teeth, their rings, their boots, their identity papers . . ."

"Where is he now?"

"I think they've killed him in the electric chair. They took him back to America. He'd have had a future here in Marseilles, for he had ideas. The Americans have done well in this war and I suppose myself that they represented the right and the Germans represented the wrong, broadly speaking. Yet on the whole the Germans, when they were here in Marseilles, behaved better than the Americans. That's a funny thing. It perplexes people. Nothing makes sense nowadays." It was one more screw of puzzlement in the coffin that smothered the French nation.

"The man who has the best ideas and who represents a sane kind of life is not necessarily better-mannered than the man who represents the black market or than the owner of a slave gang," Isabel said.

"No, that's true enough; and whatever the Americans do, they do it. Now just look at Joey-le-Noir. . . . One day he was driving down the Cannebière and he saw a woman who took his fancy. He said, with his hat in his hand: 'Can I give you a lift, madame?' After a little arguing here and there, she climbed into the car. She had shown such strength of character that Joey-le-Noir decided to have a look at her home, and he drove her there as he had promised to do . . ."

Our van stopped at a street-crossing, and I saw an American come out of a third-rate hotel. I saw from his walk and clothing that he was a merchant seaman. He had a decent, quiet face, and he was going back to his ship after a night and a bath on shore. . . .

"Well, they sat down in the salon, Joey-le-Noir, the woman, and her husband. 'You have a fine wife,' Joey observed to the husband. 'How much do you want for her?' The husband was insulted; but his protests weakened when Joey opened the bidding at 250,000 francs. The husband declared, properly enough, that a man did not sell his wife for any kind of money. Joey raised the bidding to 1,000,000 francs. The husband and wife went to the far end of the room, and in whispers they discussed that generous proposal. They decided that the negro would not stay long in Marseilles because the American troops were being withdrawn, and that it would be worth putting up with a little discomfort to have 1,000,000 francs in the bank. 'First let me see your 1,000,000,' the husband said. Joey left the house; he returned in less than an hour, and counted out 1,000,000 in thousand-franc notes. 'There is one thing I forgot to mention,' he said to the husband, 'I want your house as well; it pleases me.' Husband and wife went off to the end of the room and whispered together. 'Furnished or unfurnished?' the husband asked. 'Furnished, just as it is,' Joey said, looking around. They whispered some more and then the husband told Joey that the house would cost another 300,000 francs. '250,000,' Joey said, 'and not a centime more.' 'Done!' the husband said. He took another 250,000 from Joey and walked out of the room. Joey spent only one night in that house, and the next morning he left and never went back. The woman was one of the first to testify against him, it is said."

"What complaint had she?"

"A week after Joey-le-Noir left her she found her husband in her own cellar. Joey's confederates had stabbed him as he left the room, had taken their money from the bag he carried and had hidden the body under some old bottles; it is said that when Joey-le-Noir was confronted by her he said: 'You set too high a value on yourself and the house. If you had asked for 125,000 for yourself and another 125,000 for the house your husband would be alive to-day. Although I admit that everybody has to live,' Joey said, 'I don't pay women; women pay me.' "

With profound relief we left the mobile oven and entered the insurance agents' offices, dark and quiet, with an Australian and a Scot sitting talking sensibly about their business problems behind school ties, a calendar, and a silver ash-tray; both clean and carefully dressed, members of the same species as Joey-le-Noir, men like him, yet living life to a different set of rules. When I went to the window I could see the crowds pushing up the hill away from the harbour and down the hill towards the harbour, into the bar across the road, out of the bar across the road; and down by the street corner a cinema hoarding showed the word *FRÉNÉZIE*! The street appealed to me with its warmth and colour and stench. I adore the vivid people of Marseilles; I always have and always shall. We hurried back to the boat, because things have a way of vanishing in Marseilles; a 125 lbs. woman, a thirty-one-ton ketch, a three-ton truck, the values of the first two vary, but the stock black-market price for the latter was commonly known to every decent person in the city.

"There was one peculiar aspect in the case of Joey-le-Noir," Torse-nu said as he drove us back to the Entreprises Navarro. "He was totally unknown when he came to Marseilles. I mean that in the Army he was a truck driver, and before that he worked on an American farm. It took Marseilles to bring out his character."

"Where do you come from? Not from the Midi, I know."

"No. I'm from Normandy, but I'm not going back. There is no place like Marseilles."

When we returned to the boat we took cold drinks from the refrigerator. The temperature was nearly 100 (F.) in the wheelhouse. The yard was silent because all the men had gone away to eat. We enjoyed a few valuable moments of calm.

The afternoon was a period of madness, because I had decided, since the Entreprises Navarro could help me with a small crane and plenty of manpower, to put *Truant's* masts in position. I was still struggling to identify and arrange the different cordages when the men arrived, thirteen of them. Exclamations of astonishment bubbled from the quay. The two masts appeared to be smothered, and all the deck as well, in a litter of steel wire, rope and blocks. Although when we laid low the masts at Rouen I had labelled most of the rigging and had stowed it away as neatly as I could, I was neither sufficiently expert a sailor nor well enough acquainted with my boat to realise at once where and how everything should be disposed. I asked if any of the men knew about sailing boats and how they were rigged.

"Don't let that worry you," the foreman said. "Three of us are divers."

"Good!" I could not see how that simplified things, but divers should be brave and resourceful men. We set to work on the mainmast, a very handsome hollow spar. I had difficulty in making the men treat it with the respect that it seemed inertly to demand. If I succeeded in persuading the man on the crane to work steadily the men on deck became impatient, and if all was going well on deck the man on the crane would either be found talking to a Chinese lady, who had strayed down to watch the proceedings, or would decide that it was time to finish the job with a rush. At length the mast was in place, and stayed sufficiently to be quite safe. Streaming with sweat, scorched by the sun, dizzy from expenditure of effort and exhortation, I went below and swallowed glass after glass of water from the galley tap. The mizzen, being smaller and having simpler appendages than the mainmast, might have been expected to give less trouble. But my helpers were tiring, and were beginning to pick quarrels with each other. Many of them had been drinking, it seemed, and a smell of strong alcohol refused to disperse from the layer of exhausted atmosphere over the deck. The foreman approached me tactfully, pointed out that the men were only working on a Saturday afternoon to do me a favour (he did not think it necessary to mention the special overtime rates of pay), and suggested that it might be a good idea if I rewarded them with a bottle of pastisse, to be consumed on the spot. How much would that cost? Oh, it could be got for 800 francs. There was a good deal more to be done, and some of the men were showing a tendency to lie down to rest in the coal-dust on the deck. The pastisse put new life into a few of them, while others, after languidly raising their heads to drink, relapsed into still deeper reveries. Several mistakes had been made before the masts were raised into position. I climbed once to the mainmast truck, and found myself so exhausted that I decided to make others do such work. There were no volunteers, but I was able, by taunts and challenges to their competitive ardour, to persuade three of the youngest to make ascents. I thus managed to get the boat rigged in what I judged to be a satisfactory manner, and when the men had all dribbled away I allowed a deep sense of satisfaction to soak away my fatigue. There was to be no rest. The ewe-necked director asked me to step over to the office to pay my account. I had not time to clean myself, and went, naked but for a pair of shorts, my hands and shoulders bleeding from straining at ropes and wires and climbing in the rigging. A fat girl and a clerk with a shade over his eyes were putting the finishing elaborate touches to my account, which had been made out in triplicate. The ewe-necked director said: "You will see that we have been most considerate, Monsieur Millar. Your account is reasonable, I'm convinced, taking

142

into consideration the price of all things to-day. You have seen your rudder?"

"Yes. You have made a good job of it."

"And the repairs to your bulwarks?"

"Excellent."

"Good. Now this afternoon you had sixteen men helping you to erect your masts . . ."

"Thirteen."

"Oh, well, we'll not quarrel over three men but you realise that they worked on a Saturday as a favour to you. And if you care to give them the money to buy themselves a bottle of pastisse in which to drink your health I am sure that such a gesture would be greatly appreciated . . ."

"I shall consider it."

"Here is your bill. The total, as you see, is only 27,000 francs."

"Preposterous! I refuse to pay."

"I beg your pardon?"

"It is robbery! Coming up the Seine we had the boat hauled out of the water at one of the most famous yacht yards in France, and their bill was less than 8,000 francs."

"Ah, but that was in the north of France. Things are easier there."

"Permit me to correct you, but things are not easier in the north."

"I stand corrected. I should be grateful if you would take the account item by item and explain which charges seem excessive. It is best in these matters to be of a devastating frankness."

"Very well. Firstly, then, for the assistance of the chalutier 8,000 francs is charged, yet soon after the assistance had been given your managing director quoted me 2,000 francs. Why has that sum been quadrupled in the intervening thirty-six hours?"

"There were eight men on the chalutier, to say nothing of six men and the chief engineer on your yacht. The assisting operations lasted forty minutes. We feel that the charge is most reasonable, and I am sure that— with the best of wills and the most honest of intentions—you are mistaken when you say that the managing director quoted 2,000; the sum that he quoted was 8,000."

"We shall leave that point for the moment, then. Here is an item, 'Diver's submarine investigations, frs. 2,000,' yet I told you personally as well as the chief engineer that I did not want the services of a diver and this is the first intimation I have had that any diver was employed . . ."

He held up a pencil in one well-manicured hand. "The diver will be struck off the account," he said.

143

"Thirdly: for 'repairs to rudder' you charge 12,000 francs. Do you not find that excessive?"

"It is a lot of money," he agreed. "But then we did a lot of work; you said yourself that it was well done. And it was done quickly. We had sixteen men on the job . . ."

"I don't see how they all managed to get near the rudder . . ."

"Sixteen men . . . I can give you their names . . ."

"That will not be necessary . . ."

"And they worked half-way through the night. Now, when we work out the man-hours and the overtime, and multiply by sixteen we find that . . ." Plainly their system for overcharging was to multiply the supposed number of men employed on your behalf. At this moment I was relieved to see a fat excuse for a diversion in the shape of an Italian ice-cream vendor, who nodded in the heat beneath a scarlet awning while a donkey drew his cart along the tramlines. I told the ewe-necked director that I must hand the matter over to the insurance agents, as I could not authorise so large a bill. I halted the donkey and ordered a quantity of ice-cream. The Italian sighed, and climbed down from his box. He had a healthy polish on his skin and humorous, sleep-soaked brown eyes. What was I to do? We had to leave Marseilles early next morning, to meet Mary at Bandol, yet I did not care to leave without settling with the Entreprises Navarro, and as I had chosen to run aground on a Friday there would be nobody in the insurance agent's offices until the following Monday. When the Italian had spooned out my ice-cream he pulled a frosted bottle from the inside of the conveyance and drank from it, rolling back his head.

"Water?" I asked.

"Yes," he winked jovially.

At that moment good fortune smiled on us, and I felt inclined to shake the Italian's plump hand; the head man from the insurance office arrived in a car with his son and a very young woman. My physical condition and my lack of clothing were incongruous to say the least of it. They wanted to see our boat, and when I got them on board, apologising for the dirt that the workmen had carried to every corner, I showed the bill to the insurance man. He did not find it "exorbitantly exorbitant", and he agreed to take over negotiations with the Entreprises Navarro. Soon we were left in peace to wash the decks. At 11 p.m. we were still washing. This was our last night in the inland waterways. As we slept the open sea swayed against the breakwater, fifty yards from our cabin; next day we were to venture on it.

144

12

THE rocky coastline from Marseilles to Bandol is interesting on the land, but from the sea is only forbidding. We rolled along, some three miles offshore, with the starboard engine pushing us at five knots into an east wind. Isabel stretched herself on a mattress on deck. Bandol harbour was comfortably empty. It is a roomy expanse of sheltered water, and we dropped anchor in the centre of it, in two fathoms. The anchor was barely down when we heard a powerful "Cooee!" from the shore, and when I swept the quays with binoculars I soon saw Mary, my relative from Scotland, sitting on the edge with her feet near the water. Even at that distance, she looked terribly scorched by the sun. I went ashore in the dinghy and brought her out to *Truant*.

Mary had been in Bandol for a month—all but one day—and she said that it was lovely. But as she says that everything is lovely unless it is worse than atrocious, this was no guide to her feeling about the place. A little later she admitted that she would be quite glad to leave, although she qualified this by saying that she had had a wonderful time and the sun was a joy. When we went ashore with her I was interested to learn that a woman whom I had associated with almost Lutheran sobriety had in twenty-nine short days adopted the habits of drinking pastisse before meals and chain-smoking French cigarettes after them.

"It's very harmless stuff, it doesn't really taste like a drink at all, and I find it most refreshing," she said of the pastisse. "And as for the cigarettes, they allow you to buy your ration, and James didn't want his, so it seemed a waste not to smoke them; and I must confess that I rather like the taste—although the tobacco's black they're not strong."

Mary is usually to be seen in Scotland or in London, two parts of Britain for which she has unfathomable addictions. In Scotland she wears tweeds until seven-thirty and then a long dress, and in London I remembered her in black with furs; in Bandol when we met she wore some kind of red-and-blue handkerchief tied around the upper part of her body, a skirt of a maroon colour which she would consider more than a little "loud" in Britain, and sandals matching the upper garment in colour. I realised, of course, that Mary was an open-minded woman and prone to put foreigners at their ease by dressing as they might expect her to dress.

Bandol was packed that Sunday with visitors from the large towns of Marseilles and Toulon between which it is situated. On the Seine it had been the men's bathing costumes that had mildly surprised us, here it was the everyday wear of the women, many of whom wore what Isabel and I took to be underclothing of pink artificial silk, but Mary assured us that these were "sunbathing outfits", which were, she agreed, "appalling."

"Most unsuitable for dancing," she said. "Last night at la Poupoune one girl lost her top (of course I'm sure that her partner was fiddling with it while they danced, I felt so sorry for her), but she just picked it off the floor and put it on again as though nothing had happened. *Comic!*"

We dined in her hotel. The dining-room was a balcony and there was good vin rosé. We went to la Poupoune. The hot air from the dancers flapped in our faces like a dishcloth that had been dipped in greasy boiling water. We walked out into the cool space where fishing-nets were drying, spread out over the ground. In the centre of the space a flower-stall, a cube of illuminated glass with water running down the vertical sides, stood like an iceberg with succulents, roses, gladioli, and a woman knitting in its heart. We had left the Poupoune but not, alas, the voice of the youth who sang into its microphone, a voice which boomed inexorably across the water until four in the morning with one brief interlude when some tourist showed what he could do and sang, in a kind of English:

> "Oh Johnny! Oh Johnny!
> How you can love!
> Oh Johnny! Oh Johnny!
> Heavens above!
> You're not handsome, it's true,
> But when I look at you—
> Oh Johnny! Oh Johnny!
> Oh!"

The mosquitoes were bad too, and several of them penetrated the defences of our sleeping cabin.

* * * *

Mary had paid her pension charges for a full month at 800 francs (then the equivalent of £1 13 4d.) a day, and although I knew her to be the most generous of women, I knew that nothing would cause her greater anguish than to leave without staying out the full period for which she had contracted. Therefore another day and night had to be spent at Bandol.

However, I was able to complete the rigging of *Truant*, and to bend on the sails, and I was very proud of myself when this was accomplished. In the evening I went ashore to fill the water cans from the tap by the yacht club. Six yachts were moored near the floating structure of the club; each of them had a stern gangway to the quay, and one of them was being watered with a hose leading from the tap. I sat down on a can to wait until the tap should be free. While I waited an elderly man with a profusion of trimmed, trained and brushed grey hair, accompanied by a curved young woman in a bathing suit, approached the tap and set down beside it an ordinary bucket. This pair had come from a small motor-boat. The grey-haired man shot a glance at me, sitting on my can, and he ran a fiery look along the hosepipe to the yacht. His companion, sunburned to a mahogany-brown, and of an exaggeratedly sensuous appearance, adopted a well-planned attitude and waited. At length the grey-haired man emitted a savage exclamation, and wrenching the hosepipe from the tap, he set his own bucket beneath the stream of water. He looked angrily at the yacht for the reaction which was not slow in coming. There were shouts of rage from below, and in an instant a very large man in khaki shorts, a singlet, and a thick gold chain worn round the base of the neck, was with us.

"I have never in all my life encountered a more arbitrary rudeness," he said to the grey-haired man.

"No rudeness at all on my part," was the answer.

"The Englishman, here, sits quietly waiting for his water while my hose runs, and he has a very big boat out there. But you, you from the two-francs-fifty *pétrolette* there, you violate my hosepipe and the laws of sport . . ."

"Did you pay for the water?" asked the other. "Ah! You see. You are nonplussed. What can you reply? But I paid. Neither you nor your Englishman is a member of the club. I am a member." His bucket was filled to the brim. He raised it high into the air, poured the contents carefully over the brown shoulders of his companion, and returned with her to their motor-boat. The man with the gold chain readjusted his hosepipe on the tap.

"I feel like taking out a subscription just to be even with that mackerel," he said to me.

*   *   *   *

Mary slept in the saloon on a mattress set on the port settee, for I was not prepared to clear the after cabin, even for her. She adjusted herself with ease to the change in her circumstances, and said that she had slept better in the saloon than she ever did in her hotel, where she had had two obstacles to sleep, the snores of the hotel-keeper's mother from Bar-le-Duc, and the mosquitoes. Not even mosquitoes could make Mary shut her windows for although she was prepared to believe that "our magnificent sailors" could have sound, refreshing sleep in submerged submarines, she refused to believe that any human being could sleep in a room without an open window. Against the mosquitoes she used an invention called Red Dragon, a spiral that smouldered with a papist odour through the night.

"It sends them to sleep, you know," Mary explained. "And when they go to sleep, I can, or rather I could but for that awful old mother. I had my room changed twice, but the snoring seemed to be just as loud all over the hotel. The head waiter says it is because the walls are hollow, but I could have sworn that the woman was following me."

"Did you try cotton wool in your ears?"

"I think that would be rather unhealthy, don't you? Janet says that if you cannot get to sleep the best thing is to wind a cold compress around your tummy, but somehow it does not seem right to use cold compresses on holiday, and they make such a wet mess of the bed. Oh, it was quite all right, you know; I had plenty of good books to read. But the maître d'hôtel says that unless they can do something about the mother's snoring they will be in serious straits with the hotel. There have been many complaints, it seems. Monsieur Voltaire, the proprietor, is rather frightened of her because she sank capital in the hotel. The head waiter says that the son did approach his mother tactfully, telling her that there had been a complaint or two about snoring, and all she said was: 'Then whoever snores must get out, because in the hotel business the clients always have the right on their side.' One day I asked her whether she slept on her back. She answered that she had slept very little since the death of her husband . . ."

There was a mistral blowing sharply across the harbour on the morning that we sailed. Two small boats left the harbour with reefed Bermudian mainsails, and I saw that they were considerably over-canvased when they cleared the mole. One of them came running back; the white hull and sails seemed to be etched round with black lines, an effect of the mistral weather. We left harbour under staysail and mizzen only, and when we got outside we heeled sharply even under that slight canvas. *Truant* was not as stiff as I would have liked. When we were far out, off the great bay into which Toulon harbour is tucked behind a much-fortified spit of land, the wind veered to our quarter. Isabel and I hoisted mainsail and jib

148

while Mary, who regarded the wheel as though saying: "Now, don't bite," steered. *Truant* behaved well with the stiff following wind and sea, and we charged along in a mattress of foam with the sun burning down on us, Isabel, uncomfortable with the motion of the boat, stretched out on the cabin-top. Mary repeated, with a certain lack of tact: "Isn't this *heavenly*? I *love* the sea." We took the narrow passage between Porquerolles, first and largest of the Hyères Islands, and the mainland. In the narrows both sea and wind increased, and we should have been much more comfortable with our squaresail for we were obliged to gybe at the narrowest part, and the boom came over with more speed and weight than I cared for. In the lee of the island the wind dropped, and between that island and the next, Port Cros, it headed us. Visibility was so bad that we could see the mainland, seven miles distant, only as a pale-blue haze. We entered the deep bay of Port Man, at the north-eastern end of Port Cros, and dropped anchor at 3.30 p.m., having made the respectable average of seven knots for the thirty-five miles. Our anchor went down in three fathoms of water so clear that we saw the ploughshare dig itself into the sandy bottom and bright fishes swim up in the hope that the commotion had provided some interesting morsels. When the rattle of the chain had stopped, the sound of the crickets in the trees filled the hot, salty air. Port Man is a paradise, a quiet anchorage that seems far removed indeed from the brassy harbours of the French Riviera, a deep bay offering shelter in all but east winds, surrounded on three sides by slopes 700 feet in height and grown densely with pines, oaks, aromatic bushes, herbs, and flowers. At the end of the promontory which protects the bay from the passage between Port Cros and the third island of the Hyères group, the Ile du Levant, there is an old fort with a cylindrical tower and battlements set in creeper. We were disappointed to find another yacht in the anchorage; she was a small white cutter, a narrow, deep-draft boat with a high topmast that went ill with her name, *Zouzou II*, and with the family party and the two yacht hands in shorts and white-piqué-covered caps who were all fishing over her rails. Mary insisted on having her money's worth of anything unobtainable in Britain, and a minute after I had stopped the engine she was up on deck in a strangely revealing two-piece costume.

"Where did you get that bathing-suit?" I asked.

"Isn't it nice? James bought it for me in Bandol."

"I would hardly call it nice. Are you sure the bottom bit is tied properly?"

"Of course I am; the woman in the shop showed me how."

"It looks very skimpy to me."

"Everybody wears them skimpy now. And very sensible too! When we get so little of the sun why should we cover up our bodies with great woollen clouts? Can you tell me how to get into the water, please?" I showed her the steps in the transom. She lowered herself gently and cast off, moving at a slant, with the legs below giving a steady, rhythmic kick and the arms sweeping round in dignified unison, the head well back, the blue eyes full of goodwill and delight. How often had I seen that forging swimmer breasting the waters of some frigid loch or burn in the Clyde estuary or in the Cairngorm Mountains! "It's *love*-ly," she used to trumpet from the water as we children, thigh-deep, hesitated to take the shuffling steps that would make immersion final and the purgatory of enjoyment complete. "It's *love*-ly. Come on *in* . . ." Here, in the warm, clear water—so clear that when I looked over the side of the boat I felt that the height from the bottom of the sea was trying to pull me over—she did not cry out her swimming song: "It's love-ly," but allowed soft expressions of wonder to escape her lips. Soon there was a splash from the stern, and I saw Isabel, a slender line flitting along the surface, for while the more solid Mary seemed to walk in, and confidently master, the water, the smaller woman rather frisked along the top of it with a white puff of foam at her feet.

13

WE decided to spend our first day exploring the island of Port Cros and foraging for vegetables, which had been unobtainable in sufficient quantities in Bandol. By nine o'clock we were rowing to the head of the bay. Five fishing boats and the white cutter's dinghy were clustered at the jetty that tottered on sun-rotted timbers into the shallow water. The two yacht hands were White Russians. One of them asked me to lend him a sail needle. We walked from the jetty up a path cutting through bamboos twelve feet high and came out beside a ruined farm. An artist influenced, like the Impressionists, by the Japanese had painted murals on the crumbling walls of the upper room. Fishermen were camping there with women, possibly their wives. We met two of the women, slatternly in loose dresses, at the well.

"How is the water?" I asked.

"Ferruginous, but potable."

Mary and Isabel wore linen dresses, and Mary, who sometimes has "trouble" with her feet, stamped along on rope-soled espadrilles upturned at the toes like the shoes of gnomes. There was an excellent path. The sun beat hotly on the trees around us, and the heat from the day before still rose trembling from the rock beneath the thin coating of soil and roots, but where our faces passed, in that shaded space between the foliage and the ground, there was a hint of the night's condensation and of the freshness of the sea. When we had walked over the hills for an hour we slithered down the path, suddenly unwooded and offering a treacherous surface of loose stones, to the village, which is dominated, but not obscenely, by the hotel. On the hotel terrace a few visitors were considering going out to bathe as they felt the sun nipping at their skins. I ordered lunch with a lobster supplement. The meal would not be cooked for two hours, and we had stupidly forgotten to carry our bathing things. The fishermen's wives and children looked at me without curiosity when I entered their houses to ask if we might hire a boat. We pushed off in a white canoe, Isabel and I at either end with stupid, double-bladed paddles. We rounded the first point of the narrow bay, and came to a place where we saw no people. It was a rocky inlet, and the water looked so good that, although a path which ran round the head of the inlet led, we knew, to the favourite bathing place of the island, and was undoubtedly much frequented, we beached the canoe and began to undress behind rocks. The water was shallow beside my rock, and as I ran into it I felt an almost unbearable pain. I had stepped on a sea-urchin and his spikes had penetrated deep into the ball of my foot. I pulled out a dozen of the longer ones in the water, and the pain became so intense that I had to retire to my rock again and sit picking at the spikes with the pin of Isabel's brooch. While thus engaged, I heard Mary exclaim: "Gracious me! That looks terribly like Humbert Snoddross." It was Humbert. Wearing grey flannel trousers, rubber-soled sneakers, a white flannel shirt and a brown straw hat of round shape with a silk handkerchief tied about it in place of the ribbon in a more normal hat, he was approaching our inlet at his usual lethargic but inevitable pace.

Humbert was born into a British family which thought well of itself, and he grew up even less than his brothers and sisters. Like the rest of the Snoddross men he entered the Army, joined the Cavalry Club, and shot, hunted, and fished. But he could have been little interested in anything except the Cavalry Club, for which he professed a fierce and partisan loyalty. He was soon invalided out of the Army, and he had enough money to live where he pleased so long as he spent occasional periods rent-free with his aged parents down in the country. I had been introduced to him by a Cambridge friend who doubtless worked on the principle that if you know a persistent bore it is best to spread him over as many of your acquaintances as possible. He was so friendly and so good-humoured that there was no way of getting rid of him. His were the tactics of endless persistence. We knew him at Cambridge as "See-you-in-your-bath". Humbert lived in lodgings, and was officially unconnected with the university except that he had himself been an undergraduate there some twenty years earlier. He very often dropped in on an acquaintance about tea-time, but, perhaps because he was lonely and stupid and had an intense longing for companionship, he usually came at least an hour before tea, at that time when the young man upon whom he was inflicting himself was often on the point of visiting the college bath-house to wash away traces of the games arenas.

"Please excuse me, I must have a bath."

"I'll come along and chat to you while you have it, if I may," Humbert would answer.

Mary knew him, for she had met him in London, and heartily disliked him because she dislikes people who constantly smile, and Humbert is one of those. Isabel had never met him. It seemed a strange turn of fate that Humbert should arrive at the moment when, stark naked, and only

152

partially concealed by a rock, I was picking spikes from my foot with the pin of a regimental brooch.

"Why," he cried. "Isn't it? . . . Isn't it? . . . Yes, it is!" He paused on the edge of the path, eyeing the rocks, slippery with seaweed, that led to the place where I crouched.

"Be with you in a minute, Humbert," I said. "I stepped on an *oursin*."

"Of all the luck," he said. "What brings you here?"

"Mr. Snoddross," Mary called sharply from that part of the sea where she was making jerky circles in the water, "will you please go away and let us come out and get dressed?"

"Dressed? Oh yes, how d'you do. What brings you here? What brings you here? Are you staying at the hotel? When did you arrive? Funny; didn't see your name in the office on the list of expected arrivals . . ."

"See you in the hotel," I said to him.

"How lucky we met so soon, for I had been thinking of making an expedition to le Lavandou to-day. What a stroke of luck! I can put you up to all sorts of useful wrinkles about this place. There are one or two fellows in the hotel who are not of the right sort. Definitely not good exports. I mean, if the Labour Government are all that keen on exports they should only export Conservatives, shouldn't they? It's awfully bad publicity to allow the other sort out of the country. See what I mean? D'you know, I saw one English girl going off for a walk in the woods, and what d'you think she was wearing? *High heels!*" He looked at us. Now it was our turn to entertain and educate him. Friendship with Humbert could be no one-sided contact.

"Please go away, Humbert," I said. "Can't you see that we want to get dressed now."

"What?" he said. "Oh! Not got any bathing suits. Oh! How uncomfortable for you. Well, I'll be trotting along. See you in the hotel, see you there. Don't go into lunch without seeing me, now; there are several tips I can give you about the quee-zeen . . ."

As our canoe drew near the beach, past the long jetty on which hotel people lay sunbathing, we saw Humbert edging round the shore to be the first man to greet us. The smile, fixed on his face, gave it a striped appearance. He had a very tender skin, and it had burned red except for the score of smile wrinkles that formed white chasms in the beef-like surface, like crevasses filled with snow set in a hot hillside.

"Are you here all alone?" Mary asked, although she knew well enough that he was always alone.

"Yes," the smile grew a little wider, then relapsed to normal, "still an eligible bachelor, still hoping that one day the right girl will come along."

"You'll lunch with us, of course," I said.

"Delighted, George. Well, well. Just like old times. Those were the days, those were the days . . ."

"Were they?"

"Do you often go back to Cambridge?"

"Never!"

"I still go there once or twice a year, you know. Cambridge doesn't alter very much, although it was a little depressing during the war with all the fellows rushing away to join up and so many getting stuck in the ranks, you know."

When the meal was over I asked the maid to ask the chef to fill my big rucksack with vegetables and 1,000 grams of bread.

"You certainly cannot carry that thing," Humbert said when she staggered back with the loaded rucksack.

"Why not?"

He shook with laughter. "Rather like going for a walking tour, you know, like those German cads who wandered from hostel to hostel before the war. Here, give me the thing and I'll get a fisherman to row it round to you this evening." Thanking him, I swung the rucksack hastily to my shoulders. I had a vision of Humbert arriving with "the thing" in the fisherman's boat, and if he once came on board I did not see how we would get rid of him. I suspected that he was too lazy to face the walk, and too careful with his money to hire a boat on his own account unless desperate for company, and surely he had company enough in that hotel.

The crickets were so active that they did not look where they were jumping, and sometimes they hit our heads and shoulders as we walked three abreast along the woody paths. Their noise was almost deafening in the woods, yet it faded into a background as we became accustomed to the place. They made the noise, Mary said, by rubbing their back legs together, but I thought that they rubbed the membranes on their wings; we all agreed that the noise was their mating call. "Otherwise they'd get bored with it," Mary said. We bathed from the yacht when we returned. One of the yacht hands from *Zouzou II* rowed across to us with a bowl of small fresh fish. When we had accepted this gift, the Russian reminded me that I had promised to give him a sail needle.

"I'll lend you one," I said.

"You mean, you need it back."

"I'm afraid so."

"Pity. They're unobtainable in Cannes. Can you spare us any English varnish?"

"Sorry."

"Poor *Zouzou*, she badly needs paint and varnish, and we can't get hold of any."

"I suppose she's on charter?"

"Yes. She's chartered by the month from Cannes this season. Hard work for us. I'd rather have an owner on board. When you're on charter the passengers are always determined to get their money's worth, and then they often eat such a lot, it keeps us busy cooking."

"She's a strange-looking boat."

"Nothing the matter with *Zouzou*. She sailed the Atlantic, from South America. She's very deep draft, and sails well. Do you like lobsters?"

"Yes."

"We have two creels down, and if we catch one to-night I'll let you have it. Are you catching many fish?"

"We don't bother to fish. We don't like the smell fish makes when it is cooking, and so we rarely eat it, but to-night we'll cook your fish in white wine."

"Where did you find the wine?"

"Bandol."

"How much?"

"Three hundred the litre."

"It's cruel!" he exclaimed angrily. "Unless the price of wine comes down there'll be revolution. Where did you buy it in Bandol? My patron is rich. Maybe we can persuade him to go there." I told him and he rowed himself away in the pram, shaking his head dolefully at the thought of the price of wine.

* * * *

We lay still in Port Man harbour and allowed time to race past us. One afternoon we decided that we must get some bread. The nearest baker was on the Ile du Levant. All three of us got into the dinghy; Isabel, the smallest, sat forward beside the dagger plate, and Mary was right aft, uncomfortably squatting in a pool of water. There was enough chop outside our bay to stop the dinghy from sailing fast, and we had a long beat to clear the point of our island. After an hour's sail, we approached a jetty where we could see several fishing-boats and the movement of people. I scarcely knew what to expect from the island, although the fishermen in Port Man had told me that it was still a nudist colony, and I was aware

155

that a French doctor had endeavoured to found a "naturist" settlement there in 1931.

The island is long and rugged, with precipitous sides, and little soil. Much of its surface is covered with scrub. At the far end from Port Cros there is a semaphore station, and at the near end the forbidding hill face is dotted with gimcrack villas which are surmounted by a fort. As we neared the jetty we saw a nude figure, posed in a reclining attitude against the smooth rocks. Some argument arose, in whispers, as to the sex of the reclining person, who, for all his or her nudity, was lying modestly, revealing a great expanse of white back and thigh, and a head covered with hair that was curly and neither short nor long.

"It's a man," Mary said.

"No it's not. It's a woman."

"Yes, I think it's a woman."

"Well, I'm still sure it's a man."

It was a woman. She turned a Byronic profile and a black eye heavy with self-conscious moodiness to glance at us, and Isabel and Mary struggled politely to stifle and conceal their laughter. A man, naked I assumed, thrust head and shoulders from the aperture of an orange-coloured tent, looked at us a little wildly, and withdrew. Two elderly women sat perched on a bank on our left; the bank had a sordid appearance because it was untidy with the temporarily discarded garments of a few people who were in the water, with the dead cooking fires of picnic parties of yesterday, and with empty cans that had crossed to the old world from the new. One of the elderly women was in the act of putting on shorts and a brassière. Mingled with the nudists were some normally dressed people; three small boys playing at the edge of the sea wore swimming trunks although it would have been normal enough for them to have gone without. Lying on the jetty itself, and at the place where we were obliged by water conditions to land and tie up, was a dark woman. The least familiar parts of her body were candidly disposed so that they lay directly in our line of advance. Her dog, a mongrel with Bedlington tendencies and a curly grey coat which seemed to exaggerate his mistress's bareness, gambolled around her, licking her face and hands. She moved her eyes, shaded by sun-glasses, to look at us. Isabel was to allege that I had glanced at the unwelcoming human doormat more frequently than was necessary, but the truth was that I was too upset by the unusual circumstances to feel other than embarrassed, so embarrassed that while making fast the dinghy I nearly tied the painter to one arching leg.

We regarded Mary as our passport to the Ile du Levant, for she wore her

Bandol bathing suit, which at least offered a generous compromise to nudity. Isabel wore a decent and attractive bathing suit which had been sent to her from Honolulu, while I was in an old pair of Army shorts. As we left the jetty we met the elderly woman who had been dressing on the bank. She told me that the shops were right on the top of the hill. "Everything is inconvenient here except the climate," she added. All three of us were without shoes. The track which mounted the hill was part dust part stones. The smells of the island were suspect, beginning with a farm, splashed on either side of the track, where there was an overpowering stench of goat and hen; later the air was heavy with the smell of sewage. The afternoon was exceptionally warm and we were exposed to sudden draughts of heat coming from the rock face. Some of the small villas were drowned in purple floods of bougainvillaea, but our general impression as we panted uphill was of tawdriness. Before the baker's shop, *Panification du Levant*, stood a somewhat faded notice-board stating: *Le Nu Intégral est Défendu.* As though illustrating the adjective *intégral* several men and youths passed wearing those small bags tied with string which we had first noticed on the Seine. We saw three or four German prisoners, apparently as idle as everybody else, and even they wore their Army trousers coloured like rats' bodies shortened to the absolute minimum. The baker's wife was very rude. She looked on us with obvious suspicion and disfavour, and told us that we would get no bread before 7 p.m.

"It's eat, eat, eat all day long," she said. "You nudists are always hungry." Mary flushed hotly, and tightened the ties of her bathing suit. We drank a mixture called "grape juice" which a youth poured from an unmarked bottle in one of the island's bars. The bar was a strangely British room; not overclean, very stuffy, with a black fireplace painted to imitate marble and holding a pendulum clock set in a case made of glass and fumed oak, it was reminiscent of the dining-rooms of small Scottish hotels. Each table had its own seedy floral decoration of stiffened paper. The proprietors were unsympathetic.

"I can give you no bread," the patron said. "We had forty people for dinner last night, forty! Greedy people, clamouring for food." He was so annoyed by this that you would have thought that he, and not they, paid for the meals. In the grocer's shop still higher on the ridge, we were able to buy two melons. I asked the grocer about the notice forbidding le nu intégral.

"It has always been forbidden," he said. "And most of the nudists obey the rule in the village, only exposing themselves in the undergrowth or on the beaches. If I were mayor a very different state of affairs would exist.

Our island is rotting because it is overpopulated and nobody except the shopkeepers does any work. It is a moral collapse resulting from the occupation. Yes, the Germans had a garrison here. When they left the island they blew our fort to pieces and sacked many of the houses. These cannot yet be rebuilt; but our population has risen from one thousand to two thousand. It is difficult to feed two thousand, when every scrap of food has to be brought here by boat, and you probably realise how complicated the markets are on the mainland. When the weather is bad the boats do not arrive for days. Fortunately most of the visitors only demand fruit and vegetables. They are a queer lot, decent enough in the main, but still a queer lot . . ." The tradespeople of the island presumably came from Toulon and Hyères at a time when it seemed that large profits might be made out of the doctor's disciples. The tradespeople are conservative, and they dislike nudity and their own nudists. While the grocer talked to us a tall, white-haired man fidgeted in the rear of the shop. He looked like a respectable lawyer, I thought, and although, judging by his neck, he was well over sixty years of age, his body was still firm and well-balanced. He ran after us when we had left the shop.

"My wife and daughter would be greatly honoured if you would visit our house and allow us to provide you with the bread you need," he said in slow Swiss French. He led us through a gate and down a narrow path to a villa more solid than any we had seen, well screened from its surroundings, and open only to the west, with a magnificent view which included *Truant* lying at her anchorage in Port Man bay. His wife and daughter sat in a large square room commanding the view through windows made of glass which, our host quickly assured us, in no way robbed the sun's rays of their vitamins.

"We are here, partly for our health, and partly from conviction," he said. When we entered the house he had taken off the grey woollen pants which he wore in the street, and hung them on a coat stand in the hall. His wife and daughter were naked, and I imagined that the rattan chairs in which they sat must be rather prickly. These were earnest people. Mary's French is not fluent; they spoke to her politely in English, talking with some degree of ease about the weather, conditions in France, their home in Switzerland, and our method of travel. A boat seemed to them an extraordinary conveyance, something fraught with mystery and danger. We did not notice their nudity, because it was taken for granted, and was something to be acquiesced in, like the religion of a Mussulman or a devout Christian. They brought home-made tomato-juice to quench our thirst. When we departed the old man lingered behind to pull on his pants in

158

the hall before accompanying us to the top of the track.

"We are going to have more wind," he said, "mistral, I think, but perhaps not for a day or two."

"How do you know that?"

"By the feel of the air on my skin."

We had a following wind from the jetty, and boiled back to *Truant* at such a speed that the dinghy would have planed had it been less heavily weighted. As we entered the harbour we saw *Zouzou II*, preparing to depart, and it was only as her narrow hull disappeared round the point that I remembered that the Russian sailor had not returned my sail needle. I put this down to purposeful forgetfulness.

*   *   *   *

At noon Humbert stepped to our deck from that of a small, motor-propelled fishing-boat.

"Well done! Well done!" he exclaimed somewhat unintelligibly (although we gathered that he was speaking for the benefit of the people in the fishing-boat). "Welcome, welcome. So glad to see you. Very fine show indeed!" He wore long blue shorts of the type often seen on English rugby footballers, and a limp tennis-shirt. "Now let me introduce you all. . . . Come out of the boat, you chaps, come on! Millar may be a little eccentric, but he's by way of being a chum of mine, and I assure you he won't eat you."

Three people climbed from the boat, and shook hands gingerly with us. They were introduced as: "Bill and Agnes Dundonald-Smythe and their son, William D.-S. Now I'll give you the plan," Humbert rattled on. "I happened to know that these good people had hired this motor-boat for the day and intended to picnic on one of the beaches with Marius, the fisherman bloke who owns it—*ness pa, Mary-ooze?*"

"Mais oui, monsieur," answered a gloomy voice from the boat.

"Well, at petty dayjnay this morning I put it to Bill and Agnes that it would be ridiculous to go and picnic on a silly old beach when they could picnic on an English yacht. We've brought the delicatessen with us, and more than enough for you as well as ourselves—dry Martinis in thermos flasks, sticks of bread, bouillabaisse made by Marius in a jolly old iron pot that's probably thoroughly insanitary, but never mind. . . ."

"A splendid idea," I said faintly.

"We knew you'd think so," Humbert said. "You must be infernally sick of sitting here day after day, with only water and bushes to look at."

"It seems awful cheek, sir, bursting in on you like this," young William said to me. He was a tall, thin youth in the awkward stage between boy-hood and manhood, and he spoke in a voice resolutely held on the lowest notes of his register. His father and mother also murmured apologies, but Humbert cut them short.

"Now then! Now then!" he said. "You'd think the Millars were doing *us* the favour."

Isabel had already been in consultation with Marius, and she and the fisherman carried the provisions below to the galley, where the latter set to work, cooking his bouillabaisse.

"Prosit!" Humbert cried, raising his glass. "Now this is what I call a real dry Martini. I stood by the barman fellow all the time he was mixing. 'Encore doo gin,' I said to him, 'encore, encore.' And, 'Sec, sec, sec,' I said to him. Unless you do that they'll give you a drink that tastes like sugared buttermilk."

Humbert made us all bathe before we ate. He insisted that there was nothing like a dip for building an appetite for bouillabaisse.

"Then why don't you bathe yourself?" Mary asked.

"I have a touch of lumbago again to-day." He seated himself com-fortably in a deck chair, a small French cigar—a "Voltigeur"—in his mouth, a thermos flask at his elbow. "Don't argue the toss," he said. "The men will change in the after cabin, and you women in Isabel's cabin—better lock the door, ladies, because, don't forget, *the Frenchman is down there in the galley.*"

When we had eaten, Humbert said that we must fish. The three Dundonald-Smythes obediently took lines from the fishing-boat, and rowed away in *Truant's* dinghy. Marius settled down to sleep in the bottom of his boat.

"Bill Dundonald-Smythe is the whale of a fine fellow, and absolutely sound," Humbert said to me. "Wife's a good sort too. Son thinks he's clever, but he'll grow up; all he needs is a few sensible chaps around to laugh him out of it—rag him a bit, you know. He goes up to Cats next term, so I shan't entirely lose sight of him. I've promised Bill to keep an eye on the lad at Cambridge, and Bill's gratitude is quite touching. When they arrived Bill was a little worried because they had all paused to buy reading matter at Victoria Station bookstall, and instead of getting a few magazines or something intelligible, William bought Osbert Sitwell's autobiography. I told Bill not to worry: lads of that age are still feeling their feet, and they're apt to show off. . . . *Catching anything young William?*" Humbert yelled at the dinghy. The youth held up some small object. "*Good lad!*"

I told Humbert about our trip the previous day to the nudists' island. One of his habits is to produce a curious noise accompaniment while you talk to him; a good many listeners intersperse your words with "hms", or "mms", or "mm-hms"; Humbert produces a steady moan. When I mentioned the nudists, he said: "There ought to be a law—not that there aren't too many of the damned things already—to stop it, or at least they should confine such nonsense to clubs, don't you think?" and his moan was interrupted by such exclamations as: "The blinking limit! You say there are nippers there too! Infamous! Barbaric! D. H. Lawrence simply isn't in it!" When I had finished, he said: "It's a damned shame I can't take advantage of this motor-boat to visit your Eel doo Levong to-day. I may organise a trip with one or two of the more decent fellows at the hotel. But I must say, George, I'm surprised that you took your women-folk. I may be old-fashioned, but I believe in shielding women from such sights."

At this point Marius—whose name be for ever blessed—awoke with a succession of wet snorts, and announced angrily that he must return to Port Cros because he had promised to take a fishing party out in the evening.

"What cheek!" said Humbert (who was not paying for the hire of the boat). "I had been looking forward to a decent cup of tea on this little hunk of England," he slapped the wheelhouse heartily, hurting his hand on the bell, "but there you are, that's the French all over—riddled with Communism, and Bolshier than the Bolshies."

Marius was in no mood to listen to arguments. He started his noisy engine, and the Dundonald-Smythes came hurrying back in the dinghy. Soon the motor-boat vanished round the point, and we were allowed to enjoy the "water and bushes", undisturbed.

Before daylight next morning I got the anchor, and *Truant* gathered way a little stiffly under light-weather jib, staysail, mainsail, and mizzen.

14

"EL MARTES ni te cases ni te embarques," Isabel said; but our journey to St. Tropez went well enough. We logged more than seven knots with the following wind past Cap Camarat, which has sandy indents on either side of its thin neck—good places for picnics—past Pamplonne, the only fine beach between Marseilles and Genoa, and into the Gulf of St. Tropez, where a mistral came flogging from the hills and Mary had to look after the wheel while we got the sails down. Our arrival was difficult, thanks to the American soldier, General Patch, who landed the armour of his VIIth Army at St. Tropez, with the result that the sheltering moles were gutted and all the quays crumbled. A few yachts were riding with their sterns to the Café de Paris, and we were about to put ourselves alongside them when a man wearing a yachting cap but no shoes ran to the edge and shouted to us that there were "rocks" in that place. We made another circuit of the harbour, and with the greatest difficulty put *Truant* in the berth that he indicated with two anchors down and stern lines to the quay. The mistral raised a curtain of dust between us and the houses, and whipped shore dirt and spray to our deck. We were told that the best place to eat was a new restaurant some distance from the harbour. The food was astonishingly good. The Crown Prince of Sweden had eaten there the day before, we were told by the squat, bow-legged, utterly charming Italian maid; like us, the prince had asked for garlic in his salad.

Early the following morning I took the four water-cans to the pump at the end of the quay. I waited in a queue of housewives each of whom, when she had filled her pitchers, held her bare feet for a moment in the jet from the fountain, which was one of those equipped with a knob and a whirling disc to draw the water.

We spent much of the morning in the Café de Paris. The wind had dropped sufficiently to allow the social ebb and flow of St. Tropez to have its way. A rough eagerness for physical things seemed to characterise the strollers. Although the quays on which they set their sandalled feet had been battered by guns and bombs and possibly rockets and had rumbled to the onrush of an army since my last visit, little seemed to have altered in the place. I could pick out familiar figures, for example the swarthy, narrow-hipped man in striped singlet, white cap, white trousers wide over

162

the feet, trying to walk like a tiger and towing a brindled great dane. At St. Tropez the men are extravagantly male (with a few notable exceptions); they are men burlesquing men, while the women tend to burlesque women.

"I must be getting back home," Mary said in the Café de Paris.

"Why not come with us into Italy?"

"No, you've had quite enough of me, and besides, I must get back. I've so much to do."

"What is there to do?"

"There are always things to do when you have a house to run. I don't know whether they've got their bread-rationing cards—I'm sure that I forgot to sign some paper—and the telephone bill hasn't been paid, and I hope Isa has enough money, and if Janet's family runs wild over the house Isa may not like it and Mina may give notice . . ."

Salade Niçoise, made with unripe tomatoes, peppers, cucumber, boiled eggs, black olives, anchovies, parsley, chervil, a little garlic, lemon juice instead of vinegar, and good olive oil; bouillabaisse, made with red mullets, rascasses, langoustes, eels; ice-cream made with fresh cherries and kirsch; strong black coffee; good vin rosé and ice floating in the glasses: after all that, as I toiled in the heat to get in our two anchors, the harbour seemed to stand on its head and on mine.

The sun was dazzling. The mistral had blown itself out. Our port anchor came up easily enough, although the anchor and some fifteen fathoms of the chain were covered with glutinous mud. The starboard anchor was fouled by one of the chains of a superb ketch built just before the war in England and owned, we were told (I suspect mistakenly), by the grocer, Félix Potin. After a lot of hard work we brought the anchor and Potin's chain to the surface, and I was able to get a rope round the latter and so clear the anchor.

Outside there was a slight heave on the water and no wind at all. Our sails hung slack, and we motored along the coast. It was well on into a fine evening when we passed the islands off Cannes. With the binoculars we could clearly see the upper floors of the hotels in Cannes, the lower portions being hidden by the curve of the earth. Here we first saw the foothills of the Alpine chain, and Cannes, in my opinion, only looks well when seen from far out at sea. Passing Cap d'Antibes we got the evening puff of wind. There was light enough to distinguish the large house near the point then occupied by the Duke and Duchess of Windsor, a pale, quiet house squinting down at the sea through a vista cut in the pines. At the edge of the water there was evidently a swimming pool for use in bad weather, when bathing from the rocks would be dangerous, and, lower than the

163

pool, a kind of niche lined with seats and canopies. A servant in white linen jacket and black trousers was putting things away for the night.

*   *   *   *

When we sought to approach the quay at Nice a puff of wind, helped perhaps by some current, pushed us away. I was so hard put to it with the bow warp, which had slipped from the bitts, that I tore much of the skin from the palms of my hands. Meanwhile, I had told Mary to hold on to the stern warp and only looked astern just in time to shout to her: "Let go!" She was obeying my injunction too literally, and while she held with the utmost determination to the end of the rope she was being drawn bodily overboard.

I was gingerly—with my sore hands—erecting the awnings when a car came to a cowboy halt beside me, tearing long grooves in the gravel as the brakes were applied, and Bob jumped out followed by his oldest son, Jackie, and two strangers. Bob was pale, with deep indigo pouches beneath his eyes. He is tuberculous and has one collapsed lung. Nice suits him well enough in the winter, but the climate is too enervating for him from April to November.

"We have not had rain for three months," he said, panting. They came below and drank whisky and asked a lot of questions. I had the impression that they suspected us of being "spies". In Nice, one of the crime centres of France, everybody suspects everybody of being something, but usually, as in our case, the suspicions are too flattering.

On August 18th, two days after our arrival, a storm broke, bringing with it the torrents of the rain for which Bob had been praying. He slept better than he had for months. He had been going around for two days in his raincoat, for he had been convinced that at last the rain was coming. The laundress had taken our bundle that afternoon: "N'ayez pas peur," she had said when she promised to return the lot within forty-eight hours. "Nous sommes équipées pour les grands bateaux, et les navigateurs sont toujours pressés."

We walked into the new part of Nice to cash cheques, to eat ice-cream, and to reserve Mary's seat on the aeroplane. We saw the big hotels sprawling their inflated stucco rumps on palmy beds with fine views of the sea and a green hill dotted with villas, and Rolls Royce taxis and horse-drawn landaus passing the doors. In the old part of Nice we passed shop-keepers perched on hard chairs outside the dark Genoese doorways of their shops, their shoes lying beside their hot, stockinged feet on the pavement. If we entered a shop the owner followed us in, complaining of the heat. Opposite *Truant* there was a bar called Le Nautique, which adopted us—on a strictly financial basis—and which accepted messages from all in Nice who knew of us. The woman behind the counter was described in flattering terms on a White Ensign which was the bar's most prized souvenir of the war; it had been left there by six members of a naval commando who had arrived in Nice before the Germans had evacuated the town and who had wisely hidden beneath that hospitable roof. They had signed the Ensign with the names, Sam, Jock, Bill, Laurence, Smasher, and Cole. She was a dark woman with a jutting chest, a warm, apparently genuine smile, and a voice deeper than any ordinary man's. One evening she came out and shouted across the street: "Ahoy, *Truant*! Lord Beaverbrook wants you on the phone; he won't wait, that one."

We were sitting reading in our saloon when there was a thunderous clatter on the deck above and a cry of rage or pain or triumph. It was at that hour when bed is near and the nerves are finely drawn, and for a moment I cursed myself for allowing Isabel to pack away my big automatic pistol at the bottom and the back of the linen cupboard so that it would take me at least four minutes to dislodge it; and the shotgun was under our berth. I climbed gently up the companion. The noises continued on deck and a figure caught me by the arm. I retreated to the light rising from our hatch, and looked at a swarthily handsome head wearing—as was the fashion at that time with a certain not uncolourful section of the Riviera populace—a scarlet handkerchief swathing the skull and falling down the nape of the neck, pirate fashion. The visitor had another blaze of scarlet, a sash, tightly wound round his waist. Otherwise he wore white trousers and a white shirt unbuttoned to expose portions of a bronzed chest and stomach.

"I came to see my yacht," he said, with a flourish of his hand towards a small sailing-boat with an outboard engine which had, unknown to me, come alongside *Truant* and made fast. He then proceeded to have an argument with the sailor on his yacht. They were talking about the possibility of proceeding the following day across the bay to Antibes. The man on the boat said that the mistral was blowing and that he was damned if he was going to Antibes. "Do you then regulate the winds?" hissed the pirate.

"No," replied the other. "But I regulate the possibility of drowning myself on behalf of people like you."

"This," said the pirate, "is a breach of contract."

"It is no breach. I am a man of honour."

165

"I demand that you sign a paper refusing to take your boat to Antibes to-morrow."

"That I will do, provided you insert a clause that my refusal is caused by the dangers of the weather."

The pirate whirled round on me, and brusquely asked me to give him paper, pen and light.

"Come below," I said. He came down, followed by the man from the boat.

"Mon dieu, quel luxe!" the pirate exclaimed. "I thought this was a patrol vessel, but it is a yacht. A million apologies for this intrusion. Take off that hat," he barked at the sailor, but he himself made no gesture to remove the scarlet bandana, or to button his clothing; it seemed that his disarray was contrived and permanent. When the paper had been made out and both had signed it they left, the pirate with profuse apologies to Isabel, Mary, and myself. I went on deck to see them off the boat, for their arrival had made me suspicious. The pirate had some people waiting for him on the quay, two women and a man, all exotically dressed. There was some chaff directed at him for his manner of jumping to our boat, and in order to show them that he was perfectly capable of behaving à la Hollywood as he put it, he made the leap again, landing on our planking as heavily as an avalanche in a monastery refectory, a display of energy that found no favour with me and that drew sneers from the sailor in the little boat.

"A braggart," he said, "and miserly into the bargain." He explained that the pirate and his three friends had chartered his small boat for a week. "And every day it is, 'leave Antibes and go to Nice,' or, 'leave Nice and go to Antibes,' but they do not travel on the boat, they go in their car; and sometimes when I arrive here in Nice they telephone me and say: 'Eh, Marius! We have stopped in Antibes and are enjoying ourselves. Return immediately.'"

We certainly never expected or intended to renew acquaintance with the pirate, but next day the three of us went to the offices of Air France to complete arrangements for Mary's passage to London, and there he was, still in the same exotic costume. He at once pounced on Isabel.

"So we are to be camarades-de-voyage," he said in a most friendly manner. Isabel said that it was Mary who was travelling and he gallantly bent his head, adorned beneath the scarlet handkerchief with curved black sidewhiskers, and handed Mary a large visiting card. He told her that the manager of the airline was a dear friend, and so, when their aeroplane arrived at Le Bourget, since she had been unable to arrange a through booking to London, he would simply make a coup-de-telephone and presto, the ticket would materialise. "I am a movie actor, as you see from my visiting card," he added. "I have studio commitments here in Nice and also in Paris."

"How nice!" Mary responded weakly. Her face admirably expressed the struggle that she was having to achieve another of life's compromises.

*   *   *   *

Mary and the female baritone at the Bar Nautique became good friends. "Votre pastisse est magnifique," I heard Mary, president of her local Conservative Association, tell the patronne.

"Ça vous plaît?"

"Wee, wee. Beaucoup, beaucoup!"

"Vous-aimez la bouillabaisse?"

"Wee, wee. C'est—delicious."

"Alors, votre dernier repas à Nice vous viendrez chez moi manger la bouillabaisse, hein?"

So we carried Mary's suitcases to the Bar Nautique. The good-looking youth whom we took to be the female baritone's son (although we scarcely liked to inquire) had laid the table in the corner with a white cloth, white bread (then extremely rare) and three bottles of wine, one white, one red, and one rosé.

"Vous aimez la soupe aux poissons?" Madame asked Mary.

"Wee. Beaucoup."

"C'est *delicious*?"

"Wee, wee."

The baritone explained that she had not been able to find the right type of fish for making bouillabaisse. "Only one man in the whole market caught any fish to-day. It was very expensive, and so the bill will be bigger than I care to ask. I told the fisherman, who happens to be a good friend of mine, that I needed the fish to celebrate the christening of my grandson. He answered that if the fish was needed to celebrate the shaving of the prophet, the price was still 600 the kilo . . ."

We ate hors d'œuvres, then the rich gluey fish soup, and then course after course of the fish which had given up their juices to make the soup. It seemed that dishes of strange-looking fish, arranged according to species, would continue to arrive for the rest of the afternoon.

"Ce n'est pas bon?" the woman boomed anxiously from behind the bar. "Vous, Madame, ça ne vous plaît pas?"

"Wee, merci, c'est très bon. Seulement, je n'ai plus faim . . ."

'Comment, vous n'avez plus faim! Vous mangez comme un petit oiseau. Jean! Trois verres de vodka. . . . Il faut manger . . ."

Mary drank the vodka and wearily turned to the fish. "It does seem an awful waste not to eat it," she said, "and I'd loathe to hurt her feelings. I don't know whether this aeroplane 'will ever manage to take off with me inside. And if it comes down in the sea I can surely expect no mercy from the fishes."

With the last assortment of fish the waiter brought us a marble bowl of ailloli, that pungent but heavenly sauce. Mary at first refused it. "I should stink of garlic," she said. "It wouldn't be fair to the other passengers." But the baritone was so persuasive that she agreed, "just to taste a little." After that, we were only faced with green figs, coffee and liqueurs. We staggered out into the sunshine, spurning taxis because the thought of sitting in a taxi was unbearable.

"I feel as though my inside is swimming away," Mary said. "I did not know that it was possible to eat so much fish and live." We left her sitting heavily, her eyes half-shut, in the bus that was to take her, the pirate, and their fellow-travellers to the aeroplane. We returned to the boat and I pulled the bicycles out from the after cabin, for we had arranged to call on Lord Beaverbrook.

Bob had told us that it was impossible to go on bicycles from Nice to Cap d'Ail, because, he explained in his correct English, "the road traverses mountains". But it is unwise when Isabel is near to use the word impossible. She looked at the roads which were marked on several of our charts, and saw that there were three, the coastal road, the Moyenne Corniche, and the Grande Corniche. She thought that the Moyenne Corniche would be the best, and it certainly looked the shortest on charts which took no account of the mileage that the road climbs and descends between the two points, a mileage that must almost equal the horizontal distance between them. At 5 o'clock, when we should have been at Beaverbrook's villa at sea level, we were surrounded by fleecy clouds while I pushed our two bicycles up yet another hill and approached the entrance of yet another tunnel. All the height that we had struggled for was lost in four kilometres of dazzling descent. Beaverbrook had just reached Cap d'Ail from England, and he had a dinner engagement along the coast at Beaulieu. He had been pacing beneath the pergola when we arrived and he led us to a sheltered terrace where he offered us figs and whisky. He found time to rattle off the series of questions and statements that I associate with all our meetings. He and Isabel argued strongly over an American-owned island in the Pacific which Beaverbrook described as "providing all that man could desire", and Isabel (who had lived there) as "the ugliest civilisation on earth". Our legs were aching when we mounted for the ride back to Nice, but this time we had a sirocco on our backs and we followed the coastal road. Our German lights cast white jets ahead. When we had travelled a few miles Beaverbrook's car passed us, carrying him to his engagement. The light was on in the back of the car, and he appeared to be reading! Back in *Truant*, we cooked ourselves a fine meal; this had reached the dessert stage when we heard footsteps on deck, followed by guttural, but unmistakably feminine, cries: "Monsieur, madame."

It was the woman who had agreed to do our laundry, a heavily-built person with broad shoulders, broad hips, thick arms and thick lips, a face that could not accurately be described as ugly, and a mane of strong hair from which all colour had been drawn by the use of some powerful bleaching agent.

"I'm in danger, real danger, monsieur, madame," she announced, descending into the well-lit saloon.

"Sit down, madame, and have a glass of cognac." The hand that she stretched out shook with rather more violence than could be accounted for by emotion alone, and I realised, though too late, that in offering her cognac I was dropping incendiary bombs into a house that already burned.

"You are generous and noble," she replied.

"Have some coffee," Isabel said.

"Ah, madame. I knew that you would not hear my plea in silence, I knew that you would place yourselves at my side."

"We have not yet heard your plea . . ."

"No, no . . . not yet . . ." She dropped her face for a moment over her well-filled blouse, sipped her brandy and snatched a quick, embarrassed look around our cabin. "What a lovely place you have here," she observed and then, speaking more brusquely, "I've been a good wife through twenty years of marriage and my kids would be the first to cry in chorus: 'Our mother is a saint.'" Neither of us could think of any comment. She proceeded: "If any breath of scandal were to be associated with my name the neighbours would seize it as hungry dogs seize mutton bones, they would delight in it, knowing that I am what they can never be themselves . . ."

"We can well believe that," Isabel said, wondering, no doubt, if some misfortune had befallen our laundry.

"But the fact is," she said in a calmer voice, "I am not a stone. Yes, I am human, and I have sinned. And where some women of naturally loose disposition may slip a hundred times with impunity, it looks as though one slip, the first, will be the end of me. . . . My husband is a well-known figure in Nice. He is a sailor on the steamship *Néron* which carries passengers and cargo to the islands of Corsica, Sardinia and Sicily. My married life has been happy. My man being a sailor, I don't expect him to be a saint, and I have never lacked opportunities, but I had never stretched my marriage vows.

"My cousin Arthur lives up in the hills. He's a farmer. He and I were boy and girl together. He opposed my marriage, but I thought so little of his opposition that I came to forget it with the passage of the years. I'm a woman who has room in her heart for only one man. When the war came, and hunger with it, Arthur returned to my life in the guise of an angel. He brought us eggs, ham, butter, potatoes, yes, and olive oil. For some years we were only able to live by reason of Arthur's bounty. I thought that it was bounty freely given from cousinly and avuncular affection. How should I know that he expected a return for every egg, for every kilo of ham? It was only when my husband left for Sardinia, nearly fifteen days ago, that Arthur came out into the open. I nearly went out of my mind . . ."

"You're hard pressed for money? You would like us to pay our laundry in advance?"

"Money! He didn't ask for money. He required payment in another currency, and any less exacting man would agree that he'd been paid in full. But now he refuses to leave my house, and there will be the devil to pay, for the *Néron* is expected to arrive in this harbour any minute . . . I can't describe to you the carnage that may follow if you don't help me. I know I've no right to ask this of you, but I'm desperate . . ."

"Why do you come to us?"

"Because you're strangers. To whom else should I go? To the good people across the street at the Bar Nautique? To the men and women who share the building in which I live? To the police? If I go to any of those my life as a respectable woman with a respectable laundry is ended. No, in this fix, monsieur, and sad I am to have to say it, I can do no better than seek you out, two strangers . . ." She sank her chin on her blouse and sniffed a little.

Isabel crossed the cabin and sat beside her. "We aren't strangers, we're your clients," she said. "It was very brave of you to come to us, and I'm sure that we shall be able to help you."

"Is Arthur very big?" I asked.

"Big?" she answered. "Not he. So you will really come with me?" She led us through the streets until we were nearly a mile from the harbour and some two hundred feet above it. As we turned up the last street she

170

pointed over the rooftops to the sea where a little tree-shaped cluster of lights was moving towards the harbour mouth.

"The *Néron*," she said. "We've no time to lose." It was all shamelessly melodramatic.

She led us into the hall of a tenement building, and up two flights of stone stairs to a door, which she unlocked with a large key. The door opened directly into one room which combined the duties of bedroom, living-room, kitchen, and laundry. Hanging all over the place were my clothes, and Isabel's. It struck me as bizarre that I should see my own shirts and socks hanging in that foreign interior, and our own linen sheets beautifully laundered and folded, stacked on the table with tissue paper neatly pinned around them to guard them from dust. I wondered what other stories my shirts could tell me? How many houses had they visited without me? How many women had washed them and what problems had they considered as they washed?

"That gentleman from the yacht and his lady have come to see you," the laundress announced. At first it was difficult to perceive a recipient for this information. There were three beds in the room, two of them small, and one, a billowing sea of a bed with a well-stuffed feather mattress, set in a recess. When she had spoken there was some movement from the soft interior of the big bed and a man slowly turned from his side to his back. He put on his boots, which had been disposed, for greater comfort, near his head. He was, I should have said, five to eight years younger than the woman, with a body and face well charged with beef and muscle. There was a smell in the room of wine and recently-cooked food; the man's face was unnaturally flushed, and his speech was low, thick, but fairly precise. He looked an awkward customer, and a glance at his shoulders was enough to convince me that there would be no possibility of evicting him from the room if he did not choose to leave. Although he looked a decent enough fellow, there was something in the carriage of his head that set me against him. His grey eyes, much inflamed, looked up at us miserably, looking through fair, bushy eyebrows, or sideways, in the shortest of glances, from under the jutting bone structure of his lined forehead.

"We saw the *Néron* entering the port," she told him.

"Suits me," he answered.

The woman gave a short sigh, a sigh that was both impatient and resigned, it seemed to me, and crossed to a cupboard where she found a bottle and four glasses. Then she moved to the flat cooking stove in which a wood fire still glowed. She added wood and set water to boil. "I'll make coffee," she said. "He'll most likely want some coffee when he comes home."

171

"If you make coffee then I'll have some," the man said.

"Now, Arthur, I've told the lady and gentleman our story, and they have come here to persuade you to clear out of this place, and not to make a mess of my life."

"Is that true?" Arthur asked me.

"Yes."

"Now just let me put my point of view before you," he said. He had a ponderous way of speaking, and I had the feeling that he was one of those men who never quite grow up, but who wander round fields and villages, children in men's bodies. "I'm thirty-three, and I know what I want. I have money and I have land. I can feed her and her children and be a good man to her. The other's no good for her. He leaves her to work in the laundry and he seldom brings money home. I can go away if I want and leave him to come back and take her. For fifteen days I've slept in this room, and now the *Néron* comes back and he's to occupy the dent I've made in the plumard. This wouldn't be good for him and it wouldn't be good for me, and it wouldn't be good for her. I am thirty-three, and I know what I want. . . . Your good health, Monsieur, Mesdames."

"He'll kill you," the laundress said, stretching up a hand to one of my shirts, to feel if it was dry.

"He's no more anxious for the guillotine than I am," was the reply. "I know my mind. I know what I want, and I'd be willing to pay him for an arrangement, so long as he lets you be."

"How would you pay him? With land? He could never interest himself in vineyards, only what they produce."

"Never you mind how I could pay him. That's for him and me to decide."

"But the children," Isabel said. "Madame told us that she had two children."

"They're up at Grasse with their granny," the laundress said. She poured out coffee for all of us, and set an extra, a fifth, cup on the table.

"Have you thought about the children?" I asked Arthur.

"I know what I want," he answered, "and nobody's going to scare me out of here before he arrives." He rolled and lit a cigarette and scowled fixedly at one corner of the room. He had not combed his hair since he rose from the bed, and the sleeves of his shirt were dirty where they pushed out from the arm-holes of his waistcoat. We sat for some time and then the woman suddenly shouted at him.

"For God's sake get out!" she shouted. "I'll come to you to-morrow. We'll have it out then. Ah, you stubborn one! Then wait in the street

172

below, and I'll come down when he's arrived and when I see how things are. Just clear out now, Arthur. To please me . . ."

"When my mind's made up, it's made up."

"And you say that you love me!"

"I affirm it."

"You love only yourself, or you could never put me in this situation, you could never humiliate me in front of these kind people."

"As for them, you dragged them into this yourself. And I warn you all now, when he comes I'm going to speak out my mind."

The woman looked at me. "What are we to do, monsieur?" She stiffened. We all heard steps in the street below, a man's voice saying: "Good evening."

We heard the concierge's bell ring just inside the front door. "Promise you'll say nothing to him. Promise you'll let us be," she said to Arthur.

"I make no promises."

She began to speak very loudly, talking about some trip that she had once made in a motor-boat to the Iles des Lérins. "And when we got there," she said, "the engine conked. Just imagine that! We might have had to wait for days. But the mechanic was a good one. He called us to him. 'Any of you ladies got a nice strong garter,' he said. 'Something really strong, something pre-war . . .' " There was a rap on the door.

A man in the uniform of a ship's steward entered the room.

"Evening all," he said.

"Good evening."

"Your husband did not rejoin the ship at Genoa," he told the laundress. "Captain told me to call in on my way home and say you can collect the pay at the office to-morrow morning . . ."

She poured him out the coffee and a glass of brandy. It was a moment or two before she could speak. "What happened to him?" she said at last.

"Caught his finger in one of the deck winches. It went septic. He's in hospital in Genoa. But they'll tell you all about it at the office. You call at the office to-morrow morning. O.K.?"

"O.K.," she answered.

"Must be going, now. I'm late to-night. We took a long time coming in."

"Yes," she said. "You took a long time."

"Well, good night all."

"Good night."

Arthur filled his own glass. Isabel and I soon followed the steward out of the building, and when I looked up at the window I saw the light go out.

15

THE motor-boats plying from Nice harbour eastward to Monte Carlo and westward to the Iles des Lérins remained in harbour that day because of the sirocco. But we had had enough of Nice and I telephoned the shipyard at Antibes to say that we should arrive that evening.

The laundress brought our laundry in a handsome old perambulator which travelled with a limp because one of the larger wheels was buckled. We walked across to the Bar Nautique.

"What would you like to drink, madame?"

"Red wine, please."

"You look tired, madame."

"That Arthur!"

"Has he gone?"

"No. He knows what he wants." The female baritone refilled our glasses. "I've had to work so hard I just can't think any more to-day." The laundress ran one hand over her bleached hair. "And there is Arthur, drum-drum-drumming at me. Sometimes I could wish I were under the ground." She smacked her lips juicily when she had drained her glass.

In the harbour entrance we slammed into a remarkably steep swell. I set jib, staysail and mizzen and stopped the engine. The beam sea did not impede *Truant*, and there was enough wind to push her along. We had been eating perhaps too well in the old quarter of Nice, and the boat's liveliness annoyed us both. By this time I had fully realised that rough weather is amusing enough on other people's yachts, but not on your own.

The slipway is excellent at Antibes, and is well situated near the entrance to that attractive harbour. There was no difficulty in hauling us out, although I was not taken with the foreman who directed the operations, a tall, dirty-looking man with a coarse tongue. His face was deeply indented on either side of a gat-toothed mouth, and he frequently spat a wide brown jet over the side.

I was beneath the boat with the foreman, examining the bottom, which, we were delighted to see, had collected no marine growths, and showed no scars despite all its groundings in the canals, when I heard a stranger inquire for me by name. Wiping tendrils of seaweed from my person, I emerged, and faced a chauffeur. Almost unwillingly, incredulous that his

174

mission should be to anyone so dishevelled, he handed me an envelope, saying that he had been instructed to wait for a reply. The letter was an invitation to swim and lunch at a private house the following day.

The yard's sirens called the men to work at 6.55 a.m. and again at 7. The foreman arrived soon after the second call. The bottom had already been washed with fresh water. He and I set to work, scraping and rubbing with sandpaper. As the men arrived they joined us apathetically. Because I used my own scrapers, and these were superior to the local tools, and because I was interested in advancing the work since our time on the slip was limited, I worked faster than any of the others. I tried to stifle my annoyance at their lethargy, reminding myself that if I showed too much impatience all might well be lost.

A painter arrived, a slick young man with a sardonic expression. He was very freshly dressed in a white shirt, grey flannel trousers, and white espadrilles. He changed into working overalls before approaching *Truant*, which he appraised in the unsuitable words: "Oh! the cow!" I forgave him this, for the director of the yard, himself a designer, had just been speaking of the boat's shape in most flattering terms. The painter began to indent the edges of the white line around *Truant's* boot top. He was breathing distastefully through his nose, and I could see that he was trying to think of another wounding remark.

"It's sacrilege to work to-day," he said at length.

"It's never sacrilege to work," I answered falsely.

"It's sacrilege to-day," he reaffirmed. "You may not know it, but to-day's the anniversary of the liberation of Antibes. Not a few of our comrades fell on this day." I reflected that the liberation seemed to pursue us eastwards along the coast, for we had watched St. Tropez celebrate its liberation on August 15th. It was not until August 24th that an American platoon was sent to Antibes. A few sleepy German soldiers had exploded at the last moment the charges that damaged Antibes harbour. But the painter did not know that I knew these things. The painting began. The undercoat for the anti-fouling was coloured a bilious brown, and was easy to slap on. The sun was rising and the day was hot. Isabel went away to the post office. While they worked the men talked, and their brushes moved at inverse speed to the tempo of their speech. Frequently all the brushes were still. I splashed myself liberally with paint as I endeavoured to show them by example that if all persevered the work would soon be done. In the shed there was a bottle of pastisse which belonged to an elderly man wearing a petty officer's cap, one of my workmen. He required his friends to pay him twenty-five francs for each drink from the

175

bottle. The liquor was so precious that every time one of the workers felt inclined for more the elderly man also had to leave his work to see that the measure taken was not over-generous. As the bottle neared its end the arguments about the price charged became acrimonious. The elderly man had been in the navy, and the simplest way to annoy him was to criticise his service. Soon blows seemed to be near. The foreman was in it with the rest; in fact it was he who had most savagely criticised the navy. I intervened to point out that no painting was being done. The general flow of bad feeling at once turned against me. Many remarks were passed to the effect that they were only working to do me a favour. I mentioned the very considerable hourly sum which I was paying the yard for their services. They told me that they despised money. Relations still further deteriorated when the foreman proposed, before the painting of the first coat had been completed, to start two men on the second coat. I refused to agree to this because I did not think that any of the first coat had thoroughly dried. Addressing me as "Mon pauvre ami", the foreman led me to that part of the bottom which had been first painted. "Look! It's drier than the Sahara." He dragged the back of his hand down the surface.

"It's by no means dry; there's paint on your hand."

"Have we come here to enable an Englishman to defecate upon us?" asked the slick painter. I climbed the ladder to the deck to collect the anti-fouling paint for the second coat. Months previously in England Isabel and I had hunted for this paint, the best of its kind in the world. We had gone down on our knees to the director of the manufacturers' Southampton branch, and he had scoured his warehouse to oblige us. He had been able to supply us with the necessary quantity of undercoating in one large tin, but he could only give us the "finish" in the smallest tins—twenty-three half-pound tins and six one-pound tins. When I appeared with the twenty-nine tins in a rope bag the foreman thought that he saw his chance.

"Ah ça! Non!" he shouted.

"What's the matter?"

"It'll take all day to open ces sacrées boîtes."

"Each painter can work with one tin at a time," I argued. "It will be a little inconvenient. But under the circumstances . . ."

"It'll be impossible."

"Do you recognise this brand of paint?"

"Of course. It's the best. I was at this game before you were born."

"It's unobtainable in France?"

"Naturally. We haven't seen it since 1939."

"Let me tell you that supplies are so limited in England that when

176

I bought those tins I thought them more precious than jewels."

"That doesn't in any way alter the fact that we can't paint from the bloody tins. What do you expect us to paint with? Toothpicks? I'm fed up with this job."

Isabel was walking down the harbour's edge, carrying two string bags filled with vegetables and fruit. "You're a lot of sodden women who have not even the spirit to waggle paint-brushes," I shouted at them.

"We can't all be Englishmen," the painter remarked.

The foreman was startled by my anger. Realisation of his bewilderment spurred me on. "I've had enough of you all," I shouted. "More than enough."

"Give me the tins, then," the foreman said.

"No." How could I go off to lunch and leave the twenty-nine tins in their charge. The paint was irreplaceable: in their present mood they would at best thin it down and pocket half of it. I glanced at *Truant*. The painter had finished the white line, and his work was excellently done; the first coat of anti-fouling had been completed. I allowed my anger to take its course. "Foutez-moi le camp!" I was shouting when Isabel came through the gates of the yard.

"You understand that if we go now we won't return to-day?" the foreman said.

"Yes."

"Also that to-morrow's Sunday, and nobody here works on a Sunday?"

"I understand that you have all just finished fifteen days of holiday, yet you are on holiday while you pretend to work. Clear out."

"Listen. We have our professional consciences as workmen. At 7 on Monday morning this boat must go back in the water to make room on the slip for the big bateau-de-commerce from Monte Carlo. You realise that?"

"Yes."

"Then who'll paint the bottom of your boat? If you put it back in the water as it is, the worms will rejoice, and in one month you'll drown."

"The best solution . . ." said one of his assistants.

"It's forbidden to employ non-union workers," continued the foreman.

"My wife and I will paint it ourselves, and be damned to you!"

"You'll never do it. You'll never get your boat painted like that. And you're treating us abominably. It's only 11 o'clock. D'you call that a day's work. Just let us get on with it until 12, anyway. Then we get paid for a half-day."

"None of you will touch my boat; but to show you that I bear no

177

rancour I won't mention this matter to your director provided you agree to lend me your large paint-brushes for the work." He was giving me the brushes when the young painter, who had washed under the pump and had dolled himself out again in white and grey, intervened.

"They've no right to do the work themselves," he said.

"Mais si," the foreman shouted, taking my part for a change. After a stormy argument the brushes were handed over to me.

Isabel was calling me; it was already time to clean myself for a public appearance. Wondering at the coincidence which had brought an invitation to bathe on a morning when most of my anatomy had been splashed with brown anti-fouling undercoating, I cleaned myself in three stages; with cotton waste and turpentine in the engine-room; with a remarkably efficient patent household preparation which Isabel used for cleaning her pots and pans in the galley; and finally with soap and water in the bathroom. Isabel had laid out a thin suit and a white shirt for me to wear. I put on the shirt, and then knocked into the anchor chain as I was washing my hands for the last time. The chain planted a dirty mark on the shirt, the last clean one available. Isabel scrubbed the mark, and we set the shirt in the sun to dry until the moment of departure. I tied the bicycles to the jib sheets, and lowered them to the ground. We rode through the Roman gates of the harbour, pushed our bicycles up the narrow streets climbing to the ramparts of the old town and, mounting again, hurried along the shore to Cap d'Antibes. It was perhaps thirty minutes ride. The morning was still hot, but there was more than a hint of mistral, for the sky was glazing and fingers of pale cirrus were appearing to the north-west. Stoneeagles sat on columns at the entrance wearing boas and bloomers of green creeper. We negotiated an avenue deeply gravelled and clearly not laid for the convenience of cyclists. Iron gates barred our passage, and the lodge-keeper opened one of them to let us through. Isabel was in favour of riding on, but I persuaded her that it would be easier to leave the bicycles at the lodge and follow footpaths to the house. A pelouse formed a wide vista to the front door. An elderly gardener was planted in the middle of the grass like a statue with a slow clockwork movement. Near him a watering machine cast its glistening lance into the sunlight.

After lunch we hurried back to the boat on our bicycles, dressed ourselves in old rags, and set to work. I had dismissed the workers assuming with too ready optimism that the second coat of anti-fouling would be as easy to put on as the first. But the new paint was treacly. The paint-brushes had to be pushed with two-handed jabs, and it was most difficult to cover the surface in anything like a thorough manner. While Isabel, brave spirit, was struggling with her brush the foreman came back to the yard to jeer at us. If he had been agreeable then, and if he had offered to bring back his men, we should have accepted, but his meanness strengthened and embittered our resolve. We worked until darkness made it impossible to see the brushes in our hands, and we tumbled into bed with only one-seventh of the bottom painted. But while we slept my brain, like a states-man's, sought compromise.

The answer was a chemical one. At 5 a.m. I was doctoring the anti-fouling, thinning the paint with petrol. I thinned as much as I dared, bearing in mind that the anti-fouling was our only protection against the boring worm, the teredo, that infests the warmer seas. We both worked in leather gloves, for our hands had blistered the night before. At 11 a.m. Isabel brought a dish of peaches, greengages, melons, and green figs. We stopped work for ten minutes to ward off thirst and hunger. I was again covered with paint, but Isabel, a clean worker, remained almost spotless. When we resumed work she began to paint the difficult bit, cutting into the white waterline, while I struggled on with the bottom. It was nearly completed at 2 p.m., when we ate a loaf of bread, a six-egg omelette and more fruit, and drank a litre of claret. We had finished the serious work, and had knocked off to consume a late tea when Maso Waleners was lifted from his car, placed in an invalid chair, and wheeled into *Truant's* shadow. Isabel carried a cup of tea down the ladder to him, and suggested that we knew him well enough to talk to him while we continued with our work, which had to be finished before nightfall. His face had always been inscrutable and now, because of the terrible illness which had attacked him during the war years when he had been obliged to leave France and return to his native America, the remainder of his heavy body matched the face in immobility. Tired though we were, he must have envied us our activity. While we worked he told us of a broken marriage and of his new recipe for fruits raffraichis. The recipe was scarcely delivered when the Admiral arrived to ask most kindly if he might be of any assistance. The Admiral is tall and active, with grey hair, beautiful manners, and a resounding naval voice. He spoke with warm approval of the action of the American Government in sending its largest aircraft carrier, the *Franklin D. Roose-velt*, on a visit to Jugoslavian waters following the loss of an American civilian aeroplane, shot down in peacetime by Marshal Tito's fighter aircraft.

"That is what I call diplomacy," he said. "There isn't enough of it nowadays."

Isabel and I went on with our work, keeping our opinion of such

179

"diplomacy" to ourselves. But Maso appeared to agree.

"We've entered the age of refrigerated discomfort, streamlined ugliness and expensive incompetence, and it's a relief, a pleasant whiff from the past, to hear of such a delightfully Victorian manœuvre as this mission of the *Franklin D. Roosevelt*," he said. "Take my case, to explain what I mean. When I got ill in America it was decided that I should have the services of a male nurse. The first male nurse got drunk and was sick over my bed. The second male nurse got drunk and beat me up. The third male nurse was paid fifteen dollars a day; he was untrained, and he had to have five afternoons off in the week because he was taking ballet lessons; he had a broken nose and bad breath. Don't you think that's an awful story?"

*   *   *   *

When the 7 a.m. hooter went on Monday we were both on deck to watch the arrival of the workmen. Their laborious pretence not to notice *Truant's* smartly finished bottom was some repayment for two days of hard work. In a few moments we had raced down the slips into the water, and at once three painters began to prepare our topsides for fresh coats of black paint, while an electrician began to alter the wiring in the engine-room. The painters chipped and scraped away all the blisters and then covered over certain places with lead paint. Isabel was greatly upset by the temporarily spotty appearance of *Truant*.

"Better to have patches of grey paint than all the blisters," I argued.

"It may be better from the technical point of view, but it looks as though it has measles, or has been badly camouflaged."

The Duke of Windsor drove himself along the quay that evening. His arrival coincided with the drawing-up on the slip of the bateau-de-commerce from Monte Carlo, which was the largest vessel ever to be hauled out there. A crowd which had gathered to witness the operation unanimously transferred its attention to the Duke and, turning with curious cries, surged towards *Truant* and ringed round her gangway. They were almost instantly dispersed by three tremendous explosions from the mole near-by, where engineers were still detonating the German-laid mines, and in places were blasting the ancient walls so that they might be safely rebuilt. Stones showered over our decks and the quay; when these had ceased to fall, a German prisoner, who was working on the motor-boat lying next to *Truant*, began to smooth down ten square feet of rough mahogany with a rotating electrical device. The Duke took all of this most calmly, but his cairn terrier was sorely distressed, and had to be carried to the car before he would be silent. There could be no doubt about the

Duke's interest in the boat. Nobody, including myself and the surveyor, ever examined *Truant* more carefully. When he had seen the working parts he climbed across our berth to read the titles of the books on a shelf. The Duchess, who arrived a little later, was shocked, although she struggled politely to conceal it, by the smallness of *Truant*, and she frequently urged me not to go too far away from land, and to take Isabel into a port every night.

✼   ✼   ✿   ✻

The concierge at the yard was a handsome fellow with a straight back and a straight eye in his head. He had passed his youth and early middle age in the cavalry and for many years before the war had been a member of the Garde Républicaine, which recruits no man lower than a non-commissioned officer in the French Army. When the Germans arrived in Paris they took full advantage of the horses of the Garde Républicaine, and our friend found that he was frequently detailed to act as a groom for the conquerors, taking horses out to the shady alleys of the Bois de Boulogne and waiting there until they were returned, lathered, by the German officers. So he resigned from the regiment, and moved down to the Midi, where at least there were no Germans to offend his racial pride.

"If the director of the yard hadn't given me this job we should have been in grave difficulties. It isn't a highly paid position; all the same, there's a house with it, and it carries a lot of responsibility. But no sooner were we settled here than the Germans occupied the whole of France, and I had them around me once more. I might just as well have stayed on in the regiment."

"You'll return to it."

"No. They won't have me back. Those who stayed on can't understand why I left."

His wife did our laundry. One day while she was ironing she put a sheaf of photographs into my hand. Most of them were group photographs showing units of the Garde Républicaine, very stiff, handsome, and disciplined. In many of the treasured photographs the husband did not figure; but his captain did, or his colonel, or other members of his troop or squadron. There in the boat-yard they were far, far from the stables and the jingling walk of the cavalrymen. I reflected that if the world survives the next century or two and a state of peace exists, then the faithful love of a man for his regiment will be one of the small things that will go to swell the worthwhile price of peace.

16

WE sailed from Antibes on August 30th; the east wind teased the sea into intoxicating greens and whites to show off our new coat of black and gold and the sunshine caught in our white sails. *Truant* was the poorest of performers to windward, but the day was too splendid for motors, so we wallowed far out to sea and, hours later, approached the land to the west of Cap d'Ail.

I looked at the rash of villas along the littoral. Villas in plots, like cabbages, like turnips and parsnips and beetroot; like tombs, like incinerators, like chapels, like factories for making false hair, imitation leather, chromium-plating, mass-produced tobacco, and unspeakably sordid rubber goods; like a dispersed, bomb-proof system for destroying mankind. In that area the more sensible towns appeared to have taken refuge from the contagious rash sprouting so profusely near the sea; those towns which still lived crouched on the points of hills, and the bigger agglomerations near the sea were no longer towns, but places conquered by the villas and taken over, another part of the dispersed, bomb-proof system for self-annihilation. The visitors to the villas floated, decayed— but never quite worthless—débris, where the sea met the land.

Both of us were tired of nights in harbour. But the weather was uncertain. We made for Monte Carlo.

Monte Carlo harbour is approximately square in plan; it is spacious and the water inside is clear and bright blue; solid quays, clean and prosperous, surround it, and from them the town appears to climb in a rococo staircase to some kind of heaven. Yachts were lying on our starboard hand as we entered. They were a more impressive collection than any we had seen since leaving England. *Elpis* lay among them. Fortunately we had studied the *Mediterranean Pilot*, which had informed us that the water in that harbour is exceptionally deep. We dropped anchor closer to the quay than usual, and Isabel took *Truant* astern with supreme artistry. Mr. Bundy, following English practice, had made our stern gangway on the strong and the heavy side. However, I had fitted a sling to the outer end, the top of the sling was shackled to the mizzen halyards purchase, and Isabel was able to hold the weight of the gangway with the purchase while I pushed it outboard and dropped its inboard swivelling hinge into the socket in the transom.

Our immediate neighbours that evening were the small cutter, *Winibelle*, in which the Frenchman, Marin Marie, had sailed across the Atlantic single-handed, and a schooner of about twice *Truant's* size which had formerly been owned by an Englishman and which still, though under new ownership, flew the Red Ensign (perhaps because the luxury tax on French citizens owning yachts is extremely heavy). *Winibelle* had changed hands after her Atlantic crossing and was occupied by a French trio whose acquaintance we had made in Antibes. The owners were a handsome young married couple and the third party on board was a curly-haired youth who seldom was dressed in anything more than was strictly necessary to cover his reproductive organs, and who was apparently the paid crew, since he was always referred to by the owners as "the mousse". He did most of the work on board, even cooking, when the owners had not gone away in their car to some more fashionable spot. *Winibelle* is of Norwegian double-ended shape, and as they had no stern gangway but chose to lie stern-on like the rest of us, they had nailed a piece of motor-car tyre to the upper parts of their rudder, and they hauled in on their stern lines until the rudder, protected superficially by the tyre, rubbed against the quay. Poor *Winibelle's* deck was so badly in need of caulking that when rain came, as we were to see later, the occupants only kept moderately dry by taking all the sails and spreading them over the yacht.

Further along the line was the handsome Bermudian ketch, *San Domenico*, built in Italy to an English design with a British officer of the Naval Reserve on board, his Italian wife and her fair-haired son, who, at the age of five, could haul himself hand over hand up the bare steel wire of the forestay. They had two delightful Neapolitan yacht hands.

Then came the big schooner *Aloha*, French-built and with many harbour comforts. We could watch dinner parties held on deck there, beneath the sky-blue awnings and with lights gleaming on silver and glass and white linen, and the faces and shoulders of the sunburned women looking almost negroid against their pale clothes.

Next to that luxurious boat was a more interesting one, a small Breton yawl from la Rochelle. She had sailed round the coast with two youths on board, and they were having the hell of a time. The Bretons had just returned from a trip with two women to the island of Corsica. One of the youths described the trip to me in a few words. "First day, the wind came. Second day the wind increased and the tarts, who'd been sick from the outset, began to scream. Third day we sighted Corsica, but the engine wouldn't go so we sailed around the island. Fourth day we decided to return to Monte Carlo. Seventh day we dropped anchor here. It was all right; but those tarts were only a damned nuisance." Their boat was beamy, rather box-shaped, with rough, black topsides. Isabel christened her "the baby *Truant*", a fairly apt description. The Bretons were in no way dazzled by the opulent yachts surrounding them, but the owners, passengers and crews of the big yachts were not sure of the Bretons, regarding them rather as cheap and dangerous interlopers and possibly as an annoying challenge to adventure. For the majority of the rich men's yachts on that coast are very little used except in harbour.

One very big black schooner, Clyde-built to a Fife design, flew the Monegasque flag, belonged, it was said, to an Italian nobleman, and was chartered by an English industrialist. Her skipper, a Jugoslav, looked more like a lowland Scot than any Scot I ever saw. I wanted to ask him if he had Scottish blood in his parentage, but fought shy of doing so as he was an excessively muscular man who gave the impression that he held his emotions in check only by strong pressure of the muscles at each end of the jawbone. I preferred to think that he had come to have a Scottish look from caring for the old boat; her teak decks and hatches bore evidence to the skill, selection and patience that went into vessels built on the Clyde sixty years ago. Another yacht, almost as big, was a more modern but less beautiful Dutch staysail schooner, with a strange, inflated roundness to her. She flew the Swiss flag, and her owners, who also possessed motorcars over-garnished with that peculiarly hideous plating, chromium, were sometimes seen in her high deck house.

As I walked along the quay studying the different boats, and looking for practical hints in their rigging, I realised that I would not change old *Truant* for any of them, and that I found in *Elpis*, *Truant*, and the Breton yawl, qualities of strength and character absent from the opulent harbour crawlers. I deduced that I was beginning to learn something about boats.

The early night was serene but we were both awakened by a grinding noise from astern, a noise so terrible to my ears that it drowned the screeches of the wind, the hiss of rain, and the slap of waves. Pulling on my oilskin, I ran on deck. *Truant* had slewed round through eighty degrees, and was bumping her port quarter on the quay and her port side against *Winibelle*. I hauled in the anchor chain, tightening it with the gravest misgivings, for I had been told that much of the bottom of Monte Carlo harbour is stone, and affords poor holding ground. I had forgotten in my haste to button the oilskin and my body was soon streaming with cold rainwater. Isabel came to help, well covered in her yellow oilskin and sou'-wester.

"What time is it?" I shouted as we worked together on the windlass.

184

"Midnight. What's happened?"

"It's the mistral again."

"Do look at Douglas and Gwenda."

"The baby *Truant's* dragged her anchor by the look of it. She's swung round into *Elpis*. Gwenda doesn't sound pleased."

"Where did she learn those words?"

"Motor-racing, I expect."

"Well, I'm going below to bed. Come on."

"I'll have to wait and see if the anchor's dragging."

"If it drags we'll only bump into the quay again. Then you can come up and do something else." She went below. On all sides of us I saw men rowing forward into the darkness, paying out rope as they went. I remembered that two large mooring buoys were set out there. I got out a new coil of two-inch manilla from the sail-locker, dumped the coil in the dinghy, making fast one end to *Truant*, and rowed off. There was enough rope in the coil to take it through the ring of the buoy and have a double thickness. I saw that the Bretons had done likewise to the other buoy, and now *Elpis* was swinging into them. Gwenda was busy with a large coir fender. I went to bed. The rain was coming through the deck in a few places, two or three of them over our bunk. But the night was warm and I was soon asleep.

The wind had not abated in the morning, and we were glad to get off the boat, which was jumping in an irritating manner. The mistral has an unpleasantly wild strength in that harbour, for it penetrates the land defences, whistling down the twisted valley between the old town of Monaco and the hillside stringing that town and the new one of Monte Carlo into one agglomeration. We began the day well by pushing our bicycles up the hill to a shop where, Gwenda had informed us, we could buy red wine with our ration tickets. We had not been able to do this since being issued with the tickets at Rouen. Loading bottles into my rucksack and every conceivable receptacle that could be hung on a bicycle, we launched ourselves on the steep hillside, and descended rapidly to the harbour, our bottles clanking, our brakes squealing under the unusual weight, and pedestrians smiling at two foreigners so laden with one of the advantages of life in France. We rode off to Beaverbrook's villa, where we had hot baths. When we came out into the sunshine by the swimming pool Beaverbrook, stretched out in a chair in a blue-and-white linen cap, shaped somewhat like a jockey's cap but with a higher crown, hastily buttoned up his only garment, a pair of shorts.

"Was the water hot?" he asked.

"Boiling."

"Now you will want to bathe in the pool, I expect. It is too rough to swim in the sea to-day. You would be battered to pieces on the rocks."

Obediently, we undressed once more. When we left the pool Beaverbrook was still in his chair, a satyr only slightly overblown by advancing years. Strong grey hairs writhed over each pectoral bulge like snakes on the head of Medusa. He had told us ten days earlier that he intended to make a long stay in that "beneficial sunshine", yet we learned that he was already on the point of departure.

"I suppose that I prefer the life of action to the life of contemplation," he said, with the half-jovial, half-cynical smile that often inhabits or flickers across the lower half of his face. "Do you know how to use those French telephones, George?"

"No," I lied, for I knew that there were many more efficient helpers at hand. He soon had someone else putting in calls to Nice, Paris and London, and while he waited urgently for these calls to come through, he stood, bare toes splaying over the carpet, spouting memoranda into the dictaphone which darkly gleamed beside an antique desk.

The following day we rode our bicycles to Cap Ferrat with the intention of calling upon Somerset Maugham. It was a long, hard ride against the mistral. We circled the end of the Cap and then, gravity taking charge, swept downhill past the former house of Leopold II, King of the Belgians, and so to water level at the port of St. Jean. We chose to eat at a very small restaurant. The only other clients were a pair of lovers. Both had faces that looked to be near explosion point, the explosives being a compound of red meat, red wine, spleen, and lust. Their conversation pursued no even tenor.

"Let me be," she said. "I haven't finished my salad yet, and it's good for me."

"Don't talk in my embrace."

"Ssh! Why can't you behave like a shontelmann?"

"Shall we try the camembert?"

"No. As for me, I want framboises à la crème."

"You're joking! Framboises à la crème cost 110 francs. You know you can have anything you want within reason."

"Is reason enthroned again? Oh! you men of business! When you have ordered the framboises à la crème you may kiss me."

"Anything else, but not framboises."

"Very well then. I'll have crêpes Robespierre."

"One hundred and eighty!" he said peevishly. "It makes me giddy.

You used to get the earth for that. You could live carefully for three days in Paris for that. You wish to spend it on crêpes Robespierre which will only be an inferior product of the pharmacist's laboratory! No, no, and no! It is not as though we came here to have a luxurious meal. We came to mix pleasure with a little food. One thing at a time, my friend, and remember that this little holiday is in the nature of a partnership. When my money—or at least the money set aside for this purpose—is gone, back I go to my desk and you to your work. That was agreed, was it not?"

"Haven't I made you happy?"

"Most happy. Is that any reason why I should throw away my money on crêpes Robespierre?"

"Last night you declared that you would lay the earth at my feet."

"And so I would. But in order to conquer the earth I need judgment and the knowledge when to say no."

"So it is 'no' to my crêpes Robespierre?"

"It is emphatically 'no' to your crêpes Robespierre."

"Think again on that point, my friend, I advise you." She had withdrawn from all contact with him, and sat rigidly upright, her thick young fingers resting on the edge of the table as though she were playing the piano and leaning on a chord.

"Listen to me. When I have made up my mind, my mind is made up."

"Try to be clever; that's right. You think that you can laugh at me. Well, let me tell you, I can laugh at you. You're mean, and there's nothing more shoddy than a mean fellow. Yesterday when we examined the windows with their little shoes and dresses and ornaments did you think that I was so stupid that I didn't notice how relieved you looked when I lied and said that nothing pleased me? You hadn't even offered to buy me a handkerchief or a small cup with a design on it. Digest this, my friend, nothing in the world is free, not even meanness. And this time your meanness is going to cost you . . . *me*! Good-bye." She rose from the table, a dumpy, soft figure, turned on him a face flushed unbecomingly with the effort of so long a declamation and stamped from the room. He waited until the sound of her high, wooden-soled shoes had died. Then he called for coffee and his bill and turned to look at our table. Chancing to catch my eye, he winked.

"Les femmes! Les femmes!" he said, not bitterly, but with a certain philosophical delight in the waywardness of women that quite took my fancy. When he had left the restaurant the waiter came for our orders.

* * * *

187

The sea was much too grey for bathing; the afternoon was sultry, and Alpine teeth stretched up to the vulnerable, damp bellies of thunderclouds. We sat digestively in deck chairs set on the strip of pebbles that passed by the name of *plage*. From the café immediately behind us tawdry music came from a machine. When it was time to go we roused each other with a great deal of stretching and liverish yawning, and I pushed the bicycles up the hill.

Considering that he had not the slightest idea what had brought us there beyond a perhaps impertinent curiosity, and with the name of mutual friends as our only introduction, Mr. Maugham was very polite. He gave us tea.

We had gone to see Maugham because I admire his work. I liked him; and the realisation of his presence in no way spoiled but rather enhanced my appreciation for what he has accomplished. He had been charming to us. But I could not help feeling as we left the house that ability, character and good manners surround a man—especially at tea-time—with barriers that no stranger can pass; it was as though he stood on the highest ramparts of a castle, and I on the ground, at the outer edge of the moat, and we conversed according to the formulæ of chivalry. It was certainly true that, although I knew all of Maugham's writings that had been published and there is a very large amount of himself in them, I felt that I knew him less well than the rather unpleasant person who had chanced to occupy the next table in the restaurant at St. Jean, and whose only words to me had been, "Les femmes! les femmes!"

*   *   *   *

This was not my first visit to Monte Carlo, and I was disconcerted to realise how much I liked the place. From our home on the lively water of the harbour we were able to make not over-prolonged excursions to savour the strangenesses and the comforts of the town. While we were in that harbour the autumn month of September came in. We saw and heard of people leaving for the winter countries where money is made and business done.

The French authorities are usually at pains to make the interiors of their post offices as dismal as possible, dark, dull caverns of masonry smelling of dust and sour bodies, with savagely ill-tempered faces emerging from the gloom behind the guichets. In the period following the war the faces were more savage than ever, for post office salaries were sadly inadequate to cope with the increased costs of living. Monte Carlo, though, tries hard to remember that it is Monte Carlo and, as you would expect, the main post office, there, is more light and airy than most. The place is usually very full of customers, many of them English, old gentlemen and old ladies from another century; narrow trousers, long skirts; high white collars, opal tie-pins, curly-brimmed bowlers; lorgnettes, black stockings, a black patch on a white-powdered chin; watch-chains and lockets, lavender gloves and gardenias; a cane from Malacca, card cases from India, sable stoles from Russia. They move slowly to the counters and their hearts are stiffened to the abuse that may come with a stamp for two francs fifty or a letter from the Poste Restante. Some of the old people are comfortably off, and some are desperately poor. Some have soft, angelic faces, and others the expressions of turtles about to be fed. Some have servants or paid companions or expectant relatives to help them have done with life, while others are surrounded by that touching nimbus of a loneliness that is feeble and unreprisive, the loneliness that comes to old people sensitive enough to realise that they are no longer wanted by those whom they have loved. Those are the people who are most at home in Monte Carlo. They are the complement to the horse carriages for hire, old horses and drivers nodding in the sun, to the stucco buildings that were erected to express gaiety and wealth and somehow succeed in hinting at the transience of riches, to the black, Scottish-built schooner flying the Monegasque flag, skippered by a Jugoslav, owned by an Italian, and chartered by an Englishman, and to the unblinking, reptilian good manners of the professional staff of the casino. But even at Monte Carlo the swinging door of the post office will do its best to hit you in the face unless you hurry nimbly through. . . .

17

A HALF-DECKED fishing-boat moved from a berth at the far side of the harbour and came noisily alongside *Truant* during the night. The owner thrust his head out of the blankets at dawn, when I began to wash our deck.

"What will the weather be?" I asked him.

"East wind. That's why I moved. Not going to-day, are you?"

"Yes."

"How's the barometer?"

"Rising."

"That's bad, with the east wind. Very bad."

I filled our fresh-water tanks with a hose-pipe borrowed from the schooner *Aloha*. There was not enough wind to stir our burgee; the sunshine was yellow and warm. We were excited at the prospect of Italy. Isabel helped me lustily with the windlass. For those on land the sea does not fully exist; it is only something to look at or to smell or touch, a cooling agent, a nerve tonic, an aphrodisiac. Even for those in harbour the sea outside only half exists. At the harbour mouth we were astonished to find the sea black and menacing. The east wind that had blown during the night had but abated for the morning lull. It soon hastened back, whipping up an unpleasant head sea. We ran both engines, but conditions were such that we could go no faster than three knots. *Truant*, with her considerable beam, behaved in a manner that gave us confidence. The decks were too wet for Isabel to lie on her mattress. She was very ill. Between bouts she explained that so far we had travelled unintelligently on the sea; we had made our departures correspond with our interests on land. In future, she said, we should travel on smooth days with following or fair winds, and the weather—instead of social engagements—would dictate our movements.

An extraordinary Englishwoman who had stepped from her Rolls Royce in Monte Carlo to ask us: "What about giving us a ride on your yacht?" had volunteered a good deal of information about San Remo, across the Italian frontier. She said that it made her "flaming mad", the amount of food that she had seen there, and the quantities of clothing in the shops. "Of course," she had added, "you won't be able to go there because there's no harbour; there was one, but the Germans blocked it with a big ship, and the Italians are doing nothing about it."

We had great difficulty in distinguishing the harbour mouth in the line of foam surmounted by spindrift that marked the shore, and we were obliged to move on, well to the east of it, before putting about to take the high seas under us for the run in. When we approached the damaged mole we saw the wreck of which the Englishwoman had spoken, a big ship, sunk close inshore, with all the deck-line showing above the waves. Only a narrow entrance channel remained, but obstacles that are plainly seen are seldom to be feared. The sea worsened, as seas usually do in shoal water, and I was glad that it was Isabel, and not I, who steered us into the narrows. Inside, we saw only one short undamaged length of quay, and that was occupied by the smart ketch *San Domenico* and by the sloop *Cyrano*, which we had seen at St. Tropez. *Elpis* was anchored in the middle of the harbour, and Gwenda, cupping her hands, shouted to us that they had tried lying at the quay but had found it "fiendishly uncomfortable". Isabel brought *Truant* round in a tight circle, and I dropped anchor in four fathoms, well sheltered by the German wreck.

Although we had only travelled seventeen miles, and there is more Italian blood and influence in the south of France than either France or Italy cares to admit, we were in a vastly different land. The first thing that struck us was the number of men at work on the harbour repairs and the vigour and spirit with which they attacked the work. We could not but feel that before their impetus the port would come alive again and the terrible wounds showing in the buildings of San Remo would soon heal. The same energy was going into the repairing of a coastal steamer which had been salvaged from the bottom of the harbour. The fishermen did not scull from the stern like those across the frontier, but stood swinging behind two narrow-bladed oars, the blades of which faced nearly skywards through the stroke. I had spent two years as a prisoner-of-war in Italy, and as a prisoner I had learned to love the country and its people. It was with the deepest excitement, the utmost sense of privilege, that I set a free foot on the quay of San Remo.

The harbour master, young, and conscious of his responsibilities and the smart blue-and-gold uniform that went with them, wrote down endless details about us and our boat. "You will need eleven lire to pay the customs," he said to me, "and as you will have had no opportunity to obtain Italian money and the banks are closed to-day, do me the honour of permitting me to give you the eleven lire." He was worried that we had no Admiralty instructions about the minefields. "I should be doing less than my duty if I allowed you to sail from here without full details of the mine agglomerations. Will you promise me to go straight from here to Oneglia down the coast? The commandante del porto there will give you further assistance." I promised. "Word of honour?"

"Yes."

"You have made me very happy."

Soon after we arrived the Hawkes hoisted their pretty tanned mainsail and departed for Oneglia.

During the night a yellowish dust settled on *Truant* and covered every surface so closely that when I went on deck to wash down I at first took the dust for salt that had dried on the boat after her rough passage from France. We went into the market and bought vegetables and fruit and well-remembered but long untasted delicacies like gorgonzola and bel paese, salami and prosciuto crudo. Italy being a vanquished country, the exchange was more in our favour than in France, and all the goods we bought were about half as expensive as in France. We had intended to wait another day in San Remo, but in the evening the tawny dust from the ruins began to choke us, and we decided that we could stay no longer. After a glance at the burgee, I hoisted the mainsail, and went joyfully forward to get the anchor. Shouts from the wheelhouse attracted my attention. Hard puffs of wind, which were being reflected in some manner from the harbour works, were filling the mainsail, and pushing *Truant* against the wreck. Fortunately Isabel did not wait for any answer from me. Starting both engines, she somehow managed to bundle *Truant* into the entrance channel, and we did no worse than scrape the rusty side of the wreck with the squaresail yard and the end of the boom. We had managed to slide out of an awkward predicament which taught me a good deal about how and when to hoist the mainsail in a constricted space.

Oneglia lies nineteen sea miles to the east of San Remo, and we soon realised that it had been the height of folly to sail so late in the day because, apart from the danger of floating mines, which can easily be avoided in daylight, we had been told that the port of Oneglia had not sufficiently recovered from its war-time battering to show any light. We kept well out to sea, carefully studying the coastline with the help of our charts and the outlines shown in the *Mediterranean Pilot*. As the light died we were able to get a bearing on what we judged to be the harbour entrance, still some eight miles distant. We lit the navigation lights, and steered into the darkness with considerable misgivings. After several false alarms, for imaginary coastlines kept appearing in the darkness ahead, we knew that we really were approaching the shore by the shortening and stiffening of the swell beneath us. I stood in the bows, the lead line in my hands; we moved gently ahead, using one engine. I heard Isabel's voice.

"What is it?" I called aft. Through a wheelhouse window I saw her face, ethereal in the gentle, rising light from the binnacle.

"Can you smell smoke?"

A light flickered ahead, flickered again, nearer, nearer. I saw that it came from the phosphorescent puddles made by two oarblades. I shone a torch into a boat-load of fishermen.

"You are in great danger," one of them said when we had finished with preliminaries and introductions.

"I thought so."

"A big ship is sunk in the harbour entrance. You must follow us and we will guide you in."

They rowed so slowly that we were unable to follow them and keep steerage way.

"Faster," I kept shouting to them. "Go a little faster, please." Then I would have to signal with my torch to Isabel, for she was unable to see them from the wheelhouse. Suddenly there were yells from ahead.

"*Terra! Terra!*"

"Astern!" I shouted, and white water frothed past the bows as both engines jerked us back. Swinging the torch ahead, I made out the silhouette not of land but of the masts, funnel and bridge structure of a sunken ship. The fishermen led us over to a corner of the harbour where *Elpis* was anchored. We were thankful to hear the chain run out. Gwenda and Douglas came rowing hastily across, rather annoyed with us.

"You must be mad," Gwenda said in her penetrating voice. "Fancy trying to enter such a place after dark!"

*   *   *   *

When it was day we awoke and went out on deck, and looked sadly around us at ruins. The most cheerful sight in the harbour, apart from our two slightly incongruous yachts, was a line of minesweepers, corvettes handed over by the British to the Italian Navy, lying side by side at a quay like so many toy ships made of lead. A message came from the commandante del porto. Would I have the goodness to report immediately with my ship's papers and the identity papers of the crew. He was a stout, wheezy man, with a sad expression and an automatic pencil of which he was inordinately proud.

"What a way to travel with your wife!" he said when he had taken all the necessary details concerning our birth, parentage, marks and scars, and reasons for the journey. "I cannot see myself making such a journey on a boat, and after all, I am in the Navy, a sailor by profession."

"Where would you go if you had free choice?"

"To Milan," he said, moving his automatic pencil swiftly across the blotting paper, and drawing a tramcar that seemed to shudder with movement, to tremble and nearly burst with the expanding pressure of the people inside it "Supposing I could go to Milan, I'd want the money to go into production. I've no political beliefs, but I'm full of theories on man-management. Labour problems are all-engrossing to me, so long as I'm free to look at them from the employer's point of view, of course. I'd manufacture soap or cigarettes or sausage or wine, anything useful . . ."

"You draw well," I said. "Your tramcar is very good. I can hear it and smell it."

"That's a child's scribble," he said scornfully. "You're interested in art?"

"Yes."

"Then I'll show you something. I'm no amateur. I sell my pictures." He walked to the back of the office, where two beds of the type usually seen in hospitals, with tubular metal ends, white-enamelled, stood in a recess. He kept his water-colours in a big folder between the springs and the mattress of his bed. "This was my last ship. Four funnels, you see, giving it a formidable appearance, but the food was poor. This is a war memorial, a country one, near Legnago. And this is a belfry in Oneglia. Although these are only sketches, they show you what I can do." They did: his tramcar was infinitely better than any of the three careful water-colours. "If I had a little capital I might make a great thing of life in Milan," he said. "But destiny probably rules that I remain in this office until my eyes fall from their sockets and my will rots." He had been tiresomely officious over the business of our papers.

"What happens to all this information that you have collected from me?" I asked. "Who requires to know that my father's names were Thomas Andrew, and that I was born in the year that the King Emperor George V ascended his throne?"

He pushed the automatic pencil into one ear and looked sideways at me. He was a good fellow, and he could not resist telling me how important it all was. "It's telegraphed to Rome, *in cipher*," he said.

"But the same information was taken from us the day before yesterday at San Remo. Would that also be telegraphed to Rome?"

"Without a doubt."

"How long will it take you to code the message?"

"About one hour."

"I regret that we give you so much trouble."

"Oh, for that matter, I have little else to do; the minesweepers look after themselves, and the rest of the harbour is no trouble at all." He ran his pencil savagely through the tramcar. "Do you like to go to the cinema?"

"Occasionally."

"There's a film to-night, an American film with an actress who, my assistant assures me, shows great powers of emotion. Will you and your wife come as my guests?"

"Thank you very much, but we're going to work on our boat all day, and then we'll go early to bed, for to-morrow we must leave Oneglia."

"Would you like me to find an Italian sailor for you? He'd cost you very little above his food, and he'd do all the work."

"We prefer to do it ourselves."

He looked at me to see if I was making game of him, and beneath his uniform his stomach heaved in a long sigh of incomprehension and frustration. He had not been able to tell me much about the mine-fields, but he had drawn on my chart the swept route to the next port, Savona. Beyond Savona? he shrugged his shoulders. On leaving his office I walked a little through the town. It was Sunday, and the young people, freshly washed, were pacing the harbour front and the narrow streets behind. It broke my heart to see them so cheerful and natural among the ruins, and I hurried back to the boat.

We left Oneglia at six in the morning, under mizzen and headsails only. We were headed by another east wind, and we were obliged to keep to the narrow channel between the flagged buoys marking the inshore limits of the outer minefields and the lines on my chart indicating, according to the commandante del porto, the locations of clumps of shallow, anti-invasion mines. During the morning I saw *Elpis*, looking like a long pole, upright in the sea eight miles astern, but the distance separating us gradually widened until she was lost to view. Although the Mediterranean is tideless enough to make navigation wonderfully simple, currents are frequently met, and that day we found the sea very disturbed off the headlands. We entered Savona harbour in the early afternoon, pushed on through into the inner basins, and hastily put about, for the place was an inferno. When I had taken careful soundings to find a stretch of bottom unfouled by wreckage, we dropped anchor in the outer harbour. Isabel began to cook a meal, and I rowed into the harbour in the dinghy. I passed American and South African freighters and was bombarded with proposals from sailors who wished to sell me cigarettes, bread, meat and chocolate. I climbed from the dinghy at some curved steps so handsome that they ennobled every boat that approached them. A great many small boats were bobbing near the steps, and I made the dinghy fast among them.

Two young Italian naval captains sat in a long office. The windows offered a spectacular view of the port, lying below like a mortally wounded animal with its entrails spilling from its body, and ants and larger scaly insects bustling over, round, and in, the corpse. I talked to the two officers for a considerable time in my doubtful Italian. They said that the mine situation was "very gloomy". There was a channel leading down the coast which had been swept, and which was daily patrolled by aircraft. We must follow that channel, they said, and then each port had a narrower channel leading into it from the main trunk. They gave me printed directions from the British Admiralty stating the courses that must be steamed from point to point. Then, as a crowning gesture of goodwill they presented to me their office's only up-to-date master chart of the minefields. "Think nothing of it," one of them said. "I shall order a car and go to look for another chart in Genoa to-morrow. You are doing us a favour by accepting this chart, for a trip to Genoa makes a pleasant change from Savona." Elated by my small success, I hurried back to the handsome steps. The dinghy had disappeared. The harbour was big, and very busy with small boats. When I had looked for a considerable time, I saw our dinghy about half a mile away. Three small boys were in it; they did not know how to row with British sculls and rowlocks, and they were bumping heartily into the boats around them. A row of people stood behind me, on the higher level immediately above the steps. I cleared my throat, confused between anger and embarrassment.

"Do any of you ladies and gentlemen know the three boys who have taken my little boat?" Their faces became solemn and dead. Some of them stared at me, while others looked uneasily in the direction of the boat. "How can I get my little boat back?" I asked plaintively.

"Only by shouting," suggested a scraggy little man, and forthwith he began to shout himself. If I had not feared that I might offend him with my clumsy Italian, I should have asked him to stop. His voice was weak, and he looked under-nourished. He kept moving nearer the boat, rising on his toes each time that he shouted. Occasionally he would look round at me, and I would smile, and nod encouragingly.

Since I had been a prisoner in Italy, my instinctive reaction on seeing a carabiniere was to slink away, but when a carabiniere roughly ordered my shouting friend to be silent I felt that I must intervene. I explained the situation to the policeman. He looked slowly at the dinghy, twitched the carbine with its folded bayonet that swung on a yellow-leather strap from his shoulder, thrust his hands into hairy (surely excruciatingly hairy) grey-blue breeches, and told me that the water was not his province. My small helper renewed his shouts. I caught the carabiniere by the arm, and told him that unless he took steps to recover my dinghy for me I would report him to "my friend" the commandante del porto as well as to the American authorities, and I would also see that the three boys were imprisoned for the theft of my boat.

"Whose is the boat?" asked the carabiniere.

"It is mine."

"Where was it made? How did it get here? What's your name?" But as he was beginning to trundle his mind along trained official channels a large woman stepped from the row behind the steps.

"If I get you your boatlet will you take no reprisals against the boys?"

"None, signora, only get me the boat."

She opened her mouth and roared. Her voice gushed and billowed from the depths of her body. As she shouted children gathered around her, impudent, ragged boys and girls, shy, clever and vicious, like small collie dogs. The noise took a little time to reach the comprehension of the three boys in the dinghy. Then we saw them turn to look in our direction. The woman continued to shout. They clumsily turned the boat and began to move nearer. But as they approached the steps, they halted with increasing frequency to look doubtfully at me, at the woman, at the carabiniere, and then down at the strange boat that they had borrowed, a boat with oddly clean yellow planking, dark-brown thwarts, and a little brass plate with some foreign words on it let into the transom. At last they came nervously to the steps. There were dirty foot-prints all over the dinghy, and one of the oar-blades was chipped. The three boys cringed back as I leaned forward and caught hold of the painter.

"Get out!" I said. I was enraged by the dirt on the boat, and their cringing further angered me. "Get out!" I caught hold of the nearest by his collar, and heaved him to the bottom step. He was so light for his size that my anger fizzled out. The other two scowled at me as sharply fierce as weasels. "I won't hurt you," I said. "If you'd asked me to let you take the boat for a few minutes I'd have lent it to you . . ." There was a clatter, the dinghy rocked under my hand, and the two were gone, racing up the steps, showing bare feet and rent trousers. I pushed off from the steps, feeling the oar-handles greasy and unfamiliar in my hands. I remembered the little man who had shouted so kindly on my behalf.

"Momento, signor!" I fished in my pocket for the only thing of value

197

that I had brought with me from *Truant*, a packet of cigarettes. He beamed with pleasure when he saw the packet, with its picture of a bearded sailor. He moved to a quieter part of the quay, and gestured to me to throw the cigarettes to him. My aim was true enough; the packet sailed through the air, but there was a whizzing noise from one side, and as it was about to fall into the little man's hands one of the boys rushed between him and and me, snatched the packet out of the air, and continued down the street, swerving and dodging and never slackening speed. The little man took a few hesitating steps in pursuit, then stopped, and slowly turned to me. I showed him by signs that I had no more cigarettes. He blinked, and gave me a warm smile.

As I rowed back to *Truant* I looked at the shore, and it seemed that the ruins breathed with the vitality of tens of thousands of brats, vicious, hungry, rickety, but representing life reaching out its cunning fingers to survive.

*　　*　　*　　*

In the late evening we saw *Elpis* rolling outside the harbour mouth, with Douglas and Gwenda struggling to get the mainsail down. They were having trouble with the gaff jaws, which had jammed. We never had any difficulty of that kind because our gaff was hinged to a metal sleeve, a foot deep and lined with leather which I kept well greased. I doubt if Isabel and I could have sailed *Elpis*, for despite her deeper draft she was very unsteady compared with *Truant*, and there was no room in which to make mistakes on her narrower decks. Her rigging, generally, was more modern and more complicated than *Truant's*; also *Truant* was fitted with ratlines, and I think it is impossible to exaggerate the benefit to be derived from ratlines by a small crew on a long voyage. Almost every day I went aloft for some reason, and these constant visits to the airy part of the boat enabled me to watch the running and standing rigging so well that we only had one bad case of chafe, and that was in the halyard holding the heavy square-sail yard. It is easy enough, of course, to climb up the mast-hoops, if your mainsail is fitted with those old-fashioned but serviceable appendages, but when you climb up the hoops your position is precarious enough to prevent you from doing much useful work. The first time that I climbed to the masthead at Bursledon I was extremely scared by my exposed position, but when we reached Italy I had become accustomed to the exercise, and had no hesitation in going aloft in any conditions.

Elpis anchored near us, and Gwenda began to clean vegetables for their evening meal. Douglas came over in the pram to take a note of the minefields. He agreed with me that Savona offered the worst anchorage we had struck in the Mediterranean. The east wind was making things uncomfortable for us as it rolled a sea into the outer harbour.

At 3.39 a.m. Isabel woke me. "Hasn't the wind changed?" I went quickly on deck, and found that she was right. Our bowsprit, instead of pointing at the harbour mouth, pointed at the black silhouette of the land; there was an offshore breeze. We hoisted the mainsail, wound in the chain, pushed *Truant's* head round by holding the staysail aback, and sailed out of the harbour. We had worked in silence, for although we were now devoted to Douglas and Gwenda and their fine boat, there was always a certain rivalry between us, and we had not forgotten Gwenda's prognostication when they first met us at Corbeil, on the Seine, that they would easily outstrip us in the Mediterranean.

Truant, well-equipped with electric light, was a handy boat for night sailing. Few sensations could be more wonderful than sailing off an unknown coast on so fine a night. Isabel took the wheel while I set more sail. The offshore breeze was steady and warm. The coastline of the Gulf of Genoa displayed a surprising amount of artificial light. The northern curve showed in an arc that dipped below the horizon until, when we had sailed for two hours, the diadem that represented Genoa itself rose cluster by cluster from the dark sea.

While we were enjoying this spectacle and talking in half-tones, for even at sea night brings the feeling that there are eavesdroppers, we were hit by a tremendous gust of wind which must have rocketed out of the mountains, thirty miles to the north-east of our position. For a moment that seemed interminable *Truant* lay flat on her starboard side. The port preventer backstay carried away. A fierce sea, the worst by far that we had yet experienced, rose almost instantly. Isabel started both engines, and even with their aid had the greatest difficulty in holding the boat into the wind, for the sea rushed at us unevenly, beating our bows first to one side and then the other, and so the large headsails were constantly filling or, far worse, being taken aback and pressing us down again on the vicious water. The darkness was intense. It took me thirty minutes, fighting with every ounce of energy and intelligence, to get the mainsail down and lashed. Then the jib halyards jammed and the head of the sail wrapped itself around the standing rigging so firmly that I had to go aloft with a spike and unshackle it, while the loose sail shook at the boat as though it had determined to be the end of us. Then I found that the dinghy tow-rope, a new length of two-inch manilla, had wrapped itself round the starboard propeller. I hoisted the small staysail, and the moment it was sheeted-in I felt Isabel get control of the boat for the first time in a terrible hour, and off we went, sailing like mad with that insignificant sail. When we steadied on our course, which now had a good deal of south in it, I realised that the dawn had come during our ordeal, that Genoa from far out on that wild sea was very beautiful, and that Isabel—who said that she had been too frightened and too busy—had not been seasick. We gained the usual satisfaction from such an encounter with the elements, for although we had been stupidly caught napping in the Gulf of Genoa, we had managed to survive the fight, and (for an hour or so) we were duly grateful for the gift of life.

But the Mediterranean is a most fretful sea, and when the sun came bustling into the gulf with the heat of the day the wind abruptly left us. We started the port engine, and, rolling abominably on an oily swell that would not have disgraced the North Atlantic, made for the hammer-headed promontory behind which Portofino lies.

When we rounded the headland we seemed to turn a page. Portofino did not show a scratch from the war. The sea, shaped like a curved and pointed horn, pushed into the steep land. The inner edge of the curve was lined by the village itself, a quay with a background of high, delicately-coloured houses bending with the edge of the water to a small, three-sided cobbled square with a café and four restaurants, all with tables outside and awnings, and shops showing scarlet tomatoes and yellow oranges beneath an arcade. Boats were being painted and repaired on the fourth side of the square, which sloped to the sea. The point of the horn of water was filled with scores of small craft: fishing-boats, motor-boats, speed-boats, sailing-boats. The yachts lay out on the other side, where the woods came down to the sea, their bows pointing to the entrance and the Gulf of Rapallo beyond it, and their stern lines taken to rings in a rock that rose from the deep water of the harbour. We saw at once that the place was a shade over-dressed in the part of a simple fishing village; that extravagantly clothed men and women lay drinking on the balconies of the "simple fishermen's houses" along the quay; that the restaurants were clamorous for custom; but we breathed delightedly at every whiff of prosperity that came to us from the shore and the surrounding yachts, for we could swallow comfort, no matter how banal, after the ruins of San Remo, Oneglia and Savona.

It was fortunate for us, since the starboard engine was out of action and there was no wind, that this was an easy harbour to enter. We dropped anchor in fourteen fathoms and I carried off two warps in the dinghy, making them fast to the rock, and so we hauled her stern round. I dressed for bathing and dropped into the water to examine the propeller. I soon had the rope clear by pulling at the loose end and getting Isabel to give a few turns astern with that engine; we had had unmerited good fortune, for the bronze blades of the propeller were undamaged. I was able to examine the propeller almost as clearly as if the boat floated in air, and I swam under the length of the hull, which floated above me like some orange world. Before going ashore we erected the awnings and washed the deck. We ate in a cool restaurant with a floor of chequered tiles. The food was copious, and the wine was good; but after eating in France the cooking lacked edge. Looking at the provision shops in Italy, we saw that although there were more goods of all kinds, they were less carefully brought to market and less skilfully displayed than in post-war France.

We slept the afternoon away on deck. Sometimes the flutter of voices would ruffle my sleep, and once I heard, half-waking, the splash of an anchor and the rattle of chain. We woke in the evening when the dew was wetting our awnings. *Elpis* came chugging in, her sails beautifully stowed. When I had taken their stern lines ashore Douglas and Gwenda were full of their wild day's sailing in the Gulf.

Portofino is theatrical at night. There are two or three neon signs in the square; the lights are as soft beneath the awnings as the liquid voices of the people in and round the inlet. Lighted windows mysteriously float among the stars, the windows of villas high up on the hills, villas which during the day remain in hiding among the foliage.

*   *   *   *

Snuffling, and constantly dry-washing her hands, the proprietress waited for us in her dark shop. She explained that she had been in Genoa to buy scarves and sandals, shirts, shorts, and linen trousers, and she had been informed that we had several times found her shop door locked. She hoped that we understood; the thieves were so numerous and so adroit these days that each evening when she left the shop she was obliged to remove all the stock and set a "burglar-proof" alarm: "Otherwise they would take the floor and the counter, to say nothing of the looking-glasses and the electric light fittings. First it was the bombers, then the Germans, then the partisans, then the Allied soldiers, and now our own thieves. How lucky you are to come from a rich country." When we told her that Britain too had been impoverished by the war she laughed until the tears ran down her face, not with delight at this information, but because she did not believe us, and our protestations of poverty fitted her conception of the dissimulating Anglo-Saxon character. It often occurred to me as we sailed down the Italian coast to tell Italians how fortunate I thought they were to live in so lovely a country. Few of them would agree with this, some because they had never been able to compare their own with uglier lands, some because they were poor and hungry, some because they were rich and wanted to be richer.

*　　　*　　　*　　　*

An American who had been reared in New York, but who had flown away and settled in the north of Italy, once saw my sister at a dance in Scotland and said to his hostess: "Introduce me to that beautiful blonde." Hearing of his request a little later—and having what we are told is a normal and healthy unawareness of my sister's physical charms—I thought that the man who made it must be a little soft in the head. He was a smallish man, thickset and muscular, with a soft voice, a liking for navy-blue, and a kindly way of looking at people and life. He moved a little shyly among the downright, approachable, money-conscious Scottish bourgeois, who were probably not unlike the American people by whom he had been reared. He was very correct. There was nothing of the beachcomber about him in Scotland except perhaps his name, Harry Careless, and his liking for poetry that did not rhyme. He did not smoke, and he drank nothing but claret, sherry and port. "I've knocked off drink," he used to say. "I'm on the wine-wagon." But however kindly the people who offered Harry Careless hospitality, they soon dug out his rather strange background, and few people get more savour from saying ill of somebody behind his back than members of the Scottish middle-classes. At any rate, back there in Scotland I first heard the outline of the following story.

Harry had knocked about the north of Italy for some considerable time before he finally came to a stop in Rapallo, where he began to drink himself to death, a strangely positive occupation in that half-fossilised town. A rich old lady was beguiled by Harry's gentle ways, and by his blue eyes which were so naturally bright that no amount of brandy could dim them. She was very old, opinionative and self-confident, and on hearing one day that Harry had soused himself insensible, she went to his rescue. She drove in her carriage to the inn where he lived. Harry lay on his bed, too weak to move, sadly plagued by his recumbent position and by the state of his person, for his manners generally were impeccable. Before he knew what was happening he had taken several nosefuls of smelling salts, and had agreed to be moved as a guest to her villa.

"But you must sign the pledge," she said.

202

"Does that include wine?"

"Well, no, I suppose that you will have to drink a little wine with your meals."

"It's a deal, ma'm."

For a time Harry Careless was exceedingly unhappy and ill at the big villa. Would he play contract? No. L'Attaque? No. Mah Jong? No. Golf? No. Perhaps he liked sailing? No. Swimming? No. Why not go for a nice little walk? O.K. Harry's walks led him in certain fixed directions, and quite often when he returned to the villa there would be a bulge in one pocket, or he would carry some smooth object carefully wrapped in his overcoat. He became a show-piece at the villa, and the old lady was so glad to have his gentle, handsome presence in her house that she managed to convince herself that if dear Harry did possibly take a little nip now and then, he never took too much. Harry, for his part, did his best to cherish her illusions. But one day, when he had not appeared for breakfast, lunch, or tea, the old lady tapped on his bedroom door and, receiving no answer, went in. Harry lay unconscious on his bed. The room smelled atrociously of brandy. Three bottles, two of them emptied to the last drop, stood on the bedside table; a fourth floated, half-empty, in the cold soapy water of the bath in which he had been immersed when he decided to take a nap. She searched the room, finding seven more brandy bottles in different hiding places. Then she sent for her doctor, who advised her that it was a case of kill or cure, and not another drop. When Harry awoke from his coma, he took a drink from the glass at his bedside and tasted, for the first time in his life, barley water. "Can't I even have a glass of wine with my meals?" he asked a few days later. "No wine for the present, dear," the old lady answered. "Now drink your nice barley water." The doctor had insisted that, for Harry's sake, she must be the soul of firmness. He had told her that "the heart" was weak, and that more drink might kill the patient. She looked upon Harry as a sacred charge. She watched his movements. If he went out of doors she followed him. She was an active person for her age, and she was able to walk as fast and as far as her dear boy. Harry pined away under her care. The eyes that drink could not dim became small, angry, blue slits, and although he never lost his gentle good manners with the old lady, she heard that he was beginning to snap at the servants. Sometimes he would fall ill, and would lie sweating on his bed with his heart thumping so that she could see it if she turned back his pyjama jacket. The doctor maintained that it was a battle of wills, and that the old lady would win if she persevered. Perhaps she would have won if Harry had not broken the rules of their fiercely-friendly private battle. . . . One hot afternoon they went for a very long walk, and when they returned they drank iced tea in the loggia. Harry had been quiet all day. He was thirsty after his walk, and he accepted a second glass of tea, which was unusual for him. Then he asked to be excused, saying that he must go to his room. The old lady wondered why he had barely touched the second glass of tea, and why he had left a whole cucumber sandwich on his plate. After tea, she climbed to her own bedroom, listening as she passed Harry's door. She heard the dear boy moving inside. He really was such a good, sweet boy. But she was tired after that fine long walk, a little tired. . . .

She was brusquely awakened by a most unusual commotion. Somebody was ringing the brass hand-bell that had never been used since the children attained an age when they could be trusted to remember meal-times. And as she sat up in bed, wondering whether the world and her villa were coming to an end, the butler ran unceremoniously into the room and told her that the house was on fire. "Everybody must go outside," she said at once. "Human life is the only irreplaceable possession, and everything is thoroughly insured." On her way downstairs she opened Harry's door. The room was tidy and empty; so was his bathroom. She picked up the ivory-backed hairbrushes she had given him and threw them out of the window. When she went out into the mellow evening sunlight she saw Harry sitting on the urn in the centre of the gravel sweep. She hurried out to join him, but her words of joy at his safety were choked as she turned to look at her villa. Both ends were burning. The main central block was as yet undamaged.

"The fire brigade!" she exclaimed. "Where is that fire brigade?"

"It was the tea in the glass," Harry said. "It looked like brandy and ginger ale. Jeepers!"

She had no time to savour his strange remark. The Rapallo fire brigade, brassy, almost melting with heat and excitement, swept up the avenue. The chief jumped from the leading engine and began to issue a stream of orders in a loud voice. Everything was reassuringly efficient. From time to time the chief would turn to insist to the old lady that soon the water would come through the pipes, and then the fire would be soused. When the water did come nobody was holding the hose, but the chief himself picked up the nozzle to direct the water at the flames. Then Harry showed that he was in a very abnormal state of mind. He ran out from behind the old lady, and bit the chief's ear. He bit so fiercely that quite a large piece of ear came away in his mouth, and a lot of precious water spilled uselessly over the gravel and soused the flower beds.

It took the chief of police, the chief of the fire brigade, the doctor, and Harry a long time and much lucid argument and confession to convince the old lady that it had been Harry who had started the fire. She refused to send him to a "mental home"; instead she sent him to some friends in Scotland, and that was how I met Harry Careless. We met him in the summer, and that winter my sister and most of my family were in London. Harry also moved to London. He stayed in an ugly hotel in Piccadilly. He was an undemonstrative man, too intense, and perhaps a little too old for my sister, who had not then developed the character that was later to make her such a remarkable woman. I saw him from time to time in my mother's house, or in the Café Royal, where he frequently ate in the grill or sat in the café, drinking a glass of wine at a table near that often occupied, in those days, by Mr. Constant Lambert. Then somebody asked: "Where's Harry Careless?" and my sister said that he had returned to Italy, to Rapallo.

* * * *

Rapallo was within easy cycling distance of Portofino. I told Isabel about Harry, and we set off to look for him. It was a fine ride, with such a sparkle in the air that summer seemed everlasting. Rapallo was old-fashioned, smug, busy. We inquired in a tourist office, two banks, a restaurant, and eight bars for Harry Careless—the name was awkward to pronounce in Italian—but nobody appeared to be able to think back much before the war, and we picked up no trace of him. Then Isabel had the sensible idea that we should ask at the establishment of an English and American chemist. "The kind of shop that makes pick-me-ups," she said. The chemist and his son came from the back of the shop to look at us curiously.

"Harry Careless?" the son said. "Beveva molto?"

"That's him."

"Did you know him?"

"Yes. Where is he? Do you know?"

"He's here, in Rapallo."

"Good!"

"Wait. When he came back from Scotland he was quiet for a time, and only took a glass of wine with his food. He was painting, and often he made excursions into the country. The old lady with whom he had formerly stayed had gone, moved to Switzerland. He was always going to join her there—she kept on sending him postcards—but it was always "next week" with Harry. Well, one day we heard he was dead. He bought two dozen bottles of cognac, and he drank so much so fast that nothing could pull him round. He died drunk. He was a good scout. Some of us here clubbed together and bought him flowers and a stone. We tried to bury him like a gentleman. Want to see the grave?"

The stone was of that spongy pitted texture that you see in rock gardens. A marble plaque showed in gold Roman lettering the words:

HARRY CARELESS

OF

NEW YORK

We rode back to Santa Margherita. For years I had not given him a thought, yet that afternoon I would have given anything to have had him alive. We sat at a table beneath a sturdy arcade, and drank white vermouth. The café waiter led us to a restaurant in a back street. It was a good restaurant; the other clients were all commercial travellers. The two obscure little rooms with boarded floors and walls were hung with photographs of actors and actresses, singers and jugglers, all of whom appeared to have faced the lens in moods of ruminative sadness. We chose a table near the street door. A fruit stall was set in the arcade some ten yards from our door. A single, middle-aged man approached the stall. He looked a little timid, but he picked out his tomatoes one by one, and placed them in the weighing scales himself. The owner of the stall watched him carefully without a word. How often had Harry bought fruit for himself? Had he ever been in this street, in this restaurant? I longed to lay my head on the table and weep for Harry Careless.

*   *   *   *

We made a great many Italian friends, good and bad, in a few days at Portofino; we swam; we sailed in boats more responsive to the light airs than *Truant*; we sat in the café; we ate large meals and talked. We had a holiday.

18

It seemed that Portofino was unwilling to let us go, for our anchor hooked itself across the fluke of a mooring anchor of staggering dimensions, which we were just able to see, eighty feet below, when we put our heads close to the water. Several yacht hands helped to get the anchor clear, and their help cost us our last packet of cigarettes; from then on we should have to reward such helpers with money, a much less popular currency with recipients as well as with donors.

The sea was calm, with a slight swell, and we had no wind all day. A big aircraft carrier passed us, far out. She was American, and she did not bother us with signals. Isabel was in high spirits, and ate a good meal, bread, butter, salami, gorgonzola, tomatoes, peaches, grapes. When we were clearing the dishes we passed an Italian salvage ship, a converted trawler, made fast to a whole circle of rusty mooring buoys. She was working on the wreck below her, using a diver hung over the side in a steel observation chamber. Not long before we passed that way Allied aircraft had dived to machine-gun and shell the coasting schooners and fishing-boats with the crews of which we were now so friendly. At 3 in the afternoon, thirty-five miles from Portofino, we turned through the narrowest of passes to Porto Venere, at the mouth of that important naval base, the Gulf of Spezia. Porto Venere tumbled about a harbour so crowded that there was no room for *Truant*. We anchored in the roadstead, under the balconies of the Albergo Belvedere. Isabel went below to cook; I rigged a table on deck and began the unpleasant task of correcting proofs sent to me from Paris. All the windows of the Albergo were open to my inspection. The evening was sultry, and the occupants of the rooms did not care to lower the venetian blinds. I saw the separate ménages washing, scratching, yawning, titivating, making tentative gestures of love, laughing, arguing, and then, later, all seated primly below the bedrooms on the balcony which served as dining-room in the warm weather.

The water was calm when we went to bed, but a heavy swell disturbed us during the night; finding the breeze offshore at dawn, we set mainsail, mizzen and jib, and ran out through the channel to the sea. I did not like the look of the swell inshore, and decided that we should find better conditions far out. We sailed with a free wind all day, first from the land

207

and then, after the shortest of lulls in the early afternoon, from the sea. We steered a compass course, and scarcely sighted land. From Spezia to the island of Elba the Italian coast is flat and dull, showing two shallow indents, with Leghorn set between them. We covered ninety sea miles under canvas and without a turn of an engine that day, our longest day's run since crossing the English Channel. Dusk found us within a few miles of Porto Baratti, and dusk turned into night as though a black cloth had dropped over the sun. We ghosted into a bay under mainsail alone and with the light on in the wheelhouse so that Isabel could check my soundings on the chart. I stood forward, heaving a light lead on a cotton line; I had placed knotted cords at the fathom intervals, with five knots on the five-fathom mark, and so on, since this method seemed to me to be more practical at night than the orthodox marks. We anchored on clean sand in only one-and-a-half fathoms, with the surf all round us.

We left the bay, which was isolated and lovely in the daylight, at 7 a.m. A man in a grey uniform rode along the beach on a bicycle and stood on a rock shouting at us until we were out of earshot. We thought we heard the word *terra*, but in that clear water we ran no risk of grounding, so decided that it would be foolish to heed his shouts. Passing about one mile from Porto Baratti, we saw *Elpis*. She was the only vessel in the harbour. We knew that Douglas and Gwenda had been ashore for dinner the previous night, because their pram dinghy—which they called "the you-you"—was bobbing in the water instead of lying, bottom-up on the cabin top. *Elpis* had left Portofino one day before us. We had agreed with Douglas and Gwenda to meet at Civitavecchia, where they would guard *Truant* while we went to Rome to arrange petrol supplies for both boats.

Elba appeared, close on the starboard hand, an exceptionally beautiful island, varied in outline, and well wooded. This was our first day of perfect conditions on the sea. A steady breeze, with enough weight in it to move *Truant* along, only ruffled the flat surface of the water; the good sun above us was doubtless too hot for less fortunate beings on land. This was one of the few days in which my vision, when I stood wearing an overcoat on *Truant* in Moody's yard and noted the curve of the deck, was realised. Soon after lunch Isabel went to sleep on deck, clasping in her arms the two-litre chianti flask, as she suspected that I was drinking more wine than might be good for the navigation. For a time I enjoyed myself with the boat, watching it, listening to it sail, then I carefully lashed the tiller and lay down beside Isabel to sleep. I wished that the night and the harbour might never come.

The breeze pushed us right up to the entrance to Giglio, a village with a good harbour set in an island of the same name. We had sailed fifty sea miles, and were a little dazed by the quiet day in the sun, a little shy of human contact after it. A man shouted to us in fluent American idiom from a fishing-boat. The speaker, a sergeant on leave from the American Army, was ingenuously delighted to see us. He explained, while we were near his small boat in the still water, that his mother lived in "that big white house beyond the village;" he said that there was plenty of water for us on the empty side of the harbour, and had he been in the navy I should have believed him. We were just able to scrape in, and when I checked with the lead we had barely two inches of water beneath our rudder. The clamorous, war-vitiated urchins of the village clustered around us in boats, pestering us. One boy carried the lines ashore, while another made them fast. Both instantly demanded payment, and I gave each twenty lire, saddened that they had not allowed the reward to be spontaneous. Meanwhile older boys and young men began to bathe from the end of the quay astern of us, the American sergeant among them and noticeably much fatter than any of his Giglio friends. Illogically, we were displeased by the contrast between the sergeant's plumpness and the bare ribs of his companions. Nevertheless, he was a fine young man. He met us in the street when we went ashore to buy provisions, and, shuffling his parachutist's high-laced brown boots in the dust and ashes and hen manure that formed the ground, he told us in a few short sentences the story of his life. He was born in Texas, the first child of immigrant parents. Six years later his father decided that he had made enough money for the family to return to his home, Giglio. He brought them back to the finest house in the village, white, rather ugly, standing back a little from the other houses and with its own vineyard. The sergeant spent his boyhood in Giglio, and he was happy there. He had no memories of America; but his mother remembered. When her husband died the boy was sixteen, already a man by the standards of the island, and ready for the heavy toil of fishing, and cultivation among the rocks. The boy did not want to leave for America even when she told him that life was easy there, and that great rewards and happiness were free to be grasped by any sensible boy who would work and save. He was an obedient son; within one year he was an American and, by the look of him, a good one. He had a wide, affectionate, lumpy face, curly hair, a wide body and strong hands. He stood talking to us with his arm around the shoulders of his younger brother, stunted, thin, spotty-faced, with wits sharpened in Italy. The sergeant said that in a couple of months he would take his mother, his sister, and his brother away

209

to Texas. They would sell the house his father had built.

While we were searching for bread we met the Brenciaglias, and, by a strange coincidence, they represented a direct contrast to the case of the family in the white house. Winifred Brenciaglia, a handsome woman of the type that you might expect to meet at a don's tea-party in Oxford, heard us asking for bread, and took us to the hotel where she was staying with her Roman husband, Mario, and their three small boys. The hotel was kept by a stiff-backed sailor with an imposing grey moustache, a most dignified man. His hotel looked more like a fisherman's cottage than hotels usually do. He agreed at once to have bread baked for us. We sat down on the terrace, and Mario Brenciaglia ordered biscuits and local wine of an unusually alcoholic nature, and the colour of diluted beef essence.

Winifred Brenciaglia was a Canadian, born in Toronto, who first came to Europe on a sight-seeing journey with her mother and her younger sister. The younger girl was left at a school in Switzerland. Winifred and her mother went south, to the French Riviera, but they did not care for that, so they travelled south again, to Rome. Rome was the most wonderful place on earth. Winifred met Mario there, and they fell in love, and married. She spoke Italian with a Canadian accent and was thoroughly herself in Italy, more than happy in her family, their house on the Via Flaminia, the north road built in 220 B.C. by Flaminius, the conqueror of Cisalpine Gaul, and their farm at Canino, near Viterbo, city of fountains and fine women. She retained an affection for Toronto, which she and Mario had visited several times since their marriage. Soon, she thought, they would have to pull themselves together and take the boys to Canada for a year, for all three had forgotten their English. During the war they had been obliged to speak only Italian.

One of the hotel-keeper's sons came on board with our bread. I searched in the cupboards and managed to find him one cigarette. He drank a glass of eau-de-vie, standing up, looking quickly around him at the structure and fittings of the boat. He and his six brothers were sailors. "Sailors on big ships," he said. "We like big ships and deep water, as our father did before he retired. Now all of us are home on the island. There are no big ships left in Italy."

"What do you do on the island?"

"Shoot rabbits, and wait for the big ships to come back."

Giglio had three fine trading schooners in the water and three more being repaired and painted, propped up on the hard. The boat that ran a daily service, weather permitting, to the mainland was a black-hulled

Dutch yacht with clipper bows and twin engines. The Italians had taken out her original masts and fitted two stumpy ones of equal size. She looked terrible.

It had been a fine day, and it was a fine night. Giglio boasts no night clubs. Red mullet cruised around the harbour, their top fins just stirring the skin on the surface of the phosphorescent water. When we went to bed we heard a strange crackling in the sea around us.

*　　*　　*　　*

Next morning it was sirocco weather. When we were outside the harbour I noticed that our large compass had a new and enormous error, of nearly fifty degrees; the under-glass had cracked, and most of the alcohol had leaked out. For some time I had been keeping a small life-boat's compass swung in gimballs inside a wooden box on the wheelhouse seat, and during our different journeys I had been able to form a very good idea of the small compass's errors, which were not considerable. Although I had the big compass repaired in Naples it was never quite satisfactory, and most of our courses from that day on were steered on the other, which had cost seven shillings and sixpence.

Although they called it sirocco weather, the sirocco itself was absent, and it was a windless day, warm, hazy, and waiting for a storm. Objects on the horizon were strangely distorted. A fishing schooner appeared in the misty distance as a queer high erection in two planes, the upper apparently divorced from the lower, and later in the day we were both puzzled by what we made out to be eight large buoys with horizontal arms sticking from their barrels as though to signal a lane between them. We took a close interest in the problem they presented, as at that time we were passing through an area profusely dotted with buoys which indicated mined areas. As we approached such buoys we had to guess whether they marked a danger area to be avoided or a swept passage to be followed. At times we were assisted in this guessing game by small patrol vessels of the Italian Navy whose courses we were able to follow. While we were in the middle of this rather worrying patch of sea I recalled the chart of the mine-fields which the naval officers had given to me in Savona. I searched the wheelhouse bookshelves, and I searched among the charts, kept impeccably in their order by Isabel in spaces below the chart table.

"What are you looking for?" she asked.

"For the chart of the mine-fields."

"You mean the coloured one that you got in Savona?"

"Yes."

211

She laughed heartily. "I tore it up and threw it overboard between Savona and Portofino. We are far better off without all that rubbish."

My attention was distracted by the eight objects we had taken for buoys, which suddenly resolved themselves into eight warships coming towards us in a line abreast. They looked like British ships, and I ran to hoist our ensign, but they were only mine-sweepers, corvettes flying the Italian flag, and they passed harmlessly on our starboard hand. Harmlessly? I remembered just in time that they were probably towing paravanes, and sheered quickly away to port as fast as *Truant* would move with sails and both engines. Sirocco weather is fatiguing, and we had sailed two hundred miles from Portofino in four days. We hoped that we should be able to have a pleasant rest in Civitavecchia.

"A medium-sized seaport, pop. 40,000, part ancient, part modern, the port for Rome and the main Italian port for commerce with Sardinia . . ." I read aloud from the *Sailing Directions*. There was a fort designed by Bramante, and later completed and embellished by the divine Michelangelo; there was an inner basin designed by Brunelleschi.

"For all that, it looks horribly big," Isabel said, examining the shore through glasses. "And I'm afraid it's been badly bombed. Shall I help you with the mainsail?"

"Yes, please." We had become more proficient, naturally enough, in handling the sails, and I could now—in reasonable weather—stow the mainsail quite quickly and neatly on my own, and still better with her help.

Airmen looking down on Civitavecchia harbour must have had the impression that the place had been eaten and regurgitated by mastodons. From water level it was an unpleasant representation of hell: rubble and ruin everywhere; troglodytes, eyes gleaming though surrounded by a fourth skin of dirt, bodies half-naked below the dust, half-covered with sordid rags, heaving, sweating, straining, yelling among the rubble; a continuous pounding of concrete mixers, ships' winches, stone crushers; the rush of coal unloading into metal lighters, powdered coal to make briquettes; explosions of demolition charges; water covered with a layer of stinking oil that bubbled from the dead ships rotting at the bottom of the sea; what was that swollen carcass in the scum? the body of an illegitimate baby? Incongruously clean, *Truant* nosed round the shattered basins, a film of dirt settling greedily on her white canvas, scrubbed decks, and still-gleaming black paint. The more obvious berths were occupied by ships of the Italian Navy, Brunelleschi's little basin had been so crumpled by aerial bombardment that we could not bear to enter it. We anchored in the main harbour, between a ruined quay and the rusting hulk of a half-

212

submerged freighter. The eight minesweepers came gliding swiftly in as I hung out our riding light.

The following day we erected awnings to give some protection against the flying dirt. We shut the hatches and portholes, and remained below. We knew that we could not expect the *Elpis*, for the sirocco had begun to howl, and we heard the thunder of the sea in the pitted caverns of the outer mole.

Thursday, September 19th, was my birthday, and since I hate birthdays, Saint's days, anniversaries, Christmases and New Years, I was half pleased to enter on my thirty-sixth year in so unpleasant a port. I am glad, moreover, that we entered Civitavecchia in 1946, for I learned a good deal there about the spirit that is in man.

The harbour area was divided from the remainder of the town by barbed-wire fences guarded by the police. The purpose of the division was to prevent too open black-market activities and too flagrant immorality on the part of the foreign sailors who brought cargoes of coal and food to the port. Life in Civitavecchia had relapsed to the primitive, and when the men from fatter countries, and from townships which still had transport and sewage, saw how life went in Civitavecchia they were unhealthily excited. It seemed that some of the foreigners were a little stifled by the trappings of civilisation, and when they saw a piece of civilisation that had been smashed into temporary primitiveness, their instinct was to leap into it, as though into a bath. When they saw the rags and the ruins their thoughts slid into dark places like the alleys off Gin Lane; the immediate cost of copulation was food or tobacco, the ultimate cost venereal disease.

At 7 each morning thousands of Italian labourers burst through the dockside gates, and divided into the gangs that worked on reconstruction. They were fantastic figures, often shamelessly underclad to an inhibited eye, and with coloured handkerchiefs around their heads and hanging down their necks to prevent sunstroke. They were men from another age, or they were cinema pirates. We thought at first, mistakenly, that they must be convicts. A gang came past *Truant* each morning in a barge. Twice we saw savage fights in the barge, and often one wild man would be haranguing his fellows. But in the evening, when the barge carried them back to the ruined town, there was no fighting and little talking, and many of the bodies hung damp, limp with exhaustion. I never saw men work as those did. They worked viciously, attacking the ruins as though some piles of rubble and contorted masonry were all that there was to hate in the world. But when a mason began to set a pale new stone he sang, and so did the boys tending the rotating concrete mixers and the stone crushers that drummed an accompaniment to days of work and madness.

We felt a bitter guilt in that place, for English-speaking peoples had made the explosives and dropped the bombs, and some of them had exulted as they destroyed or as they heard tell of the destruction. We saw no rancour against us in the wild men who were working to put things right; they behaved in the most friendly and agreeable manner, and I had no hesitation in leaving Isabel alone on the yacht while I went ashore to attempt to buy food. I left the dinghy in charge of a fisherman in what remained of the Brunelleschi basin—the water was still there—and climbed over the rubble to the harbour entrance, where the carabinieri politely let me through when I explained that I came from the black yacht. For some time I hunted among the ruins for food shops. There were other shops set in queer caves in the masonry, where strong arches had maintained hollow spaces beneath a cataract of stone, or where floor constructions of extra strength had held all the walls and upper floors of buildings. I saw tailors, blacksmiths, tinsmiths, ironmongers, plumbers, even dressmakers and drinking shops—these last well patronised—set in the irregular, unglazed caverns. At length a middle-aged woman, showing her toes like freshly dug potatoes through the shredded uppers of her carpet slippers, led me to the market. The squalor of the place disinclined me to buy anything, and indeed apart from grapes there was little to buy. I entered a crowded space with the web of a blasted roof hanging overhead. The space served as meat and fish market, and I backed away from the stench and the sight of the intestines and viscera offered on the wet slabs. I could scarcely believe that this market was in the same country as the market of San Remo. Superficial tourists and journalists were very full at the time of the prosperity of Italy. Civitavecchia was an example of how war and defeat had split the country up into units, units of family and degree as well as units of city and region; superficial watchers had no cause, and sometimes no heart, to see the misery. I had great difficulty in buying bread, and the baker only sold me some as a personal favour to the woman in carpet slippers. It was a round loaf of black bread, an object heavy and hard enough to use as a weapon against fellow-man as well as stomach.

The dinghy was so badly in need of varnish that weed had grown on its bottom. This repulsive sight overcame my laziness and my reluctance to varnish it in so unsuitable a place. I hauled it up outside the standing rigging by attaching the painter to the throat halyards, laid it across the deck, straddling the windlass, and scraped and varnished it. I was finishing the first coat when I saw *Elpis* enter the port.

"We thought you would want to get to Rome on your birthday,"

214

Gwenda shouted as she stood forward by the anchor while Douglas made a sweep to approach us.

"We won't be able to leave before to-morrow morning," I shouted back. "It'll take me till then to clean myself."

"What a hellish place," she said.

I called to some of the workers in the vicinity, asking about train services to Rome.

"There are two trains in the day, one at five in the morning and the other two hours later."

*   *   *   *

Gwenda's alarm clock woke us at five. We breakfasted in bed and left at six in their you-you, Isabel in the bows, a little nervous about her dress and stockings—with some reason, for the you-you was built to take not more than two persons, and the oily surface of the water was within an inch of the gunwale—and Gwenda perched in the stern with our suitcase on her knees. We were obliged to stop and turn the bows to the wash of any passing boat. Landing was a gymnastic feat. We promised Gwenda that we would return in two days, and picked our way past shunting coal-wagons. The road to the station was a river of soft dust. A car sank to the axles; carts went more easily, but the horses and mules held their heads stiffly above the dust and stepped nervously.

Dark patches around the building were human beings, waiting in clumps for the train to Rome. Most of them sat on bundles of luggage in attitudes of nervous dejection; some jostled and fought in four lines leading to two holes in the wall through which tickets were obtained. I dared not add myself to the fighting lines; pushing through the vestibule, we came to the railway tracks. There was a long, and ill-tempered, queue for the *Donne*. Thirty minutes after the train was supposed to leave for Rome, one carriage which, even empty, leaned to the left as though it had been built with one set of wheels bigger than the other, was shunted at us. In a tornado of energy, we flung ourselves at the carriage, pushing, tearing, shouting. Just missing a wooden seat, Isabel and I were pinned in a corner of the corridor, and thought that we had done well. The pressure around us augmented as body after body forced its way into the leaning coach. We were wedged between a party of three men who discussed politics and ethics until we arrived in Rome, and three women who giggled and enjoyed themselves in the examination and re-examination of our person. Beyond the women there was a lavatory which, as the voyage proceeded, made itself increasingly obvious in a most unpleasant manner although it could not be

215

asked to fulfil its function since it was occupied by an elderly man, three women and two children, one of the latter unweaned. Sometimes a man would fight his way down the corridor to the lavatory door and his expression or, still better, his disappointed remarks on arriving there and witnessing the over-populated interior constituted an excellent joke in the lavatory itself and in our corridor. We were a full hour late in leaving Civitavecchia; our coach stood in a siding until the Genoa-Rome express came in, and we were attached to the back of that superior train.

The journey to Rome, a distance of some forty miles, lasted two hours. At first the country was flat and arid. We saw men riding fiery little horses across the dusty fields. Nearer Rome we entered the Campagna that I knew well from the paintings of the Scottish artist, McWhirter, great, gloomy canvases in the town house of my Millar grandfather, and from the train I saw the things that McWhirter had painted, sections of a two-tiered aqueduct, sheep, goats, and lonely trees swelling to the silhouettes of long-stemmed mushrooms, the colour of brown tea-pots, with a hint of gold from the touch of the sun on the brown.

From the station we emerged into a square where there were many taxis and carriages for hire. While in London during and after the war so many citizens and visitors could afford to take taxis that there were never any available, in Rome the taxis were in the habit of demanding such prices that they were always at hand. Climbing into an open carriage, we were jolted away into the warm, imposing, adorable city. As the capital of Italy, Rome was the mecca for cigarette worshippers. Our carriage was surrounded for a time by small boys holding trays on which they arranged and re-arranged, with darting, delicate touches of their beige fingers, the different packets. Some of the acolytes reverently pronounced, in a kind of litany, the holy names: "Camel, Chesterfield, Crah-venn; Philip Morris, Players; Gold Flack, Lookee, Abdoolla . . ." The handling of the cigarettes fascinated me. All over the streets of Rome the boys were to be seen with their trays. Sometimes we watched them fitting cellophane wrappers on the packets, or taking off the wrappers; we watched them sniff at the drab tobacco inside the paper cylinders; we watched them buy from furtive soldiers and sell to unfurtive civilians; and always the delicate beige fingers fluttered reverently among the packets.

We were shocked to find Rome transformed into an Allied camp. The noble streets, the heavenly squares, the palazzi with their sombre grace, St. Peter's, the Atlantic liner of cathedrals, formed a strange background to that malaise that follows each great war, while men are still acting to the rhythm and impetus of the devil dance, and truth is a weak convalescent.

216

We saw all kinds of uniforms, for the soldiers were everywhere, and uniforms were also worn by many others, the business men, the officials of relief organisations, the airline employees, the temporary hangers-on of embassies, the journalists, the members of Allied missions and commissions. A vehicle of military aspect and bearing the letters, T.W.A., stopped beside our carriage at a traffic light. The single occupant was hatless, but otherwise wore a uniform corresponding to that of an American officer, without rank badges.

"What does 'T.W.A.' mean?" I asked him.

"Where have you been? It means Trans-World Airlines."

"Good heavens!" I found something unpleasantly remote in the title. Inhabitants of the moon might thus talk of their aeroplane or rocket services to the sun.

The Italian petrol supplies were controlled by an organisation known as 'Cheep' (C.I.P.); in the offices of Cheep we had the good fortune to meet Commandante Enrico Insom, a thin man, youngish yet grey-haired, with a light voice and the most exquisite manners. Commandante Insom sat behind an overgrown desk in a veneered room of the type that appears in nine months when a drawing-room makes love to an office. The pictures on the panelling represented the tanker vessels which he had controlled prior to the war. Isabel quickly laid our needs before him, and it was arranged that a truck would leave Rome to meet us at Anzio with one thousand litres of petrol for *Truant* and two hundred litres for *Elpis*. Our suitcase stood beside us while these arrangements were completed, and Commandante Insom asked if we had been able to reserve accommodation in Rome. "I will give you the best man to find you rooms," he said. "But I cannot hold out any hope." He introduced us to Count Achille Larussa, who swept us from the building and into a car. Larussa also made no secret of the fact that we should be extremely fortunate if we found a room for the night. And as for a bath! The Americans had requisitioned nearly all the hotels, and we knew how the Americans felt about baths? They had requisitioned all the baths.

"What about the Ambasciatori?"

"Requisitioned by the Americans."

"The Excelsior?"

"Requisitioned by the Americans."

"The Quirinale? The Reale? The Plaza? There never was a town with so many hotels as Rome."

"Listen. You heard of the Spanish Inquisition. I am sorry to pun at such a serious moment, but here we have the Roman Requisition.

There never was a town with so many requisitioners."

"But they must leave a few hotels for people who are passing through, if only as overflows for their own people."

"Yes, there are the Grand and the Regina." But both the Grand and the Regina had been filled to the attics with the members of an Allied Commission of unbounded importance and armed with sheaves of what were called "priorities". At length Larussa said: "There is only one chance left. I know the manager of an albergo near our office. In fact I have a good deal of influence in that quarter, since my brother is the manager's lawyer."

There was a long explanation from Larussa of my importance and the great significance for Italy of my presence in Rome. The manager was affable until the point was reached at which it was intimated that I required a double room and bath. Impossible! The only room-and-bath vacant was booked for a colonel who was arriving from Verona that evening. Larussa leaned across the counter, took both of the manager's hands in his, and spoke for a long time so quickly and so softly that I only heard the sound of his voice and the swift intakes of breath.

"All right," the manager said.

"What did you say to him?" I asked Larussa as we went out to the car. He shrugged his wide shoulders.

"We often say more than we mean to say."

*   *   *   *

When we returned to our hotel at night my feet were raw from wearing shoes and socks. After living barefoot on the boat the soles of my feet were leathery, but the upper skin had become delicate. While enjoying a bath, I noticed that that hotel had also been occupied by soldiers, for a long, rusty nail had been crudely hammered into the white-tiled surface above the bath. Who had hammered in the nail? German? Austrian? Italian? American? Englishman? Frenchman, New Zealander, Moroccan, Indian? Hawaiian-Japanese, Cypriot, Cingalese, Pole?

Unused to the night noise of a city, I had nightmare after nightmare, dreaming most vividly that Mr. Churchill had thrown me down a well, and was inciting a million enemies to drop yachts on top of me.

*   *   *   *

In the course of the next morning I had to collect a letter of credit which was waiting for me at the head office of one of the biggest of the Italian banks. When I had summoned energy to visit the bank we were

218

directed to a counter before which a considerable number of men and women waited. I told a young man behind the counter of my errand, but the politest way to describe his reaction would be to say that he ignored me. When we had waited for some twenty minutes with no further opportunity even to say what we required, I decided that we must try another avenue of approach. A hired carriage took us to the offices of Cheep, where Commandante Insom telephoned on our behalf to the managing director of the bank. This time we were met at the main doors by an attendant who led us up an imposing staircase to a waiting room furnished with pompous sumptuosity. Two directors of the bank came to us, the senior an elderly gentleman and his junior a romantic young man with a small moustache and large black eyes. We had a very agreeable conversation. The younger director vanished, and soon returned with my letter of credit. Would we like any cash? Then if we would not mind accompanying him for one moment. . . . The older man wished us good-bye, bowing at the top of the stairs. The romantic director led us to the identical counter at which we had waited before, but now the clerk who had ignored me rushed shamelessly forward, deserting another, less fortunate, client, and in surprisingly perfect English made himself agreeable. While the business was transacted the romantic director made conversation. "Yehss . . . Ischia is nah-ice. . . . But Cah-pri is paradah-ise." We departed with our money. I found this method of banking charmingly historical. It had not changed from the days of Marco Polo. It lent to the humble act of cashing twenty pounds the glamour of a Venetian transaction in houris and amethysts.

Although I took the most expensive tickets available (second class), and we arrived at the train ninety minutes before it was due to depart and one hundred and fifty minutes before its departure, I was only able to secure for Isabel a guard's strapontin. But there was room for me beside her on the floor.

In the late evening we hurried to the docks at Civitavecchia. The weather was bad, we were horrified to see. Rome had been airless, but here the sirocco nipped the smoke from the funnel-tops of the mine-sweepers, all of which lay roosting in their harbour berths. The Hawkes had taken their trusteeship with characteristic energy and efficiency, and had lashed *Truant* and *Elpis* together. Gwenda was typing letters in *Truant's* saloon when we arrived, and Douglas was working on his engine. We gave them the good news that they would get petrol, and the more doubtful news that they would have to go fifty-five miles the next day to get it. We were overjoyed to be back on *Truant*. I gave the dinghy another coat of varnish while Isabel cooked dinner.

*   *   *   *

The clanking of the hydraulic windlass on *Elpis* accompanied by Gwenda's vivid running commentary awoke me at 5.30 a.m. I twisted to one side and looked through a porthole. They had hoisted their dark mainsail, and *Elpis* was bow-on, the end of her bowsprit close to my face. Gwenda, tall and slender, with her trousers rolled up to the knees revealing white legs and narrow bare feet, was coiling the tripping line while the automatic windlass hauled in the chain with inhuman regularity. Gwenda worked in a vocal manner, talking now to the rope, now, over her shoulder, to Douglas, who was busy at the after end of the boat, and finally to the small C.Q.R. anchor, which she addressed in by no means endearing terms. An hour later we left Civitavecchia. Isabel had to jockey with an immense swell at the harbour bar, continuing straight out to sea until we were in deep water, and the sea was easy enough to allow us to turn on our course. The sirocco had fallen to a puffy headwind. We ran on with one engine and jib, staysail, main and mizzen, the sails making little difference to our progress. After three hours we passed *Elpis*. We were short of petrol, and Douglas, who had even less, was saving his last pint to take him into Anzio harbour. In the afternoon the breeze freshened and veered to the south; we were able to shut off the engine.

The coast from Civitavecchia to Anzio is straight, dull and dangerous. We passed ten miles to seaward of Ostia, and sailed on the dividing line between the spread fan of brown Tiber water and the vivid blue sea. The Sailing Directions warned us of overfalls there, but we saw no more than a few unnatural ripples on the water. We stowed our mainsail as we passed the ancient port of Nero at Anzio and, veering to port under headsails alone, sailed gently into the wide new harbour, a good anchorage except—and it is a big except—that it is exposed to south and south-east winds. The fifty-five miles had taken us nine hours.

Anzio had been the scene of a landing during the Italian campaign, while Civitavecchia had merely been a target. Yet Anzio presented a lively front, with music and crowds on the quaysides, and rows of freshly-painted villas with striped sunblinds. A number of small yachts lay in an inner basin, but we elected to drop anchor near the centre of the outer harbour, since we felt inclined after Civitavecchia to remain in the cleanest water available.

"Meester Meellerss! Meester Meellerss! Meester Meellerss!" We looked round the harbour, and saw that a tall youth was gesticulating to us from the end of the quay to which the other yachts were made fast. "Meester Meellerss! Commandante Insom is come!" And there indeed, was Insom, behind the tall youth and a little embarrassed, perhaps, by the noise. They soon came rowing out to us, Commandante Insom, the English-speaking youth, another like him but a year or so younger, and a young girl wearing pigtails secured at the ends with thin elastic bands, all three being the children of a certain Alberto Sciolari, whom we had met in Rome. We went with them to the Sciolari villa where, it seemed, we were awaited for tea. Sciolari paterfamilias, in white sea-side clothes with a round-necked singlet of soft white wool revealing a gold chain around his neck, introduced us to his wife, to his mother-in-law, to a few more children, all younger than the three whom we already knew, and to Signora Insom, tall, composed, and rather silent beside all the Sciolari family. We were told that tea was waiting for us; but, delightful surprise, we moved to basket chairs surrounding a long table on a loggia and a pale golden wine was poured into tumblers. The wine was iced, and had a wonderful fragrance. A long day in the salt air builds a thirst; I drank the wine quickly, thinking it to be the lightest I had ever tasted, and then, as I accepted a second glass, I felt it tap at my head, and asked Sciolari how strong it was. Fourteen degrees, he answered; it came from a vineyard between Anzio and Rome, and was extremely difficult to obtain. I wondered that it was not requisitioned. There was to be an interval between that pleasant and unusual fore-runner to tea, the wine, and tea itself, and Sciolari profited from the delay to show us over his week-end refuge from the toil of commerce in Rome. The villa and its garden occupy that section of a sloping hill which was, we were told, the axis of the main Allied landing on the Anzio bridgehead. Two landing craft and a tank, all three red with rust and gashed by shell-fire or mines, lay on the beach across the garden wall, but there were astonishingly few signs that the Allied assault troops followed by a mass of consolidating infantry had passed through the steep garden. It was difficult to believe that the villa and its surroundings had been bombed by the Allies, then shelled by their ships, and by the amphibious tanks, and then a little later had been shelled and bombed by the Germans. The garden was of the complicated variety, with a network of tap-water streams running from top to bottom and passing through basins designed to display Etruscan stone and pottery fragments. The house, which was being repaired while the family lived in an annexe at the foot of the garden, still lacked the major part of its façade. A mastiff was tethered on a long chain in the dining-room to keep thieves away from such of the fittings and decorations as remained. The Sciolari tea-table was covered with confections of remarkable variety and richness; Isabel and I had eaten little in the course of our long day, and we willingly settled ourselves on the circumference. The oldest Sciolari boy evidently wished to keep "Meester Meellerss" happily talking, while an Italian who had just returned from a visit to Toledo sought to convince Isabel and the rest of us regarding the astounding fluency of his Spanish. Before we could pierce these social obstacles and attack the spread, a great company of strangers arrived, all spectacularly dressed and in holiday spirits. The introductions were long and thorough, and when I had time to look at the tea-table all the places were occupied and good manners dictated that I should listen to the views, comments, and questions of the newcomers. One of them, another naval commandante, greeted Insom in a manner of gushing friendliness and then greeted me with equal warmth but more familiarity, being under the impression that I was Insom's son, aged twenty-five. Soon after this Insom announced his impending departure for Rome, and we were able to leave with him and his wife. *Elpis* sailed into harbour as we were leaving, and her tanned sails and workmanlike rig seemed to disappoint some of our companions, who perhaps knew even less about such matters than I did. As we drove away from the villa in Insom's car we met Douglas and Gwenda, who were wrathfully trudging down the road, accompanying a stout Italian yacht hand. Commandante Insom stopped his car. Gwenda was outspoken.

"We don't know what the devil this creature wants," she said, indicating the yacht hand. "He dragged us off our boat by force, and we are too tired for such pranks." Leaping from the car, I explained to them swiftly that Insom's importance was only matched by his kindliness, and that he spoke excellent English.

"Then ask him where we should eat," Douglas said to me hoarsely when they had shaken hands. And Gwenda added: "All we want to do is go quietly to a good restaurant."

It appeared that the yacht hand had been ordered by the all-powerful Alberto Sciolari to lie in wait for *Elpis* and to bring her crew to the tea-party at the villa the moment the anchor was down. The man, a loyal servant, had taken his orders literally. We managed to convince him that it would be wisest to guide his querulous flock to the best restaurant in the town. We took the Insoms aboard *Truant*, and spent an agreeable evening with them.

"Meester Meellerss!" Had our ears deceived us? No, for there was the creak of an oar against a thole-pin. "Meester Meellerss!" Isabel and I lay rigid, scarcely daring to breathe. "Meester Meellerss, Meester Meellerss,

222

MEESTER MEELLERSS!" The voice was inexorable. I put on a dressing-gown and went on deck. It was the Sciolari heir, of course, and he was accompanied by his father and the younger boy. They came below to the saloon, and accepted whisky. Explaining that it was unthinkable that Isabel should prepare food while their own large domestic staff was so near at hand, they invited us to luncheon or dinner or both the following day.

"I am extremely sorry," I said, "but we are going to Rome."

"Ah! Then we shall be travelling companions on the train," said the older son.

"I am afraid not, because Commandante Insom is sending a car to take us to Rome."

"Ah! I regret that I shall not be able to accompany you from Anzio to Rome, for there is a girl with whom I want to have companionship on the train to-morrow morning. But I shall telephone Commandante Insom when we return now to the villa and ask him if I may travel in the car from Rome to-morrow evening. Then I shall be able to show you all things of interest on the road down, and when we get here you will dine with us. After dinner I will show you Anzio." I stood on the deck, watching them row away, clearly visible in the darkness, for against the chill of the night all three had put on white linen garments with short sleeves.

We did not sleep well; soon after the Sciolaris left us a sharp swell from the south-east entered the harbour, making *Truant* roll and clatter. At first light we moved alongside a very dirty quay, to prepare for the arrival of our petrol, and because the quay offered some protection from the swell. While petrol was being poured into *Truant* and *Elpis* Douglas invited a man who called himself a ships' chandler to fill *Elpis's* drinking-water tanks. The water was brought in five-gallon cans made for the British Army, and there was something of an altercation at the end because the man demanded payment of seventy lire for the contents of each can. Douglas, who had seen them filling the cans at the public fountain, was indignantly surprised, and the chandler took this in good part, immediately halving his demand.

Between Anzio and Rome we crossed a dry plain offering little cover, and it seemed that the Allies had suffered heavily in their advance over it. The armoured vehicles that lay broken on the dusty soil, constituting now only eyesores and obstructions to the plough, were of types that I had used myself in the Army; their presence reminded me of the price that had been paid by some of my former companions for this pleasant trip to Rome. High up, near the Villa Borghese we lunched with the Insoms. With the

223

long windows open to the garden and existence inside so calm, so regulated, so decent, so like the equivalent interiors in England or America or Germany, I wondered at the fantastic stupidity of our world. The Insoms' only son, who bore my name, Giorgio, was there, a virile young man who refused to work in his father's oil company, but instead had taken employment with Trans-World Airlines. For a considerable period Giorgio and I had fought on opposite sides in North Africa. He was a parachutist. And at the end of the war, when he had parachuted behind the German lines to work for the Allies, we had been in different branches of the same organisation. He had been wounded and almost killed on the last day of the war. Signora Insom heard the news of peace in Italy and, almost immediately after it, the news that her son was believed to be dying. Giorgio brought us a slab of metal, the head of a German anti-tank shell, which an American surgeon had extracted from his body, and X-ray photographs showing the metal as it was before the operation, pressing up against his beating heart. All afternoon we were able to drive round Rome, unguided, stopping where we felt inclined, and in the evening our car stopped outside one of the Sciolari establishments and the son ran forth and joined us. On the way to Anzio we told him that we should not be able to dine with him because the Hawkes had been good enough to watch our boat for us all day, and in return we must watch *Elpis* for them while they went out in the evening. When we arrived at the quay he pressed our hands and vanished into the crowd of trippers who stood gaping at the yachts. Douglas and Gwenda followed him, making for a restaurant, and after a light meal we went to bed.

We were not properly in the sheets when, from the quay above, we heard "Meester Meellerss, Meester Meellerss!" This time he had brought his mother who, since we could not go to dinner, felt that she must come to say good-bye and to see our boat. We both rose in dressing-gowns to greet them. But Signora Sciolari was no sooner below than she felt seasick, so she hastily left us, followed by the youth, who murmured as he bent to kiss Isabel's slender hand: "A rivederla, Meeses Meellerss."

19

W E pushed *Truant* out from the quay and hoisted the mainsail, then staysail, jib, mizzen. She steadied, and sailed from Anzio. A mile away we saw *Elpis*, heading straight out to sea to take advantage of the breeze, a white Genoa showing against her tanned jib and mainsail. Douglas was making for the island of Ponza, thirty miles south of Anzio, but the day looked promising, and we felt inclined to go farther than Ponza. We soon lost sight of land.

When we had eaten, Isabel became engrossed in calculations with charts and dividers—which she called by the Spanish word *pinzas*—calculations which entailed dragging one hundred and sixty charts from the space below the chart table, and spreading some ten of them about the wheelhouse. She exclaimed after thirty minutes of this unusual behaviour that we had done enough "hanging about", and asked if it would not be best to sail from the toe of Italy direct to the Gulf of Corinth.

"We could sail from the Straits of Messina to Cephalonia—is that called Kephalonia or Sephalonia, I wonder—and that would mean sailing across—where are my pinzas?—across just over two hundred miles of open sea. Whereas if we crawl along the southern coast of Italy and then go round by Corfu . . ."

"I want to see Corfu. I want to see the Governor's Palace there."

"Yes, but wait till you hear how much farther round it is if we go to Corfu. From Capri to Cephalonia *my* way is 420 sea miles; from Capri to Cephalonia via Corfu is 570 sea miles. One hundred and fifty miles longer! What do you think of that?"

"I don't know what to think." Isabel likes to arrange the future neatly; I prefer to let the future mould itself. While she was rearranging the charts I looked at the *Mediterranean Pilot* to find out what kind of place we were heading for, and although on the chart the island of Ventotene looked pleasant enough, the *Pilot* was not reassuring.

"It's a convict settlement," I told Isabel. "The port was cut from the rock by the Romans, who used the island as a dumping ground for political prisoners . . ."

"Isn't there another anchorage?"

"It says that when there are southerly gales the supply ship puts in at a bay on the north side . . ."

"That would be this bay," she said, examining the chart. "It looks all right, but there are a lot of beastly crosses round it."

"Rocks?"

"Yes. Still, it would be nice to be in a quiet anchorage, with no people staring at us."

"That looks like Ventotene ahead."

"Yes, that would be it. A queer shape . . . like a box."

"With nothing inside it but stone."

We were surrounded by cliffs rising sheer from the water to a height of two hundred feet. There was a constant splashing as the sea penetrated into deep holes and washed over submerged and half-submerged rocks which reached out to us from the edges of the anchorage. As the day darkened the cliffs seemed to draw closer round us and we heard shouting above. Isabel drew my attention to a line of heads looking over the edge of the precipice, and in the centre of the line one strange figure that appeared to be dancing in black robes. When we examined the dancer through binoculars we saw that he was a tall priest who was talking to his companions, who—less brave than he—lay on their bellies with their heads at the edge of the drop. The priest waved his arms and even jumped into the air in his excitement. There could be little doubt that it was our presence in the cove that interested him, for now and then he would dramatically point one long black arm in our direction. While Isabel was cooking a swell began to roll into the anchorage. I was uneasy about our position, for I could see the anchor underfoot, and the rocky ground was not good holding. *Truant* rolled so badly that she almost wet her decks, and the riding light described great arcs against the sky. Both of us were nervous, imagining glistening, otter-like convicts swimming out with knives between their teeth to board us. At 2 a.m. I woke Isabel and suggested that, as we could get little good sleep in that place, we might have breakfast and then sail on to Ischia. She agreed; in less than an hour we were feeling our way out to sea through the cordon of rocks. When we had turned to head for Ischia I steered on a star, occasionally switching on the binnacle light to check the course. Isabel took the wheel while I hoisted staysail and mizzen; the sails hung flabbily, and I hurried back to the wheelhouse, for the night air was piercing. The impression of our ghoulish anchorage was still with us, and we both jerked nervously when a very big fish jumped near us. To pass the time, I tried to calculate the relation in size of a floating mine to the surface area of the Mediterranean. I could do no better than say that the odds were more than a million to one against our hitting a mine. Isabel said that she thought those odds might be a little generous, as she had heard that each week one fishing-boat from Civita-vecchia was lost in the mine-fields. After that we discussed our lives before we had met each other. Words and ideas seem important as the dawn approaches, and are passionately laid forth. Our wheelhouse was a good place, and the gentle tick of the engine was friendly company, in the darkness. When the dawn came we first saw on the starboard bow the highest peak of Ischia, for it achieved the clear air above the mist. Then slowly the coastline of the island fitted itself together; the last thing to be visible was the seashore. Ischia looked entrancing, a green, well-wooded, prosperous, volcanic island. The houses were whiter than any we had yet seen from *Truant*, the verdure more tropical. Ischia, like Capri, is formed of a younger sister of the volcano Vesuvius; the Ischia volcano, Epomeo, is now believed to be extinct. There can be no doubt that the islands in the bay of Naples have, and always have had, a peculiarly languorous charm for men and women—but I think for men in particular. Ischia was developed by the Greeks, was taken in 326 by the Romans, and then was given by Augustus to the Neapolitans in exchange for another island that had taken his fancy, Capri. The next masters were the Saracens, who successfully attacked it in 813 and again in 847. The Pisans landed there in 1135. Epomeo, as though men were not making enough commotion over the place, erupted seriously in 1302. The great pirate Khair-ed-din Barbarossa, the renegade Greek from Mitylene who flayed the Christian powers as a Turkish corsair, sacked the island in 1543, and—judging it rich enough to yield an annual harvest—again in 1544, when he shipped a selection of Ischia's most prepossessing virgins for his Triumph in Constantinople. Three years after Barbarossa's second visit, "Balafré", the scarfaced Duc de Guise, called on the islanders in a most violent manner in the course of his 1556-57 expedition against Naples. The next visitors, who were perhaps a little more gentle and less unfriendly than Barbarossa and Balafré, were Nelson's sailors. Then there were the earthquakes of 1881 and 1883; the second, and the more terrible, nearly obliterated the watering place Casamicciola, which sits in a valley on the north side of the volcano. By contrast with all these alarums, Ischia passed calmly through the two great European wars. Indeed to us, as the fishing-boats came streaming out from the ports, and the sun warmed the lively, gay northern flank of the island, it looked a soothing place. We passed through the single narrow entrance to the elliptically-shaped harbour which is the crater of an ancient volcano, and were most gravely disappointed to find the place occupied by our own people. Air-sea rescue craft of the Royal Air Force, high, black-and-yellow boats with humped bows and multiple machine-guns in transparent gun-turrets, were clustered around the quays, and as we dropped anchor near two yachts we swung our stern towards an Air Force encampment surrounded by a barbed-wire fence; greasy smoke from the cook-house, preparing an English breakfast, rose into the air; thousands of horse-power muttered, moaned, whined and roared about us as the mechanics tested and warmed their engines before the morning patrol. The smooth water of the port was black with oil and shot with the rainbow colours of high-octane petrol. Since the morning showed promise of great heat, we erected our awnings before we went ashore to buy provisions. The shops were squalid, and even the fruit was poor by the standards to which we had become accustomed. We returned to the boat, and ate curried salmon with rice, pimento, raisins, and herbs, an iced bottle of good Riesling, salad, fruit, and coffee. A man working on the yacht alongside us, a fine Bermudian cutter of about *Truant's* size, was scraping teak hatches that sadly needed varnish or linseed oil, and singing meanwhile in a penetrating tenor voice. When he had gone ashore for lunch we turned on our radio, and heard the voices of Naples, voices with Africa in them as well as Europe.

* * * *

Greatly refreshed by an afternoon of siesta stretched into a night of sleep—we had not again ventured ashore—we set sail in the cool of the morning for Naples. A slight breeze flowed into Naples bay, gently puffing the heat-haze before it. I had bent our biggest squaresail to the yard, and when we were clear of the land I broke it out, 400 square feet of white cotton that fell to within a foot of the deck. It pleased us to use that old-fashioned and comfortable sail. Our movement was imperceptible, but we could hear the water bubbling at the bows, and when we timed our progress past the islands we learned that we were sailing at three knots. *Truant's* arrival in the Bay of Naples with this uncommon sail aroused a wide and fully-expressed curiosity. Steamers and motor-boats hurrying to the great port with cargo and passengers altered course to steam close— often too close—to us, and their grinning, swarthy passengers hurled us gifts, oranges, boiled sweets wrapped in bright papers, small pieces of chocolate that tasted, delightfully, of coffee. (It would be dishonest to conceal that a great many of these large-hearted travellers asked us with shouts and pantomime if we could repay their generosity with tobacco.) There were fishing-boats by the hundred in the misty bay, most of them feluccas with pointed sails made from frail cotton. Some managed to sail up to us, while others, less nimble on the wind, brought out sweeps with

228

which they frenziedly sought to approach us. The men shouted, "Engleesh? You spik Engleesh? Hi, Joe, what you got to sell? Sigarette? You like feesh? Two sigarette one feesh? Two feesh one sigaretta. Three feesh one sigaretta? What the matter with you?" We saw the heights and the smoking cone of Vesuvius above the haze.

Four years earlier I had arrived at Naples in a cargo of prisoners from North Africa, filthy men, still degraded by capture, weak with dysentery and other diseases, spat upon and reviled by the populace. I must confess that my second arrival was coloured for me by memory of the first, and when the fishermen asked, "What the matter with you?" I caught myself wondering if the water was hot and ready for us in the delousing station by the docks, and whether we should again be marched through the streets.

Mario Brenciaglia had advised us to go to the small harbour of Santa Lucia if we had occasion to visit Naples. Isabel searched busily, but in vain, on our charts and in the pilot books for the location of Santa Lucia, which is too small a harbour to interest commercial craft; at length she found it on a map of Naples in that able French publication for tourists, the *Guide Bleu*. We had dreaded the arrival at Naples, a port of which many evil things are constantly repeated, but like other arrivals, it was more pleasant than we had anticipated. Santa Lucia is a narrow, rectangular harbour tucked into the outline of the town and shielded from the dusty streets by two restaurants, "Zi' Teresa" and "Bersagliera", and several nautical and pseudo-nautical clubs, which splash awnings, drinks, Neapolitans and foreigners over the wide quay. That end of the harbour was filled with small, but by no means inferior, yachts, the largest of them eight metres. We anchored in the centre of the rectangle and hauled our stern round with two lines to a breakwater so low that we had an uninterrupted view of the bay. The barracks across the harbour was occupied by a British battalion and a "working party" of Jugoslavs under British supervision. The Jugoslavs, who (and we thought this distinctly tactless of their British employers) patrolled the military area carrying long and solid cudgels with which to belabour any Neapolitan thief who might pay an unauthorised business call, were wildly excited by our arrival, but the British tommies were stolid county troops, and no ripple affected the glassy surface of their phlegm although a yacht from England, with a beautiful girl on it protected only by a weedy young man of slightly effeminate aspect, should have been an interesting sight and one calculated to whet the imaginations of virile soldiers. I found their apathy restful and pleasant, and so—no doubt—did Isabel; we were inclined to call it good manners, but having spent a few years in the British Army myself, I put it down to boredom and the heat. When I had coiled ropes, trimmed the squaresail yard, and made the decks look half-decent, I hurried ashore.

A few days previously I had used for the first time some paraffin bought in France, and had found it to be of such poor quality that even our cookers—let alone the sensitive and aristocratic refrigerator—were inclined to cough repeatedly and to blow black fumes round the galley. The weather was the most torrid that we had encountered since the passage through the canals, and life without a refrigerator would have been unpleasant, if not intolerable. I took a carriage to the head office of Cheep in Naples.

In the Naples streets all the cigarette vendors were girls, and not boys as in Rome. I asked the driver why this should be. "A short time ago they began to prevent the people from smoking American and British tobacco," he said. "The newspapers said that if we smoked less tobacco from America we'd be able to have more bandages and chloroform in the hospitals. But the smokers answered: 'Now our need is for tobacco, and when we require bandages and chloroform we will see what can be done about paying for them; and in any case, if we don't buy the tobacco others will.' Then the police were told to arrest those who bought in the streets. But if that went on there was soon going to be no room in the prisons, which are over-full in any case. The police were told to change their tactics and to arrest the boys. This was more profitable for the police, for each boy arrested yielded a tray-full of cigarettes. The police were never more zealous. A couple of days of it and there were no cigarette vendors. So then they sent out girls instead of boys. The girls are still there."

"Do you mean that the police are too chivalrous to arrest the girls? Your story would have pleased King Arthur and the Knights of the Round Table, but somehow . . ."

"Nothing will come of all those Peace Conferences," he interrupted me. "And what is more, Italy will never get a square deal. What was the war fought for, if things are not to be done squarely once it's over? Round tables are no good."

There was stimulation in his truculence. I found the cynical Italian attitude-in-the-street to the late war most pleasant after wading in France through all the maze of sentiment in which the French—otherwise logical people—swaddle every war that strikes their country, whether it be lost or won. The Frenchman would say to us, truthfully or untruthfully: "I was of the Résistance: we suffered under the Boches!" the Italian would say: "I collaborated," (with the Allies) "but damn-all have I got for my collaboration. Is there no justice in this world?" A hero is often a very dull stick—even when he is genuine—so give me a cynical coward or a scally-wag any time that there is no war to be fought, and especially when war has to be discussed.

The director of Cheep placed a car and a chauffeur at my disposal, and a most intelligent guide, Dottore Antonino Gargiulo. It was as well that I had such strong support, for although I only required ten gallons of good-quality paraffin, we drove sixty miles round and about Naples to get it. The paraffin itself presented no great difficulty, provided you had the authority to buy it, but although there were millions of suitable con-tainers lying on the dumps each drum had been checked and counter-checked, and lay with its fellows in a zareba of barbed wire protected by sentries. Eventually we were lucky to wheedle three cans out of a friendly American at a Standard Oil depot. Dottore Gargiulo was eager to practise his English. I could imagine nobody less like what is considered to be the typical Neapolitan; thin, with a bony, serious face below close-cropped dark hair, he talked to me of politics and economics, of kingship and caste, and finally, when we were rowing out to *Truant* with our three drums of oil, he was asking me exactly what constitutional powers were vested in the English throne, and whether such powers were ever used, and, more important, misused. I should have preferred the Dottore to have been in less serious mood, for Naples is an intriguing town, and the frivolous and picturesquely vicious atmosphere of the streets went ill with his urgency for solid information.

That night they were playing tango music at Teresa's. We tied our dinghy to a post beside our table. The maître d'hôtel suggested haddock Monte Carlo, and the sommelier brought a bottle of Rhine wine. "Property of the Wehrmacht," he said with a wink. *Truant* was only some fifty yards away from us across the still water, and behind her was the wide bay. The night was hot, and although the restaurant was crowded, few people had the energy to dance; the wind players shone with sweat, and often shook their waterlogged instruments; the two violinists held the violins sagging, away from their chins, and wet patches appeared on their white coats beneath the bowing arms; the tall man who swayed before the band like a delphinium in a high wind held a baton in his right hand, a white silk handkerchief in his left. The musicians' lassitude improved that type of cheap music which, outside of Spain and Latin America, takes on too jigging and hasty a rhythm; they dragged it out, fluted, weakened and strained it until it was almost as tango music should be, resembling the phrase, *no sabes esperar.*

231

"I believe that I've seen that man before," I said, indicating to Isabel a British major who was dancing assiduously, "but I can't remember where . . ." Nor did I wish to remember. He was a tall young man with a bloodless skin, sandy hair, pale eyes, and a graceful body. Carefully dressed in the wide-trousered service dress of a north-country regiment he danced with exceptional smoothness and intricate variety of movement, but in a manner which neglected one of the important rules of more frivolous dances like the minuet, the quadrille, and even the waltz, that the male, however well he dances for his partner, must still preserve for the assembly his outer dignity and grace.

The young major came towards us. He held his partner by the hand in a manner which seemed to me to sit ill with his uniform and his pale, sand-coloured face.

"Aren't you Millar?" he asked. "I see that you don't remember me, and there's no earthly reason why you should, but we were officer cadets together at Pwllheli. Good old Pwllheli!" He introduced us to his partner, who appeared to be a little bewildered by his continued grasp of her left hand. "She doesn't speak a word of English," he said, and before we quite realised his intention, he had pulled two chairs to our table, and we were four. He returned, with the conversational and reminiscent gusto which some men reserve for such memories, to the subject of the officer-training school at Pwllheli. "Good Lord, old chap! where did you learn to parley the lingo?" he asked when I had ordered something to drink.

"In prison."

"Of course, I forgot—stupid of me—you were in the bag in Italy. I suppose there was nothing better to do than learn the language. Well, even so, I'm glad I wasn't in the bag here. You see, if I had been, I should have been bitter and hated Italy now, while as it is I only came here at the end of the Italian campaign. I had no time to get to hate the Eyeties. And I must say, I don't know what I'd do without Italy."

The Italian girl and Isabel were talking in Spanish.

"A lovely, lovely dress," the girl said. "Harry here told me you could not get beautiful things in London, but I couldn't get a dress like that in Naples or Rome or Milan."

"So glad you like it. You can get clothes provided you have the coupons and the patience to wait for them to be made."

"I would so like to go to London."

"To England, yes, to the country. Don't go to London. London will take many years to recover from the war."

"Well, that's a bit of luck," the young man said. "Mrs. Millar and my girl having a language in common, I mean. I don't mind admitting that even with so pretty a girl it becomes a bit heavy just sitting around and then dancing all the evening. She learned English at school, but she won't speak a word, while my little Italian servant chap natters away like nobody's business though he's only been with me a month."

"I expect your servant is less self-conscious."

"That's it. You've hit the nail on the head. She's shy about it, even alone with me, while if she comes to the mess, well, she's by far the best-looking woman there, but nobody except the I.O. can get a damned word out of her. What I feel is that Italian is such a dead end of a language; I mean that French takes you most places, and Spanish is useful in South America, but what's the good of Italian? Oh hell! I suppose I shall have to settle down and swot at it. I'm thinking of stopping here, you know, when I'm demobbed."

"Are you really?"

"You're surprised, I can see that. But although I'm pretty young to be a major, and I've had a fairly good time during the war, I can't bear the idea of staying on any longer in the Army. I'd have to come down to lieutenant, and I'm thoroughly browned off with Army life anyway."

"You don't want to go back to England?"

"Good God, no! Do you?"

"I do indeed."

"But the chaps who've been home say that life is hell there now, that one leads the life of a coolie."

"The only people in Britain who used to lead approximations to the lives of coolies are now better off than ever before."

"But it doesn't make sense. Why are you here if you think life so wonderful there? It's all very well for you to say things are going well when you can escape from them on a bleeding yacht!"

"I didn't say that life was wonderful there at this moment, but on the whole it's better in England than in most places in Europe, although that's not why I want to go back. I like travelling well enough and I like foreign places and people; but after a time abroad I feel that I want to live again in the country where I really belong and that really belongs to me; I get tired of being thought of as a stranger and I find it comfortable to be in England again."

"But be honest now: there's nothing like all this in Britain, now is there? like this restaurant even the bay there, Capri, nothing half so—super."

"Nothing like it, no."

"Well," he said definitely. "I'm damned if I want to leave all this, these blue skies and the pretty places and the girls and the bathing, and go back to Liverpool. Not that Liverpool isn't all right in its way; up to last year I still thought there was no place like it. But I know that I'd be discontented if I went back there after this. If only I had a private income I'd settle here for the rest of my life."

"Perhaps the blue skies would pall after a time. They do for most people, you know . . ."

"But not for me."

"How do you propose to stay here?"

"My girl has an uncle who's a big wholesale grocer. He used to do a good deal of business with London. Of course, that's fallen away to nothing, and it hasn't even begun to pick up yet. He's said that he'd take me on as an agent, but he wouldn't pay me a salary; all he'd do would be to give me a percentage; they're pretty tight about money, you know, although in other ways they're so decent. I know nothing at all about business, and I'd have to learn this damned lingo. I can see that the job's risky and it would mean a couple of years before I was earning anything at all. I've saved a good bit during the war, but all my savings would go in the two years because, as you probably know, just living costs the earth here. On the other hand, if I went back home I suppose I could put the savings into the bank and in two years I might use them to get married or to improve my position, buy a partnership or something. I took a degree in engineering. I was supposed to be a mining engineer like my father. I expect they're crying out for chaps with my training in England now."

"Almost certainly."

"What I like about the Italians," he said, "is that they aren't snobs."

"Oh?"

"What exactly do you mean by 'Oh'?"

"I thought that there were snobs in every nation. They're international; isn't that one of the nicer things about them? And then, I'm not sure that I would enjoy a world without snobs; it would certainly be a less amusing world."

"I know, I know: you are one of those chaps who have to have plenty of Worcester Sauce with their humour. Well, I haven't noticed any snobs here, and believe me I like it. When I meet strangers in England I'm always on edge. Even in the Army, one never knows when one's going to meet some of those superior asses who've enjoyed all the advantages one hasn't had oneself, and Christ! can't they make you feel small? Now here, people take you at your face value."

234

"I don't want to tarnish any of your beliefs, but do you think that the Italians' attitude towards you will remain unchanged when the Army leaves Italy, as it soon must, and you're a lonely civilian?"

"I'll take a chance on that."

"Well, if you decide to stay, I certainly wish you the best of luck."

"You think it's a good idea, then?"

"A very good idea."

"By jove, that's grand. All the chaps in the mess are on t'other side, you know. They prophesy disaster right, left and centre. I know what I'll do: I'll buy an Italian grammar book first thing to-morrow morning . . ."

They stood waving by the table as we went down to the dark edge of the water.

"An Italian grammar!" Isabel said.

"What was the girl like?"

"I rather liked her. Very good-looking, didn't you think?"

"Well, quite. What did she say about him."

"She said that he was handsome, rich, and a wonderful dancer."

"Anything else?"

"Yes. She asked me. . . . Here we are . . ." She caught hold of *Truant's* ladder. I made the dinghy fast, and followed her below.

"What did she ask?"

"Oh, that. She asked if he was a gentleman."

"What did you tell her?"

"That he was."

* * * *

When I endeavoured to draw water for our breakfast tea I learned that the fresh-water tanks, last filled twenty-two days previously in Monte Carlo harbour, were dry. I took two water cans ashore in the dinghy. I heard full-noted snoring from the married quarters above the offices on the quayside. The Jugoslavs who mounted guard came forward to me, smiling. They said that Trinkwasser—they spoke no foreign language but German—was easily obtainable, and showed me to their own, extremely bare quarters, where I filled the cans from the tap at which the non-commissioned officers were shaving. When I reached the dinghy with my cans I saw a sergeant and a private in the Royal Army Service Corps, who were washing down a silly-looking, pale-blue launch. Noticing that they were using a fresh-water hose, I approached, and falsely admired the launch.

"Oh, you're the fellow off the black ketch," the sergeant said. "Yes,

235

she's a lovely thing," he said, referring to the blue launch. "She belonged to the King of Italy, and she has six hundred horsepower in her."

"Who owns her now?"

"Our commander-in-chief. But she's being handed back to the Eyeties next month. Damned shame I call it; they'll only knock her to bits."

Although I entirely disagreed with him, I restrained my argument, and asked for the use of his hose.

"You're welcome. The brigadier and his wife are going out in the launch to-day, and I don't suppose they'll want to come back before tea-time. You just bring your boat alongside here any time before tea, and I'll leave the hose coiled up handy behind that door."

When we had bought provisions in Naples, we hurried back to *Truant*, for the day was so perfect that we could only think of leaving the big town and hurrying off to sea, and to Capri. An American battleship had anchored out in the bay and naval pinnaces—I can never see them without a smile since the day that my infant nephew repeatedly mispronounced the word "pinnaces" in a thoroughly embarrassing manner—were dashing across the intervening water, fanning out, as though for an assault on the town. We had great difficulty with our anchor, which had entangled itself in a wire hawser stretched on the bottom. By combined effort we tautened the chain underfoot until I was able to see that the sharp edge of the *charrue de la mer* was beginning to cut through the rusty hawser. Both of us went right forward and, jumping in unison, we managed to bounce *Truant* so effectively that we cut the hawser. This triumph was but accomplished when I saw to my disgust that the King of Italy's launch was re-entering the harbour. The brigadier had decided to return to Naples for lunch. As they went by us the sergeant, who stood steering, while a smart soldier held a boat-hook on either side of him, hailed me: "Had your water yet?"

"Not yet."

"Just slip in after us and we'll fix you up."

We allowed the brigadier and his wife a moment to land, and then Isabel began to coax *Truant* to the small vacant space at the quay, but an American pinnace with an Admiral on board rushed by and occupied the space. Isabel flung both engines astern; the starboard propeller fished a small mooring, and refused to function. We drifted straight for the pinnace. The Admiral looked round at us, and instead of cursing as I expected, he growled at his boat's crew: "There's a lady on that boat. Don't stand looking at me!" Several pairs of arms and several boat-hooks stretched out to take our weight, while one sailor leaped across the water, then lay on our deck and fended off with his feet. While we took water I was able to free our propeller with the tool that we had made to remove weed in the canals. We were hauling away from the quay when *Elpis* sailed into the harbour. Douglas shouted that they intended to swing their compass in the main harbour of Naples—which is specially buoyed for that purpose—and then to follow us to Capri.

Capri appeared ahead as soon as we had cleared Santa Lucia harbour. The island is only sixteen miles from Naples. We had a sharp heading breeze all the way, and it took us most of the remainder of the day to get there. We lashed the helm, and lunched on deck as soon as we had hoisted sufficient sail to take us steadily along. When we had eaten I lay down forward and enjoyed a siesta, warmed by the sun, cooled by the breeze. Through the splash, tumble and hiss of the water I heard Isabel singing at the tiller, aft.

"*Great slabs of fat, run off my hips . . . Hairy Mary, had a canary. . . .* Don't you think . . ."

"Yes," I called lazily.

"I was only thinking that we might do better with the bigger jib . . ."

"Oh." I looked over the bulwark, and got a tongue of salt water in my eye. The singing had begun again. "We seem to be moving," I called. There was a pause, then singing again. "Anyway, we shall soon be there at this pace," I pleaded. When I awoke she was standing looking down at me and the boat was still.

"We're within half a mile of the island and it has shut the wind away from us," she said. We lay inside a semi-circle of glassy blue water in which every tree and every white dwelling on the high land ahead was reflected. Two hundred feet astern the sea was rippled where the breeze touched it. Ahead was Marina Grande, the man-made port of Capri, and as I looked at the walls a boat came out from them, impelled by no fewer than eight oars. It was a narrow-hulled boat, dirty white, with an azure waterline, and a great acetylene lamp, the size of a street light in Baden-Baden, drooped and wobbled over the stern. The eight fishermen, four of them elderly and four very young, stood looking ahead and rowing with swinging harmony. They paid little heed to us, but rowed steadily, swiftly on, concentrating perhaps on thoughts of the fish they would catch, the money they would make by selling the fish, the food and wine and enjoyment that would be bought with the money.

20

ISABEL, always the more capable and energetic when plans had to be made, pointed out that we had long delayed in French and Italian waters, and that soon we might expect the weather to deteriorate; we could spend no more than one week in Capri, and a part of our time there must be set aside for preparing *Truant* to face the rough times ahead. We agreed that the engines, the decks, and the rigging claimed attention.

"Can we do all that in a week?" she asked.

"Yes, I think we can."

"In that case, let's make to-day a holiday."

"Good!"

The sun cannot reach Marina Grande in the early morning; the dew is most profuse on the decks of the boats, and the air is like a cold compress. We waited only for the arrival of a laundress commissioned to work for us by the commandante del porto's interpreter, Giovanni Catuogno (Napoli). Isabel had reasoned wisely in England when she maintained that we must take all our sheets and towels because the less regular your laundry service, the more linen you require. Nearly a boatful went ashore at Capri.

We pulled the dinghy up a shingle beach near the entry to the funicular which climbs from Marina Grande to the town of Capri. The railway was built by a Swiss firm long ago; it contrives to retain a good deal of the glamour that attached to even the most ordinary mechanical device when machines were hand-made novelties pressed into the service of man.

I knew the instant that we disembarked from the funicular and walked into the Piazza Umberto, so absurdly like a scene from opera, that Capri pleased me just as much as it had pleased all those who had bored me with their praises of it. Narrow lanes that were indeed, as the romantic director of the bank in Rome had claimed, remarkably clean and well-constructed, led us through the close-built shops and houses. We noticed the window of a bedroom in which a pair of silk stockings and a man's necktie were suspended from a piece of elastic, doubtless to dry in the draught which made them bob and curtsey grotesquely, while from the room behind them came the sound of passionate altercation in Dutch, Danish, or Swedish, we were unable to decide which. Four steps down the lane we paused before a café in which a young girl was pounding an upright piano and singing: "W'en a buddy, meets a buddy, comin' through the rye, should a buddy greet a buddy, coming through the rye? W'en a buddy meets a buddy, comin' . . .' "

"What about learning the right words?" A stout man had spoken from behind a table on which stood a half-gallon tankard of beer. He wore the uniform cap of the Royal Army Medical Corps, and his tunic, with rank badges showing him to be a captain, hung over the edge of the table. Judging by his accent, he had been reared in or near Glasgow.

"Who'll learn me them?"

"Surely it goes, 'Gin a body, meet a body, coming through the rye, should a body . . .' Dash it. They've slipped me. Where's your mother? Mother!"

"She's washing her bathing suit."

"Play 'The Road to the Isles', that's the best by a mile."

"It is not. The other's a love song."

"You're not the age to be thinking of such things." He took a long drink, squinting into the gassing liquid with an air of embarrassment.

Round the corner we came on another aspect of the Allied occupation forces. The Grand Hotel Quisisana was a "rest camp" for American airmen, of whom there were several hundreds on the island. Even these men, the most boisterous soldiers of the different kinds in Europe, plainly felt the influence of Capri (an influence that therefore would seem to be stronger than that of London or Paris). The American airmen on Capri were apt to be quiet, ruminative, and lazy. They were liable to form touchingly unmartial habits, like carrying walking-sticks or putting blue flowers in their hats, or chewing at the stems of roses while the blooms hung below their chins; once we met a brawny sergeant who walked barefoot down the lanes carrying a dirty urchin on one shoulder. A dozen of them were lying on the steps of the Quisisana and as we walked past they lifted heavy-lidded eyes to look appreciatively at my wife. Two of them mounted on plump donkeys followed us down the street, and we heard one say to his companion, who burdened the air with lusty sighs: "You in love again?"

"Yeah."

"Who with?"

"I don't know."

While Isabel went to be measured for sandals, I entered an establishment marked, *Barber Shop*. The man in the other chair was a French operatic tenor of forceful appearance and dimensions. The chairs rotated freely, and instead of manœuvring around me the young barber whirled me, so that one moment I looked at my own reflection in the looking-glass, the next at the soapy jowl of the humming tenor, and the next at an advertisement for an unguent that was stated to prevent, and often to cure, certain diseases which lurked—the advertisement warned—in the home and in the street. My hair had not been cut since we were in Lyons, and was a little wild, even for Capri, where wild hair was in fashion. I learned in conversation with the barber that the island had, shortly before our arrival, been purged of "certain elements less guilty and depraved than many supposed to be the case". It seemed that a dance had been given to which no women were invited, but certain of the male guests did their best to remedy the deficiency by impersonating the other sex with convincing skill. My informant said that everybody who had attended that affair had spoken so highly of it that many of the women on the island had joined forces to seduce, bully and cajole the authorities into the purge that had followed. "It makes one wonder why a war was fought," the barber said. "Is this liberty, or is it despotism?"

The doe-eyed youth who had shaved the tenor withdrew from the powdered chin asking: "Ça va bien, Monsieur?"

"Très, très bien," he shouted, rolling the rs, and in a voice that rattled the mugs, the jars of brilliantine, the bottles of friction, the tins and boxes of talcum powder, the devices for corns and hernia, he sang of a woman and her lover who were passengers in a taxi which struck and killed a pedestrian; all ended according to happy convention, for they discovered to their relief that the dead man was only the woman's husband, who had been following them. The tenor adjusted a beret, a tinted eyeglass, a silk scarf, hung a knotted cherrywood stick over one arm, and sauntered from the shop. His singing was audible for a long time after the door had ceased to swing behind him.

We lunched alone beneath a great vine in a stone courtyard, and then, feeling the heat, descended to the sea and went off in our dinghy. A mile from the harbour mouth we dropped the sail and entered the water. Isabel floated and swam until she had no strength left to climb into the dinghy. I hoisted the sail and towed her. Her two small hands on the transom and two languidly trailing brown feet were all that I saw of her as I crouched amidships to trim the boat.

We were happy in the Marina Grande. The main mole juts from the shoreline and then runs parallel to it in a long L and to narrow the entrance a small breakwater comes out from the shore until it nearly meets the top of the L, thus forming a rectangular basin, rather shallow before the fishermen's houses which line the waterfront and which, unlike the

240

somewhat similar houses in Portofino, have not been "developed" or improved internally by rich strangers, because on Capri Marina Grande is only the place of arrival and departure, and the place to which visitors descend to make excursions in small boats—at fixed rates of payment if they are wise—around the island and to the celebrated grottoes. At the moment of arrival a curly-headed man had rowed vigorously to us and had succeeded in thrusting a printed card into one of my busy hands. The card gave his name as Giovanni Catuogno (Napoli). He suggested that we should moor *Truant* beside one of the main quays.

"Oh, don't you think they look a little crowded, Mr. Catuogno?" Isabel said.

"Yes, fine and crowded. Plenty people."

"But we don't like crowds. Supposing we attach our stern to that little breakwater."

"Suppose the east wind come, Signora, then he catches your boat back-sides."

"But if we prefer to take that risk."

"Ah! You prefer! That's different."

"So we have your permission to moor there?"

"*Cerr*tainly."

The result was that we lay apart from the other traffic, except for the fishing-boats, which gathered round us before going out at night and when they returned in the morning. Only ten feet from our port side a rock rose suddenly from the bottom to within two feet of the surface, but as Catuogno had pointed out, we were well placed in anything but an east wind.

*   *   *   *

I had to spend all one morning in the engine-room, a place that I still disliked. Isabel rowed herself ashore to do the marketing. In the afternoon we scraped, sandpapered and varnished the foredeck. While we worked we watched with amusement the Sunday traffic that came to the island, boat-load after boat-load of British and American soldiers, launch after launch filled with officers. Our friend the R.A.S.C. sergeant was at the wheel of the former King's pale-blue boat, which entered the harbour noisily. The Commander-in-Chief, Italy, was the first to jump to the quay. We saw him wet his forefinger and hold it up to gauge the wind. He ordered a box to be carried from the launch and supervised the erection and the lighting of a portable cooking-stove. The Commander-in-Chief's party, stiff and rurally English, settled down to making tea. The sea wall behind them was painted with out-of-date slogans in lettering ten feet high,

241

calling upon Italians to vote for King Umberto in the election in which the majority of Italians had voted the other way. We saw *Elpis* sail up to the harbour-mouth, where Gwenda had another fight with their stubborn gaff. Even the gaff, however, had the sense to yield to Gwenda, who did not spare her comments on it for its show of obstinacy. They motored in, and anchored beyond us. Later we rowed across to them. They were dining, and seemed to be in high spirits. The first thing that Gwenda said when we had exchanged greeting and had settled down was: "Some douglas, Beans?" They had found some excellent red wine in Naples. We sampled the wine and ate toast, butter, and part of a magnificent gorgonzola. Excavating with the cheese-knife, I uncovered the nest of a translucent green worm, an inch long, and the colour of fine jade. Douglas, Gwenda and Isabel took an instant dislike to the cheese; it was handed to me, and at subsequent meals I had many moments of enjoyment from it. I dropped the worm overboard, but none of the fishes would touch him, although several approached to have a look—or a sniff.

The following morning, our third in Capri, we worked hard on our deck, and managed to scrape, sandpaper and varnish all of the starboard side. *Truant* had a fine deck, but it had been caulked in Bursledon at a time when the weather was unsuitable, and the men had been obliged to work quickly between rainstorms. Deck seams are first caulked with cotton and then paid with marine glue, which must be heated until it runs smoothly and then is poured steadily into each seam. If this operation is hurried bubbles form in the glue, and in hot weather these rise to the surface and form blisters. We had a thick crop of such blisters on the deck and on the cabin-top. They were easy to scrape off, but when I had scraped the length of the deck I found that the small particles of black glue which had jumped from the blade of the scraper to my torso had melted there, and had become so much a part of that long-wearing surface that I had the utmost difficulty in removing them. Before I varnished the deck I filled in any obvious holes in the seams with an admirable plastic glue which does not need to be heated, and can simply be pressed into any crack or broken blister which is a suspected source of trouble. The last thing Mr. Moody, senior, had done before I left his yard was to press into my right hand a tin of black plastic glue, and into my left a tin of teak-coloured. I could have had no two more useful presents.

That evening Douglas introduced us in Vuotto's to a tall, savage and opulently-dressed woman, Madame de Quelquechose. Her ideas of conversation seemed to be a little stagy and inflated. She said to Douglas that she could not make up her mind whether he was a man in God's image or a god in man's image, and Gwenda laughed until the tears ran from the corners of her eyes; Douglas inscrutably ordered dry martinis and camparigins. Occasionally when the Frenchwoman became excited by her own florid usage of the English language she would lay a large, slightly yellow hand on Douglas's. Around her wrist was a multiple gold bracelet to which were attached small gold objects which she began to show him in detail. "Look here," she said. "This is a little gold valise, you see. I open it, thus, and look what it contains: a tiny golden brassière et d'autres bricoles très amusantes . . ."

"Très amusantes," Douglas echoed absent-mindedly, keeping one expressionless eye on Gwenda, who was at pains to pretend that a small fly had been engulfed in her throat. When Douglas lit her cigarette, Madame de Q. grabbed his wrist and glared into his eyes. But when politics were mentioned I was drawn into the discussion, which at once assumed the lines of an argument. In England men and women were free to choose their own political leanings, and it was strangely annoying in Italy to find that all persons wealthy beyond a certain degree took it for granted that an Englishman was a Russophobe.

"Within a year we shall be fighting the Soviet," she cried. "And I am not afraid to say so."

"The idea seems to gratify you, madame. I don't intend to fight anybody . . ."

"Not even the Russians?"

"Having just fought for some years as their ally, I should require very much stronger arguments than any that are likely to be produced to convince me that it was necessary to turn about and fight against them."

"Then God help your British Empire if there are many more long-haired young pacifists like you!"

I called the waiter for I wished to pay my part of the bill. This was construed by the lady as an overtly hostile—perhaps even a communist-inspired—act. She leaped to her feet and hastened to a neighbouring table where she loudly inveighed in perfectly comprehensible Italian against "long-haired pacifists, and communists disguised as Englishmen". Gwenda laughed all the way down in the funicular.

"What strange friends you make," she said to Douglas. "Where did you find her?"

"We met in the bank, and she wouldn't cast off."

During the night a heavy swell rolled into Marina Grande, the first that had bothered us there. When I went on deck I saw Gwenda shaking her head as she sluiced and scrubbed at *Elpis's* white teak.

"This swell means foul weather," she said.

We had forgotten how handsome our decks looked when freshly varnished. Douglas had told me that I should sprinkle sand over the varnish while it was sticky, to make the decks less slippery when wet, but I could not bear to do it, for he admitted that the sand would not look well. I had bought some aluminium paint in the town, and with it I painted the rail stanchions and the rigging screws. Isabel, who dislikes anything new, did not care for the result for a few days, and Gwenda described it as "rather vulgar".

We walked out of Capri, taking the path to the Villa Jovis. Unshaded for the most part, and perfectly built of masonry inlaid with small cobbles, the path climbs some four hundred feet past vineyards and small farms to the eastern peak of the island. However admirable the paths of Capri may be, they reflect all the heat that the sun may throw upon them. It was only when we were half-way to the Villa that Isabel revealed that she had a headache. Workers in the vineyards were snipping off bunches of grapes. They said that it would be a good year for the wine. When we reached the Villa, Isabel lay down to rest on a bank in the garden. I picked my way with awe through the traces of that theatrical palace, examining what remains of the banqueting hall, the solarium, the baths, the cisterns, the intricate pattern of aqueducts taking to different parts of the building the water by which the Romans, like their spiritual descendants, the twentieth-century North Americans, set such store. I followed an aqueduct into what I thought might have been a treasure chamber. The walls were vastly thick, and the place was lit only through the smallest of embrasures, high up, near the barrel vault. It was disconcerting that others should have chosen such a place in which to relieve themselves, I was reflecting, when a voice boomed out a great: "Sonny Jim!"

"Hullo?" I answered doubtfully, and then I saw an eye and part of its surrounding human territory looking at me through one of the embrasures. Thoughts of prisoners in towers entered my head, but when I walked out of the doorway and turned the angle of the wall I found a steep, grassy bank, which rose so close to the top of the treasure chamber that the man who had called out had been able to watch me while he lay on the grass. He was an ugly person, extravagantly dressed in ultra-blue blues and ultra-white whites, and he lay now on his back, with one arm round the neck of a generously proportioned woman whose naturally fair hair was dyed to a reddish tinge.

"You're the English boy from the black yacht, aren't you?" he said. "They call me G., and this is Signora Volpi. Where is your pretty little wife?"

"She had a headache on the way up, and she's resting in the garden."

"Bring her round to meet us, there's a good scout." His over-colloquial English was spoken with a slight accent. I did not take to him, but I told myself that his patronising attitude was only another of those inferiority complexes to which—in others—we are supposed to pander. Isabel had recovered. We climbed round slowly by another route, for we wanted, before joining the others, to see the platform on which Tiberius was in the habit of consulting the stars with the professional help of his reader of oracles to discover his own destiny and to determine what directives should be flashed to the mainland to keep the Empire functioning in the desired manner. But at that high place Christians have meanly invaded the past by erecting a little church with a tronc on its door begging for alms, and a puerile statue of the Virgin Mary. The pair had not altered their position on the bank. "Sit down, young woman," G. said to Isabel. "I have just been telling Signora Volpi that you have beautiful hair, and by God, I was right." He turned for confirmation to Signora Volpi, who smiled, nodded, and looked at him with a great deal more warmth than she could spare for Isabel. "Pour us some champagne, Jimmy," he said to me. "Signora Volpi and I are sharing one glass, so that will leave the other for you and your good lady."

"You have a remarkable command of the English language," I told him, thinking how vile it sounded on his lips.

"I darned well ought to have, for I've worked with Englishmen since I was a nipper. I know the English business methods and the English business man backwards . . ." Signora Volpi tittered, and he screwed his red face round to look at her. "There's nothing funny in that," he said. "It's pure English idiom."

"So long as it's pure," she said.

He reached over and pinched one of her fat cheeks before taking the glass from me. "Skin off your nose," he said. "You've seen my yacht, of course?"

"Perhaps we have," I answered carefully, "but we've been so busy working on our own boat that we haven't had time to notice any of the other boats in the harbour."

"Now what's all this? they tell me that you and your sweet little wife, here, are managing your big boat all alone; is that true? doing it for a bet or something? Well, what's the idea? I've got two fellows working for me on my boat, and it's only an eight-metre."

"We like doing the work ourselves . . ."

"Now, my dear old Jim, there's no sense in saying such things to

245

me; nobody likes work unless he's well paid for it."

"If we had paid hands we should have to arrange our life to suit their whims, whereas, being alone, we live exactly as it pleases us to live."

"Two love-birds, eh? Who says the English are cold? You want to be alone all the time, eh?"

"Quite," I said, trying to put a great deal of frigidity into my voice.

"There, there," he said stickily. "I know you can take a joke, Jimmy. And nobody can be angry with old G., or so they always told me. Do you know Pinner?"

"I've driven through it," I said.

"Do you know Pinner, Mrs. Millar?"

"No, I'm afraid not."

"Well, before we part I'll give you a letter to some good friends of mine in Pinner, and when you get back home you just look them up and they'll see you lack nothing. Hullo! Here are our mokes." Two men were indeed hastening up the hill with two large and glossy asses. G. mounted, his face still smeared with little blurred petunias where Signora Volpi had kissed him. "To-morrow morning I'm coming to drag you both if necessary by force from your bonny black boat," G. said. "So bye-bye for the present." He seized a switch that one of the men held in his hand, and beating a tattoo on his animal's ribs, vanished at a shaking trot round the corner, and then reappeared on the lower path, followed, more gingerly, by the plump Signora Volpi. One of the two men spat on the ground and began to pack into the hamper plates, glasses, and other remnants of the picnic. The other man looked intently at me.

"You're the owner of *Truant*?" he asked.

"I am."

"Do you want a sailor, Signor?"

"No thank you."

"And they say you are going to Greece."

"Yes."

"Greece is wonderful. I was there on yachts before the war, and I would dearly like to go back. I'm on the eight-metre in the harbour now, but I don't like little boats and little journeys from Naples to Capri and Capri to Naples, from Naples to Sorrento and Sorrento to Naples. I mustn't detain you." He politely wished us good day.

We woke early, and at dawn we were both working on the port side of the deck. When the wood had been scraped and sandpapered Isabel varnished it while I attended to the teak hatches. As we worked we argued about the suitability of Capri for honeymoons. I thought that it was

246

highly suitable, a restful, suggestive place, without too many distractions, with few organised amusements, with good cafés and good wine, with a superb climate which drives people to bed for the after-lunch siesta. Isabel felt that the atmosphere was too unhealthy, that Tiberius still, after two thousand years, tinged the air with cynicism and illegal forms of love. She pointed out that the children of Capri are wizened and ratlike, and that their elders, quickly perceptive in the business sense—as behoves members of a community which lives off tourists as the mosquito sucks from such mammals as stray into his ken—seemed to be strangely slow and coarse in others. For example, the touts at the Marina Grande who attempt to persuade all strangers leaving the funicular to hire sightseeing boats, still ambushed us daily, although for a week we had been living on our own boat within one hundred yards of the place where they operated. Isabel felt that Capri was too worldly and too crowded for a honeymoon. But what was more worldly than a honeymoon, I asked. Was a honeymoon not the coating of sugar over the pill that should by ecclesiastical and even secular law be swallowed when two beings of opposite sex wish, however temporarily, to lie together? We both jumped as a deafening "Ahoy there, *Truant*!" came over the water. There was G., dressed again in blues and whites, though in a different combination, and seated in the stern of a large dinghy rowed by a yacht hand. Four children occupied the bows of the dinghy, two girls with pigtails and two dignified little boys in grey suits. They appeared to range in age from eight to thirteen. They were agog with excitement, and almost shivered with the pleasure of anticipation as they gaped at *Truant*, but when the dinghy touched the side they politely waited for G. to go first up the ladder, and then they followed, girls leading. "These are my kids," G. said carelessly, and while each of them politely shook hands and the girls did little curtseys, he added: "Now, let's see what you've got here. How much did you pay for her, and where did you find her?" When they had seen all the below-decks accommodation, had examined the rigging, and had run the engines, G. said that although *Truant* was surprisingly comfortable, he would prefer to live in a hotel or a villa. "I like my sailing straight," he said. "No auxiliary engines for me. Now you come along with me, and I'll show you some real sailing." He turned to one of the boys. "Where's Signora Volpi?"

"I see her on the quay, sir."

"Oh, so she is. Well, go and get her, put her on the yacht and bring the dinghy back for us." He turned to me with a wink. "Their mother doesn't like sailing, believe it or not, so Signora Volpi, who's a real sport, comes instead." The signora had covered her head with a silk scarf, and had already stationed herself in the small helmsman's cockpit well aft in the racing-boat. "Move over," G. said to her. "You're far too stout, my girl." He crushed in beside her. Isabel and I, the four children and one yacht hand somehow managed to dispose ourselves about the deck and in the larger working cockpit. G.'s boat was exceptionally handsome, very modern, and with a fine suit of Ratsey sails. Under mainsail and a large Genoa we hissed out of the harbour. The boat was remarkably fast in the light breezes. The two boys and the yacht hand arranged the sails to suit the vagaries of G.'s helmsmanship, for G. although he casually held the tiller was devoting all of his attention to Signora Volpi. As we rounded the end of the island he suddenly said: "By the way, Millar, haven't I heard that you've written a book? Well, there's a girl who might interest you. She writes love stories. Pretty good they are too. I get quite a kick out of them. We'll see if we can find her. This party wants livening up." Until we reached the Faraglioni we had no idea whether G. could steer or not, but when we arrived at the high rocks and he saw that he had an audience of bathers and fishermen, he showed that he was something of an expert. We charged around like a stallion in a circus ring. Round and round we went, the boom sweeping overhead, the big Genoa flapping and filling again with resounding cracks while the two boys worked hard with the wire sheets on the deck winches. While he steered G. carried on a shouted conversation with a muscular young woman who lay sunbathing on the rocks. In the end he persuaded her to join us, and then engaged a fisherman to bring her to us in a rowing-boat. When she had hoisted herself on board, and had given G. a light kiss on the cheek he introduced her to me, saying: "Now get on with it, you two, for you should have plenty to talk about." The girl and I disliked each other at sight, and after a few words with Isabel, she went forward and lay on her back beneath the jib. G. sailed the boat out to sea, passing the time, as before, with Signora Volpi. When he hove to, the hand arranged a special ladder over the side, and most of us entered the water. After the bathe the children were sent forward; the hand removed a trap in the mahogany floor boards and pulled out two insulated containers, one of which held hot Neapolitan hors d'œuvres and the other two bottles of champagne embedded in crushed ice. Food and drink were soon disposed of and G. began to sail for the eastern end of the island.

"Where are you going?" asked the writer of love stories.

"Marina Grande."

"But you promised me you'd take me back to the Faraglioni."

"Too much trouble," G. said. "I'm hungry. I want my lunch. You can take the funicular from Marina Grande and then walk."

"I'll do no such thing. Take me back to the Faraglioni or you'll regret it."

"Keep a civil tongue in your head, young woman, or you'll regret it. How would you like to have to swim back to the Faraglioni?"

"I always thought you were a swine, and now I know it. I suppose you realise, you vulgarian, that you've spoiled my entire day. You made me leave my friends, and now what will they think of me?"

"That's your own lookout. You should never have come. Should she?" he asked Signora Volpi, giving a hitch with the arm that encircled her plump, drying shoulders. Signora Volpi smiled. The writer shut her mouth, her jaw muscles working, and sulked. The four children had looked carefully out to sea while this was going on. We sometimes talked to them. How did G. come to have such pleasant children? They were very much his children; each of them resembled him; they regarded him with admiration. On his side, G. treated them with a certain brusque affection, but when he spoke to them it was usually to give an order or to reprimand one of them for some offence against the strict code of behaviour that he laid down for them.

The writer of love stories was still (since she had nothing else to wear) in her bathing costume when we entered Marina Grande; her flesh was roughened by the chill of the breeze. Isabel asked her to come aboard *Truant*, and offered to lend her some clothes, but the young woman's pent-up fury was too great to permit her to accept. G. invited us to lunch. "I've a perfectly foul villa," he said. "My wife chose it. But there should be enough to eat and drink. Come on up."

"I'm very sorry, we have another engagement."

The writer had been put ashore, and we saw her walk stiffly in her bathing suit to the line of carriages drawn up before the entrance to the funicular. She climbed into a carriage pretending to ignore the sensation that her appearance caused among the local population. G. missed none of her discomfiture. "Let that be a lesson to her," he said.

*   *   *   *

The air was cool after the heat of the day when the sun went down beyond the island and the Marina Grande was sunk in clammy peacefulness. The tourists had hurried up to Capri, where the sun still shone and the crowds gathered in the cafés; the fishermen had long ago made for the sea and the night's business. I went with Douglas to the fountain. We waited for a time in a queue of barefooted women. Above our heads the island's power station was emitting smells of hydrochloric acid and diesel oil. The fountain gave the merest trickle of water. At length Douglas said: "Just tell them, will you, that I can't wait any longer because we're going to-morrow and I've the devil of a lot to do on board." Before I had embarked on my explanation, he pushed past the queue and set a four-gallon water can beneath the spout. There were screams of protest from the women, but they were only simulated and soon turned into conversation. Some of them did not seem to have much political comprehension; they took me for a German. The inhabitants of Marina Grande who live off the fishing trade become dazed by the ebb and flow of tourists, and develop a certain aloofness from that foreign tide. We had a last drink with Douglas and Gwenda in their small saloon in which electric lights and fans worked everywhere. All four of us were sad, for we had become attached to each other, and they to our boat as we to theirs. Perhaps we should meet again; for after all we had supposed that we were exchanging final good-byes when we left them in the restaurant at Arles with the Rhône pilot, Pépé Male.

They sailed at eight the following morning. The weather was sultry and an ominous ring of cloud had gathered to the south-west.

*　　　*　　　*　　　*

It was best to go to market in the evening after the arrival of the boat from Naples which carried the majority of the fresh provisions for the island. The provision shops were in a twisting, dark lane that slid from one corner of the Piazza Umberto. We stocked there for a long journey, buying a chicken, white bread, gruyère, butter, vegetables, fruit, oil, and a dozen litres of Capri bianco. We collected the packages beside a table on the terrace of the Café Vuotto. By this time we knew most of the Vuotto regulars by sight. There were two dark sisters who arranged their hair over pads on the tops of their heads. Two cads, brothers, went around the terrace making assignations with every age, type, and nationality of woman, then returned to their own table to compare notes in public and to ogle each other's conquests. Two pink-skinned Swiss women had a habit of blushing in their ears, the lobes of which were usually constricted under round, white-china ear-rings. The muscular young woman who wrote love stories made a point of ignoring us. And Madame de Quelquechose showed ever-increasing energy in her campaign to persuade Capri—or at any rate the patrons of the Café Vuotto—that I was "nothing but a sneaking little communist.' A small, mousey-looking young man arrived early each evening and hurriedly consumed through straws iced-chocolate with whipped cream, until he was joined by two handsome and excitable young women, when all three drank gin or champagne-cocktails. Two quiet Americans with clean clothes and faces and well-bred ears and hands gave every appearance of being such timid young men that thev scarcely dared raise their voices above a whisper, even to order a drink. Another American, tall and exceptionally handsome, and wearing his hair nearly down to his shoulders, that night staged a farewell celebration at the café with six or seven young friends of both sexes. He repeatedly shouted as he entered the carriage that was to take him down to the Naples boat: "They may drag me away from Capri, but not for long, not for long." One of the waiters was sure of his own charms; he was a pretty man with tight curls, boiled shirt, black trousers, white napkin, black tie, white coat, ready civility, and only his cracked, dusty shoes revealed the weaknesses of a post-war economy on a waiter's salary. His wife and his dirty little son were hanging round the café, standing on the cobbles outside the outer ring of tables, sometimes pretending to look into a shop-window displaying things that they could not afford to buy, silver and gold rings, amulets, crucifixes. The woman carried another child in her womb. The second waiter was tall, lazy, aloofly friendly, with the face of a man who was always wondering what would win the two-thirty. The third waiter had the thin, discontented, snarling look of a revolutionary who, his views perhaps not uninfluenced by a dirty colon and an inefficient liver, would like to see the blood flow and the fortunate burn.

As we entered the upper station of the funicular we felt the early breath of a cold wind, and saw lightning play all round the sky. Thunder sounded before we had climbed into the dinghy, and as we hurried across the harbour Capri's longed-for, prayed-for autumn rain came down on us by the ton. When I had unloaded all our packages the water had mounted from the dinghy floorboards half-way to my knees. Thunder shook *Truant*, as though it put out a hand to the masthead, and lightning illuminated every detail on deck and on the island, and revealed on the still-calm sea a long string of fishing-boats—some of them with their lights burning—the occupants rowing like madmen for our harbour. I secured the dinghy carefully, and before doing so examined both of our stern warps. As I was about to go below the first wind struck us. It came from the west in one howling blow; I was relieved that it came from dead ahead, for we were riding securely to the 80 lbs. C.Q.R. anchor and some thirty fathoms of half-in. chain. For an hour the wind rose and fell, rose and fell, while the rain came in deluges. Then the wind and the rain both steadied, the latter becoming less violent. Around us the returned fishing-boats

251

rolled. We had hoped that the freshly-varnished decks would be water-proof, but although no water came through the decks, a great deal was shed on us through the seam between the deck and the cabin-top. Both of us were capable of sleeping under a few jets of water, however, and the only thing that kept me awake and trembling—though not Isabel, who after remarking: "Poor Gwenda!" closed her eyes and slept—was the infernal noise of the wind. There are men who claim to enjoy bad weather at sea. I am not one of them. A high wind over the sea at night never fails to chill me with terror. I woke at 3 a.m. with the feeling that something was very wrong. The first flash of lightning showed me that the view through our porthole had altered. I jumped from the bed so quickly that Isabel spoke to me.

"Not having a nightmare?"

"Not this time."

"But you're getting up."

"We've swung round."

"What on earth d'you mean?"

"The wind must have veered and broken our stern lines."

"Call me if you need me." She turned over. I put on a thick sweater, my oilskin and sou'wester, and went out on deck. We were swinging in the centre of the harbour, having changed position by at least one hundred yards. When I had been forward to make sure that the anchor was holding I went aft and hauled in first one four-in. warp and then the other; the bowline at the end of each was still intact, but when I looked at the break-water I saw that the warps had torn two holes in the masonry. Giovanni Catuogno had warned us that our position would be insecure in an east wind. The harbour had filled during the night with many craft, large and small. The miracle was that we had not hit any of them, and had continued to sleep as the yacht swung in the harbour. The barometers were still falling.

"We had better move to the quay," I said after breakfast.

Giovanni Catuogno was standing on the quay as Isabel took *Truant's* stern in. He caught our stern lines and made them fast.

"Not nice here," he said.

"No."

"But safe in east wind."

"Yes."

"Not possible go Blue Grotto. To-day too much waves. You want a carriage for go Anacapri?"

"No thank you."

"You like use my telephone? Do not scruple to ask me for anything."

"Thank you very much."

"All right." He walked away, wagging his curly head. We were safe in our new berth, but very uncomfortable. We took the funicular to Capri, and walked from there to Anacapri, a distance of four kilometres. The wind scoured the heights of the island and there was a glum look of autumn everywhere, especially in the pinched faces of other pedestrians and of the honeymoon couples who drove past in basket-coloured carriages with feed-buckets swinging from the axles. We ate in the garden of a delightful place called the Ristorante Cesare Augusto. We were the only clients on such a day. The boy waiter covered the marble table with a white cloth and bunches of purple grapes hung, nearly touching our heads, from a pergola that was rotting in the sun and sagging. The garden must have been unusually sweet and fresh after the rain. When we held our breaths we both thought that we heard from ground and greenery the noise of drinking. We had stumbled on a restaurant with a chef who knew how to cook. He was an elderly man, bent and sniffing, and when each course was set in front of us by the boy waiter he would step out of a door which was divided, like that of a stable, to watch us eat the first mouthfuls. He cooked over wood embers, and the entrecôte had the taste of singeing that I find particularly agreeable.

When daylight came we cast off the stern lines, wound in most of the chain, set the mainsail and staysail, and sailed our anchor out of the ground.

21

THE sea that had been somnolent when we arrived at Capri was now disturbed, like a flock of sheep that dashes this way and that, terrified by some suspected danger. We were aware that our journey was assuming a more serious nature, and leading us to wilder seas. It was soon decided, when we had seen the weather on the open sea, which was neither good nor bad, but might develop into either, that we would make that day for Punta di Palinuro, fifty-eight sea miles from Capri. While we rolled along southward with the high coastline just visible, Isabel strove to forget her malaise by discussing the isolated house with two cows which she intended to buy in England. I told her that her state of mind was one commonly induced by the sea; sailors are always likely to talk of houses in the country, of gardens and of farms. While officers of the Royal Navy dream of polo ponies and hunters, of saddle-backed pigs, shorthorns, and Labradors, officers of the Army discuss ketches and yawls, dragons, six-metres, and ocean racers. We ate our customary wheelhouse meal at midday, less good than usual for the red wine obtainable in Capri had been of poor quality, while the white, which would have gone well with oysters, lobsters, or sole, was a trifle waspish for our food.

As we ate we noticed that the whole boat had been invaded by flies which appeared to be of the common housefly variety. When we first noticed them we were some twenty miles from the land. We supposed, although we had seen no flies at Capri, that we had brought them with us from Marina Grande. We began to slaughter them with sprays and switches, and killed such numbers that we were forced to the conclusion that they were arriving on the boat as we sailed along. Had the wind been offshore we should have thought that they had been blown from the mainland, and alighted on *Truant* as a heaven-sent refuge; but what wind there was would constitute a cross wind for any fly leaving the shore to come toward us. After two hours of carnage we saw that we were gaining the upper hand, and soon the only flies that remained were corpses, which had to be swept from the wheelhouse and dumped overboard by the shovelful. Night was nearly upon us as we approached Palinuro, for the impending winter was curtailing our working day; dawn was not well up now by 7 o'clock, and darkness was on the way at 4.30. Soon, I told Isabel, the sun would be dictating a five-day week to us. As we neared the coast we saw no sign of habitation, only a smooth dark brownness, gashed here and there by river beds, and then, as I was getting down the useless mainsail, she pointed at the sea and called: "What is that, do you think?"

I thought, in the dismal failing light, that the bold line on the sea ahead represented a tidal wave. Another appeared to follow it, and another. How should we counter those unusual marine dangers? However, as we approached we saw the lines were nothing more than semi-solid masses of driftwood, herbs and dirt, possibly swept into the sea by a local river and then arranged as though for a parade by the actions of the sea currents. Punta di Palinuro is a promontory running west but with a northward hook to it, and on the inner edge of the hook there is an indent holding the few stone houses that form Marina di Palinuro, while Palinuro village itself is inland and higher. I stood forward with the lead, and sounded continuously as Isabel nosed *Truant* into the darkness. A tunny fisher, a schooner of about twice our size, was anchored at the entrance to the cove. Her crew turned out on deck and shouted to us in unison that we should go no farther as the water was shoal, but I still had four fathoms under the bow, and saw no reason why we should roll all night when shelter might be available closer inshore. As we moved in, two fishermen rowed to us in a boat full of lobster creels, and they led us close up to the shore, where I dropped anchor over yellow sand two fathoms down. Our stern swung to cover the lights of Marina di Palinuro. Above us, on the wind-shaven headland, the lighthouse turned four beams round the sky. *Truant* was steady, and the water lapped gently against her stout black sides. The fishermen came on board and we gave them brandy. One was young. The other, his uncle, an old, twisted man, looked like a pollard willow, as he stood in the cheerful saloon in his drab clothes a little green with age and with one arm upstretched, the gnarled hand with its long earthy fingernails resting on a white-enamelled cross beam of the deckhead. They asked if we would like fish. No, they had no lobsters, but they would try to get us some by the morning. The nephew told me that he had been a prisoner of war.

"Who took you prisoner?"

"Canadians, very kind, big men. They gave us a meal when we had surrendered. It was in Sicily. The noise was so bad before the Canadians came that we thought they had placed explosives beneath Sicily. Now Sicily is an island," he added, "so our situation was terrible in the extreme."

"Did they send you to Canada?"

"No, to England. At first I worked on farms in England and there was a great deal to eat. The place was alive with cows, and udders on them the size of your boat. You never saw anything like those cows. We heard that they needed all the cows to make explosives and aeroplanes. The English took the war seriously. They had discovered a way of turning milk into everything, cups and coats and white steel."

"Were the farms in the north or the south of England?"

"I don't know. Then I went to work in the docks of great ports, and we met American soldiers, coloured men who were jovial."

"What ports did you work in?"

"I don't know. We couldn't pronounce the names, and the places, although exceptionally fine, all looked alike. I have a fiancée in England, and one day I hope to return there to be a fisherman in a diesel-engined drifter."

"Where does your fiancée live?"

"I don't know. I wrote down the address before leaving England, but my uncle here used it to light his pipe, and now I'm waiting to hear from her. I wish that the English hadn't sent me away. They said that Italy was in need of food and that all fishermen must return to carry on their trade. I told them I was a dock worker, but that availed me nothing, for when I was first made prisoner by the Canadians I'd told them I was a fisherman; I never thought that the Canadians would remember to inform the English."

"What's the weather going to do?"

"It will be good to-morrow and maybe for some days."

I hope that we did not believe him. When they had gone I heard our chicken beginning to crackle in the oven and Isabel singing as she cooked. I got out the FRE-HUM volume of the *Encyclopædia* and looked up "housefly". But the writer, while describing the housefly's proboscis and other revolting organs, did not mention his powers of flight, whims of flight, and rayon d'action. I thought that I had heard somewhere that he could only fly for thirty yards.

We left that interesting and uncommon anchorage before the dawn, and soon regretted that we had done so, for the day showed us a top-heavy accumulation of greasy clouds in the west. But at first we benefited from a steady off-shore breeze, and running free under number two jib, staysail, mainsail and mizzen we headed straight out to sea, setting course for the volcanic island of Stromboli, some sixty sea miles distant. The wind veered with a speed that we thought sinister, veered to the south-west, a dangerous quarter in that part of the Mediterranean. We fussed on, plunging a good deal and often burying the port bulwarks, but it was exhilarating sailing, and the log showed that we covered nearly sixteen miles in two hours. The sea was increasing all the time, and black clouds were piling themselves so ominously behind the wind that, deciding for once to be warned, I took down the mainsail and changed the jib. Ten minutes later the wind was screaming in our rigging, and the three working sails were too much for her, with the beam sea. The staysail was the easiest canvas to reduce, so I went forward and hauled it down. There could be no thought of continuing to Stromboli. We both consulted the charts, wondering what had possessed us to leave the safe anchorage at Palinuro. We decided to run for a small place called Paolo, some distance down the coast. It was not quite clear from the chart whether Paolo had a harbour or not, but the *Mediterranean Pilot* said that the Italians had begun to build breakwaters there in 1936, so, having high opinions of the Italians as builders and of Mussolini's government as gaffers for such undertakings, we were inclined to be optimistic. We turned south-east, and the following sea came rushing under us. We were yawing and travelling rather fast under the jib and mizzen, but I did not like to take the mizzen off her because it gave me control when I wanted to turn more into the wind. After an hour or two of unpleasant running I decided that the weather was too threatening to remain at sea any longer than was absolutely necessary. I was uncertain of Paolo harbour, and it was still far away. I altered course again and headed for a small island called the Isolotto Cirella, which the *Pilot* stated was "sometimes used as an anchorage by small craft with local knowledge seeking shelter from gales". The Isolotto was difficult to see, but my navigation on dead reckoning proved to be accurate, and when we were still eight miles offshore we saw it ahead as a lighter patch against the mainland. A small bird in the last agonising stages of exhaustion perched himself on the boom within three feet of the wheelhouse. He looked something like a wren. When he had rested for a while he tried to fly on, moving in jerks close over the big waves; but he was not strong enough, and he returned to perch on our rail, puffing and bedraggled, and keeping one eye warily fixed on us. Isabel sent me below to get the six large volumes of Bree's *European Birds*, and while she hunted in vain for a portrait of our visitor we rolled across the last miles to the island. We had spent a good part of a day covering fifty miles and sailing three sides of a square, one side out to sea, the next closing slightly with the coast, and the third turning inshore at right angles; the Isolotto Cirella was only some sixteen miles from Punta di Palinuro, an infinitely superior anchorage. The island is some four hundred yards long and one hundred and fifty yards across. It lies lengthwise along the coast, but the channel between it and the land is eight hundred yards wide, and in such weather we could hope for shelter from the wind behind the island, but not from the sea. It is an uninhabited, rounded projection of rock sparsely covered with scrub and surmounted by an ancient tower. Sweeping round the lee end in a really vicious sea, we turned into the channel. A current ran between the island and the shore, and the swell where we anchored in about four fathoms was appalling. There could be no question in either of our minds about remaining on board in such conditions. The holding ground (sand and weed) was good. I put down the second anchor, and decided that we could leave *Truant*. But where were we to go? It would be impossible to land on the Isolotto Cirella, for the rocks around it were covered in creamy foam as the sea hurled itself at them in an infantry commander's ideal of an attack in depth, each new wave crashing on the objective while it still reverberated to the weight of the last assailant. As for the mainland, the long beach looked most inviting from *Truant's* deck, but the breakers seemed to increase their speed as they approached it, and at the edge there was a great deal of foam. We locked the hatches, put our sandals in a French marketing basket, rolled up our trousers, and dropped into the dinghy. I had underestimated the strength of the swell on the beach. We rushed inshore as though the boat were a surfboard. As the bow touched bottom I jumped out and, with the water up to my waist, held the dinghy against the backwash. The next wave hurled us inshore. Isabel had the good sense to jump out at the right moment and on the dry side, and together we managed to haul the dinghy clear. When we had rested a little we pulled it twenty yards up the shingle. We put on our shoes. Isabel arranged her face and I struggled to disentangle with her comb the reef-knots and topsail-halyard bends that had formed in my hair. It was wonderful to be on warm, solid earth after that day's work on the water. We felt a little mean when we looked at old *Truant* rolling her mast-heads round the sky. "To hell with the sea," Isabel said, and I agreed with her.

We turned to see what more the land could offer us. A sombre prospect of savage brown mountains, escarpments, and dry watercourses rose before us. Up to our left was the grim citadel of Cirella Vecchia, crouching on a minor peak, blasted and contorted in ruins so spectacular that they might still be smoking from the bombardment of the French fleet that cremated the town in 1806. Down on the coast, farther to the left, was the village of Marina di Cirella, the more modern agglomeration of hovels which had housed those survivors of Cirella Vecchia who refused to leave that tragic scene. On our right, more than a mile distant, were the nicely-grouped white houses of Diamante, a place so named because it was reputed to shine out like a diamond to the navigator passing down that coast. We decided to try Diamante.

When we stood both of us swayed a little, feeling the lack of movement in the land. An electric railway and a road with deep ditches followed the fringe of flat country below the hills. Olive trees and vineyards clung to the lower slopes, but soon fell back, discouraged, as the bare rock burst through in sullen outlines. The railwayman's house at the level crossing had gauze mosquito-netting not only over door and window embrasures, but also stretched on frames across the entire veranda. Two stony wounds in the landscape were marked as "torrents" on our chart, but now, in the autumn, were dry cracks in the unhealthy earth, with rusted tins, remnants of furniture unwanted even by those impoverished people, and other refuse staining them where they passed near any dwelling. As we neared Diamante the falseness of its glittering exterior became evident, and we saw it to be a squalid town with unkempt, and outwardly bestial, inhabitants. Our judgment may have been biased by the roughness of our day and our desire for a sustaining meal and sleep in a clean place. After one glance at the main street of Diamante the most optimistic traveller could scarcely have hoped to realise such desires. The walls showed notices conjuring up ghastly medical spectres with the words: "This town out of bounds to all Allied personnel", and these were interspersed with bombastic old slogans which had never been erased with the official disgrace of the Fascists who had painted them on the stones. The population, naturally mystified by our arrival out of nowhere, regarded us with the astonishment that two gorillas dressed as royal sovereigns might be expected to evoke if they occupied a box at the opera. But it was the crowd, and not the two central figures, that was guilty of simian lack of manners. Jabbering, squalling men and women trailed after us, and sometimes, so strange was our appearance, curious hands were stretched out to touch our clothing. Because of the difficult passage in the dinghy, Isabel had broken her normal rule of wearing a skirt for shore excursions, and her blue trousers excited a good deal of hilarity. We walked down the main street and, still followed by the crowd, turned into the promenade along the sea front. Diamante is built some eighty feet above the sea on a rocky shelf. Spray was crossing the road. Our situation was slightly complicated by lack of money. Our expenditure in Capri had been higher than we expected, and it seemed unlikely that I could obtain cash on a letter of credit in Diamante or indeed within eighty miles of it. We passed a filthy tratoria and an equally dirty café, with strings of beads hanging

259

across the doorway to discourage the entry of flies. Then, at the moment when all seemed lost, we saw that the very last building on the promenade, a large concrete building which we had taken to be a warehouse, was marked in faded lettering with the word *ristorante* and the still more inspiring word *albergo*. The entrance corridor, floor, walls, ceiling of rough concrete well layered with dust, was like the entrance to a bunker; it led to a space which mounted from the foundations to the roof and around which the concrete stairs climbed. This spaciousness, instead of being admirable, showed up the poor materials used by the builders and the dirt which lay thick on the concrete. On the lintel of a doorway on the first landing we found a small enamelled sign, of the type that you can buy (with two screw nails thrown in) at any continental ironmonger's. *Albergo*. A young man sat in front of a table littered with textbooks and notebooks in the room to which the albergo door opened. His round black head was bent close over the print; it was nearly dark in the room. He rose, blinking, and said in a soft, puzzled voice, as though he were a medium, waking exhausted from a trance: "Yes, of course; I'll go and find my mother if you will be good enough to wait here." As he left the room he turned on the light, a single, naked electric bulb with a sticky fly-paper hanging from it. His mother was friendly, tousled, and depressed. The room she showed us was bare to the point of sightliness, furnished with two small beds (the major end of each bed showing storks conferring over a spittoon), a commode, one chair, a wardrobe. One window looked straight out over the enraged sea, the other opened to a balcony. The sea pervaded and overpowered the room with its sound.

"How much will the room cost?" I asked her. "I must warn you that we haven't much money."

"Would three hundred be too much?"

"No, three hundred is reasonable for such a pleasant room."

"The view is splendid, is it not, for those who like the sea? The water closet is at the end of the corridor, and I'll bring you another chair and a table."

"We're very hungry. What can we have to eat?"

"Anything that you may desire. We have many beautifully fresh eggs. Then the fish is always good here. The meat, on the other hand, is very bad indeed."

"Who is the cook?"

"My husband."

"Then ask him to prepare an omelette containing at least six eggs, also potatoes, fish, vegetables or salad, cheese, fruit and a bottle of his best wine . . ."

"Ah, wine. At least we can be proud of our wine."

"We are starving." When she had gone I added to Isabel: "If we can't pay I'll sell my watch."

Her husband, a clean-living man by the look of him, with snowy hair and a jutting chin, met us in the kitchen which was also the foyer to his restaurant. They had carefully prepared a table with a clean white cloth in the very centre of the dining-room. The dining-room had been a garage, for on the seaward side there were huge doors, closed and double-bolted but allowing the wind to whistle through a score of crevices, the floor was stained with patches of oil where cars had stood, and one wall was honeycombed with pigeon-holes containing the odds and ends of a poor garage: used inner tubes, used fragments of emery paper, old sparking plugs, bolts that had lost their threads. The contrast between our table and its surroundings deeply touched us. The glasses and cutlery, the pieces of bread, the tall bottle of white wine, the carafe of water, and the cruets, seemed to represent a gallant struggle against Diamante, and I thought that we should eat well.

"We might have some potatoes with the omelette," I called to him, "and have you a corkscrew?"

"I'll open the wine," he answered. "But we've no potatoes. There, we can give you a decent bottle of wine anyway."

"This wine is sweet. Rather too sweet to drink with food."

"Oh no. The wine is buonissimo. This is expensive wine. You permit that I try it?" He poured out a little and smacked his lips over it. "Good wine. Nothing the matter with that."

"Have you no other?"

"Only the red."

"Then bring us some of the red, and we'll drink the white after dinner, with our fruit."

"I would not dare to set the red before you. Ourselves we are not drinking it this year. It is worse than vinegar and mustard mixed. It would burn out your lady's stomach."

After such a warning we continued with the non-inflammable white wine. He brought two omelettes which were no more than small pancakes. Then he appeared with two segments of sour-smelling white cheese.

"Where is the fish that we ordered?"

"In the sea. For days the fishermen have been unable to launch their boats." He said that he might manage to find a slice or two of salami and some tomato salad. We laughed a good deal over our hunger, and ate as much black bread as they would set before us. The man sat down with us, and drank some of the sweet wine. Isabel told him that he must not think we were always so greedy. We had eaten nothing all day, and had been out in the storm. Next day, he said, he would show us that he really could cook; he would make us pollo in brodo and tagliatelle "home-made with eggs" Unexcited by such a prospect, we paid for the meal and said good-night. As we climbed the staircase he stood at the bottom, his eyes still alight with his vision, and he called after us: "Pollo! in brodo! Tagliatelle made by my own hand, and containing many eggs."

Our room was cool, almost chilly. We did not like to ask for blankets in case they should have the embarrassment of saying that they had none in the hotel. The sheets were amazingly rough. The noise of the sea was too near and too wild. Soon both of us were scratching at bites, real and imaginary, and the lavatory down the corridor stank with penetrating vileness against which walls and door could offer little protection. Tired though we were, we could not sleep. I worried, as I lay and scratched, about the launching of the dinghy. I had read some advice on that subject from Mr. Conor O'Brien, but I could not remember clearly what the Irish sage had written, and I could not see how book-learning would help us to get away through the breakers. The wind dropped a little during the night, but only a little. It would be folly to sail in such weather; I did not want to put Isabel back on the rolling *Truant*, and yet I could not envisage another day on the mainland. We must try to camp on the Isolotto Cirella.

At six o'clock we ran into our host at the front door.

"I've left the money for our room on the table upstairs," I told him.

"So you're going?"

"We feel that we mustn't leave our boat unattended."

"What am I to do about the pollo in brodo?"

"You know what you can do with it."

"I beg your pardon?"

"Let the pollo live."

"And you will eat it the next time?"

"Yes, the next time."

We parted the bead curtains of the café and drank minute cups of caffè espresso, good coffee, even in that place, but sweetened with liquid saccharine. Dirty little children came in to buy sweets. Each child only had one lira, and for that he or she got one boiled sweet from the glass bottle.

"Do they ever have more than one lira?" Isabel asked the dark young man behind the bar.

"No, signora. The parents have to defend themselves. If one parent gave five lire to his child then all the kids in the town would soon know of it and would make commensurate demands on their own fathers. Besides, a lira is a lira."

"Then I want to bring down the price of the sweets, at any rate temporarily." She handed him a thousand-lire note. He slipped the note into a drawer in the cash register and rang the bell. A small girl came in and handed over an inexpressibly sordid one-lira note.

"Hold out your hands." He put six sweets in her palms, two crimson, two yellow, and two emerald. She stood for a moment, and then her fingers closed convulsively. After a sharp glance at us, she bolted from the café.

It was a great relief to leave Diamante. The air outside tasted remarkably fresh. We walked, two strangers in a trickle of peasants, most of them mounted on mules or donkeys and most of them wearing articles of American or British uniform. Our dinghy still lay on the beach, and its two sculls were safe along the thwarts.

"Do you think we shall manage to launch it?" Isabel asked.

"With luck, yes."

"The island looks peaceful."

"It does indeed."

"I'd like to walk on to Marina Cirella and try to buy some fresh food to eat on the island. The only thing is, I believe I spent all the money in the café. But stand still."

"Why?"

"I'm going to search your pockets." It is a joke with us that if she searches my pockets when we think that we have no money, money is found. "There!" she said, pulling a thousand-lire note from my hip pocket. "A whole pound! What on earth did you do before you married me? Pounds and pounds must have gone to the laundries and the cleaners." We scrambled back to the road, and continued to Marina Cirella. The single shop was a dark place with a bed in the inner room, the floor of which was two-feet-deep in unroasted peanuts. A man was lying on the bed as we entered. He jumped up and waded in bare feet through the peanuts.

"Excuse me," he said. "When there's nothing to do, do nothing, that's what I say." He was young and quick-witted. We bought a kilo of black grapes, wine grapes with a strange sickly-sweet flavour; a loaf of black bread, a kilo of tomatoes of the oval kind, and four eggs. The eggs were very expensive. Isabel was parched with thirst. We bought a drink of wine and water and he invited us to taste a marsala with egg in it. All of the purchases were stowed with our sandals in the marketing basket, and when we reached the dinghy I used my handkerchief to tie the basket securely to the ring in the bows. We dragged the dinghy to the edge of the surf, turned it round, and rolled up our trousers as far as possible. We rested and uneasily studied the surf. I had remarked when we were under way in bad weather that the fiercest waves came in groups of three to five, and were then succeeded by an indefinite number of less harmful ones. This rule was proving itself on the beach. The beach was of fine gravel, and the undertow had carved it out steeply about fifteen feet from the landward edge of the foam. It looked a very dangerous beach.

I took the bow, Isabel the stern, and we waded out. I was able to hold the dinghy straight, and assist it with a lift over each wave that rolled at us. I was wet to the chin before we came to the sill at the edge of the deep water and yet I was hot with my efforts. On the edge of the sill we stood, fighting to retain our balance, to hold the dinghy straight and to wait for a calmer patch. I counted seven large breakers, and was on the point of calling for a retreat when I saw that the backwash from the seventh breaker was smothering and flattening the eighth. Isabel jumped into the boat and took the oars, I thrust the dinghy forward and then hurled myself over the stern, pushing madly at the oar handles while she pulled. For a long time we seemed to hover on the crest of the wave, and then a few extra hard jabs with the oars sent us over and into the trough beyond. Three more strokes and we were away. I landed Isabel with the utmost difficulty on the Isolotto Cirella. A narrow ramp had been cut in the rock leading up from the ledge where she landed. She skipped up the ramp to explore the island while I rowed back to *Truant*, rather worried that she should be alone, and out of sight, in so wild a place. As I prepared the food and gear that I intended to take to the island I repeatedly imagined that I heard cries. On the last of those occasions Isabel really was shouting. She stood on the top of the island by the tower, holding a bundle of rushes in one hand, and signalling to remind me that we should need matches to light a fire. By that time I had hard-boiled our fresh eggs and had put together food and drink for four meals and bedding for the night. I anchored the dinghy off the rocks on a miniature C.Q.R. made of copper-bronze and a long heaving line and then sculled the stern in just far enough to be able to throw the different packages to Isabel. But I could not climb out of the dinghy myself without the risk of cracking its side. Accordingly I took off my clothes and threw them to her, allowed the dinghy to swing to its anchor, some thirty yards clear of the island, and swam to the rocks carrying another line with me. We loaded ourselves, and she led me up a well-made path to the top of the island. Not far from the tower there was a bothy in a fair state of repair and containing a heap of cleanish straw. It had evidently been used by a goatherd, while his goats passed the nights in the tower, but I did not like the look of some reptiles resembling scorpions which scurried into holes in the walls as I entered. We set our mattresses and blankets in a circle of shade beneath a stunted thorn tree. Near-by a fig tree offered some small but excellent fruit which we ate. That side of the island was covered with bushes growing to a height of three to four feet, and in appearance rather like cranberry bushes. It seemed that no man had been there for a considerable time. A great many sea-hawks had risen when Isabel arrived, and some of them hovered persistently over the island. The place was prolifically populated by lizards, red and black ants, ordinary flies and small stinging gnats which attacked our bare legs. To drive away the insects I built a large fire. Isabel had a headache, probably caused by the heat and the wind; the latter never ceased to buffet us. When we had eaten we explored the island. Two gun sites had been constructed of stones and red earth on the seaward side, but there was no evidence that any guns had ever been placed there. Down near sea level in the north-west corner where the sea was fiercest we found small pools which had been filled with salt spray and then warmed by the sun, some of them to approximately the temperature of a hot bath. We spent much of the afternoon there, lying in the warm water, and trying to rid our bodies of the memory of Diamante. The wind increased that afternoon, and when we next looked at *Truant* she was rolling wildly, and the currents had swung her so that her anchor chains were crossed. After tea we were both reading, and darkness was falling when I heard a diesel engine. Running to the edge of the summit, I saw that two beamy fishing-boats were struggling into the channel, and were about to anchor near *Truant*. Out at sea, but plainly also intending to anchor for the night in the "shelter" offered by our island, was a trading schooner, a fine old ship. The arrival of the strange boats worried us, since both *Truant* and the dinghy lay there at the mercy of the sailors, supposing that they should feel acquisitive. We ate a light evening meal, and disposed ourselves to sleep, but the moon was dazzling and swarms of vicious mosquitoes would not leave us alone. After midnight rain fell in large, noisy drops. We crouched beneath the semi-waterproof coverlet I had taken from our berth, but very soon all our bedding was soaked, and our wet clothes chilled us. We had been so persecuted by the mosquitoes that we were thankful for a good excuse to leave that place. We gathered together all our waterlogged belongings and with a great effort carried them to the sea. The red earth that we had admired earlier had turned with the first raindrops into a thin spread of slime upon the rock. I carried two mattresses on my head, a rucksack filled with plates and tins and books on my back, and a bundle of sheets and pillows in one hand. To add to my difficulties, the straps of my sandals broke under the strain of holding my weight back on the slopes. My passage to sea level was only accomplished with groans, cadenzas of semi-hysterical laughter, and several rests. At the bottom it was too risky to haul the dinghy alongside the rocks, and I was obliged to slide naked into the black water and swim to it. Somehow we managed to load our gear, and then we rowed swiftly to *Truant*. The swell had greatly eased with the heavy rain, and it was splendid to be once more in *Truant's* clean, bright and mosquitoless interior, surrounded by the homely inventions and fabrications of man. I lit every stove in the boat and heated water. We both bathed and washed our hair. When we met in the saloon we burst out laughing. The mosquitoes in that place must be exceptionally venomous, for both our faces were greatly swollen after their attentions. I had a bulbous forehead and positively mongol cheek-bones. We went to bed with two oilskins over the sheets; rain continued to fall in torrents, and I "had not found time" to caulk the one leaking seam. We slept very soundly, late into the morning.

*   *   *   *

Although the sun was high, and the three other boats in the anchorage had moved long before we went on deck, we were still tired when we had breakfasted; we decided that we must immediately put a distance between *Truant* and the Isolotto Cirella, but that the twenty miles separating it from Paola would be quite sufficient. Conditions were most unpleasant; no wind and an extremely high, fast-moving swell. We pushed ahead on one engine and although I optimistically set headsails and mizzen to steady us, they hung flaccid, the sheets slatting. A great disillusionment awaited us at Paola, for as we approached that accursed place we saw that the "harbour works begun in 1936" had remained at the stage of dumping quantities of black stones on the straight beach. A schooner was anchored close inshore, unloading timber for Paola into small boats, but her situation looked to me both uncomfortable and dangerous, and I could not think that she would risk spending the night there. We turned once more in exasperation to the charts. Whereas from Marseilles to Genoa, on the wealthy Riviera coast, a man-made harbour appears every few miles, down south of Salerno for one hundred and forty miles there is no proper harbour until Vibo Valentia Marina in the Gulf of Sant' Eufemia. We knew that Vibo Valentia was outside our range in daylight. Isabel

266

calculated that just before dark we should reach Cape Suvero, at the northern end of the Gulf of Sant' Eufemia. We possessed a large-scale chart of that coast, and she examined every inlet around Cape Suvero until she found one which she thought might give protection from the south-westerly swell. She settled down to sleep on the chart table. I steered in silence for the rest of the day, and that day even I did not feel inclined to eat or drink. I thought that Suvero would never come. We passed along a tormented coastline. The forbidding mountains were cut frequently by ugly, dry, red watercourses, and here and there a fantastic jumble of houses tottered on the edge of a precipice or squatted on a miniature peak. At 5 o'clock I had Cape Suvero in view, and I switched on the second engine, realising that we must find our anchorage in daylight or not at all. Our speed came up to nine knots. Past the cape the shoreline changed completely, becoming low and sandy, with a flat delta behind it, and resembling Norfolk more than southern Italy. We found our sandy creek, and crept cautiously round the bar, taking soundings every few yards. The water quickly shoaled from five fathoms to two and then to one and a half, but at that depth we were able to find excellent shelter, well tucked in, and with sand all around us. We saw what was apparently a narrow channel leading to an inner lake about one hundred yards long, and Isabel encouraged me to go off in the dinghy to see if the channel was navigable, but I had not rowed far when the dinghy ran aground. There was heavenly silence and peace. The nearest village, Sant' Eufemia, was more than two miles away. The air was sweet and still, the sky clear, the barometer steady. We were so pleased with our creek that we felt like staying there for ever. We lit two primuses, and I cooked a six-egg omelette on the starboard side, while Isabel, to port, cooked in butter, potatoes and numerous choice vegetables and fungi.

The next day dawned in tranquillity. We were breakfasting when three fishermen sailed up in a nice felucca and called me out on deck to beg for cigarettes, to ask where we were from, and to try to sell us fish. We decided that we might spend a whole day in the creek. Checking over the rigging, I found that the tremendous rolling of the past three days had chafed the squaresail halyard above the yard until that heavy spar was hanging by less than one strand. At 9 o'clock, while I was preparing a new halyard and had several other small tasks in mind Isabel called from the saloon: "The barograph's behaving most peculiarly."

"What's it doing?"

"Shooting down. Perhaps you ought to check it with the barometer."

I dropped the halyard and went to the wheelhouse. "The barometer's fallen about a mile. But the day looks wonderful, and the big ketch is still taking cargo off Santa Eufemia. Surely they'd clear out if they suspected bad weather?"

"They probably have no instruments to warn them."

"We ought to move, I know. There must be something really bad coming. Hullo!"

"What is it?"

"A carabiniere in a boat." He was a garrulous and oily policeman. He asked me to report at the village to give details of the boat and her crew.

"I fear that we must leave almost immediately," I said.

"Not before you have lodged the required information, surely," he answered, climbing on board without my permission. "I think that I would like to bring my wife to your yacht to show her how luxuriously every little detail is arranged." Isabel had begun to cook. The carabiniere opened the door of the oven and looked in. "Most delicious!" he said. "When I see that I know that you will still be here in an hour or two. I go back for my wife." He rowed away. His visit had determined us to leave at once, but still I fiddled away with little details on deck, and Isabel cooked.

"We shall eat on the way across the gulf," she said. "After all, it's only thirteen miles."

We left the creek, using the port engine. I intended to hoist the mainsail, thinking that the pleasant morning airs would dry it out nicely, but Isabel persuaded me that it was too much trouble in such zephyrs and for so short a run. I compromised with a light-weather jib "to pull us along". No sooner had the jib set firmly than it was flapping, and then it was taken aback. The light breeze had puffed from the north-east and had changed almost instantly to an equally light breeze from the south-west. I did not like that. The barometer was still falling. In a couple of minutes I was obliged to take the jib off her, for the sheet was cracking with the strain on it, and there was already far too much wind for light canvas. I switched on the other engine.

"There's going to be terrible weather," I said. "We must waste no time in crossing to that harbour." In five minutes the wind pressure on our bare poles heeled us over as though we carried full sail. It was the hardest blow we had yet encountered, and although the sea had not had time to rise the wind was so fierce that spray came solidly over our bow and smashed against the closed doors and windows of the wheelhouse. In fifteen minutes the sea was beginning to be serious. We left the creek at 11 o'clock, and before 11.30 a gale was blowing into the gulf. We had made few of our normal preparations for sailing because the harbour for which we were bound was visible from the creek, and a trip of thirteen miles seemed ridiculously short after the distances to which we had become accustomed; for the first time since we left England I had not even bothered to lash the anchor; we were towing the dinghy instead of carrying it on deck, and we had not closed the lower portholes. We were obliged to throttle down to avoid slamming too hard into the waves, and to head more and more into the weather, which meant that we progressed slowly out to sea instead of across the gulf. We soon saw three other boats in the same uncomfortable plight, one beamy fishing-boat and two coasters, all rolling about in the most devilish manner although they headed into the sea like ourselves. But the big steel ketch that had been lying inshore, close to Sant' Eufemia, came thrashing up astern of us, sailing close to the wind with four reefs tied in her gaff mainsail, two in her small leg-of-mutton mizzen, and one in a handkerchief of a staysail. She passed very near us, and Isabel was nauseated by the sight, for the ship showed most of her rusty bottom as she rose on the crests and leaped from them into the hollows. She seemed to have nearly twenty men in her crew, and they were all clustered near the wheelhouse, and holding on for life. Her sails were dirty grey and her fat hull was badly in need of paint, her crew were in rags, and I could hear her frames and spars grunting as she passed, but she was a brave sight, and I envied her the men to set the sails and the bulk that held her steady in such weather. She carried as little canvas as we would under fully reefed mainsail, and storm staysail, and her hull was some six times the size of ours, yet she sailed quite swiftly away from us out to sea, then went about, heading for the port. How her crew must have despised us, with our engines! The sky for a time showed a fearsome black bunch of cloud with thunder and lightning in it as well as wind and rain. After an hour or two the clouds passed, and we were left in bright sunshine. But now the wind stiffened in the west, and the sea grew constantly worse. We had never imagined anything like it.

We saw that our dinghy was making a very poor attempt to ride the waves, for it had soon been half-filled with spray, and then, in such a sea, it sank lower and lower until the gunwale was awash. Isabel was in stout heart in this, our most serious trial, and tended merely to be a shade ill-tempered, the best of all signs in a human being when an emergency has to be faced and overcome. She took the wheel, and I went aft to see to the dinghy. I strained for about twenty minutes at the back-breaking task of hauling the waterlogged boat up to *Truant's* stern. Now and then Isabel would shout aft: "Look out! here's a big one!" and I would cling to the nearest solid object while *Truant* stood on her heels and then on her head.

I saw that I had not the strength to haul the boat in single-handed, let alone lift it from the water; but if I did not get it on board fairly quickly I might just as well cut the tow-rope and let it go; and how would we get another dinghy on that desolate coast? I took a stout line from the windlass through a block by the forward fairlead and then aft to the end of the tow-rope. It was difficult to work forward, and while I was shackling the block I fell over backwards, and just saved myself from going overboard by taking a fearful knock on the windlass. When I rose to my feet, more than a little dazed, the first thing that I saw was Isabel's furious face peering through the wheelhouse window. She shook her fist at me and shouted something which could not reach me against the wind. She had to neutralise the starboard engine while I winched the dinghy past that propeller. We had lost the oars and the small cover to the dagger-plate housing, I saw, but those were minor losses. When I got the dinghy level with the shrouds I made the painter fast to the throat halyards' purchase and heaved away on that, using one of the winches at the foot of the mast. The weight of the dinghy, filled with water, was leaden, but once I had it half lifted the water spilled. After a long struggle, with some terrible bumps for *Truant*, the dinghy and me, I got the thing down on the cabin top and securely lashed. When I returned to the wheelhouse I was astonished to find that the afternoon was wearing out. The sea was worsening, and so was the wind. Isabel clutched my arm, pointing at the three boats to the south of us. A rocket had just gone up from the largest of them, a tunny fisher of about twice our size. She seemed to be very low in the water, and sluggish in her movements as though sagging to the blows of the waves. We could see men running about her decks, and the other two boats were closing in on her. But whenever we looked away from the sea ahead of us we allowed *Truant* to be caught by extra large waves, and then it seemed that we would roll right over. For a time we were busy looking after ourselves, and when we looked back the tunny fisher had gone, and we saw two of her crew being hauled out of the water, strange bedraggled objects that looked more like stockings or sausages than men.

"I wonder what happened?" Isabel said. "How could it sink like that?"

"Probably she had some rotten wood in her hull, and it would not stand up to this pounding."

"Are we making any water?"

"No."

"Do you want something to eat, darling? Are you hungry?"

"No. How do you feel?"

"Terrible!"

"Would you like some brandy?"

"Ugh!"

"I'm going to have a drink, anyway. I'm cold."

"What are we going to do? How long is this weather going to last?"

"Perhaps for days, by the look of it. I've never seen the glass so low."

What were we going to do? We read and re-read the *Mediterranean Pilot*, examined and re-examined our charts. We were now well beyond Vibo Valentia Marina. That harbour is not highly recommended by the *Mediterranean Pilot*, which explains that, while sheltered from the west by a mole, the place is "rendered uncomfortable" by a westerly sea rebounding off the beach, and that a strong current from the Straits of Messina enters round the end of the mole. The next harbour, Tropea, was only twelve miles farther along the coast, but of that harbour the Pilot said: "Should not be approached or used in anything like bad weather". I began to experiment by taking the seas a shade more on the beam, thinking that we might drift back and then edge in towards Vibo Valentia, but the increase in our rolling at once made Isabel actively ill, and as she refused to be ill in a safe manner—the cleanly habits of a life-time prevailing even in that hell—I turned into the wind again, fearing that she would go overboard. Then I saw a steamer of some 800 tons running down the coast, obviously for Vibo Valentia Marina. If she could get into the harbour in that sea I was sure that we could. We staggered on, accustomed now to the wildness of the sea, and not so afraid of it because a little numbed by it. We occasionally exchanged the rather bitter jokes that seem to go with such circumstances. At 5.15 by the wheelhouse chronometer I told her that I intended to put about and run for Vibo Valentia Marina. She thought that we would turn over if we tried to put about. I argued, seeking to convince myself as well as her, that we would never turn over, and that the alternative to running for it was to stay out as we were, certainly all night, and perhaps for days. She lay back on the chart table, and asked me to make up my own mind, and please not to bother her. I told her that I was going below to get the life-jackets from the bathroom shelf. She poured scorn on the life-jackets, saying that if the boat sank we should be sucked under. I argued that sucking-under was a theory exploited in children's books. I went below, and got the life-jackets. She laughed hoarsely at me while I pushed her into one of them. As for me, I felt theatrical, but a great deal safer, in mine. She looked very sweet.

I waited for a few of the smaller seas, then slammed the port engine full astern, the starboard full ahead. She came about fairly quickly, gave one tremendous roll, and steadied with the seas under her quarter. I slowed the engines to their minimum revolutions, but the sea hurtled us towards the coast at a speed that we found terrifying. Soon we made out the long mole of Vibo Valentia Marina. The next real danger was the entrance to the harbour, for the worst seas would be there, and we did not know whether, like so many other Italian harbours, it would be sown with wrecks. I determined to keep the seas on the starboard quarter, and to make a quick turn in the harbour entrance, trusting to our reserve of power under both engines to get us through any obstacles. At the end of the mole the water was a filthy yellow, discoloured with churned-up sand. We crossed three sharp yellow waves, opened the throttles and swung the starboard bulwark into the sea as we veered sharply and raced into sheltered water. A stiff wind whipped across the harbour, but the water was comparatively flat.

We saw a fine, big harbour, and it needed to be big, for there were at least fifty boats anchored there, the majority of them sturdy coasting schooners and cutters. Isabel steered past all of them to the inner end of the harbour, and I let go first the starboard anchor and then the port so that we rode securely to a wide V of chain. While I straightened the tangle on deck and prepared the riding light, Isabel, extraordinary woman, descended to her galley and cooked a magnificent dinner based on the preparations for the lunch that we had never eaten. I was a great deal more shaken than she by the day's experiences, and from that day any reverence that I felt for the sea was peppered with hatred and salted with fear.

When we were about to eat, a boat bumped clumsily into *Truant's* side, and a man climbed on board whom I saw to be a naval officer; he was the harbour-master, and exceedingly polite, so I invited him below. He insisted that he must send to Rome all details of us and our boat without even a night's delay.

"It is like this," he said. "My position is not ill-paid; it is absolutely all that I have got, and without it I starve. If I allowed myself to be lax, who knows? Someone may envy me my authority, and if they reported my slip to Rome I should be out."

"In that case, have a glass of wine, and if you don't mind we shall continue with our dinner, for we have had a fatiguing day."

"This is wonderful wine."

"It comes from Capri."

"Then it is even better than I estimated." He had startled young eyes, and fuzzy hair thinning out on the top of the skull. He was terribly embarrassed.

*   *   *   *

Vibo Valentia **Marina** is an unpretentiously ugly port, a haphazard clump of drab houses squatting at the end of the harbour behind a sand beach which boasts a line of bathing boxes and a small band-stand built, like the huts, of unpainted wood. The hills allow the town a corner to exist in, but they dwarf it, torment it with sudden whiffs of dusty wind, with torrents of water at the time of the melting snows, and supply it with grapes and raisins, timber and gravel, marble and curdled cheeses, for cargoes. We were lucky to strike so uninteresting a port in bad weather— although we should scarcely have called there had the weather been good —because it was full of ships, and these, since ninety-five per cent of them were sailing vessels, were of great interest and beauty. Most of the crews were glad of the weather, for it gave them a respite from work, and also enabled them to patch their already patched canvas and rigging. The quality of the rope on their boats was pitiful, and they begged for any old piece that I discarded from our running rigging. We went ashore on our first morning there to send a telegram to Rome. This cost us 217 lire, which left exactly 139 lire—or three shillings and one penny—in our combined purses. We spend all but one lira of that sum on two kilos of potatoes, one-and-a-half kilos of onions, and one kilo of grapes. That evening the harbour was swept by a gale from the east, although we had thought ourselves sheltered on that side by the high hills. We had our two anchors down, but since they had been laid for a west wind, the chains were necessarily crossed when we swung to face the east. I should dearly have liked to have placed the anchors better, but we could not tamper with them in such conditions, and could merely pray that they would not drag. During the afternoon I had noticed that most of the Italian vessels lifted their second anchors, and now that the wind had settled in from the other side they were able to drop again and lie securely to two. The new wind was so cold that we had to close the hatches and put on corduroy trousers and winter sweaters. All night we heard the wind, the grating of one anchor chain on the other, the yells of sailors returning drunk to their boats, the vicious slap of the waves, the hissing of spume and rain, and the rattle of hailstones.

In the morning the weather was even worse. When we left England I had wondered if our barograph worked very sensitively, for it always seemed to draw a straight line with only the smoothest of variations; now it had drawn a series of serrated peaks and hollows, and the general movement was still downward. Isabel stayed in bed all morning, reading a tome about Australia, which she said was "very depressing and wonderfully soothing under the circumstances". I lay down on one of the settees, and read too.

273

I should not have bothered to eat, but Isabel suggested that a meal would pass the time. The day dragged past without improvement in the weather. We were continually swinging unpleasantly near to other boats, and I had more confidence in our ground gear than I had in theirs. This was our sixth night out of Capri, and our peaceful, comfortable days in Marina Grande seemed years distant, and roseate with the sentiment of quiet days out of the past. We often wondered what had happened to Douglas and Gwenda.

On Sunday morning, October 13th, when it had blown remorselessly for two days and half a day, the easterly gale dropped in strength. A man who occupies a bedroom surrounded by shunting trains at Crewe is astonished and perturbed by the silence when his daughter invites him to spend a long week-end with her family in a boarding-house at Llandudno; he finds difficulty in sleeping without the clatter of bogies and points and buffers, the shouts of the men marshalling the trucks; he finds the comparative silence at Llandudno unearthly. So, when the wind stopped, we went quietly around as though it had blown our senses away. We spent nearly half a day wrapped up in thick clothes before we realised that the weather had become warm even for the south of Italy. It was strange to see all the boats that yesterday had trembled in unison, facing the east as cows orientate themselves toward the gate of a field when the milking hour approaches, to-day nodding around in circles, facing each other. It was time to straighten out our anchor chains. The port one was so heavy against the windlass that I strained one shoulder, and still could make no impression on it. So I took up the starboard. My manœuvres had by no means passed unobserved, and two sailors from one of the coasters that had lain near *Truant* during our night on the Isolotto Cirella came pushing across to us in their rough tender. I was glad to have their help, for my shoulder hurt infernally. One of them was a Sardinian, stony-faced, with black, deepset, enamelled eyes; his companion, a Calabrese, was curly-haired and talkatively amiable. With their help at the windlass we soon made out that our port anchor had dragged in the gale until it had fouled the chain of the *Samia*, a 350-ton steamship which had anchored itself off the quay and then warped alongside to take cargo. The *Samia* was a top-heavy coaster, built in the Italian manner, and looked—for all that she was unloading bricks and cement powder—like a floating ice-cream barrow. Her captain and crew were from Tuscany, and to the Calabrese and the Sardinian, and apparently to the majority of the crews on the sailing vessels in the harbour, the Tuscans and their steamship were foreign and detestable, for when our Calabrese hailed them, asking their captain to

274

slack off his port anchor chain so that we might free ourselves, and the captain answered that he would be damned if he would make his crew work on a Sunday, a mutter rose from all the decks around us as well as from our own, and the mutter rose to a growl, and the growl to a crackling outburst of shouted criticism. Our Calabrese, after taking counsel with me, shouted to the *Samia* that the Englishman was on friendly terms with the harbour-master, and would be able to force any ship in the harbour to change berth if he so desired. At that *Samia's* mate appeared on deck with four sailors. The mate wore carpet slippers and pyjama trousers; he scratched viciously at his dark torso as he came out and he spat with pointed animosity in our direction. I felt very sorry for him, but his spit drew yells of hatred from our Calabrese and from others like him. The mate stood still and grinned sardonically down at them. After a while he held up his hand, with considerable dignity.

"None of you like to be called out to work on a Sunday?" he observed, "and I only want to point out to the Englishman that as we have no steam up we shall be obliged to perform the operation by hand. Well, Mr. Englishman, what do you require?"

I began to protest that I was sorry to bother him and his crew on the day of rest, but the Calabrese dug me so hard in the back and muttered so forcefully behind me that my protestation died away in a muddle of bad Italian. "If you would have the goodness to tighten your anchor chain," I said to the mate, "we may be able to get our anchor from beneath it."

"What's needed is a bucket," the Calabrese said behind me. "Have you a bucket?"

"Yes, several." I showed him two canvas buckets and a metal bucket.

"No use," he said, and turning to the Sardinian said: "Go and get our bucket."

"Go yourself," the Sardinian answered, but he dropped into their boat, and went for the bucket. Meanwhile the mate and his four men were slowly clanking in their anchor chain, and the *Samia* was edging out from the quay. The Italian boats there in the south have see-saw capstans; the men look as though they are working the pumps as they swing their weight on a long lever. The Sardinian returned with a metal-bound oak bucket, half filled with pebbles. They attached the handle to a rope, lowered the bucket down beside the *Samia's* chain, to which our stockless anchor was firmly hooked, and emptied the pebbles from it with a jerk on the rope, so that the bucket passed beneath the chain, and slowly floated to the surface. We thus had a bight around the *Samia's* chain, and were easily able to disentangle our anchor. I had had another lesson in practical

275

seamanship. When the Calabrese saw our anchors and solid chain he laughed at us.

"Such anchors would hold a boat many times your size and I don't know why you always put down two."

"We only put down two in very bad weather."

"But both here and at the Isolotto Cirella you could see quite well that the weather was at its worst, and could blow no harder. Then why not put down one anchor, and if that holds leave it alone? And in both these places there is much current, which swings the ship and twists the chains if there are two anchors down."

"You forget that we are strangers here. We cannot tell like you where there are currents and where there are none, nor can we say when the wind is going to blow harder."

"You mean that you've never been here before?"

"Never."

"Then you're not brave, you're lunatics!" he exclaimed, and looked for confirmation at the less loquacious Sardinian, who wisely nodded his head. When we had talked for a while about *Truant's* gear, of which they heartily approved, the Sardinian nudged the Calabrese and said between his teeth: "Ask them how they find their way about."

"Yes," the curly-headed man said. "That's it. How do you find your way about if you've never been here before?"

"We have maps," Isabel said, and she pulled a few charts from below the table. They looked at the charts dully, as I might study a page of Chinese script. "And we've the compass," she added.

"Ah yes, the compass," the Calabrese said. "We've a compass on the schooner, only we seldom have to fall back on it save at night, and then we usually steer on the lights. The Italian lights are terrific."

"They are indeed. We're very much impressed by the Italian light-houses, for they differ a lot from our own and the French. The British and French lighthouses are built like great candles stuck on the rocks or the earth, but the Italian ones are set on headlands and they stand square as though they'd been erected by men used to building palaces and churches."

"Fancy you noticing that now," the Calabrese said to her. "My wife is a sharp woman enough but she could go to sea for ten years without ever noticing a thing like that."

"Sometimes there is nothing else to notice. Going through the French canals was wonderful, because there were trees and birds and fields to watch, but just sailing along on the sea is the dullest way of getting from one place to another. I hate travelling in an aeroplane, but I think

276

even that is preferable to sailing because it gets you there quicker."

"Yes, it's fantastically dull, sailing the sea, as you say," the Calabrese agreed. "I expect you play a lot of cards, you and your husband, as you go along? No? I don't know what we would do without a pack or two of cards."

The Sardinian nudged him again. "Ask her why she sails if she doesn't like it. Say we have to do it because we work."

"Ah yes. My friend here points out that we're all obliged to go to sea to earn our living and support our families. But you, why do you come so far from your homes, and in a boat which demands much work?"

"At least in a boat we travel in our home, and when we arrive in Vibo Valentia Marina we aren't obliged to go to the hotel."

"So you don't like the boat when it's moving, but you like it when it's arrived at some place?"

"Yes."

"That's like our engineer. I don't know why the captain keeps him, for often he takes the engine to pieces in port so that we needn't move. He's a good engineer so far as we sailors are concerned, for any man in his senses prefers rest to work. His mother was a negress and his father was a Neapolitan, or so he claims, and of good birth too, a pharmacist. He keeps lizards in his bunk; and this is by no means a bad idea on a boat, for it seems to keep other animals, smaller ones, at a distance . . ."

The Sardinian nudged him again. "Say good-bye for us both."

It was a sultry, clouded day, without wind but with pale grey tendrils creeping up into the western sky, shaped like the veins beneath the skin on the shoulder of a racehorse, and believed to show threat of a ponente, the wind that we were told was dangerous in the Straits of Messina. The barograph had begun to draw an upward curve, and we were most anxious to be off. We were varnishing the interior of the dinghy when the Sardinian and the Calabrese with a third man came rowing, clearly with the idea of paying a formal visit.

"I knew that you would be feeling a little dull, with nothing to do and no money to spend," the Calabrese said (every sailor in the harbour had somehow learned that we were without funds, although we neither knew nor cared whether they believed that this was a temporary or a permanent state of affairs), "so I brought along my two friends to divert you. This," he added, pulling the third man forward by the shoulder, "is Giorgio, another sailor, also from Calabria." Giorgio, who was young and tall, was over-conscious when we met him of the flourishing crop of spots that shone on his brow and around the chiselled nose with its mobile nostrils. They

277

were overwhelmed by the luxury they found below-decks, and when they got themselves down the companion they all three sat stiffly on one settee, slowly taking off their caps. They refused to have a drink, and would barely touch the wine that I set before them.

"We've agreed that if you'd like us to come as sailors on your boat, you can have the three of us for thirty thousand lire a month," the curly-headed one said. "You'd also pay for our food, wine and tobacco." I replied that we were greatly honoured, but we preferred to work the boat ourselves, and that if they came with us their future would be very insecure, since Isabel and I did not intend to remain afloat for more than one year at the outside. "As for insecurity, that wouldn't worry us, and we'd be confident that your susceptibilities would guarantee our well-being in any arrangement you might make for our future," he said, becoming a little involved. "For instance, if you decided to leave the boat in Greece, you could just turn it over to us, we'd demand no more payment; we'd load up with a cargo of tobacco or sugar, and return to Italy. And you needn't worry about taking us away from our homes. The Sardinian here hasn't seen his wife for three years."

"Why not?" Isabel asked. There was a whispered conversation with the Sardinian.

"He says that he sends a proportion of his earnings to his wife and family, but that his work never permits him to go home. If he decided to go back to the island he would lose his job, and on the island there's no work."

"He must hate being separated from his family."

The curly-headed Calabrese hastily consulted the Sardinian in whispers. "Yes. He greatly misses his wife and his bambini, but he doesn't want to return to Sardinia."

"How many bambini?"

More whispers. "Six," the Calabrese said. And the Sardinian nodded and uttered a grunt of pride or agreement, his black eyes resting on us, his face dark and stony. When we had convinced them that we wanted no paid hands they changed the conversation to political levels. They spoke with admiration both of King Umberto and of Benito Mussolini. Of Umberto the curly-headed man said: "All Italy except the accursed inhabitants of Milan and Turin wanted the King to stay. If Britain and America had only played their parts and given us another election we'd have kept our King, for this time we'd have shown the other side that if the election was to be crooked we could outdo them in illegal methods." Giorgio spoke of Mussolini, insisting vehemently that the Americans had been greatly put out by his assassination. "The Duce was so artful and industrious," he said, "that Roosevelt and Churchill intended to elevate him as leader of the western world and supreme opponent of Russia. Ah! How the world now misses his clear brain and leonine courage!" The others nodded solemnly in agreement. "The proof of it," he continued, "is that the Americans have settled Mussolini's heir in Switzerland, where he lives like a prince at their expense."

"No, you're wrong," Isabel said. "For I've just read somewhere that Mussolini's son is in Ischia, and is playing in a dance band there to earn his living." She hunted among the periodicals that had arrived with our last mail, and found the article she sought in one of the more reliable American magazines. Even when confronted with the picture of the swarthy young guitarist, our three well-informed guests would not retract.

"That's propaganda," the young man said. "But we all know the hand that the Americans are really playing, and we know what use they would have made of Mussolini had he not been murdered in the north. Mussolini was molto intelligente, that nobody could deny."

We denied it most strenuously, arguing that no man who connived at war in the twentieth century could be molto intelligente.

"Ah!" curly-head exclaimed, "but he won every war until the last one and he'd even have won that if Hitler hadn't been a fool, for Mussolini tried to change sides half-way through, and he tried to make Germany change sides too. But there, Hitler was an ass. You can do nothing with Germans."

They invited us to be their guests at the local cinema, but we refused, saying that we intended to go early to bed. We made them a present of six tins of the internationally celebrated "corn-edd beef", and they replied with a very greasy aluminium soup plate piled high with grapes from the hills above Vibo Valentia, monstrous purple grapes, crescent-shaped, with leathery skins which retained a whiff of tar from a ship's hold.

22

THE wind was light from the north when we breakfasted. We moved before any of the other boats showed signs of life. Soon after we had sailed into the gulf we sighted the smoking outline of Stromboli, a burning beehive set on the sea, the beehive that we had hoped to reach direct from Punta di Palinuro a week earlier. Our course now lay far inside it. When we cleared the gulf we turned our transom to the swell and made good progress which was uncomfortable for Isabel. To cheer her, I read aloud from the warnings—they amounted to threats—of the *Mediterranean Pilot* regarding the dangers of the Straits of Messina. Even the charts, always infinitely less doleful than the *Pilot*, showed melodramatic spirals indicating the presence of Scylla, Charybdis, and other less historic whirlpools which function in and near the Straits. There was every sign of a fairly permanent moderation in the weather. Passing the town of Scylla, an attractive place built in three sections, above and on either side of a rock, and remembering the frequently repeated warnings of our friends in Vibo Valentia Marina, I lowered the mainsail and the jib. When we reached the mouth of the Straits I switched off the engine I had started when the mainsail came down, because the north-east wind increased suddenly so that the staysail sheet twanged and keen water hissed against the side of the boat.

Far from the Straits being dangerous in such fine weather, we saw open boats little bigger and much less seaworthy than our dinghy sailing across to Sicily from the mainland. Such whirlpools as were turning that day were no more fearsome than the swirl that would be formed if the contents of an ordinary swimming pool were allowed to escape through a pipe six inches in diameter. We sailed into Messina in the early afternoon. It was a pretentious harbour, and the war had left it as shattered as the harbour of Civitavecchia, yet somehow more squalid, more obviously accusing and unprepossessing, beneath the hot sun and the sweeping mountains of Sicily. A motor-boat flying the pilot's flag followed us across the harbour, and an official in civilian clothes bounded from it to our deck. In Vibo, Capri, Naples, Anzio, Portofino, we had been warned about Messina, a port which is renowned—one might almost say admired—throughout Italy for the skill and industry of its thieves. So we were determined not to

280

set *Truant* against a quay, while the pilot was equally determined that we must not drop an anchor because of the wrecks which, he said, covered the bottom of the harbour. While this impasse reigned two motor-boats darted at us. The first contained a well-dressed business man who handed me a visiting card which described him as a chandler. I asked for the address of his establishment, thinking that he might sell me a pair of oars for the dinghy, and he told me that I could find him at any time of any day in the Café Netuno. He then offered to sell me all the petrol I might require or any other "rationed" commodity, also American and British money. He said that he would be willing to buy any gold, jewels, or sugar of which I might care to dispose. The second motor-boat contained another black-market operator of the same type. I knew that the only easy way to be rid of them was to make appointments to see them, and this was swiftly done. Appointments are easily broken, but a persistent Italian commercial gentleman is difficult to dislodge when he seeks business. At length the pilot compromised, and said that we might anchor in a corner near a coal wharf, and take two stern ropes to a bollard. Neither of us liked the look of the place, but we launched the dinghy, and then went confidently in, to dispose ourselves as he had indicated. Isabel put the bow just where I wanted it, and I let go the anchor. She swung round the stern, and I jumped into the dinghy, congratulating myself that we were becoming so much more proficient in handling our boat. Our berth was near the place whence the train-ferry service left for the mainland, and a crowd had gathered to watch our arrival. My self-satisfaction soon changed to dismay, for although I could see that *Truant* was going astern and Isabel was keeping control of her in the usual admirable manner, the yacht was in fact moving no nearer the quay. I sculled with the spare oars, which were small and quite inadequate, until I was at the full length of one of the big stern lines, and I was still some ten feet from the quay. Then one of the oars broke. To make things worse the dinghy, which we must have damaged in the storm in the Gulf of Sant' Eufemia, was leaking badly. The crowd were amused by my predicament. Isabel saw quite well what was happening to me, and she came out on deck to pass me more rope, but the moment that she left the engines *Truant* slewed dangerously to one side. Too late we realised that a strong tide rip was entering the harbour and rebounding from the quays we sought to approach. For some moments, while urchins, black-market dignitaries in pseudo-American costume, and slatternly dockside harlots, yelled at me, I was standing in a sinking dinghy, desperately clutching one of *Truant's* big warps under one bare foot while Isabel darted from the controls to the deck and back to the controls again, seeking to hold *Truant* away from the battered walls with their dangerous projections of steel and masonry. One thing we had learned by experience, we did not shout at each other. At length the tide won, and *Truant* was swept to the wall. Isabel compromised at the last moment and kicked the engines ahead so that the yacht jolted into the wooden side of a pontoon from which divers had been operating earlier in the day. A man with a toothbrush moustache, and a boy, whose face was marked by smallpox, came to our assistance. With their aid we got *Truant* securely lashed to the pontoon, which was lined by spectators, eager to examine every detail of our boat. The pilot chose this moment to return, his launch filled to capacity with Italian officials, some in civilian clothes, some in uniform. Without asking our permission these gentry jumped on board, gritting their shoes on our deck. There were so many of them that beneath their weight *Truant* took a decided list to starboard. A man among them introduced himself as a detective, and announced that he intended to search below decks.

"What for?" I asked.

"What for? For nothing. Just a routine search."

"I forbid such a search, and warn you that if you carry it out you will hear more of the matter."

He shrugged his shoulders, and grinned, but he did not search. The others began to take down the usual details that had to be cabled to Rome. The secret police demanded our passport. They took perhaps thirty minutes to examine that document, while the crowd looked on, occasionally hailing me with a "Hey, Joe, what you got to sell?" The pockmarked boy and the man with the moustache stood on deck, looking hungrily at me. I made them a little speech, saying that I had nothing on board with which to recompense them for their unstinted assistance, and asking them to return the following afternoon. They both shook hands with us and left quite cheerfully. Isabel and I sat on deck to rest and take breath. We were beset from all sides with proposals, all of a commercial nature, and these goaded us into summoning energy to moor ourselves in a more isolated position. One of the men who pestered us, an elderly sea-dog with a scarred, ill-tempered face, who was rowed by a youth with a partially withered neck and a great wart, like a sapphire ring, on one finger, took our stern lines to the bollard that we had attempted to reach before, and since the current had lessened we moved ourselves without any further difficulty. The sea-dog, like the other helpers, agreed to return the following day for his reward—you get nothing for nothing in Messina harbour—and we were free to go below and eat. I brought my .45 Colt automatic from the linen cupboard, and checked the mechanism of the pistol and its three loaded magazines. I decided to leave the dinghy in the water in the hope that the leak would "take up", but I thought it wise to pass a thin chain around the thwart and take both ends of the chain through the porthole to our bunk. Some of the harbour officials had warned me—with more than a hint of pride in their warnings—that two-thirds of the cargo of a relief ship with sugar from America had been stolen that day.

*　　*　　*　　*

Such havoc as the Germans, the Americans, and the British, had wreaked was little more thorough, after all, than the work of earlier peoples who fought for that fine, sickle-shaped harbour and the town that grows so easily on the narrow strip of land beside it, beneath the hills from which gush fruit and wine and olives. The Carthaginians (twice), the Romans, the Saracens, the Normans, the Neapolitans and the Sardinians all laid waste the town. Then the Sicilian Vespers massacre raged there in 1282, the plague in 1743, earthquake in 1783, and earthquake again in 1908.

When dawn broke a line of people shuffled to the nearest quay to watch us, and some of them remained there until we departed from Messina. Four men of criminal aspect brought fishing lines, which they dangled in the filthy water though their eyes were steadily focused in greedy speculation on our boat. Boys and trollops shouted their: "Hey, Joe! What you got to sell?" When I went ashore Isabel, contrary to our usual custom, remained on board. She sat on deck writing letters with the big automatic lying ostentatiously on the cabin roof near her right hand. We floated in slime, oozing up from the sunken wrecks, and our dinghy, freshly varnished at Vibo Valentia Marina, was covered with stains too hideous to contemplate.

The Cheep oil men, while anxious to please a client who came with recommendations from Rome, were not inclined to be paternal, and they handed me over to the Moscatelli Brothers, who would be responsible, I was told, for delivering the fuel and anything else that I might require. Santi Moscatelli, the elder, fastened to me with the enthusiasm of a leach which by hazard comes in contact with a bloodshot nose. He was a slender man of medium height and athletic outline clothed in a worn, grey-worsted coat and white linen trousers. His hair, sparse on the domed head, but thick stubble on the champing jowl, was iron-grey. His face was almost diamond-shaped, and he had fine dark eyes sadly tinged by some kind of ill-health, which he explained by telling me "frankly" that because of his

283

anti-fascist sympathies he had decided, before the war, to banish himself in Assawa, and had only returned to his native Messina one month before our arrival. His firm, he told me as we footed it through the dust on our different errands, was responsible for a great deal of haulage work in Messina and other places. He took an early opportunity to hand me the type of visiting card that southern Italians have printed or engraved before they consider acquiring an office, a secretary or a business. "MOSCATELLI BROS." the expensive pasteboard proclaimed in English . . . "Ship-owners—Agents & Brokers". And each of the four corners had its message: "Branches at all Sicilian ports CCIA Messina n. 34557 . . . Telegrams MOSBROS MESSINA, Telephone 23672 . . . Head Office MESSINA, Piazza Municipio, 20–22 . . . AUGUSTA, Via Pr. Umberto, 309, Telefono n. 81 . . ."

Pipa Moscatelli, younger and with a hint of the eagle in his dark face, dashed around us in wide circles on a bicycle; he had been detailed by Santi to obtain the necessary permission from the customs officers for *Truant* to take petrol and paraffin free of tax. Santi led me to the bank in the centre of the town where I might obtain cash with my letter of credit. Pipa occasionally hovered near us on his bicycle, as though he could not long forbear a glance at so luscious a prey as the Englishman. I had to wait two hours and thirty minutes to cash £20, for the bank's system was even more antiquated and considerably less impressive than the rococo interior with its cream-coloured, coffered ceiling. "Don't worry," Santi Moscatelli said when he saw me lift my shoes to examine the soles. "This bank smells thus; it always has done and it always will." He was so eager to handle the money that I drew that he himself took it from the cashier. Yet his own pockets, as he soon showed me, were filled with dollar bills and pound notes, and there was almost nothing that he did not offer to sell to me or to buy from me. I found a kind of gruesome relish in his company and his conversation. He had evidently at one time been connected with the sea, for when we reached the dinghy he thrust the paddle over the transom and sculled powerfully to *Truant*, and once on board he occupied himself to such purpose with the stern lines that we soon hauled the boat alongside the quay. The watching fishermen parted to make space for us. Two of them were level with the bowsprit, and the other two with the rudder.

Isabel had to go marketing, and Santi accompanied her. I asked him to get us some good wine, and to my astonishment he advised me not to buy in Messina, but to go to Reggio di Calabria, on the other side of the Straits. "Here the wine is no good this year," he said. "And me, I never touch it. Neither wine nor tobacco since I visited that accursed Assawa,

284

where the climate poignarded my kidneys and scorched my spleen." While they were gone I spliced a new painter for the dinghy, cleared the shaft of the port engine, which had become tangled with a ball of tarred twine, and wrote letters. Seeing me thus occupied was not enough to deter the hyenas on the quay and on the water. Boys refused to believe me when I assured them that I had no cigarettes, no British, American, or Swiss currency, no candy, and no naphtha, for sale. Three barbers refused to believe that I did not want a hair-cut, and that I had adequately shaved myself that morning. Isabel returned with a huge load of food, carried in a hired donkey-cart. I walked to the Cheep offices. Rounding a bend I came on the Moscatelli Bros. They stood with their backs to me, arguing in loud voices about how much they ought to make us pay. Santi was of the opinion (I gathered before they turned round and saw me) that it would be best to charge us reasonably, and obtain from me a letter to the Cheep in Rome. I agreed, with some misgivings, to give them such a letter, comforting myself with the knowledge that neither could read English. The petrol was to arrive at two o'clock; we faced the prospect with equanimity because Isabel had done well in the market. The grapes were golden and slightly hooked in shape; the figs were opulent and sweet; the sausage was full of ham, the salad crisp, the bread white with a good crust on it.

The advance guard of the Moscatelli Bros.' supply train was composed of two ragged but intelligent urchins carrying thirty litres of paraffin. Next came a flat cart, drooping on one spring, creaking under the weight of two drums of petrol and drawn by an aged donkey wearing a brown-and-yellow nose-bag. While the fuelling slowly proceeded the persons who had aided us the day before arrived for their rewards. The boy with the pitted face received 200 lire from me, but the man with the moustache was ill-advised enough to tell his story to Santi Moscatelli, who gave him only 100 and sent him packing while I was below. The old sea-dog who had taken our warps got 200, but still loitered near us, pretending to help with the delivery of the petrol. When this was completed, and the donkey-cart had withdrawn, I invited the Moscatelli Bros. below, gave them a drink, and asked for their account. They required 1,500 lire (about thirty shillings) for delivering the petrol—the cost of which I had paid direct to the oil association—90 for delivering the paraffin, and 1,500 for customs fees. I paid what they asked, thinking that the charges might have been worse, and gave them my carefully-worded letter to Cheep in Rome while Isabel presented Santi with a large packet of tea from a Piccadilly establishment.

When the payment had been made the Moscatellis stood around with gentle, Christian smiles, saying that if we were contented and pleased with their services, then that was all that mattered. I said that we were most contented, and I was leaving it at that; but Isabel saw that they considered, or pretended to consider, that they had been underpaid. They admitted, under pressure, that they were "prepared to lose money on this deal" or rather "not to make any profit at all" because we were so sympathetic, and because we had given them the letter of introduction. Next time, Santi said, perhaps they would permit themselves to take a tiny profit, but since this was our first meeting, let us meet as gentlemen, with no hint of commerce thrown in. Of course, if Mr. Millar insisted that he had not paid enough, that would be different. When I weakly brought out another 1,000 lire note, he snatched it surprisingly quickly from my hand, as though overcome with embarrassment. The old sea-dog, who was on terms of intimacy with the Moscatelli Bros., and who had, I suspected, advised them of our arrival in the port, helped us with the anchor chain. There was a great deal of chain out, and the work at the windlass was heavy because the anchor had collected a long bight of wire rope. I gave him 100 lire when the work was done.

"Ah, no!" he cried. "You insult me!"

"Why?" I asked. "If I had 100 lire for every time I wound in that chain and catted that anchor I should be a rich man."

He dropped into his boat, shrieking at the Moscatelli Bros. that he had been swindled, but they only laughed at him. He rowed in our wake as we moved to the harbour mouth, and his shouts of protest became louder and more violent until suddenly he saw that we really intended to sail without handing out any more money; then he smiled warmly and shouted to me: "So long, Joe."

Isabel steered out of the port, and steadied on a compass course for Reggio di Calabria on the mainland while I washed the deck. Reggio was obscured by mist. I heard Isabel whistling in the wheelhouse, but soon she lashed the wheel and came to help me, flipping the canvas bucket over the side for water and sluicing the deck while I scrubbed. Sometimes we paused to look at the strange little whirlpools occasioned, according to the *Mediterranean Pilot*, by the uneven nature of the bottom, and the speed of the main currents in the Straits.

Reggio has a drab, sullen harbour, but we were relieved to see that it was almost undamaged. A uniformed officer ran out of the Capitaneria showing us where to berth; but he wanted us to go alongside the quays, and this we refused to do. He would not hear of us anchoring and swinging in the harbour, because, he said, they were expecting many ships, and the train-ferry would object to our presence in the fairway. Finally, we anchored off the inner quay with two lines to it from our stern. As I threw out the lines I got my hands and bare legs smeared with heavy oil which had clung to the ropes after their immersion in the filthy water at Messina. This maddened me, for I had become proud of the four-inch rope, whitened and beautified by constant use in salt water and sun. My irritation boiled over when the officer asked me to step ashore immediately and comply with the usual formalities at the Capitaneria. With angry shouts and gestures I told him that these formalities had been complied with at fifteen Italian ports—naming them individually, to the delight of the listening crowd— and that we had not been so stupidly misused in any country but Italy, a country where there were still far too many police. At this I actually had growls of sympathy and approval from the crowd, and the young man very properly reminded me: "I am not a policeman, but a naval officer."

He went away, but returned shortly to ask for the name of the yacht and her tonnage, and then left us alone for the night. Isabel remarked, while she was cooking dinner, that I had become uncharacteristically irritable with strangers; she wondered if the effect of owning and sailing a boat would be to make me permanently crotchety. I replied that the Italian crowd enjoys a certain display of temper, and thinks no less of a man because he bursts through his reserve. But I secretly resolved to keep more control of myself in future.

We found an exceptionally charming and helpful commandante del porto when we went ashore the next morning. He was able to recommend a marine carpenter, who said that for 1,600 lire he would make a pair of oars for our dinghy.

"You will want English-type oars," he said.

"No, Italian-type," I answered, thinking that it would be best if he did not experiment but worked in his accustomed manner.

"Yes, Italian-type but a little more *robusto*, that is English-type. I quite understand what you want."

"But I want the Italian shape, and I abominate heavy oars."

"Yes, yes. The Italian shape, only more spoonlike in the blade; we call that the *tipo inglese*."

A soldier in uniform bespattered with the insignia of the British Pioneer Corps waited for us on the quay. He did not speak English, but he clung to us as though he wished to adopt us, as though we were England itself. His name was Ercolino Esposito. He was the son of a farmer in the Calabrian hills. He had volunteered to join the British Army after seeing Field-Marshal Montgomery drive through Reggio in his jeep the day that the British landed there.

"I'm English, like you," he said. "My naturalisation papers are stamped, and I'm only here on leave."

"You will be sorry to return to England?"

"Only a very little sorry because I've over-spent my leave, and when I get back this will cause pain to everybody, including myself. But I like Britain because the life is spread more evenly there. Here, you've plenty of money, you've plenty of food; there, everybody has food. Here, everybody gets mad with somebody else; there, nobody gets mad at all. I'm going to get married in England, and then I'll leave the Army and go to an amusement centre in London. Already I've saved money enough to buy two amusement machines, pin-tables. When I've six machines I can make a start in business. The day will perhaps dawn when I'll have a million pin-tables."

We walked with him down the apparently interminable Corso Garibaldi to the post office. Then we walked to the other end of the Corso Garibaldi, searching for good wine and olive oil. We discovered that we conversed more easily in French than in Italian for he had spent three years in North Africa, and spoke a brutish Algerian French. His company was stationed at Ipswich, a small English town which he greatly admired—although Isabel and I both preferred Reggio di Calabria—and if only he could have his fiancée with him in Ipswich, all would be well. His fiancée was called Janet, and she lived in Anniesland, "which is an arrondissement or rather a banlieu of Glasgow—a very beautiful place," he told us. He was a little worried about Janet, for although she was a sensible girl and had a steady job making telescopes, she should surely write to him occasionally, and he had not heard from her for three months.

"Do you think something's wrong?" he asked.

"How long is it since you saw her?"

"I last saw her three months ago when my company left Glasgow for Ipswich."

"Then she's never written?"

"Never. But it would be difficult, I suppose, for I can't understand English and she can't understand Italian."

"Then how do you know you're engaged?"

"There could be no two ways of thinking about that," he answered with a most villainous wink at me. "She's a fine strong girl and she appeals to me. I'll never find another like her. Will you assist me in this matter, for I read in the paper that you're something of a writer, and then I determined to ask your help."

"Of course I'll help, if I can."

We dived into a grocer's store, dark, lined with square pigeon-holes containing farinaceous foods and beans of all colours and sizes, and hung with fine hams. Isabel bought a two-litre fiasco of pure olive oil, a kilo of gorgonzola, and a kilo of butter. We were leaving Italy as soon as the weather seemed favourable, and she intended to finish our Italian money. The shop seethed with excitement at her bold purchases, and Ercolino swaggered about winking at the shopkeeper and his sons We sampled the contents of several barrels of wine, all three of us tasting from each barrel. We said that we would collect bottles from the boat, and have them filled there. Then we repaired to a small businessman's café where we ate ice-cream and drank vermouth. It was a sultry day, and after asking our permission Ercolino took off his tie, and opened his shirt. He called for paper, pen and ink, and set the writing materials before me.

"Write to her from me," he said.

"But you must tell me what to say."

"All right. Say this: 'My fine, big, white flower: do you remember your Ercolino Esposito and the long Saturday afternoon that we walked by the canal with the men fishing so tranquilly in the water and the small racing dogs crouching behind them in the grass?' What are they called those small racing dogs?"

"Whippets. But I like the sound of 'small racing dogs'."

"Very well then, continue: 'When I have left you I have gone to Ipswich, a place of many taverns, but with tea and fried fish greatly inferior to those which we enjoyed together in Anniesland. I like Ipswich nevertheless, but I would like it more than heaven if you could be there to see me when the hours of work are finished. Two women in Ipswich have attempted to seduce me from my love for you but I have told them that I am affianced to another and they have understood. Here in Reggio I have bought for you a pair of silk stockings. I will hide the stockings below my uniform, and when I return to Britain I will post them to you. They are expensive stockings which have cost me two thousand lire—much money even in pounds—and my sisters and others have importuned me saying: "Ercolino, give me the stockings," but I have refused even to let them try the stockings on their legs, knowing well that it is one thing to allow a girl to put on a fragile stocking and another thing to take it off her. I have not spent much money in Italy because things are too expensive. I am saving money to help us when we are married and live in London. I am certain that you must also be saving. Good-bye then, my big white flower with a thousand embraces and tender thoughts from your Ercolino.' That will do well enough," he said.

"You have not asked her why she has not written."

"No. It is bad policy to chide a woman in a letter, and bad policy to praise her to her face."

We exchanged addresses with him and left him in the café, excusing ourselves from his company by inventing some business at the Capitaneria. In the afternoon a strong wind blew up. *Truant* plunged and heaved at her anchor and it seemed that we might have to move to a quieter place, for the north wind raged down the length of the harbour at us, and rain spattered intermittently on our decks. Twenty yards along the quay navvies were working on the masonry, and below them a diver was working from a float fitted with a pump which two men steadily operated. Each time that rain fell the navvies ran for shelter, and the men on the pump turned longing eyes after them but continued to press and lift the creaking arm; the crop of bubbles among the rain circles on the surface showed that the diver worked on below. Soon the little waves in the harbour became so fierce that the overseer came from his hut, nibbling at a huge sandwich containing an omelette; they called the diver to the surface, and wrapped his helmet in a cloth and folded his patched under-water suit into a white cardboard box.

We liked Reggio. The people in the streets are small, fierce, hot-looking. There is an almost Asiatic twist to the general countenance, a certain bitterness that carries passion with it. Although black clouds heavy with water sweep low between the mountains, little water falls on Reggio, its vineyards, its olive groves. But that, we found, is not the only peculiarity of Reggio's autumn climate; the wind is both strangely capricious and, it would seem from our experience, diurnal. The currents passing through the Straits and altering the temperature of the air over the water in that tunnel-shaped space suck in the winds, and if there is already a north wind it will draw strength from the *scendente*, or south-flowing stream.

Early on our second morning in Reggio while I was writing below I heard a thump on the deck, and running up suspiciously I came face to face with the small Sardinian whom we had known at Vibo Valentia Marina.

"We went to Catania to load bricks," he said. "Then we went to Messina, and we saw you in the papers. Did you ever hear the like? We'll bring you the paper this afternoon, for this morning we're unloading bricks, and I must return or the captain will be enraged. Also our captain says that the corn-edd-bayf you gave us was good. Will you gave us more corn-edd-bayf if we bring you grapes and the article in the paper?"

"Certainly."

"Our captain will be gratified. To-night we leave for Salerno. I wish

290

he'd take cargo for Sardinia, but this is never so."

Isabel was taking down the mosquito nets from the portholes and hatches. The boat looked better without them but we were sorry to see them go, for their departure was symptomatic of autumn and winter. Already we thought with considerable nostalgia of the hot days in Corbeil when the flies had made Isabel improvise the net defences. The boat-builder came with the oars he had made, two great lumps of unseasoned elm without leathers, copper, paint or varnish. I rather liked them, for they looked to me much more tipo italiano than tipo inglese, and the shape was good for sculling through the groove in the transom. I found this the best way to go ashore in Italy; none of the urchins was able to scull in that way, and it was safer to leave the dinghy with one oar in it than with two and two rowlocks.

We chose from the assembled conveyances a carriage with a faded coronet on its royal blue door and a young chestnut mare between the shafts. We told the driver to proceed slowly down the Corso Garibaldi. When we reached the far end we told him to drive slowly back again. When he was asked to turn about for the third time he said: "I am not paying and I do not wish to criticise, but there are more beautiful streets in Reggio than the Corso Garbaldi."

"I know, but a short period of my wife's adolescence was spent in America . . ."

"That explains it . . ."

"Let me finish. Walking down the Corso Garibaldi yesterday she saw in the window of some shop an American sweetmeat called a Hershey Bar. But now she cannot recognise the shop."

"Ah well," the driver said. "Now that I know there is some sense to it. . . . Forward, sluggard!" he cried to his chestnut mare.

We bought a great many eggs at 25 lire each, four bottles of white Cinzano at 300 lire each (they had been 1,000—or a £1 a bottle—in Capri), twelve litres of the red wine we had chosen with Ercolino Esposito, four kilos of bread, two splendid sausages and an even finer ham, quantities of tomatoes, green vegetables and fruit. The carriage was full, and we felt that we were well provisioned for our voyage to Greece. We ate in a bare, fly-blown room sporting similar wall pegs and standing coat-hangers to those seen in Soho. It was a restaurant which prided itself on copious dishes; two women and two men lunching at the next table ate as an entrée such quantities of spaghetti as to leave us—and themselves—breathless.

The Calabrese and the Sardinian boarded *Truant* in the evening with a plateful of grapes that were so dirty we scarcely liked to lay them in the galley, and an even dirtier copy of a newspaper called *La Sicilia* which contained a paragraph headed "Una Coppia Felice!" and stating that the yacht which had just entered Messina harbour carried young George Muller and his wife Isabella who were "happily sailing around the world." Isabel laughed heartily at this description of the purgatory she withstood so courageously when the boat was moving. I went ashore in the evening to get our bill of health and clearance papers. The commandante del porto was dealing with a party of sixty-eight naval deserters, the second officer was indenting for stores, so I was passed on to the third, a lieutenant, who gave me my clearance papers for Greece and that day's weather report from the lighthouse at Cape Spartivento, which Isabel had come to call "the jumping-off place". The report was poor, but better weather was believed to be approaching. The young lieutenant was annoyed by the difference in our situations, and compared my "romantic" life favourably with his own "underpaid" one.

I was ashore with the water-cans at 6 a.m. The single fountain which supplied drinking water to the whole harbour only ran at certain hours of the day, and was therefore in great demand. But at so early an hour there were few people about, and I was able to fill my cans in peace. My second trip was infinitely slower, since the port was waking; many boats and houses required water, and one fat man washed beneath the fountain with a great frothing of soap. "Sunlight Soap!" he told me. "I paid a great price for it on the island of Malta." At the corner by the fountain a woman and her son sold prickly pears. The pears cost two lire each; they lay in a beautiful basket beside her spatulate toes. She had carried the basket on her head from the hills. Her wooden-soled shoes were thrust to one side while she sold the fruit, and her feet arched themselves in the warm dust. Her son, a slender child, stood with a few notes of small denomination in his left hand, while his right was hooked to his mother's skirt, beneath which showed a good eight inches of flannel petticoat. The boy gave each customer his change, while the woman, who had a short, curved knife, sliced off each end of the pear, slid the interior neatly from the skin, and offered it on the point of her blade. The customer would take the wet object gingerly between thumb and forefinger and push it whole into his mouth. She looked frankly into the customer's faces, savouring their enjoyment of her fruit, and accepting with dignity and reserve such brief compliments as were paid. Few buyers ate more than one pear, but one man ate eight or nine in quick succession, as well as a large hunk of bread which he brought from his brief case. He was a business man about to

292

catch the train-ferry to Messina; over-dressed and very middle-class, he turned his back on the woman while he ate, but neither she nor the boy gave any sign of being insulted by his lack of manners. The empty skins piled behind her arching feet formed an advertisement for her wares.

Several young men, recently returned prisoners from Britain, spoke to me. Two of them claimed British fiancées, one in London and the other in Lowestoft, and I was glad to hear them all speak well of their period of imprisonment in a cold country, but perhaps they were only influenced to do so by their natural courtesy and by the southern desire to please. I doubt if so many people would have spoken to me and treated me as a friendly equal if I had not been dressed in clothes faded and worn by work in the sun, and had not, like themselves, been working. This is one of the peculiar joys of travelling on a boat without a paid crew. *Truant's* water-cans were heavy, yet when I think back over the times that I filled them in foreign places I realise that the simple task was always enjoyable, because the mere fact that I was doing something necessary gave me a place in all those varied surroundings, a place among the native peoples and the growing things. Tourists who travel in more ordinary conveyances, steamships and trains, motor-cars and aeroplanes, can have few such pleasures, because when they go abroad to enjoy themselves without working for their enjoyment they are deliberately putting themselves in another category, and they will be misfits wherever they go.

The lieutenant who envied me my life came out of the Capitaneria as I was filling the last can. He waved the weather forecast from Cape Sparti-vento in one hand, and shouted down the twin flight of steps that the morning at the cape was clear with a light north wind, and that the sea was described as *leggeramente mosso*.

In fifteen minutes I had emptied the water-cans into *Truant's* tanks, and we were off. The Straits were calm, with few signs of current. We headed into a zephyr that scarcely stirred the foresail and mizzen. A steamship passed us, steering about a mile farther out from the mainland. She was the *Corinthia*, and she flew the Greek flag. We knew that she regularly carried passengers between Marseilles and Athens. Her white paint gleamed—at any rate from that distance—and beyond her was the splendid outline of Etna, with a grilled mushroom of smoke gathered around and above the crater. As we rounded Cape del Armo—congratulating each other on having travelled the length of Italy's western seaboard—we got more wind. I hoisted the mainsail and the jib. We sailed past a desolate coast, pale and faded as watercolours done a century ago by Anglo-Indian pig-stickers. A few factories were down near the shore, the red remains of landing craft lay on the beaches, and ungainly, crumpled fighting vehicles in the dry courses of the seasonal torrents. We saw flying fishes; one dashed itself to death against the wheelhouse. In the early afternoon we passed Bova Marina, a large white village, then another village like a head of hair parted in the middle, the parting being made by a strip of woodland; and so we came to Cape Spartivento.

Bova Marina, Spartivento, all the other landmarks that we had passed that day were familiar to me, for Isabel had often discussed them while she studied the *Mediterranean Pilot* and planned our journey to Greece. I dropped anchor east of the cape, and as close inshore as we dared to venture for shelter. *Truant* wallowed abominably, and the swell rolling out on the beach behind us made a most ghoulish noise. We were a little disconcerted, for we had hoped for a good rest at Cape Spartivento before "jumping-off". Isabel lay down on her mattress on deck. I had a few things to do in the engine-room, and I bent the bigger squaresail to the yard, and checked over all the standing and running rigging. We were ready to go. I felt a mounting excitement, and so did Isabel, despite her sea-sickness. I made tea and toast, and boiled eggs. I suppose that my wife prefers lightly-boiled eggs, toast, fresh butter and salt to most other foods, and the preference is surely not ill-placed. I boiled three of the Calabrian eggs for her because they were so small that any self-respecting hen would have stamped them contemptuously to fragments. Isabel ate in bed, and could manage no more than one egg. When I had washed the dishes I went to bed too, and lay reading, listening to the waves and the many noises of a boat rolling at anchor. I noted with approval that the noises were lessened since I had re-rigged the squaresail yard with new improvements at Vibo Valentia Marina. I read until I thought that I felt tired, and then switched off the light. Isabel was already asleep. It was 7 p.m. We had agreed to weigh anchor at 3 a.m. But before going to bed I had worked out the course—210 miles on East Magnetic—and I began to see that if we had no fair wind for the passage we should be lucky if we averaged five knots, and that it would be wise to leave as early as possible to increase the likelihood of a landfall on the second day out.

"What is it?" Isabel asked sleepily.

"I'm getting up. I can't sleep, and I might as well sail the boat as lie here thinking."

"Would you like me to get up?"

"I'd rather you stayed here. I'll shout if I need you, and if I begin to fall asleep at the wheel you can take over."

"Steer where the sea looks flattest," she said.

23

I STARTED one engine, leaving it ticking over in neutral to warm up while I hoisted the mizzen to keep *Truant's* head well into the wind. A kick forward on the engine, and I wound in most of the anchor chain, quickly. Another kick, and I catted the anchor, then jumped to the stay-sail halyards; when the staysail was sheeted firmly *Truant* began to sail herself away from the thundering shore. I went to the wheelhouse, set her on her course, and lashed the wheel; forward to secure the anchor on its chocks; to the wheelhouse to adjust the helm again; aft to stream the log, below to listen to the engine and turn the cooling water through the main exhaust pipe; back to the wheelhouse to check the course; forward to see that the navigation lights were burning clearly; once round the decks with a torch to ascertain that all was secure; back to the wheelhouse, to settle down. A good many ships were steaming across our course; that part of the Italian coast, perhaps because it is harbourless, seemed to be particularly busy at night. I chose a star over the bow and steered on it, checking the course every twenty minutes, and sometimes changing stars. The barometer was rising slightly; the wind came in fitful gusts, sometimes not enough to sail us, sometimes heeling us well over so that the port-hole a foot from Isabel's head was awash. The movement was better for her now that we were away from the shore. Occasionally she would awake and call to me with her amazing voice that can be deep and gruff or softer than the voice of a pigeon; once, when I did not answer her call promptly, she pushed her head up into the wheelhouse, and then whisked back to bed, reassured. I began to feel the cold, to close the wheelhouse doors and windows, and to put on more clothes until I was steering in a shirt, a blue, high-necked sailor's jersey, a thick white "pigswhisker" jersey from the north of Scotland, corduroy trousers over my shorts, and socks to keep my feet warm. After a time the turning light from Cape Spartivento ceased to flicker into the wheelhouse and on the sails, and no more lights from ships were visible. We were alone in the blackness, and I was glad of the steady, silken noise of the turning engine. About three in the morning I began to waver from the course, drowning in patches of sleep like a blind man who, walking in the sea, stumbles into deep pools. At 4 o'clock Isabel came up, fully dressed. We had breakfast and she took the wheel. I stopped the starboard engine, to give it a rest, and started the other. There was still not enough wind to sail reasonably fast. I went below, undressed and slept until 7.10. At 8.25 when we had been moving for twelve hours, the log showed sixty-four miles, or an average of just over five knots. With the dawn what wind there was fell away, and we were left to the mercy of the swell. The day looked bad, with a great deal of cloud and some rain all round the horizon, but we had warm sun, and the barometer was high and steady. At midday a breeze came from the north and I hoisted the mainsail and a light-weather jib; we were able to switch off the engine, and to log six to seven knots in greater comfort. I cooked lunch: French beans, sweet potatoes, pimento, a little garlic, butter, all done together in the oven, stewed apples, pears and tinned cream. The wine that we had bought in Reggio was delicious. In the evening we had a very intense period of swell, and the wind dropped so much that I took the mainsail off her to reduce the chafing. We had seen nothing all day but some small birds, flying our way across the sea. Isabel began to feel very ill. It was rather cold for her on deck; we made up a bed on the chart table. This was probably a mistake, as she was lying athwartships instead of fore-and-aft, as in her bunk below, but it was better for me to feel her beside me as I steered. At 9 p.m. I was overcome by sleep, and she had to take over. After an hour I had recovered, but later in the night she had to take another long spell, leaning down from her bed with one hand on the wheel, and occasionally shining a torch at the "tell-tale" compass on the deck, near my sleeping body. Now we were 100 miles from any land, and floating on a sea deeper than the height of Mount Everest. We wondered if *Truant* was aware of all the giddy distance beneath her keel, and thought how terrifying it would be if the sea dried out while we were there, leaving us grounded in a steamy petrified forest, surrounded by expiring monsters. The second dawn began at 5.30 a.m. and we were heading into a bank of cloud so sensational and so solid in appearance that I frequently had the hallucination that I was steering straight for a beach with a fantastic background of houses, mountains, leopards, monkeys, honeysuckle, and black men with white teeth. Quite often this hallucination was so strong that Isabel had to argue with me to prevent my turning from our course. After an hour the sun rose from behind the clouds ahead, and we saw the real coast, merely a low bluish line on the horizon, and a most insignificant sight by comparison with my previous images. I had navigated to enter the channel between the islands of Zante and Cephalonia, and we found our bowsprit to be pointing at the northernmost tip of a long island which we were soon able to identify as Zante. We had planned, before leaving Italy, to make either for

296

the port of Argostoli, under Mount Nero, in Cephalonia, or for the harbour of Zante, on the inner side of the island of that name; but with the land ahead of us we both felt inclined to spend the first night in some peaceful anchorage, away from men, and we were irresistibly attracted by an inlet marked on our charts as Port Vromi, a small natural harbour far from all houses and used only occasionally, according to our *Pilot* book, by "small craft with local knowledge". We made for that place, accordingly, and were within a mile of the coast at 10 a.m., our log showing 218 miles. After our accurate navigation across a rather wide stretch of sea we had the greatest difficulty in finding Port Vromi. While, helped by an excellent chart, we were hunting for it along that strange, twisted, volcanic coast, where often there are 100 fathoms of water right under the cliffs, we saw another vessel for the first time in two days, a Greek trader, cutter-rigged, and painted white with a saffron line below her bulwarks, a fine boat. We steered towards each other, and exchanged shouts, but I was unable to understand them. Eventually, crawling along the coast only a few yards out, and searching every inlet, we found the narrow entrance to Port Vromi. We moved cautiously through an opening in the cliffs which gave way to steep hillsides covered with a kind of gorse bush and with bright, yellowish pine trees. At the inner end the water ran into two small horns, and the tip of each horn was a sandy beach on which a row-boat lay. *Truant* was too big to enter either of the horns. I anchored her on an up-and-down chain in twelve fathoms. The water was as clear as in the bay at Port Cros, and the bottom was soft white sand. When we shut off the engine the silence at first seemed to be absolute, and then we gradually heard the hum of crickets and the chirping of small birds. That was how we arrived in Greece.

24

Since Isabel rarely entered the galley while we were at sea, she was obliged soon after we had anchored to attack the chaos caused by my preparing meals during the crossing without "having time" to wash the dishes. As for me, I worked cheerfully on deck, examining the rigging for wear, giving the dinghy and its new oars a coat of varnish, and listening to a programme based on the career of Arturo Toscanini and broadcast from an Italian station. Our anchorage was a sounding board, and Beethoven's Fifth Symphony reverberated from the rocks with the most remarkable effect, as though two orchestras were playing, one a whole beat behind the other. We went early to bed with our books, and must have fallen instantly asleep, for we awoke next morning with the books still open.

My feet and ankles were stiff and sore from overwork when I climbed out of bed, and a mosquito sting planted in my left eyelid had given me a horribly corrupt appearance. We had planned to remain all day in Port Vromi, but the weather changed rapidly; when I went on deck after breakfast I saw that a south-west wind was beginning to roll a sea towards our anchorage. Within seven minutes we were under way, and hoisting sail as we motored out of the inlet. Once outside, with a strong free wind, and as yet little sea, we turned north, and fairly boiled along the coast of the island. At the fearsomely rocky northern end we turned south-east, and the wind was obliging enough to veer just sufficiently to allow us to sail close-hauled. The island of Zante is fertile on the inner side, while to the west and the open sea it presents only its cliffy battlements. The outlines of the island, sometimes rather vulgarly called "the pearl of the Levant" and sometimes "Zante, fior di Levante", now showed themselves to be sinuous and civilised, with white houses and many pines, olive groves, and olive-green fields. There was a black storm of rain. The *Maine*, a British hospital ship, lay in Zante Bay, her bows to the town and a sharp wind. Fishing-boats were sailing for shelter.

Zante harbour is spacious, and the waterfront, gloriously foreign to British eyes, is adorned with arcades, domes, minarets, Venetian palaces, and a strange dash of English Georgian—that most noble of domestic architectures—because the English once stole the place from the French, who had obtained it by treaty with Russia and Turkey, who had stolen it from the Venetians, who had no right to be there. The English colonised there for fifty-three years until, bowing frigidly to a storm of local indignation-cum-poesie, they gave the island back to the natives.

We dropped anchor off the outer mole. The bystanders helped most willingly with my stern lines, but we exchanged no words. We were obliged to close portholes and hatches against the chill wind.

No sooner had we set foot ashore the following morning than we were seized upon by a tattered ruffian aged about thirty. He spoke a few words of English, a few more of Italian, and a few less of French, and when introducing himself he laid claim (rather boastfully, we later felt), to "six languages excluding Greek". His face was seen mistily through a haze of dirt and whisker. What chance had we of seeing into his soul? I called him Alcibiades, and he agreed, willingly, that that was his name. We merely asked him to direct us to the offices of the harbour-master. Direct us? He had no intention of letting us go. He would lead us there.

The streets were of an incomparable charm, white and gracious, and built on either hand to so low a level that but for the excellent proportions you would imagine that the buildings had sunk into the ground. We passed stalls and shops apparently well-stocked with bread, eggs, mutton, vegetables, and fruit; dark cafés where glass urns of sweetmeats and nougat, cases of chocolate, stood on the zinc, side by side with bottles of liqueurs and the battered Swedish stove for making Turkish coffee. Dark and curious stares were directed at us. The children were beautiful in a fragile manner, almost spiritual after the long fasting period of the war, which had surely not damaged their eyes and hair and skin-textures although their teeth might be rotting beneath the white enamel, and tuberculosis might lurk in their blood. We entered a building of tattered but immense pretentiousness. Painted marble veins peeled damply from the Ionic columns that flanked the ceremonial staircase. We swept through the ante-room, a scarlet saloon with ornately-painted walls, Byronic portraits, and plush seats in which rooks might have nested, so musty and torn was the fabric, and so into an inner room where a man, urbane, stoutish, dark, with frayed trouser ends, sat in conclave with five underlings. I addressed these persons in French, and Alcibiades, who had no intention of leaving us although indoors his presence created great unpleasantness by reason of his pungent smell, evidently gave us an imposing introduction because the underlings vanished and the stout man behind the desk invited us with signs, liquid but incomprehensible sentences, and the international word "café" to accept his hospitality.

This was the prefect. Alcibiades, who occupied the plush chair nearest to mine, had brought us to the highest authority in Zante, and to the wrong fountainhead. One by one the satellites drifted back to continue their business with the prefect and to look at us. Facing the prefect was a yellow papier-maché frame holding an immense photograph of Mr. Winston Churchill. Behind the prefect, standing on a table, was a photograph of similar size representing the frosty torso and visage of King George of Greece. Two cups of coffee and two glasses of water were brought for us on an aluminium tray. A harbour official and an old notary were called. The notary was bent nearly double with rheumatism, and his hands shook so that they nearly rattled. He spoke French with an exquisite accent, and only the vaguest remembrance of a vocabulary with which he had probably once been familiar. With his slow aid we were able to ask the harbour official if the Corinth Canal was open.

"The Corinth Canal open!" They all stared at us for some time, and then burst into a clamour of agitated speech. The notary translated: "The harbour official says that the Corinth Canal will not be open for years unless the British or the Americans take a hand in the clearing of it. The British Air Force partially blocked it, but the Germans did the most terrible things to it before they left Greece. They filled it in so thoroughly that where there was once water there is now often solid land. And that is not all, for there are mines where the excavations should begin. Lives have been lost, and now that the war is ended lives seem very precious, not only to individuals, even to the state . . ."

Isabel and I looked at each other. In the south of France we had been assured by an Air Marshal that the Corinth Canal *was* open. "I ought to know," he had said. "My boys fly over it every day." Instead of sailing straight down the Gulf of Corinth, and passing through the interesting waterway cut through rock to the gates of Athens, we should have to sail round the Peloponnese peninsula, a place with a very foul reputation for storms. We went to the bank, where a man who spoke excellent French cashed £30 of my letter of credit, recommended the best restaurant in the town, and advised us strongly to be rid of Alcibiades, whom he described as "a man with strong criminal tendencies".

"What should I give him?" I asked.

"Say two thousand drachmae—or two shillings in your own money."

Outside the bank Alcibiades pocketed the two thousand, and remained beside us. "Well, good-bye," I said.

"Good-bye," he answered, accompanying us to the post office.

"Adieu," I said.

300

"Au revoir," he answered, shaking hands, and matching his pace to ours. "You do not understand, Alcibiades, our association, not that there ever was one, is terminated . . ."

"Terminated?"

"We would rather you left us alone."

"Alone?" His eyes were wary, but unwounded behind the mist of hair and dirt.

"Please go away."

"Me go away?"

"Yes, please."

He dropped some twenty yards behind us, and occasionally stopped to show that it was only coincidence that carried him our way, while he exchanged a few words with some acquaintance, one misty eye always turned on us.

Isabel made large purchases of fruit and vegetables, talking to the man in Spanish, Spanish-Italian, French and English. But mainly she explained her wants and her queries with her exquisite hands, which soared, like graceful butterflies or long-tailed tropical birds over the red, yellow, and green mounds of country produce. When it only remained to pay, the shopkeeper, a twisted man with a gruesome expression, wrote down the figure, 11,000. Isabel, who had kept her own tally, refused to pay. "Lista, lista," she demanded, her hands miming the movements of a scribe at work. A crowd at once gathered round us, with Alcibiades on the outskirts, and a non-commissioned officer in the Greek Police—they all seemed to be non-commissioned officers, and they were all smartly dressed in British uniform with round military caps and the Greek badge—came to ask what it was all about. Seeing this new development, the shopkeeper tore up the paper on which he had written the figure 11,000, and substituted another paper which showed 580. The policeman was determined that we should have our rights. Everything had to be taken out of the bags and meticulously weighed, sweet potatoes, French beans, figs, apples, pears, melon, onions, oranges. This time the policeman kept the lista, and the total came to 610. Nobody except us seemed to realise what had happened. It was some days before Isabel completely recovered from the effects of the greengrocer's perfidy.

The restaurant, like most restaurants that we visited in Greece, was extremely beautiful. It was a well-lit, stone-floored room, sunk a little below street level. The buff-plastered walls were hung with a few irregularly-placed pictures torn from magazines and then set in ancient frames, and the place of honour was occupied by a purple and gold

301

panoramic view of Athens. In one corner of the room was a basin for the washing of hands. Water fell from a small cylindrical tin tank secured to the wall above the basin; if any form of towel seemed to be necessary the customer used his table napkin. The proprietor, a small man with a certain look of dignity about to be injured which to that date I had associated uniquely with a famous conductor, led us from the dining-room to the kitchen, where his wife stood behind a long charcoal range, languidly turning over, with one tin spoon, the contents of the different cooking-pots. There were red mullets fried in oil, different cuts of mutton, roasted, broiled, cooked with potatoes, with beans, with tomatoes, with olives, and lastly there was a great copper vat of slimy spaghetti. We ate copiously and drank a thick white wine that looked like lime juice and tasted half as strong as it was. As we were finishing our meal a Greek ships' chandler named Spiro entered with two Englishmen from the *Maine*, the hospital ship outside. One of the Englishmen proved to be a useful acquaintance, the chief officer. He wore a small goatee beard, a Panama hat, and civilian clothes, and he was very young to occupy so important a post. Quiet of voice and manner he told us that he had a fiancée in Paignton to whose purity and absolute fidelity he earnestly swore. We begged him for some black paint for *Truant*, also anti-fouling paint, and, if possible, some marmalade. Spiro, the Greek chandler, who strangely resembled the actor, Mr. Adolph Menjou, said that he would fill our boat with "sweet water" but would quote no figure for the work. "Sweet water" is a rare commodity in Zante, so I asked him to arrange the supply, thinking that we would not care to be bothered with watering while we sailed round the Peloponnese. The chief officer came with us to drink a brandy on *Truant*. He was waiting for a friend and fellow-officer who was visiting the town that afternoon in order to view the remains of a mummified saint which, he had been told, were stored in Zante. He soon passed along the quay, and came aboard. He was bald, and his face and forehead were covered with bumps which he explained with the words: "My father was very fond of camping and when I was a baby he used me as a mallet to knock in the tent pegs." The next people to come on board were two British nurses from the hospital ship. We had earlier seen them with an elderly Englishwoman, grey-haired, stooping, and distinguished, and I hastened to ask them if Miss Crowe—for that was her name—lived on Zante, since she obviously was not part of the crew of a hospital ship.

"Oh yes," one of the nurses answered, "she is called the Queen of Zante."

"Why does she live here?"

"I don't know. She has a house here, you know, a house on a hill . . ." Accompanying the nurses—or were they accompanying him?—was a young eye specialist from Glasgow, one of the hospital ship's eight doctors. He had fine blue eyes, wore a Glasgow Academical's neck-tie, and looked more intelligent than the language he spoke, presumably because he was trying to talk a language that he thought we would understand. Our visitors had not yet mustered. The next to come on board was the Reverend Jones, a well-dressed and positive chaplain, naval model. While we were discussing Italy, a country to which Isabel and I had become deeply attached, the Reverend Jones reminded me sharply that the Italians had cost us a great deal by entering the war on the wrong side and that "we must not be soft with them". But if the Reverend was lacking a little in that unsectarian charity which was so eloquently taught by his Master, the young bearded chief officer was charitable enough, for he came tearing back in a launch with two cans of paint for me, his own week's ration of marmalade and chocolate for Isabel, and the news that everyone must be on board the *Maine* within forty minutes, for the captain had just received a signal that he must steam with all haste for Corfu. A search party hurried into the town to hunt for the bald officer who was hunting for the mummified saint. We had been a little dazed by all this social activity, too dazed to complain about the watering of *Truant*, which proceeded while the visitors were on board, Spiro's men bringing out three boat-loads of ordinary pump water in extremely rusty iron cans that had probably once contained petrol, tar, or crude oil. The two men asked for 20,000 drachma (or £1) for their work. I suggested mildly that Mr. Spiro had guaranteed that the price would not be high, and they replied quickly that Mr. Spiro unfortunately had been called away from Zante on business of an urgent nature.

The following morning we set out on foot to visit Miss Crowe. It was so windy in the harbour that life was uncomfortable on board, and it was still early when we traversed the streets of Zante. At one point, near the school, we had to push through a mob of shouting, laughing children, who were clustering round street vendors carrying nuts of all kinds—some of them heated,—figs threaded on strings, and slabs of cake. When we had found our way out of the town and were mounting the hill up a narrow road which once had been well-built, but which had deteriorated in surface until it was as rough as a watercourse, we heard the songs of birds for the first time in any chorus since we left England. We passed a blackbird, sitting shining and motionless in the heart of a pomegranate bush. The birds were singing in fruit gardens on the left of the road; on the right, grove

303

succeeded grove of olive trees so well-tended and so prolific that we could scarcely see the leaves for olives. At the top of the long hill we entered the grounds of a very handsome house, thinking that, if it did not belong to Miss Crowe, at least the inmates would be qualified to direct us to her. But the house stood empty. We walked around it, examining the garden, long neglected and stained in places by the refuse of Italian, German, British, and Greek troops, but showing such signs of breeding, such delightfully unvulgar layout, such profusion of border set in lawn, that we felt sure it had belonged to English settlers. The house itself, walled in buff stucco with a yellowish tinge, with white stone frames to the sash windows and a Greek Doric portico of the same stone, had been designed in well-proportioned rectangles and might have been an eighteenth or nineteenth century product of English architecture except that it would be rare in England to find so small a house so exquisitely built. Long neglect was affecting the building, but the climate of Greece is kind to stones, and the place was well roofed with weathered pantiles. We walked on, down a narrow lane between olive groves to another and still grander—though no better proportioned—house and garden. The wrought-iron gates and railings to this second house were masterly, far ahead of such work in London when the town was rebuilding after the great fire. From the kitchen of this second house a dark girl emerged who made nothing of my query regarding "the English lady", but the answer was given with a shout by a stoutish woman, clearly the chatelaine, who came out speaking voluble English, and who, she soon explained, would be delighted to show us to Miss Crowe's house, for Miss Crowe was a neighbour and a very dear friend, but first we must allow her to show us the view from her own terrace. Her house, wide and classically proportioned in the same yellowish and white materials, presented a façade of such clear beauty that it etherealised the tangles of bedclothes that were hanging cooling in the morning air from every first-floor window. Below us, as we leaned on the delicate stone balustrade was a lower terrace, paved with minute ancient bricks through the interstices of which white flowers exuding an unfamiliar perfume pushed stalks crowned with spiky petals. Below the brick terrace a wide stairway of stone led down in straight flights to the orange, tangerine, fig, and citrus groves belonging to the house. Even the lean-to roof of the cart-shed was supported by a row of doric columns. The chatelaine, Madame Marina, led us to Miss Crowe's gateway, an iron gateway, filled-in with metal sheets and with a blue-glass peep-hole to allow the servant to examine any person who might clamour on the Aphrodite knocker.

A small maid opened the door and three animals rushed at us, a black Grecian mongrel dog, an elderly, almost blind Pekinese bitch, and a kitten. The house, after those which we had just visited, was a disappointment. But was it? It was, as the owner was the first to admit, a Victorian bungalow. I have noticed how remarkable, indeed how beautiful, one Indian student may look when surrounded by white men, although set in his own people he would be no handsomer than they; the Victorian bungalow on Zante reminded me of verses from Barrack Room Ballads, of caraway seeds, of a gramophone record called "The Broken Melody", of raspberry wine, and other aspects of my childhood made fruitful by my elders. It was a sprawling building. The sitting-room was crammed with belongings and ornaments, books, newspapers and magazines, both new and very, very old. One lithograph showed Lord Byron (wearing Greek costume) making love in a cave to a voluminously-dressed lady, while a Greek sentry kept guard at the entrance. Miss Crowe told us that her grandfather had been Byron's banker, and that her family had long been associated with Zante. I think that she herself had been born there, and she contrived at the same time to look completely English and yet, in some indeterminate manner, less so than most Englishwomen of breeding. We found her a strikingly handsome woman, tall, with splendid eyes, white hair, and a voice that was an instrument with all that delicacy in it that seems to fade from spoken English as it feels perhaps one of the last of the virile influences from across the sea, the influences that formerly sustained it and enriched it without costing it its form and grace. Miss Crowe was possibly a little lonely in the Victorian bungalow on the Ionian island; thoughts, reflections, and descriptions of Zante, London, Rome, and Cape Town, flowed from her with irresistible melody and grace.

Before the war, we learned, she had kept the bungalow as a place in which to rest for a few months out of the annual twelve. Normally she had lived in Italy, mainly in Rome, and had paid long visits to London. When the German attack developed on Greece, Miss Crowe fled from Zante to Patras on the mainland. She left Patras with a few other refugees in a chartered caique. They sailed only by night, lying up during the day in port, while the German dive-bombers patrolled the sea outside. They were six in her party at Patras; they were sixty-five when they reached Crete, for they had picked up Allied airmen and stray soldiers on the way. Those awaiting the German attack on Crete sent Miss Crowe to Alexandria, and thence she travelled to Cape Town, where she worked in the censorship offices until the day of victory, and the liberation of Greece from the Germans, the liberation that turned into a civil war. We suspected that some of the savour had gone from her life in Zante. Perhaps she had too ardently longed for her bungalow while surrounded by the less attractive bungalows of Cape Town and by people who were inclined to think that civilisation could be bought with bombs and priced with diamonds. Perhaps, although she did not bluntly say so, she was of too downright a character to find it easy to live on an island where some of the inhabitants had found it easy to be on hospitable terms with all the troops who had occupied Zante, first the British, then the Germans, then the Italians, then the communists, then the British again, and now the Greek police in British uniform. Certainly she could not forget that after the "liberation" of the island many of the townspeople, men whom she had known at any rate by sight from their earliest days, had attacked and all but annihilated the single British platoon quartered in a house down near the harbour. But perhaps we exaggerated all those things.

From her terrace we could see *Truant* and the ruffled harbour. We stood beside a dog cemetery, with a stone effigy of a smooth-haired fox terrier at one corner of the plot holding the small graves of the faithful. Miss Crowe gave us wild irises, a red flower that she could not name in English, and a small cactus in a pot to replace one of our three that Isabel had lost in the storm near Sant' Eufemia. The cactus she gave us was less beautiful than our others, being round and dumpy in shape, but it had a sentimental interest, for it had been brought to the house by an Italian soldier who sought to be the lover of the maid who looked after the place while Miss Crowe was in the Cape Town censorship office.

Her gardener hovered within the carry of her voice. He had asked her to obtain for him a picture of Mr. Winston Churchill, and had (vain) hopes that we might be able to furnish one. "My wife hangs up pictures of all the blessed saints," he said. "Just give me one of Churchill, and I can more than hold my own."

Miss Crowe walked with us for a mile or so, showing us a short cut through her olive grove. She had to run back to pick up the blind Pekinese, which had strayed from the path and was losing itself; the black mongrel that scurried gaily around us had had a German bullet through its neck during the occupation. The gardener had saved its life and had hidden and fed it, knowing that this act would gain the approval of his absent mistress.

*   *   *   *

We felt the claws of approaching winter on October 24th, when a south-west wind came screaming across the accidented outline of the island. As you lie tossing in a boat at anchor you are apt to look around you and imagine that every stretch of water is calmer than that immediately surrounding your hull. I was able to persuade Isabel that the most comfortable berth was not in the north-eastern corner where we lay, but in the south-western corner, where there seemed to be water partially sheltered by a breakwater and by a tall, white monastery from which issued a constant trickle of Orthodox priests with square, black beards and something of the cheerful appearance of industrious warthogs. We gathered in our stern lines and motored across the wind-whipped harbour. Many people gesticulated at us and yelled advice to go this way or that, and always to go in any direction but that in which we were heading. I could see one or two caiques ahead which probably drew as much water as *Truant*, and I took soundings all the way. We dropped the big anchor on a great length of chain in two fathoms. Our move had at least taken us away from the quay, and I would rather swing free in any conditions than have my boat's stern tied to a quay and her bows held out from it. But my promises of smooth water had been false, and *Truant* jumped about considerably in the new place. We dropped into the dinghy and sculled ashore. I was getting so adept at pushing the boat along with one oar over the stern that the urchins ashore had named me "Propeller-man". Here the street was entirely arcaded along the waterfront in one band of low, white-washed buildings, the archways forming purple-black shadows in the dazzling whiteness. As we strolled haltingly along—for when she passes shops Isabel is apt to "mizzle", like Soapey Sponge down Oxford Street— a man stepped from the doorway of number fifty-four, and shouted: "Howdy, folks?" This was the opening to what proved to be a long conversation about the desirability of living in Chicago. We could not but notice that he had a prepossessingly pointed face with lively eyes and a sensitive smile. He was a middle-aged man and he told us, "Call me Danny."

Danny had spent twenty-two years in the United States of America, most of them in Chicago. He is a cabinet-maker and he managed to live well in America until there was a slump, and he returned to his father's house in Zante. But on returning he immediately noticed all that Zante lacked by comparison with Chicago. He had spent the intervening years investing Chicago with the manifold advantages with which he invested Zante while he was in Chicago. When we met him he had been working in Athens as an interpreter for the American mission which "observed" the restoration of the Greek monarchy. He had begged the Americans to arrange his passage back to their country, but they told him that if he had not considered taking out citizenship papers when he lived in Chicago for a period of twenty-two years, he was scarcely fitted to be a citizen.

"Finally," he said, "I got mad."

"What did you do?"

"I told them their attitude was un-American."

Danny was at pains to find out why, when we had been able to fit out a boat and sail for Greece, we had not instead set sail for Chicago.

"You like to swim?" he said. "You can swim in Chicago. You like to eat? You eat good in Chicago. You like girls? They got the prettiest of them in Chicago, millions of them. You like movies? Nice clean houses? Hell, I could go on all day. Why don't you go to Chicago?"

We tried to explain why neither of us would care to live in Chicago, but it would be as easy to explain the Immaculate Conception to an unbeliever.

"I know that whole town better than I know Zante, and I was born and reared in Zante," he said. "I know Chicago from one end to the other, but there are many places in this one-horse town that I don't know, and never want to know. In Chicago I wanted to know everything."

He asked if we had been to South Africa, and if it was true that there were large cities there with a plenitude of those things which were on everybody's lips after the war, modern conveniences and "high standards of living". We were able to assure him that South Africa could provide them. He gave us his card and wrote in our lettering below the Greek: "Danis Koriceanos, Fabiaror Street, 7, Athens". We went on foot out of the town, taking a long street lined with general stores showing strings of onions and garlic, yellow fan-shaped brooms, and leaning towers of new galvanised buckets from Britain; and cobblers where yellow leather hung in sheets from the walls, and second-hand British Army boots were offered at four times their original price. At length the street withered and died in a desiccated countryside. The south-west wind howled across the stones and the crumbling earth. The sun glared from every stone shooting barbs of light into our eyes, and soon we were exhausted with the dryness of it. If you stand up in Britain and let the south-west wind blow into your open mouth it will stimulate you and fill you with its sweetness; but in Zante the south-west wind smelled dead. Beside the roads, built by the British when they were fighting Napoleon, were ditches of dried mud which spread a strange odour, half incense, half decay.

*   *   *   *

I rowed them, Miss Crowe and Monsieur and Madame Marina, out to *Truant,* and thought I perceived in their faces some horror at the prospect of boarding a boat that rolled so violently. Isabel, very appetising in blue trousers and a white shirt, was waiting on the deck with a welcoming smile. I lit the primus stove, and we sat around in the saloon, waiting for the water to boil. Our conversation was interspersed with pointed remarks in Greek, exchanged between our three guests. I had little doubt as to the tenor of the asides, my only doubt being as to which of the three felt the most ill. It proved to be Madame Marina. Before the kettle boiled the poor lady was obliged, with profuse apologies, to ask me to put her ashore. As she landed on the windy quay she said with a gleam—surely not of malice?—that Miss Crowe and Monsieur Marina were also "feeling the movement", but particularly Miss Crowe. That lady, however, so completely recovered when she tasted China tea that she swept us along on a flood of bottled-up talk which made Monsieur Marina brighten and stage an equally remarkable recovery.

No sooner had I put them ashore than the wind veered with startling abruptness. We found it necessary to move *Truant* back to the north-east corner of the harbour, but the wind was now favourable for our next trip, south to Navarino, and our spirits rose with the barometer. We went ashore to buy a loaf of white bread made with the British flour supplied to the Greek police, and sold by them at a price of four shillings a loaf. Tea was reaching the Greek shops in the same way, but the shopkeepers knew so little of its properties that they were "storing" it loose, in great dusty piles on their counters. We stopped before a butcher's establishment, a muddy booth in which two carcasses hung from steel hooks.

"Take your choice," the young butcher said to me in Italian. He handed me a long knife, and pointed to one carcass: "Sheep," and the other: "Pig." Gingerly I approached the sheep and, feeling all kinds of a fool and a criminal, severed a haunch, which cost me ten shillings. The haunch felt horribly flaccid and warm.

When we returned to *Truant* I went over the leaking portion of the deck with plastic glue, and then bent the biggest squaresail to the yard. We switched on the radio, and heard that two British destroyers had entered a minefield set in Albanian waters, and that several sailors had been killed. We knew then why the hospital ship had been ordered to leave Zante for Corfu. The wind dropped as darkness came, and we had a peaceful night. There was a lot of singing in a café on the waterfront, but both the singing and the accompanying instruments had a thin, semi-oriental quality, and were conducive to sleep.

25

WE would not sail in the dark; our nervousness about the possibility of hitting a floating mine had been renewed by Alcibiades, who had remained a smelly menace in the background throughout our stay in Zante, a kind of combination of a peeping Tom and the man who may blackmail you or steal the spoons. He had paddled himself out to *Truant* on a raft and had roused us from bed on our last night by scratching with his long nails on the porthole of our cabin, to tell us that a caique had been lost that day on a mine some three miles south of Zante harbour; all that had been found of the caique and its crew of six was a jagged stave from a wine- or water-cask. Alcibiades had given his news with every appearance of grotesque relish, and had asked if I would care to give him a donation for the widows and orphans of the deceased. I learned later that the caique came from Rhodes, many hundreds of miles away, but then we never even suspected that Alcibiades' intentions were honourable as I handed over the donation and said good-bye to him more gladly than to any other part of Zante.

When the day came sufficiently to see fifty feet beyond the bowsprit we hoisted the squaresail and soon were sliding through the jaws of the breakwaters.

Although we were confident that the wind would hold for days, giving us just the weather we needed to round the Peloponnese, we had not sailed for two hours when it grew puffy, and began to take the squaresail aback. The following sea remained, however, helping to swing us along, and I set our big Genoa staysail and largest jib. The Genoa pulled well, but slightly disconcerted us that day because it greatly reduced our field of view ahead. In the afternoon the wind whistled and steadied from the east. We made excellent progress under ordinary working canvas. *Truant* jumped about a great deal, since she was travelling fast and heeled on a sea that was still following. Isabel lay on her mattress on deck, sheltering from the spray under a blue blanket, and trying to sleep the afternoon away. For the last ten miles we had a race with a coasting schooner which we slowly overhauled. The schooner was sailing and also using her diesel engine. She was heavily laden, and her captain, like us, was anxious to make Navarino Bay before dark. She seemed to carry at least fifteen of a crew. When we approached the entrance to Navarino the schooner waddled on ahead while we lowered our mainsail. The entrance was most forbidding, the sea crashing against tall black rocks, one of which is pierced by a volcanic archway, about the size of the Arc de Triomphe. Rain squalls swept over us, and we should have been cold had there not been plenty of work to do. We had averaged nearly seven knots over the distance of fifty-five miles—an excellent day's run by our standards and in those shortening days. Using the schooner as a guide we sailed slowly into a vast bay, land-locked except for the slit by the black rocks. Soon the small town of Navarino appeared on our starboard hand. The harbour was very congested; the captain of the schooner anchored off it, in about five fathoms, and we followed his example.

It seemed a pity that rain should fall during the few daylight hours that we remained in Navarino Bay. The place had been in my thoughts since, in the early 1930's, I had spent some months on a salvage ship, the *Orphir*, which had been fitted out by a Greek owner with the immediate objective of salvaging the bullion and jewels believed to lie in the sunken hull of the Cunard liner *Lusitania* (which was torpedoed off the south coast of Ireland in the First World War). That scheme was a failure, at any rate from the financial point of view. Beaten by the weather, the *Orphir* returned to its home port, Glasgow, having done no more than send a diver down to identify the wreck. The diver wore an articulated metal diving suit capable of withstanding high pressures, the invention of a Persian. The Greek was full of plans for which the ambitious project with the *Lusitania* was only to have been the forerunner. He often spoke to me of Navarino Bay, where, on October 20th, 1827, a Turkish and Egyptian fleet was annihilated by a combined British, French, and Russian fleet under the command of the British Admiral, Sir Edward Codrington. Since the Turkish warships were replete when they sank in the bay with fabulous loot from the Greek church and from wealthy Greek merchants, the present-day value of the treasure lying there, in water so clear that in fine weather the oak hulks may still be seen from the surface, is stated to be incalculable. The spoils have been guarded so far by the deep water, which puts them beyond the reach of rubber-suited divers, though not of modern equipment with metal, pressure-resisting diving-suits and observation chambers equipped with telephones and acting as the underwater eyes of ships fitted with powerful grabs. Any question of salvage is also to some extent regulated by the political situation in Greece, an element much more uncertain than the climate and the waters of Navarino Bay.

We left the bay, following the schooner behind which we had entered.

She motored close along the shore, keeping only some fifty yards from the breaker-pounded rocks. We supposed that the captain steered that course for some good reason; perhaps to escape some contrary current, of which we knew nothing, or to avoid a minefield of which we were also in happy ignorance. We had no wind, for we were in the lee of high cliffs. Soon the coast opened to the east, and we followed a channel between the mainland and some small islands, passing an ancient Venetian fortress, a military conception of incredible grandeur against the lower bastions of which lay the hulk of an American "liberty ship" sunk during the latest war. We made the most of a heavy breeze through channels which our charts showed to offer deep water right inshore on either hand, and we were in great spirits when we came to the small, barren island of Venetico, our last landmark before Cape Matapan, at the far side of the thirty-mile-wide Gulf of Kalamata. Cape Matapan has far more than a local reputation for bad weather, and we were well aware of it.

As we approached the tail of Venetico we were struck by a succession of bitter squalls, which we weathered by luffing up into the wind. At the first opportunity we reduced sail. A very stiff head sea was rising with a strong wind, and the barometer showed an ominous drop. After experimenting for a time I found that the boat was well-behaved under the mainsail reefed right down and a small staysail. The head sea was most uncomfortable, and the boat made a tremendous noise whacking her fat bottom down on it, but she sailed wonderfully well, if very, very slowly. Isabel suffered so badly from sea-sickness that there was no alternative—apart from putting about and running back to the sheltered channel near the Venetian fortress—to pushing ahead with an engine for the far side of the gulf. When I suggested turning back she poured scorn on me. The engine made our progress a great deal more uncomfortable than under sail alone, and the whole boat shuddered from the blows of the short seas, while we were permanently covered by sheets of spray. Our petrol was get'ing low, and the pitching and pounding stirred up the sludge which I had been too lazy to drain from the main tanks. It seemed that war-time, or post-war, petrol deposited a greyish sediment, and this worked its way to the carburettors. Time after time Isabel had to take the wheel and keep *Truant* sailing while I went below to the hot engine-room and cleaned one carburettor or the other. I knew that if we did not keep an engine running there could be no hope of reaching shelter that night. I lunched off a glass of whisky, gulped down in the saloon, and when I went on deck I found the wheel turning as *Truant* came up into the wind, while poor Isabel, soaked with spray, hung dangerously over the lee rail. As usual, when

312

conditions were at their worst, and a million times worse for her than for me, she was in strong spirits, and would have faced anything, burning with the rage inspired in her by the sea. We had been receiving letters from relatives and friends in countries like England and America, saying (hopefully?) that our trip was surely "a great mistake"; that we should have a surfeit of each other's company, that our marriage would be weakened. Such people can have no conception of the strengthening tonic on companionship, and still more on love, of discomforts as well as pleasures faced together, accepted and overcome with some degree of fortitude.

I had no doubts in my companion, none in the boat which ploughed steadily, if maddeningly slowly, across that thrice-damned gulf, and I had no time to have doubts about myself. Once I was ill-advised enough to say to the long-suffering Isabel that we were making good progress. She showed such wistful hope and disappointment on looking at the still distant land that I decided we must alter course. I had noticed that the sea tended to come from two directions; one sea was rolled at us by the wind, while another swept at us round the point of Cape Matapan. It seemed to me that if we sailed on the other tack, heading for the Matapan peninsula instead of for the open sea clear of the cape itself, we should be likely to find better conditions. We picked out a harbour, more or less ahead on the new tack. It was Port Mezapa, some twelve miles up the gulf from Cape Matapan, and although the *Pilot* described it with mistrust and scorn, I judged that with the east wind it should afford shelter.

As we approached the land we met a succession of really terrifying squalls. I had not known, and this was my introduction to the knowledge, that in Greek waters if you move into the lee of an unwooded shore the wind is often funnelled at you by the hills, and is stronger than on the open sea. During one of the squalls we took the mainsail off her, and it was fortunate indeed that we were now practised in that manœuvre. The nearer we came to the mountainous land the stronger the wind became. Finally our staysail, a pitifully small rag on so heavy a boat, was too much for her, and I had to haul it down, feeling while I did so that I was extremely likely to blow overboard. The force of the wind on our bare masts and our rigging was sufficient to heel us over till the lee bulwark was awash. In these nerve-wracking conditions we motored slowly into the "port". Right under the lee of the land the wind whipped the water to foam, while less than one hundred yards from the shore the sea was already rising. The *Sailing Directions* warned us that it was difficult to find bottom for anchoring in that bay chiselled out of the bare mountains.

313

We pushed on with the engine until we were close under the few poor houses of the village at the inner end of the bay. I let go the starboard anchor, Isabel made *Truant* veer sharply to port, the port anchor went out, and we dropped back until we were held on a long V of chain. Even with two excellent anchors down we felt unsafe and unreal. We hung in the wind, drumming like a weathervane that is loose on its swivel.

It was some time before I could lift my eyes from the anchor chains to the shore, from which shouts came, the frail sounds of the human voice whisking by, pellets thrown from pea-shooters but bound for the moon or infinity. When I was fairly sure that the anchors were holding I looked up in time to see figures piling into a rowing-boat, and an instant later the boat had left the shore, and was being wildly driven towards us by the wind. I did not like the look of its occupants.

"Turn out the lights below and lock the hatch as you come on deck," I shouted to Isabel. The boat thudded heavily into *Truant's* side and they climbed shouting to our deck; except for four boys they were all hirsute men dressed in British battledress but without insignia of any kind and carrying what was surely an over-profuse armament. Each man had a sub-machine-gun or a rifle slung on his back, a pistol or grenades at his belt. They smelled of stale drink and equally stale tobacco. When they had poked and pried into all the corners available they made us turn on the wheelhouse light, and the leader, a swarthy little man wearing a sergeant's stripes, sat himself on the chart table, swinging his dirty boots, while the rest clustered round. They were neither friendly nor unfriendly, but they showed a tendency to order us about which we both took unkindly. Their interpreter was the smallest of the four boys; he spoke a few words of Italian and padded them liberally with the word *si*. He told me the sergeant said I must move into the "inner harbour".

"Can you guide us in," I answered. "It's very dark."

"Si, si, si, si, si, si, si."

I set to work getting the anchors, back-breaking labour—for I had naturally let out a great deal of chain—in which I was assisted, though in a most lukewarm manner, by the two youngest boys. The men in uniform watched me without the faintest appreciation of my difficulties, and so contrived to impede Isabel, who was endeavouring to make my work lighter by pushing *Truant* ahead with the engines, that in the end I relinquished my grip of the windlass handle, hurried aft, and fairly drove them from the wheelhouse, with shouts of fury. My shouts appeared to surprise them, but they were no more amused than friendly, although they allowed themselves to be bustled out on deck. At this point the sergeant offered me a cigarette from a flat cardboard box. I refused, asking the boy interpreter to explain that I rarely smoked, and was too busy at that moment. The sergeant listened to the explanation, then roughly caught hold of one of my hands, and thrust a cigarette into the palm. When the anchors were free Isabel cautiously took *Truant* inshore, the armed men agog with wonder at the way she managed the engines. Their "inner harbour" was a cosy place, no bigger than a medium-sized swimming pool, a hole cut out of a cliff. By some miracle, for none of the local people did anything but hinder us and confuse us, we managed to moor *Truant* with one anchor dropped at the entrance, and warps going off in all directions to hold her in the centre of the pool. We were remarkably sheltered in that place, and although the wind rushed overhead it was impossible to feel it, even standing on deck. In the village above us there was considerable noisy activity; a group, composed mainly of hooded women, gathered with lanterns on the small quay at one side of the rock pool. Our uninvited passengers howled greetings and explanations.

Satisfied that we were securely tied up, Isabel and I began at once to yawn. I used the small interpreter to issue formal thanks to all—although I felt most dissatisfied with his manner of doing so—and to announce that we were exhausted by a rough day on the sea, and now asked to be left alone to sleep, but that we invited them to visit our boat at their leisure in the morning, and hoped that they would then honour us by accepting such hospitality as we were in a position to offer. All save the sergeant descended into their rowing-boat, but he caught the interpreter by one ear and, punctuating his words with loudly-resented tweaks, announced that *he* intended to see what there was to drink on board the English yacht, and that when we had finished whatever there might be on board, we would repair to the tavern ashore and drink the night away. He was a very small man. With protestations of everlasting friendship and gratitude Isabel caught one of his hands, and I the other, and pump-handling his arms most warmly, we fairly dragged him to the rail beside the rowing-boat, into which he reluctantly lowered himself. We went below, locking the hatches after us, and ate toast and boiled eggs before tumbling into bed. Over our rock-set pool the wind shrieked and bellowed, but *Truant* was motionless as a boat set in concrete.

We both slept well, but awoke wondering if our visitors of the night before intended to give us a surprise. Were they of the type called by the Government of Greece "soldiers"? or were they of the type called "bandits"? I took it that they were the former, because when I asked one of them why he carried so many arms he had replied "Communisti morti!"

and had drawn his forefinger slowly across his throat. To hell with such talk! I did not care for the way they had behaved, and I hate men who drip with weapons; indeed, during the war I had taken the ostentatious show of arms to be one sign of a bad soldier. Isabel had found our guests no more to her taste than they were to mine, and she decided that she would remain below until we managed to extricate ourselves from the place, and that if they asked for her I should say that she was ill. I had a good deal to do, sorting the tangle on deck, and cleaning out the entire petrol system in the engine-room. It was not long before we had a horde of people on board, most of them armed men. They crowded into the after cabin and hung their heads over the edge of the engine-room hatch while I took gallons of sediment from the tanks and the filters. Many questions were put to me through the same small interpreter, whose translations were—I was sure—more than dubious. One common question, which I hoped had no undue significance, was whether we had a wireless set, and if we could send messages to the British in Athens with it. Naturally, under the circumstances, I lied, stating that we could send messages, and regularly did so. They brought a handsome red dog on board, telling me that his name was "Dzonnee", and that he was "an English dog". When I called him Johnny he seemed to be excited. He spent most of his time sniffing near the curtained portholes behind which Isabel was clandestinely doing her housework. I had finished my work in the engine-room, had tested the engines, and was wondering what to do next when a fusillade of shots sounded on the hill behind the village, followed by a few haphazard reports. The men in uniform did not seem to be excited or flustered, but they soon melted away from the boat, and I was left with Michele, the interpreter, a runt-like creature with a running sore on his upper lip, and his two young brothers, even smaller and dirtier than himself. I asked Michele to help me by untying the lines attaching *Truant* to the shore. When he had done this I gave him four tins of corned beef, four of condensed milk, four of salmon, and two of jam. The three boys were wildly excited by these gifts.

"Will you be able to open the tins?" I asked.

"Never fear, captain."

"What will you do with them?"

"Hide them, captain."

Outside the rock pool the same fierce wind still raged. We hoisted stay-sail and mizzen and were bustled quickly out of the bay. We turned to port, into the shelter of a long table-land which stood above the sea with cliffs two hundred feet high. Here the water was bluer even than at Capri, royal blue. We were heading for another "port" a few miles nearer Cape Matapan, and called on our charts Port Marmari, although it was nothing more than a bay, and there were no houses near the water. I put our leg of mutton in the oven to roast along with different vegetable dishes, according to Isabel's instructions. The moment that we emerged from the shelter of the tableland the vicious offshore wind whipped at us again, bullying us so that I was obliged to take all sail off her. We were beginning to regard Cape Matapan as a kind of monster. We fought our way with an engine into Marmari, avoiding the many rocks shown on our chart, and dropped both anchors as near as I dared venture to the shore at the head of the bay. We rode there quite steadily and were comfortable enough. At least there were no men to bother us. We ate a heavy meal: tinned pâté de foie gras; mutton with roasted potatoes and braised onions; leeks cooked with milk and cheese; baked apples and cream; gorgonzola with the red Calabrian wine; coffee and brandy. It is certain that the inhabitants of the few dwellings to be seen, dwellings that looked—at any rate from a distance— red and smooth, like cisterns or cylindrical blockhouses, would have been astounded had they witnessed the weight and variety and richness of the victuals gathered on our mahogany.

We remained below, reading and resting, and occasionally looking at the barograph, which was registering a decline. In the evening Isabel made me steep my hands in hot soapy water, and then she worked on my finger-nails. I had undergone considerable physical changes during the trip, we noticed, having become thinner, harder, and more like a workman—an entirely desirable change. But my hands, Isabel said, were "appalling", and would need several periods of intensive sprucing before I would be judged fit to appear at her side in Athens.

The movement of the boat, steady enough when we went to sleep, became so excessive that it woke us both. At four in the morning, in thick darkness, I went on deck and took up the port anchor. The wind was veering, and I feared that we might get our anchor chains crossed before being thrust on to what looked like becoming a lee shore. The wind, north-east when we first anchored there, then east, had veered during the night to the south-west. An enormous sea was rolling up to the mouth of our bay. The sight of that sea, when dawn came up, would have been enough to chill far stouter hearts than mine, and I well knew that we would almost certainly be driven out into it, for the wind had veered so far that it was likely to veer still farther to the west, when our bay would be open to it, and would be absolutely untenable. The biggest seas still raced past the mouth of the bay, but the vast impetus of their passage raised, at an angle of some sixty degrees to the main axis of the advance, a swell which entered the bay to topple and disrupt in the shoaling water where we were anchored. *Truant* jumped and rolled so abominably that Isabel remained in bed. I fussed around the boat, seeing that all was ready for anything that might occur, putting extra lashings on the dinghy, stowing dishes securely in the galley, warming up the engines, re-tying the mainsail. The sky blackened, and rain fell in deluges. The only satisfaction to be derived from the weather was that our deck was now completely watertight. I decided that we should be safer in another part of the bay, on the southern side, where there was a small cove that seemed to have a little more shelter from the swell. Isabel came into the wheelhouse in her dressing-gown, and steered *Truant* over there while I looked after the anchor and took soundings which showed conclusively that the cove was not deep enough for us. If anything, we were more uncomfortable on that side than at the place from which we had moved, but I let go the anchor, and Isabel went back to bed with her book. If the wind changed still more to the west we should have to move to the other side of the cape. Looking at the chart, Cape Matapan resembled a snake with two bites in its neck, near the head and exactly level, the one with the other. The two bites were deep bays, our own Port Marmari, and another harbour, Port Kaio. As we now lay at anchor, badly in need of shelter from the west, we were only separated by a high saddle and half a mile from the refuge at Kaio. But we could not transport *Truant* over the hill, and were we obliged to quit Marmari we should have to struggle four miles round the cape, two miles with a head sea and two with the sea on our quarter.

When I had weighed this up I put the chart away, looked at the sea outside with a shudder, and settled down in the wheelhouse with Balzac's *Marriage Contract*, a book interesting enough to distract me from my gloomy forebodings. Every few pages I lifted an eye to see that we were not dragging our anchor and to watch the direction of the wind on our burgee, which stood out as firmly as a blade of quivering Toledo steel.

At 9.30 I noticed an immense cloud of spray at the south-western point, and as I watched a column of pale water-dots entered the bay resolving themselves into a waterspout, within some sixty yards of us, on the starboard hand. The somewhat wispy spiral, rising to a height of about one hundred feet, was not immensely imposing, and I presume that it was a very small waterspout, for the waters did not "boil" at its base in the best tradition of mariners' tales—although the reason for this may have been that the whole surface of the bay was almost "boiling" when it entered—but there was something eerie in the speedy twist that was apparent,

318

particularly near the top, where the spray grew thin. When it reached the rocks at the inner end of the bay it dispersed, taking a good five minutes over the process.

At 10.30 the wind definitely veered through a point or two, and came at us from the west. We were now facing the full strength and thrust of the sea, and our anchor at once began to drag. Our fate had been decided. Isabel was up and dressed in an instant, and had started the port engine before I had reached the windlass to get the chain in. I was more relieved than sorry that we must go, for I have not got that calm temperament which can resign itself to waiting in discomfort for an ordeal that seems imminent; and I would rather be smashed about on the sea than roll stupidly at anchor. Good fortune smiled upon us, for no sooner had we got the anchor than the wind eased a little in a valuable lull which lasted until we were half-way to the end of the cape. It was by far the worst sea that we ever encountered, for there are strong currents round Matapan, and the waves, always higher than our masthead, appeared to come from several directions and at completely irregular spacings. *Truant* was wildly thrown about. On occasions the whole boat seemed to be in the air, and then she would drop with a thundering crash on one side or the other. After a few minutes we were bruised, for we were hurled about the wheel-house, sometimes landing in a helpless tangle of arms and legs at one side or the other. I had never imagined anything like it. Objects which had been judged securely stowed, and which had passed all trials to that day, escaped from their places. The foghorn and the binoculars leaped from their hooks behind me; the parallel rulers slid from their rack and struck me viciously on the side of the nose; a wedge of some fifty charts thrust out from beneath the chart table and kicked me in the rump. Isabel was more ill than she had ever been before. There could be no question of her going to the rail, and indeed I got nervously enraged when she opened the door of the wheelhouse, fearing that she might be given a sudden impetus which would fling her clear of the boat. I threatened to take a lashing round her waist to prevent this, but had no time to do it. We moved with the engines turning slowly, and made gradual headway to Matapan, a barren grey outline. The lighthouse-keeper on the cape must have seen every square inch of the port side of our orange-coloured bottom, yet we never for one instant doubted that we were going to reach Kaio, for *Truant*, wonderfully buoyant with her beamy hull and her shallow draft, behaved (provided we did not try to drive her) like a life-boat, reacting so quickly to every threat of the vicious sea that, although she crashed about violently enough to shake loose the teeth in our jaws, she seldom took water on deck, and then

319

never a wave. We had a hard job to turn our quarter to the sea and the wind, which had now picked up its former strength; but by this time we had confidence in *Truant's* steadiness with a following sea, and after some fiendish rolls, we got her around the jagged end of Matapan. Two miles into the head sea from Marmari to the point took two hours, the two miles before Port Kaio, with the sea running under us and a gale pushing us on took only seventeen minutes, although I throttled the engine right back to avoid the danger of being pooped. I started the starboard engine, and warmed it up well, in preparation for the quick turn that had to be made at the entrance to Kaio, a kidney-shaped inlet protected—to some extent—by abrupt hills and by a rocky spit that forms a natural break-water shielding the best anchorage, a cove at the southern end. We shot into the harbour on the summit of a big swell, astounding the sailors there by our foreign shape and rig and by our appearance at such speed and out of such a storm. The two engines, with Isabel's deft fingers again on the throttles, brought us skidding round, and we anchored behind the caiques, in six fathoms of water, yet surprisingly near the shore. It was a pretty enough place, and after that morning's lonely trials we were glad for once to be near other boats. They were all connected to the shore with ropes and chains, and each of them had two anchors down.

Chaos confronted us when we went below: the three cacti lay among a powdering of loose earth on the carpet; one saucer had jumped from its place in the china rack, and had smashed on the galley floor, while the oven—a fitting designed to Admiralty pattern for use in small boats—had risen from the stove, struck the white deck-head with such force as to leave a clear imprint, and then landed on the débris of the saucer. One of the carpenter's canvas bags which hung on the engine-room bulkhead had left its hook, distributing over the engines spanners, pliers, screwdrivers and nails of all kinds.

Truant's movements, even in that satisfactory harbour, were so violent that we did not care to remain on board. We made sandwiches of Ryvita—given to us by Gwenda from the large store of modern "hard tack" that she carried on *Elpis*—and cold mutton, boiled some eggs, slung the dinghy over the side, and rowed ashore.

We landed on a sandy stretch of beach, some three hundred yards in length; a few impoverished stone dwellings, occupied as much by animals as by human beings, crouched in the tall rushes behind the beach. The moment that our dinghy ran through the surf and grounded men and women came from the houses to meet us. There were ten men and three women in the reception committee. They were bare-footed, and the women

320

had their heads tied in dusty black cloths. The faces looking out from the shadows of the somewhat spooky headgear were painfully lined with toil, but the eyes were amused, and the mouths parted in smiles to reveal discoloured teeth. I found that the soles of my bare feet were sufficiently hardened to keep pace with them over the pebbles and thorns to the headman's house. One of the men was supposed to speak English. He wore a town suit and pointed shoes which had been sadly battered through walking in that stony place. "I plan to go on British ships again, in a year or so," he said. "My father wants me at home here, in the village, and I am wondering if I should marry a local girl."

"And it may take you a year to make up your mind?"

"Naturally, for a farm hangs by the contract, and the girl's a virgin; one year's surely not long to consider such problems."

The headman came from his house and had two wooden chairs set for us in the yard. We sat side by side, like a foreign king and queen, surrounded by lean black pigs, leaner mongrel dogs, and still leaner fowls. The men and women formed a wider circle round us and the livestock, and the headman sat on a third chair, facing us. A woman brought a small saucer of olives for Isabel, another for me, and two pieces of dark bread. Next she brought a tin jug and six glasses. We each accepted a glass of resinated wine. Isabel did not like it, but I did. The headman behaved with considerable dignity. He had a hawk-face, with a strawberry planted in it instead of a beak. He was irascible, and would occasionally rise from his chair and stride to the corner of his house to yell an order into the terraced fields, more stone than earth. But when he had asked our ages he became jovial, and to our astonishment, he reached out a bony hand and caught hold of the woman who had brought the wine. He caught her by the skirt and then pressed his hand round her thigh, so that her leg was outlined in the rusty material. He began to shout, and all the bystanders laughed. The interpreter said: "He says he is seventy-five, that she, his third wife, is twenty-eight, and that she is the best wife in the village." We became tired by the constant scrutiny of all those dark, sympathetic eyes, and after asking if we could buy from them eggs, bread, and a chicken, and telling them that we would return in two hours, we climbed up a rough pathway, very steep, and in places dangerously precipitous. We sat down to eat on a hill overlooking the harbour. It was uncomfortable country even to sit in, for the ground was all sharp, crumbling stones, prickly scrub, and goat droppings. Goat after goat wandered across the hillside to have a supercilious look at us. Twice while we ate, Greek boys passed down the hillface, moving with the almost incredible two-footed agility that they would probably admire in us if they saw us boarding a bus, climbing out of the driving seat of a motor-car, or stepping off an escalator. Flies were persistent, and appeared to have stings as well as loud buzzing equipment. The combined petty discomforts soon drove us downhill. This country was supposed to be one of the wildest in Greece. We saw no sign of any roads, but here and there a clump of houses shaped like silos had been planted in the brown hills.

A toothless crone sat on the beach, jerking her hunkers a little nearer to us from time to time, and finally, thrusting her hands deep into some dubious recesses of her black skirt, she pulled out an object which—when she had clawed from it fluff, dust, hairs, grass, and various objects too small to be identified—proved to be a dried fig. She offered the fig first to me and then to Isabel, and when we had refused with all the graciousness at our disposal, she bit into it herself, chewing wetly, drops of saliva filling the excoriations in her chin.

The headman took us inside his house to a bare room with an earthen floor; two vast wine barrels lay uneasily, slightly tilted forward, at one end. We sat on a wooden bench and Isabel—against my advice—drank two glasses of water from his well. He gave us a large slab of their brown, home-baked bread, as heavy as timber, and some figs, but he was sorry that neither the eggs nor the chicken for which we had asked would be ready before the next day, and even then he doubted if he could supply them.

We returned to *Truant*, ate a good hot meal and drank red wine. Isabel worked on my hands for thirty minutes, and then we slept.

*   *   *   *

The captain of the caique that lay nearest to us had worked as a stevedore in San Francisco. He was a stout fellow with a round, strong face. His boat was twice the size of *Truant*, and thoroughly well-found. She was cutter-rigged with a lovely sheer, and her hull was painted café-au-lait colour with a line of bright azure beneath the deck line.

"She ought to be a good boat," he said, when I offered him my compliments, "she represents good American dollars that I worked hard to get."

"Are you sorry to be back in Greece?"

"I ain't glad and I ain't sorry. But this was my father's job, and it's good enough for me. I'm bound for Corfu to pick up my missis and kid and a load of goats."

"What are you carrying to Corfu?"

"Brandy from the Piræus."

"Are you making money?"

"I ain't losin'."

"What's the weather to-day?"

"Where you bound?"

"Athens way."

"Then it's O.K. for you, and Enna B.G. for me."

As he spoke another caique, which was evidently the only other vessel in the harbour going our way, began to haul in her anchor chain with a swinging windlass and to hoist her grey, patched sails. Isabel gave me six tins of corned beef to give to the old headman, who had refused the day before to take any payment for the bread. He received my gift in a stately manner, but as though he had not the faintest notion of its purpose. He held up a tin to smell it and rasped it against his chin. I wondered if he would try smoking it in a hookah, or spreading it over the already work-worn body of his young wife. Looking at him, I reflected gratefully that there are sensualists and sensualists.

Isabel was beginning to hoist the mainsail as I came down to the shore; she had taken the throat halyards to one windlass and the peak halyards to another; the blocks made a pleasant noise, and the white sail looked good.

It was impossible to believe that we were venturing on the same sea as that of the previous day. Now it was a blue summer sea with only the lightest of swells and a steady following breeze. Under big squaresail and raffee, mainsail and mizzen we bowled across the gulf, soon overtaking the heavy schooner that had left Port Kaio before us. This time the squaresail breeze held right through to the evening. I steered at the tiller aft, stripped to the waist, and Isabel lay sunbathing and contented near me. It was a day so heavenly as to seem unreal. We ate our meals outside on deck, far from the land, with the sails steadily filling and the bubble of our wake in our ears. As we neared Cape Malea a Greek naval vessel, a requisitioned trawler, nosed curiously towards us, but when I hoisted the Red Ensign she ran on and those on her bridge waved to us ecstatically, and watched us through glasses for a long time.

Off Cape Malea—those capes!—we were caught, flying far too much canvas, in rain-squalls with a sudden alarming weight of wind. We were obliged to jump about and "let everything go". We saved the sails, and nothing carried away except, strangely enough, the boom lacing of the mizzen. Once round the cape we had completed the worst part of our journey and could turn north-east to Ægean waters that are generally supposed to be kindly. We entered a small bay that Isabel had picked from the chart as a suitable anchorage. The water was whipped by a south-west wind coming with renewed vigour off the saddle of the cape, but the holding ground was good, and we rode comfortably to one anchor. I repaired the mizzen and tidied the decks for an early start in the morning.

Before dawn the wheelhouse thermometer registered seventy (F.) and the barometer was rising. Dawn was slow in coming, so slow that I hoisted the square sail in the half-dark, and the south-west wind carried us on our course for the island of Hydra, sixty miles away.

26

WE came to Hydra after a gusty day of invigorating sailing with islands appearing on all hands. Hydra harbour is small. It was filled with caiques, and the bones of a building caique were growing on one of the quays. Around the harbour with its plantation of squat, white-topped masts, the shops bloomed like a savage herbaceous border with great clumps of scarlet (tomatoes) and yellow (oranges). From the colour and life of the harbour the hills rise in folds covered with ancient white houses in cubic forms that seem to be made of light, continuing the ripple of the water and forming an element of the sky. The heights above the town show windmills, white, castle-pudding towers that offer to the wind wheels composed of triangular canvas vanes which can be reefed on rollers. The caiques that entered the harbour with us anchored off one quay or the other and hauled in their sterns. Each crew ate some simple meal from a communal pot and then the men went off to the taverns. Young boys sailed fishing-boats with lateen sails of flame-coloured cotton. When the moon came out the houses seemed to gather closer round the harbour, and the singing rose vinously from the taverns.

In the morning I hauled *Truant* aft until we could both step to the quay and we walked with the marketing baskets into the town. A square man was swinging a two-handed hammer at the skeleton of the caique that was building. His blows fell regularly with the whop of iron on wood, his hands and the head of the hammer curved through the air on grooves; the hammer-head was controlled by the balls and bands of muscle in his shoulders and in the small of his back. It was a cheerful place. Walking down a narrow street we heard laughter, and turning a corner we met a group of men, elderly as well as young, who walked in the opposite direction. Their laughter stopped as they studied us for a moment, then it picked up behind us and persisted, growing fainter only with distance.

Hydra bread was magnificent, the best, by far, that we had seen in Europe. It was pure white and of an extraordinary lightness, baked in golden loaves, ring-shaped like vast doughnuts and chamfered around the outer edge with the dogs-tooth ornament of Early English architecture.

We were directed to American Joe's restaurant, set in one corner of the quay. The dining-room at American Joe's is of ballroom size. Glass cases showing sponges of giant girth or suggestive shape occupy some of the wall space, and glossy pictures of generals, admirals, heroes, heroines, and naval and military engagements between noble warriors (Greeks) and dastardly cut-throats (Turks) all take part in a bold combined operation to cover the remainder. Although American Joe was reputed to be a man who had turned his dollars to good account when he returned home, even he could not find in Hydra or, it was said, in America enough tables to fill such a restaurant. He is a man of middle height, with a rubbery face white from bending into the steam from his cooking-pots and an oily black forelock that is for ever seeking contact with his nose. He ran forward to greet us, and led us into the narrow corridor behind the restaurant which serves as a kitchen. Joe spent a good many years in America, but the English language, he admits, never came easily to him, and when we met him it came only in patches. He helped us to choose our meal from the agglomeration of copper pots on the charcoal range with such phrases as: "You eat that stoff, that pretty dam' good stoff, fresh yesterday, take my opionione." And: "You like burned fish? I burn some." And: "You no like that stoff, he's letzte week; Greeks like."

We ate cold fried sardines with lemon-and-tomato salad, fried pork chops with kidneys and potatoes, and American Joe's "special" brand of Turkish Delight—which, oddly enough, was brought in by the waiter from the café next door,— and a few other indistinguishable offerings that Joe brought us with the sensible introduction: "You taste him; you no like— no call for kick my ass."

The only other patrons of the restaurant were dressed in an ultra-romantic fashion as vagabonds, fishermen, and sirens of the island. Their clothes presented a flaming hodge-podge of colour. The men's trousers were spattered with silk patches, and their white shirts were daringly ragged in places, while the girls wore low muslin bodices, reinforced to outline and emphasise their busts, and skirts flaring from the hips. They wore yellowish make-up, and were, of course, actors and actresses engaged on making the outdoor sequences of a film. For some reason Isabel christened them "the Crêpes-Suzettes". When we had drunk our coffee American Joe came out with us to the quay, where the shadows were as definite as straight-edges on white paper. Cameras were turning beside the war memorial, focusing on a boat in which stood the juvenile lead, very tall and dark and rather anxious to please, and a young woman with red hair. The director, a stout man in a German jacket of black leather which was very directorish, but otherwise quite unpractical in that heat, continually stopped proceedings in order to chase urchins from the camera's orbit. "That skirt is the younger sister in the story," Joe explained, indicating the actress in the boat. "She good girl who all a time say 'Nope!' " She was a thin young woman with a protuberant pot. Isabel thought that she was pretty. "Big sister, the star, goes bad with sailor fellows and leaves Hydra. Later she come back, marry that fellow in boat. All end happy except good girl . . ." American Joe went chuckling back to his restaurant, as though he could imagine no more suitable ending for a good girl.

Isabel had not been feeling well since we stopped at Kaio. I attributed her slight illness to the water she had drunk in the headman's house. But it was impossible to persuade her either to see a doctor or to rest. That afternoon she removed all our clothes from cupboards and tin-trunks to give them a thorough examination. The only damage was that my town suits, hanging, and swinging with the roll of the boat, had rubbed holes in the sleeves. She set to work to repair a blue coat, first sewing it delicately—for she had been educated at a convent, where they still teach girls to sew—and then dyeing it with fountain-pen ink. The interior of the boat looked like an old clothes shop and smelled of anti-moth preparations.

American Joe heard next morning—for he had his agents and spies everywhere—that I was searching for some grease for deck work and for a few small shackles. He was cooking himself and was too busy to help me, but he sent along a sponge diver who spoke enough Italian to show me where I might find what I needed.

The sponge diver was impressed by *Truant*. "Why don't you take me and my friends on board, and we can go off to North Africa, sponging?" he suggested. "All last winter I was at Benghazi in a Hydra boat. We made no money because we had to pay too much for the boat. How much did you pay for this one?" I translated the sum into Greek currency and told him. "That is very cheap," he said. "I will buy this boat for three times that value in gold pounds. But where am I to find the money, unless you lend it to me?" He did not look like good security. Perhaps it was one of his off days. Although he had the most genial expression his eyes were liverish and there was a sharp curl to his mouth, while a portion of one of his buttocks gleamed rosily through his trousers. He took me to see James Lebessis, of the customs. Lebessis, a small, neat person poking his head out of the guichet in his office listened to my requests and answered in colloquial English: "I'll fix you up."

*   *   *   *

A stoutish lady with hair the colour of Viking gold and expressive brown eyes sat with some friends at the next table in American Joe's. She asked the waiter if we were Scandinavians, the nationality we were most readily allocated by strangers, and when he told her she exclaimed: "English!" with a look at us full of kindly meaning. There could be no two ways of translating such a look, and we agreed in whispers that, willy-nilly, we were about to make a new acquaintance. While we whispered the juvenile lead of the film company came to our table and, flashing everything and a white-toothed smile at Isabel (and nearly as much at me), asked in excellent English if they might do a little filming on *Truant* that night at eleven o'clock. We explained that the project would be awkward, as we were in the habit of retiring to bed at nine o'clock. After a conference with the directors and technicians he returned to say that the idea would have to be abandoned, as the electricians said that they would have no current until midnight. With a last flashing smile he retired, part of the way backwards, to the long table where all of his companions were already consuming oily pork chops. The lady at the next table had missed none of this conversation; her interest had been so apparent and so warm that we almost felt she had taken part in all that was said. As we paid our bill she entered the kitchen—all transactions as well as the choice of menu took place in the kitchen—and she engaged us in our own language at long range, rapidly approaching to grapple. Her name, she told us, was Electra Annapolis, and she would be honoured if we would visit her at her house, as she had some lovely old furniture, much of it English, which she would delight in showing us. Still reeling from this encounter, we left the restaurant, and were pounced on by Lebessis and the sponge diver, who accompanied us back to *Truant*, carrying a large parcel of grease and a bag of shackles, both of which they sold by weight; this meant that the grease was rather cheap, by normal standards, and the shackles were very expensive. The sponge diver said, when we offered them Greek drinks, that he had never tasted whisky, and would like to try that. Lebessis knew whisky from America, where he had lived for twenty years and had taken out citizenship papers. He swallowed two straight whiskies. The sponge diver made a horrible grimace over it, but he also drank two, very fast.

"What made you come home to Greece?" Isabel asked Lebessis.

"My sister's happiness," he answered. "I married her to an American man, and she was so happy that it made me want to come home and find a Greek wife. You see it is good for an American to marry a Greek girl; that goes well, since Americans are generally wonderfully kind to their wives. But it is not good for a Greek to marry an American girl, since American women are inclined to be cruel with their husbands, and Greek men are not psychologically fitted to be as docile as American men. Also I wanted to have plenty of children if I married, and an American wife is more than likely to ration you in that respect. Lastly, I find Greek women more beautiful, naturally enough, I suppose, for I was born here, and the Hydra girls are celebrated. Well, I came home, I went into business here, I got married. Now I have a nice house, a fine wife, and four splendid kids. But in America I had become accustomed to doing business the American way; so here I was soon skinned."

He showed us a certificate signed by Field-Marshal Alexander which stated that James Lebessis had gallantly resisted the Germans and the Italians during the enemy occupation of Greece, and had sheltered British and New Zealand fugitives at great risk to himself and to his family.

The sponge diver asked for one more whisky before he left us. I gave him the drink—I was beginning to realise that the Greek working man takes a lusty pleasure in alcohol—and a pair of brown tweed trousers from which Isabel had long been trying to separate me. He was so delighted with the trousers that he offered to pilot us to Athens. "Then you have been there before?" he said when we refused his offer. We explained that we navigated with charts but he could not understand that. "How did you find your way to Benghazi?" Isabel asked him. "One man was navigator; he knew the road."

An electric bell shrilled automatically in the vitals of the Annapolis house as we opened the wrought-iron front gate with mingled feelings of shyness and anticipation. For we knew that Madame Annapolis's promises were likely to be fulfilled: although this was just one of the many fine houses in Hydra, the town itself is supremely rich for its size in remarkable furniture and interiors. The islanders are said to be of Albanian stock. To-day the men sail on small spongers and coasting caiques, but in the eighteenth century the Hydriotes were among the most daring and successful of the world's sailors. The island of Hydra is a ridge almost destitute of earth and the things that grow on it, only eleven miles long, less than two miles across at the widest point, and reaching a height of 1,960 feet. Yet in the period before the Greek War of Independence the Hydriotes numbered 28,000, and tall ships built, rigged and fitted out in Hydra harbour (then greatly expanded) sailed to Genoa, to Marseilles, to Bristol, the Hague, and Bordeaux; to Stockholm, Venice, the Canaries, the Sugar Islands, and New York. The Hydriotes could compete with the British and others for the carrying trade of the Baltic and the Black Sea. After 1770 Hydra became the nucleus of the insurgent Greeks, and the small island held out alone against the Turks. If the resistance of the

British seemed unlikely in 1940 when their island lay separated from the then invincible German Armies only by the English Channel, the resistance of Hydra was a miracle, for the channel separating that small island from the mainland is less than two miles across, and the island had few resources beyond the bravery of its inhabitants, the generosity of its merchant princes, and the skill of its shipwrights and sailors. By 1821 Hydra's population had risen to 40,000 and her fleet totalled one hundred and fifty ships. The merchants, above all the Coundouriotis family, the great sailors, the Tombazis, Tsamados, and Miaoulis, like the common Hydriotes poured forth their treasure to win the war; when it was honourably won the island was bled white, and on the seas of the world the steamships with their black plumes of coal smoke were writing in the sky the end of the Hydriotes' power on the sea. Still to-day in the houses of the great families, and in those houses that once belonged to the great, you may see treasures from the graceful world of the eighteenth century, the gifts that the seamen brought home from foreign ports. You may see English and Venetian glass, Italian mirrors, French and English furniture, dark pictures from Spain, Persian rugs, brocades from Italy, tapestries and carpets from France and striped silk hangings of the Empire period, sporting prints and silver from England, ivories, silver and jewels from the Orient, tomahawks and pipes from America, lace from Ireland and Spain and Holland.

We mounted a flight of steps between urns holding flowering shrubs. There was a creaking noise from the upper floor as Madame Annapolis heaved herself out of bed. Her blue skirt was creased when she came to the door; it was a warm day for a siesta fully dressed. She was most affable. Her brown eyes positively gushed their message of goodwill. She asked me my name, and when I told her she asked: "Just plain . . . *Mister* . . . I mean not *Lord*, or something like that?" Her furniture was glorious, gleaming with age and care, and exquisitely set against whitewashed stone walls and stone-flagged floors. Niches in the walls held small fountains. In the dining-room, we saw a fine set of Hepplewhite chairs, a table at which thirty might dine, and a white marble well-head with a marble cover to it. Here the tiled floor struck hollow underfoot, for it was laid on the top of a great cistern fed by cool mountain streams, the Hydriote corsair's notion of air-conditioning. An elderly cook was making hors d'œuvres on a succession of glowing charcoal stoves covered by a great hood that dwarfed the rest of the kitchen. Several members of the cook's family sat on the floor near the open doorway, which offered a fine view of the sea and the mainland across the channel. We ascended the stairs, and Madame

Annapolis showed us her bedroom. Silk sheets were still rumpled from the siesta. A shotgun lay on the chaise longue; although I stood beside the gun for a long time, bursting with eagerness to have the bad manners to ask our hostess why it lay there, she offered no explanation. We sat at a marble table on the colonnaded terrace. A small boy, delicate and silent in doeskin slippers, brought us sweet biscuits, cigarettes, and miniature cups of Turkish coffee. Madame Annapolis was anxious to see the interior of *Truant*, and when she thought that we were sufficiently rested she led us down through the narrow, cobbled streets which slightly resemble those of Capri. She found *Truant* "adorable", and drank a quantity of white Cinzano, a drink which she "adored", but which "one only finds in Embassies and Legations these days". She had invited a great many people to meet us at her house. "You simply cannot let me down, I promised that you would both be there. Please don't dress up, you are much more *boaty*—is there such a word?—as you are."

A wilting donkey stood by the war memorial. Madame Annapolis—to our great surprise, for somehow she did not seem to belong to the same world as donkeys—stroked the animal's emaciated quarters and said: "*Salut*, Saint Julien." She turned to us with a sweet smile. "Such a nice name, don't you think, Saint Julien? He is a good donkey. I rode him this morning to my uncle's farm in the hills. He carried me well. My old nurse used to tell me that donkeys constitute the second wonder of the world."

"And the first?" I asked.

"Sugar, I believe. Or was it the Parthenon? No, the Parthenon was the third."

The hors d'œuvres that the old cook had prepared beneath the hood were delicious, particularly circles cut from small aubergines, fried in olive oil, well sprinkled with salt and pepper, and then allowed to cool and stiffen. None of the other guests had yet arrived. The drinks were all Greek; oyzo, resinated wine, vermouth, and Greek brandy. The first arrival was a small man who was introduced as the manager of the Anglo-Greek Information Centre, a shop displaying various pamphlets explaining (advertising?) Britain and what the British were fond at that time of calling their "war effort". I was interested to meet the manager. I suspected him of having a sense of humour because the walls of the Information Centre were profusely covered with photographs of the war leader and defeated politician, Winston Churchill, but there was one immense photograph of his less photogenic successor, Clement Attlee, and this picture quite dominated the room. Some wag in the British Council

331

had had Mr. Attlee's kind face printed so darkly that it glared from the frame like the face of an unshaven Iago, a swarthy murderer, a Corsican sexual maniac, a Sicilian cutpurse, a Catalonian abortionist. The manager spoke none of our miserably few languages. He sat on a chair near the door, tucking his feet, toe to toe, under the plush seat, and smiling determinedly at Madame Annapolis and at ourselves. He frequently clinked glasses with me, an agreeable gesture of solidarity between the manager of the Anglo-Greek Information Centre and a native of the country whose taxpayers supplied his salary.

The next person to enter was announced by Madame Annapolis as an artist, more than that, as "the best artist in Greece". He had good ears, sticking out from his head and continuing the pointed lines of his chin, and he spoke French most fluently, having studied and lived in Paris. I overheard him remarking artistically to Isabel that she had a "fascinating head". A few more stragglers arrived, variously introduced in a descriptive manner, as, for example, "a shipowner", "a lady who paints linen", and "a great wag". Then ten people connected with the film company walked in. Madame Annapolis gave them a communal introduction to us saying: "None of them speaks any language you would understand, so if any of them interests you, you'll just have to talk with signs—you know—dum-dum language. But the leading man, who spoke to you in the restaurant this morning, will be here in a moment. He's in the cloak-room just now. He's a very famous and popular actor, apart from his good looks, and he owes it to his position to enter alone."

Isabel was not prepared to take Madame Annapolis's word for it that we could not communicate with the ten Crêpes Suzettes, and after she had persevered with them politely—I was sitting in the shelter of her small, but capable, shoulder—for a few moments, one young man, who proved to be a poet—they said that he was the greatest (living) poet in Greece—and to have written, and published, five books, spoke French. As the poet affably talked, most of his companions gathered courage and revealed that they also had some grasp of French. The poet was there because he was the husband of the leading lady, who sat beside him endeavouring to remember to look a little sulky, drinking oyzo, and occasionally lighting up her face with a dazzling smile that came without reason but was thoroughly agreeable. The other actress, the one whom we had watched at her work in the boat, sat beside the leading lady, and although she said nothing she frequently brought me potato chips. Next to her sat a fierce-looking man, who had written the script and who was also the brother of her fiancé. When I complimented the small director—who still wore the black-leather coat from Germany—on his important functions, he exclaimed indignantly: "But I too am an author . . . I mean, I am an author too."

The leading man appeared at a moment when the conversation was hushed. He had discarded his fisherman's clothes, and wore a London-made suit, suède shoes and a maroon tie. He told us that he made films to live, but that he lived to act in real plays, particularly those of Shakespeare. What he would really like to do would be to write poetry or novels.

It was beginning to be drummed into me that, in contrast to my own country, where any admiral, stockbroker, politician, divine, or film actor may sniff at a creative artist, literature was considered to be a most respectable career in Greece.

* * * *

We were sorry that we had left Hydra when we pushed out of the harbour inlet and found ourselves pitching in a head sea while a chilly north wind swept the decks. Madame Annapolis's drinks slopped acidly in the gloomy caverns below our ribs, and we agreed before we had covered five miles of water that nearer shelter must be found than the harbours of the Piræus, some forty miles distant up-wind. We soon decided to alter course for the island of Poros, only ten miles from Hydra and offering a vast amount of shelter that is most highly recommended by the *Sailing Directions*. The chart-work had to be accurate to enter Poros harbour by the eastern end, where a peninsula from the island comes to the mainland, leaving a navigable channel less than one hundred yards wide in places, and with the deep water close under the curve of the island. It was only when my eyes lit on Poros that I remembered the words of a distinguished and bearded English professor, who had said to me as we stood drinking among a crowd of people in Paris: "Poros is the loveliest place on earth."

In one of the books by Jean de Brunov dealing with the remarkable career of King Babar of the Elephants there is a picture of a Mediterranean port, and that is how Poros appeared to me. The houses, plain white cubes, rise in pyramidal grouping from the waterfront. The quays are the main streets. The inhabitants, often very beautiful, are all caricatures of the fishermen, the street vendors, the girls, the peasants, with whom an inspired artist would populate such a place. The town of Poros stands at the end of what is called Poros Harbour, which is in reality a large salt-water lake with two narrow entrances at opposite extremities of the island of Poros. We were particularly charmed by the trees and the general greenness of the place. The eye takes time to become accustomed to the

333

Greek scenery, and to read the fascination that lies in the never-ending lines of the hills, the gentle, yet unusual, colouring, and the clear, brittle quality of the light. But the island of Poros is heavily wooded, and to port, as we moved up the eastern channel, were extensive orange and lemon groves on the lower slopes of the mountains of the Morea. We turned to starboard in the more open water of the great natural harbour, and anchored opposite that part of the town that reaches out a filament of white houses, taverns and churches to the fine, but unobtrusive buildings of the naval college. It was a Sunday, and the people were walking the quays. A blue trickle of sailors came from the gates of the naval college, where a band was playing suety German music, and contriving to give it a debauched and thoroughly pleasant Eastern quality. Sailors patronised a tavern on the quay near us. Their singing in the tavern was reedy and sweet, but scarcely more so than the brass music coming bouncing over the water.

*   *   *   *

The ultimate stage of our journey to Athens was unpleasant. The sea rolled nastily in at the northern entrance to Poros harbour. We hauled in our sheets and began to beat into it. We were thirty miles from the Piræus, and had the choice of keeping the large island of Ægina, which lay on our direct course, either to port or to starboard. We chose the latter, thinking that on that side our chart was less profusely marked with the word "mine-fields", and that the island might offer some shelter. The wheel-house thermometer dropped to fifty-two (F.). Isabel steered, leaning against a pillow and wrapped in a blue blanket. We were both half-asleep in the wheelhouse when we heard shouts. An ugly, low-snouted schooner of German build, that did regular trips with passengers between the Piræus and the islands, was passing us, and several of the Crêpes Suzettes were waving and shouting on her deck. They were returning to Athens, and so was Madame Annapolis, who, poor lady, was lying below decks, wishing that the trip might soon end, even in disaster.

We sailed into a whitish mist, and it seemed a long time before the Piræus would appear. Then a thick shaft of sunlight lit up the agglomeration of the town, which looked to us like whitened bones spread over a sand dune.

Gwenda Hawkes had allowed us to read the books about Greece that she carried on *Elpis*. One of these had been written by an enthusiastic yachtsman and Greek scholar, who described at great length his rapture as he approached Athens in a yacht. Despite the headwind, the cold, several

334

rain showers, and the occasional stifled groans of my brave companion, I watched myself for signs of a like rapture. But the yachtsman and scholar, who had named many hills and temples and the gods and goddesses who frequented them, had contrived to give me a thoroughly false impression of the shoreline. I expected, for one thing, to see the Acropolis standing out as though spot-lighted, and the Parthenon in turn eclipsing with its radiance the other buildings on the Acropolis. But I could not see the Acropolis; in fact for a long time I could not even see Athens, which, to be truthful, is spread insignificantly, with a great deal of cheap and ugly outer development, some five miles behind the Piræus. I had read the night before a remark of Somerset Maugham's with which I found myself in agreement: "I am no sightseer." However, I was able to revert to my ordinary relish in visiting a fresh place, and if Athens from a distance looked ordinary and even squalid, why so do other towns, and I was the more prepared to find myself at ease there. I would not call Paris collectively beautiful, yet I love it.

We had been meeting boats all the way across, trading and passenger-carrying caiques, small fishing-boats, and even undecked pleasure-boats with lateen sails. Several ships were making for the port, but we bore off to starboard towards Phalerum Bay, as we had decided to stop in the smallest harbour in the Piræus, and the oldest, Turco Limano, sometimes called Munychia. Sailing round a rocky point surmounted by the club-house of the Royal Hellenic Yacht Club we found the entrance easily enough, but had great difficulty in finding a berth for *Truant*. The harbour was crescent-shaped, with the yacht club above one end of it, and above the other, flying a Union Jack, the British Consul's house. On the waterfront we saw a string of taverns and stores. A few yachts were moored fore and aft, facing the entrance; eight motor patrol vessels, British in origin, but now flying the blue-and-white flag of the Greek Navy, were made fast in a tight row, side touching side and the bows touching land; beneath the yacht club a few small sailing craft were moored, boats of the "star" class chiefly, and beside them two big caiques used as training ships for naval cadets. I did not like the way the other yachts were placed, and scarcely felt inclined to join them. On the other hand it seemed a bad idea to go anywhere near the naval ships, which had anchors on wire hawsers strewn copiously around them, and training ships are things to be avoided in any place. The edges of the harbour were all obviously shoal. So we dropped anchor in the centre, and went below to have tea. Soon there was a tap on the side of the ship and a soft voice said: "May I come aboard?" It was a dark-faced naval officer.

"Come below and have some tea."

"If I shall not trouble you, I adore tea."

He drank quickly, and soon rose to go.

"Where should we put our boat?" I asked.

"Wherever you like."

"Won't we be in the way here?"

"It will be the privilege of any craft entering the harbour to avoid you."
He bowed to each of us. "Leave nothing on deck," he said to me. "Not
even your lifebuoys. Good material is very short just now. The fishermen
might come along with a knife in the night and cut free anything that they
needed."

I lit the riding light and then rowed ashore. I found myself in a dark
lane. The air was clammy. From the houses on either side came a clattering and a sound of speech that brought with it no feeling of life. I knew
that impression from the war years. The houses had been requisitioned,
and the uncaring voices of the military billeted in them echoed in the
rooms denuded of carpets, hangings and furniture.

The head steward came from the back places of the yacht club to have a
look at me. He had the same name, Spiro, as the naval contractor whom
we had met in Zante. The other Spiro had looked like an actor named
Menjou; this one was like an amiable bishop. He took me to an elaborate
bar, and successfully pressed me to drink anything that might please me
and to eat olives and salted almonds. I telephoned from the bar to the
president of the club, M. Antoine Benaki. A gentle, confident voice came
through the telephone. If I turned my head to the left while I spoke into
the instrument I saw *Truant*, far below me, her paint and varnish shining
softly in the lights from the naval ships. If I turned to the right I looked
at a model of a member's six-metre and at an engraving of a bulbous-
faced Englishman, a Lord Yarborough. Considerable spaces of time,
outlook, and breeding separated me from him, but I took comfort from
his presence on the wall, and from his muscular calves, to which the
artist had surely done full justice. Another engraving showed Yarborough's yacht, which looked like a small ship of the line, and was
complete with gun-ports. When he had said good night to me, M.
Benaki spoke to Spiro, who had formerly been chief steward on the
Benaki yachts. He gave instructions that Isabel and I were to be regarded
as honorary members of the club and that everything the club possessed
was to be at our disposal. Spiro, he said, would be responsible for *Truant*
during our stay in Turco Limano. Spiro trembled at such a responsibility.
"Very many clever thieves here, sir," he warned me.

336

I walked down through the requisitioned houses to the meaner streets near the water. The people were sharp, and they all seemed to know where I came from. Children whispered at me from dark corners: "Hullo Dzonnee." They showed me where to buy bread and fruit, and entered the shops with me to let the vendors know that they might safely demand exorbitant prices. The children were like pretty mice with their big eyes, thin soft faces, and their chirruping: "Dzonnee, Dzonnee."

27

Sᴘɪʀᴏ was early aboard on our first morning in Athens.

"Lost anything yet, sir?" he inquired at once.

"No."

"I brought my head chef to keep watch on your boat, and to-morrow the head boatman will take over from the head chef."

The head chef was a foxy-faced little man with auburn hair and moustache, and tearful, pale-blue eyes.

"What am I going to do with your chef?" I asked Spiro.

"Well, sir, if you want to have a dinner party on board he will be useful, and when you go to Athens he will remain on the boat and see that nothing is stolen."

A dismal rain was falling, slanting before a north wind. Athens, like most towns enjoying good climates, is miserable in the rain. The people, dressed for heat and sunshine, shivered and scowled; the roads were covered with coffee-coloured slime; the men selling American dollar bills, British pound notes and "gold pounds" (sovereigns), and Swiss francs in paper and gold, retreated from the pavements into doorways and worsened their exchanges. In Athens at that time the women who had pretensions to being fashionable usually expressed them in nodding hats and flaring skirts which had been the fashion in Paris two years earlier. Isabel's clothes drew many dark stares. The Athens streets surprised us by the amount of chocolate, all of Greek manufacture, offered for sale in the booths. The shop-windows were full of goods, although the prices were such as to give them a tantalising—and, in the case of food, infuriating—unattainability to forty-nine of every fifty citizens. The British Embassy, which had many responsibilities as Greece was run at that time, had several departments which overflowed from the Embassy proper, a pink building quasi-residential in character, to an office block in a street re-named after the war—how permanently few could forecast—Winston Churchill Street. In one of the departments we received a heavy mail and looked, for the first time in months, at the British and American newspapers, generally speaking a depressing sight. The effect of dropping out of normal day-to-day existence is to sharpen the critical faculties toward all forms of entertainment such as politics, newspapers, sport, the cinema, the theatre,

338

the radio, disguised pornography, and gossip. Such of these as are part of the normal individual's life are like the tobacco habit, the addict may miss them—though I never have—for a few days or weeks, but he becomes reconciled to their absence, and when he returns to a place where they are consumed he savours them with a clean palate, and the taste is usually disagreeable.

We had numerous introductions to people in Athens. One of these was to a man who was to be extremely kind to us, Major B. Keeper-Wells, O.B.E., M.C. Most fortunately for us, Keeper-Wells was His Britannic Majesty's Consul at the Piræus, and occupied with his wife the house overlooking Turco Limano. He is a powerfully-built man, rather short-sighted with thinning grey hair. He seemed a little taken aback by our youthful appearance.

"I shouldn't have thought they'd allow you away from school to do this trip," he said to me.

"Keeper!" admonished Mrs. Keeper-Wells.

We drank gin-and-lime or whisky-and-soda in a large room decorated with drawings competently done in 6B pencil by Keeper-Wells himself and representing various kinds of sailing craft. An exceedingly kind person, and fatherly by instinct, I doubt if Keeper-Wells would have talked so much of yachts had he been aware that his professional jargon and anecdotes made me feel very ill-at-ease. I asked him where we should put *Truant* to be both in security and out of the way in the harbour below us, but I could make neither head nor tail of his highly technical advice, and was obliged to content myself with nodding and saying yes at judicious intervals. Then we inquired where we might settle in solitude for a month or so to allow me to do some work, and I told him that we had been greatly taken with Poros harbour.

"Poros is all right, now that the R.A.F. have sprayed the marshes on the mainland to down the mosquitoes," he answered quickly, for he is the type of good fellow who delights in being able to give briskly helpful advice. "Anchor in the cove by the Russian Store—remember that name, it's marked on all your charts—and be careful how you anchor, but I'll come to that in a minute. Then across the water you have the Tombazi estate, where you should be able to buy all the fruit you want and also olive oil. One day when the weather looks good, toddle across there in the *Truant*. You'll find there's a fresh-water pipe coming out from the shore; it's a first-class place to water your ship; just get the factor to have the water turned on, and there you are. But I was going to tell you. . . . Mummy! where's that sketching block? I was going to tell you something

339

remarkable. . . . When you get *Truant* across to that side keep the fresh-water pipe to port, then the shore goes like this, and about here you'll see a small jetty. Run her right in until her bows are in the weed—drop a stern anchor of course as you go in,—leave her there for forty-eight hours, and at the end of that time your bottom will be clean as a whistle. It's some amazing chemical action in the water. I did it to *Myrtle* last year so I know what I'm talking about. But are you coppered?"

"No."

"It's still well worth while."

"It sounds a little precarious."

"Just watch your weather, and oh! for the Lord's sake look out for the north wind at Poros. A yacht lying in the Russian Store cove last year had two big anchors out for'ard, and two chains aft, shackled on to trees. She needed 'em. You'll meet the Admiral, by the way. A character; lives alone and speaks remarkable English. He's in the bungalow at the corner by the cove. Then there are two artist fellows—English—in Poros, Craxton and Freud . . ."

"A descendant of Sigmund?"

"Don't ask me."

Isabel inquired about the marketing situation in Poros.

"It's a good place for vegetables and fish. You'll get meat too, and if you want chickens just ask the Tombazi factor to buy them for you on the hoof. There's quite a reasonable restaurant in Poros, but it might shut for the winter. I'll have it opened for you."

"Oh, no thank you. We don't eat much in restaurants."

"Then what do you eat? sandwiches?"

"No, of course not, I cook every day."

"Good Lord!"

The Keeper-Wells have the habit, not uncommon among active English people, of turning every place into a camp. In their hallway, we noticed as we left the house, were two primus stoves, a sou'wester, a kettle, a lifebuoy, two fishing-rods, a ball of tarred twine and part of an iron bedstead.

When we returned to *Truant* the foxy-faced little chef was sitting primly in the wheelhouse, and he pretended that he had passed the whole day there, although we had told him to make himself comfortable in the saloon and galley. He was not a very intelligent man, for he had walked in the sand at the water's edge before coming aboard that morning, and when we had rewarded him for his vigil and sent him away we found sandy foot-prints all over the carpets and floors below, even in our sleeping cabin.

340

Spiro sent the club boatman to us the following morning, to help us to moor near the "hard" owned by the club. I had not given the windlass many turns when I saw a movement on the terrace above, and knew that Keeper-Wells had come out to observe our movements. The boatman was very anxious to have *Truant* under his care, and I was equally eager to avail myself of his services, but as Isabel thrust *Truant's* stern into the space he had cleared I sounded, and the lead told me that the bottom was extremely uneven and was therefore probably fouled. Despite the boatman's arguments—seeing future tips slipping away, he warned us fiercely that the "fisher boys" would strip us of everything we possessed—we put *Truant* alongside the other yachts. Our good resolutions to have the boat safely guarded soon melted as usual, and we left her, taking no more precautions than in other places. Belongings which are unnaturally cherished are the heaviest of encumbrances for the traveller.

"What a sunny room!" I exclaimed as we entered the Keeper-Wells' house. (It had been dark when we visited them for the first time.)

"Yes, isn't it," Mrs. Keeper-Wells answered. "Keeper was pretty quick off the mark, you know. He was one of the first into the Piræus when all the fighting was going on, and he bagged this house . . ."

"Now then, Mummy, what are you saying to these good people?" said Keeper-Wells, appearing at the French windows.

"I was explaining how you bagged this house."

"The house. Yes, yes. I always say, Millar, that this house gives me the pleasures of a yacht and the comfort a home on land. Of course, I wouldn't be without my boats down in the harbour." He turned to Isabel. "I give you full marks."

"What for?"

"You handle that big ketch like a real sailor-man. I was watching this morning; and I was impressed. By the way, Millar, I have a book here that I think might interest you."

I opened the thin volume that he handed me. It concerned itself with the resistance to the German invaders of partisans in the Lake Ilmen region, and it was the work of a Russian journalist. The page which I read dealt with a supposed conversation between two German officers, one of whom was suffering from a fit of home-sickness. His companion, another German officer, advised him to: "Spill blood, Karl, spill Russian blood, that is the only recipe for cheering a man up. The more depressed you feel, the more blood you must spill. It is as simple as that." I reflected that this author-journalist had ill-served the partisan groups of the Lake Ilmen region by writing such tosh. Keeper-Wells, whose intelligence I would

341

rate extremely high, must have given me the book as a test, for he observed my reaction, and commented on it in his own way. "Come on, hand it back," he said. "I can see that it isn't quite your cup of tea. Probably you prefer P. G. Wodehouse?"

"Infinitely."

* * * *

We saw Athens in the post-war period of vendetta. Anger pounded, surged, and bubbled in the veins of all Greeks. Yet we had an impression from them of dignity and a smooth way of dealing with life. . . .

Antoine Benaki is a remarkable figure, and life would be better if there were more like him. I met him fairly frequently. I do not know him. I took great pleasure in his company. He is the most courteous of men. Every feature of Benaki is fine-drawn, yet the whole conveys an impression of strength. A British engineer remarked when he met him for the first time: "He is like a light-weight bridge; although the members look delicate, you know that he would carry a five-ton truck." He is a Greek, of course, an Athenian now, and a man of great wealth that comes from cotton. White hair is worn flat on his head. His skin is smooth, with a texture and a grading of colour which makes him look everlasting. His moustache is the longest that I have seen. It forms a horizontal equal in length to the vertical from his chin to the dome of his skull; it is whiter than Chinese white, and is waxed into two long, perfectly tapering points. Benaki is a courtier, a man of fashion, a public benefactor who prefers his generosity to be secret, a leading Boy Scout, a yachtsman, a linguist, and, above all, a connoisseur and a collector. He has turned his father's house in Athens into a museum where he shows the collection begun by his father and very greatly increased by himself. We first met him there, in the room in the basement which serves him for an office. Apart from his moustache, Benaki would give an immediate impression of gentle unobtrusiveness. His voice, sibilant and tender, can adapt itself, I am sure, to any one of half-a-dozen languages, and it certainly compasses an English that is without defect. His clothes, delicate and attenuated, are cut in a manner that suits his spare figure and his refined energy. The sleeves of his coat are turned back to expose the most immaculate of cuffs, this being, we were told, a custom of Alexandrian cotton brokers, who do not care to have any pressure on the sensitive skin of the wrists, which skin they use for testing cotton. It is an astonishing experience to be guided round the museum by Benaki himself, for although the public has the benefits of his collection, he appears to be almost boyishly embarrassed by the rarity of many of the

342

exhibits that are so thoughtfully displayed in air-tight glass cases lined with velvets of different colours or hanging on the walls of tall rooms in which a manservant raises the silk blinds as you enter, and as you leave drops them, to protect from the sun the ancient surfaces of the ikons, their gilded saints and showy, sexual horses gleaming from darknesses so dark that they seem to be cubic inches of the inevitable. Benaki showed us, on that first visit, his relics of Byron, a lock of the poet's hair, and the portable writing-desk which went with him to Missolonghi, and which was in the room when he died. It is a small folding desk of the type common in those days when letter-writing was an art, and many were able to travel in roomy private carriages. It is made of polished hardwood, with a brass handle let into either side. When opened it presents a faded red-leather slope, copiously sprinkled—by the impulsive Byron, it is said—with both ink and candle-grease. At the top of the slope is the usual arrangement, a receptacle for pens and for two square ink-bottles with stoppers made of some dark wood. It is impossible to look on so personal, so ordinary, so important, so pathetic a relic, without feeling a bond of sympathy for the self-accusing man who died in that swampy place. . . .

"How long ago?" I asked Benaki. "Do you remember?"

"Byron died on the 19th of April in the year 1824, and so has been dead—if one can truly say that of him—one hundred and twenty-two years, six months, and eighteen days."

"How did the desk come into your possession?"

"When he died, certain of his personal belongings, strange though such a procedure may now seem, were sold by auction at Missolonghi. The man who bought it at the auction, for a very small sum, I may add, sold it to another, and later I sought it out as something that I needed to have, if only to ensure its preservation from the worm and from the violence of men." Later he said: "You have heard of the collector's mania? I have it. The room in the basement where we met two hours ago serves as my office. Scarcely a day passes but some man comes to me there with something which he claims is beautiful, precious, rare. They come from all over the world, but chiefly from the Near-East. Often I fight against the longing to possess the object that is offered. I argue with the owner and with myself. I ask my wife and my helpers here in the museum to dissuade me from buying. And then I buy." He left the building with us. Not one hundred yards from the doors we came to a square of irregular shape containing a patch of grass protected by iron railings, a few trees, a kiosk with magazines of Greece, America, Hollywood, and France, vegetable shops, their earthy produce exuding to the street from doors and windows and wire baskets of Turkish eggs hanging from the lintels, taverns where men were drinking strong wine and eating the intestines of animals prepared in such a way as to make them more than appetising. I ventured the banal opinion that Athens had indeed a great deal in common with Paris, but Benaki said: "I have travelled most of the world. No other city bears comparison with this."

*   *   *   *

The war had this effect on me personally, it killed most of my convictions. At the age of sixteen, then a schoolboy at a boarding-school in Scotland, I remember feeling a desire to assassinate a man who did not stand up when, at the end of a performance in a cinema, an organist played "God Save the King". At the age of twenty-one, then an undergraduate, I used, if alone, to keep my seat through the ritual, for I felt, somewhat illogically, that by being a little rude about the National Anthem I upheld something unpolitical which I called "Equality of Birthright". At twenty-five I was a timid and unauthenticated communist. At twenty-nine, when war broke out, I thought that I was a socialist and a pacifist. That did not prevent me from flinging myself with ardour into the killing match. But when toward the end of the war I had killed a few Germans, quite unfairly with explosives, bullets, and even rockets, and had taken unthinking pleasure in my work (for I was a bright little soldier), I decided that I did not want to kill anyone or anything again. I am writing this book in a Hampshire farmhouse. I have planted certain herbs in the garden. The weather is splendid and the soil is good. The roots of the herbs flourish yet only a few lacerated shoots appear in the air because each night the rabbits enter the garden and eat all but the lovage and the apple mint. There is a shotgun in the linen cupboard, and before the war I should have slaughtered the rabbits and thought that I was doing no more than my duty. Now I do not even bother to buy and erect some wire netting. I am inclined to take the rabbits' side. And if rabbits have the sense to eat French parsley, chervil, dill, and fennel, who am I to deprive them of their pleasures? As for killing them, I now avoid killing even ants and spiders. The line of demarcation of my killing can stop at such pests as flies and mosquitoes.

When we came to Greece we came to a population split on a blood-line, and with a good many enthusiasts on either side determined to kill the members, old, young, and able-bodied, of the other. We noticed that the modern Greeks are, on the whole, an ardent and bloodthirsty race, quick to take sides, and with strong religious tendencies as well as political beliefs drawing them to one side or the other. The articulate people with whom we came in contact were all, unfortunately, of one side, the Right. When they talked politics or God or the menace of communism and Russia to me I neither believed nor disbelieved them, I neither liked them nor disliked them for their adherences, although I should have admired them more had they been unbiased, had they been able to sit on the political and religious fences. Of course there were a few Greeks, such as Benaki, who never spoke of politics or war to us. What did disconcert me considerably was that the forces of the right-wing government were clothed and trained in the British manner. During the week-days the requisitioned streets above Turco Limano, through which I had walked on the night of our arrival, resounded to the clash of arms drill and the constant pounding of metal-studded boots moving and halting in unison. The sentries by the national war memorial in Constitution Square posed and paraded in Evzone uniform like spotless powder puffs, but all around them, marching from billets and barracks to nowhere and from nowhere to barracks and billets, were Greek military columns whose equipment and whose movements I knew as well as my own feet and hands. The young Greeks of that side were going through an exactly similar military training to that which I had myself enjoyed in 1940 in the Brig o' Don barracks near Aberdeen. And although they were being trained to kill other young Greeks who had been attracted or coerced into the anti-Government forces, they were told that these other Greeks were merely bandits who represented the advance guard of Russian, Jugo-Slav, Bulgarian, and Albanian communism, a monster that would devour them, their families, and their religion.

As for the British troops in Greece, they were less numerous than was generally supposed outside Greece, and, as usual, they were inclined to be puzzled by their situation. Charges of corruption were levelled at them as a whole, which was unjust, but anybody could see that corruption was there in specific cases. Greece is a demoralising country for any person who has been reared in a place where the law is respected and obeyed, particularly if that person is a bored soldier who can see little sense in his duties. As for the right-wing Greeks, while they were annoyed with the British for refusing to send more troops, they revealed a certain dislike of the British for having troops there at all. Fun, sometimes of an acid quality, was poked at the red-faced foreign soldiers. The British were apt to repay those stings with a stolid refusal to judge the Greeks by any but British standards. Armies stationed in foreign countries are bound to breed envy, mistrust, and personal rancour.

At the same time it would be stupid to deny that there was a certain sentimental attachment between the Greeks and the British. Some of those who had fought in the clandestine manner against the Germans and the Italians gave exaggerated devotion to the British soldiers who had fought with them. One such English officer even had a voluntary body-guard of Greeks resembling the devoted souls who followed Highland chieftains before, during, and after the '45. That officer lived in a bourgeois apartment in Athens, and in a bourgeois manner, except that an armed guard slept each night on the mat outside his bedroom door. It was said, possibly by the officer's enemies, that the faithful follower's nights were complicated, for he had to know when to feign sleep while an intruder stepped over his recumbent form, and when to spring to his feet, his dagger in his fist.

We were fortunate enough to make the acquaintance of one of the British heroes (I am aware that he would not like to be described as a hero, yet I have every reason to believe that his courage and fortitude were extraordinary, and I do not write of him with sarcasm) . . .

It was a lovely morning, and Grace, who had driven down to Turco Limano to take us shopping, had opened her car. She was in a *dopo-la-guerra* mood, and it was evident from her talk as we drove to Athens that there would be little shopping done that day. "I want you to meet the British officer, X.," she said, and she went on to recount details of X.'s exploits during the war, his wounds, his unselfishness, his devotion to the cause, the price that the enemy had put on his head. She told us that he was now an unhappy man, and as she said that, X. himself walked out of British headquarters and climbed into our car. He was a tallish man with a limp and a walking-stick, carelessly dressed in a tweed coat and flannel trousers, a red face, a tuft of hair standing on the top of his head, puzzled eyes, a nervous habit of smoking cigarettes, nicotine-stained fingers, a lawyer's voice from which the war had taken any trace of pomposity. He gave me the impression of a man who is waiting for something that he does not expect to happen. His voice came in soft whispers. He was an easy person with whom to be intimate for he did not have definite re-actions to normal questions, he was interested in strangers, and he was inclined to think that most people on earth, or in Athens at any rate, had good hearts. With astonishment not untinged with admiration I heard him speak highly of an English journalist whom I had mistrusted for years. Genuine goodness of heart is a most uplifting quality to find in any chance meeting. From a tavern we moved to the bar of the Hotel Grande Bretagne, a place usually referred to by the British in Athens as "The G.B.". The long bar was clustered like a much used fly-paper with officers, women in

346

uniforms, and civilians, most of them British. X. had invited us to lunch with some charming people in the country.

"Won't they mind?"

"They'll be delighted."

"Aren't we a little late?"

"Only an hour, but I promised to take along a girl, and we must wait for her."

"Where is she?"

"She lives in this hotel; I telephoned her when we arrived here, and she was in her bedroom, but she said that she would have to keep us waiting a little. That was an hour ago." All this was said without rancour, and in the gentlest of voices, as though he were discussing the claims to sanctification of Joan of Arc.

"How late am I?" the young woman asked when she finally appeared.

"Two hours or so, my dear," he replied with a warm smile. "I *am* a little worried, though, because I promised to give Henry's wife a lift to another lunch party, and she's rather a punctual person." The clocks showed 3 p.m. when we climbed into X.'s car. He stopped the car to buy flowers in a booth near Constitution Square. Flowers were fantastically expensive, although plentiful. He bought a large bunch of white roses for our host's daughter, and three bouquets of wild cyclamens, two of which he presented to the women in the car; the third was kept to placate Henry's wife. Isabel and I remained below while X. and the young woman climbed the stairs to Henry's apartment. When we had waited for a time, X. came running down.

"You must come up," he said, "we are blowing soap-bubbles, and they are wonderfully beautiful."

We passed through an open doorway into an empty hall and then to a room lined with books. Henry's wife, a small, dark-haired woman with an intense expression, politely gave us Swedish punch to drink, but as we drifted out of the French windows to the balcony I saw a bouquet of wild cyclamens lying on the floor. The flowers were considerably mangled; they looked as though somebody had stamped on them. Henry had an old pipe and a bucket of soap, and with these crude implements was blowing the most exquisite bubbles. Pale purple, gold, and milky white, they sailed away from the balcony; some shattered themselves against the walls of the Turkish Embassy, down wind, others soared high over Athens until they were lost to view, and others, following the air currents from the hot chasms of the streets, climbed into blue trickles of wood smoke, bounced on sudden hot gushets, and then, as inexplicably, sank to make delicate

347

explosions at the feet of pedestrians. When the delight of the bubbles and the Swedish punch seemed to be palling a little our hostess suggested that it might be a good idea to keep our luncheon appointments. The car rushed out of Athens into districts that, to our uninitiated eyes, resembled the residential quarters of Putney or Kingston. Henry's wife sat in front beside the chauffeur; she faced rigidly ahead, as did the chauffeur, who also had cause to feel annoyed, for his was an Embassy car, and he had not only missed *his* lunch, he was an hour late for his next appointment. At length we stopped at a gateway and Henry's wife climbed from the front seat. She stood in the roadway, looking at all of us. "I don't know these people very well," she said. "They asked me to lunch and I'm two hours and forty-five minutes late. I suppose social convention obliges me to thank you for the lift. *But I won't!*" She slammed the door and stamped away.

"We're having tea there to-day," X. said dreamily.

"What? At the house where she's lunching?"

"Yes."

I suggested that the lady whom we had just set down there might poison the atmosphere.

"*Nothing* could poison that atmosphere," he replied.

Our host ran out to the doorstep, and X. made detailed and able apologies, taking all the blame for our lateness on himself. The apologies were accepted with the utmost urbanity. The man who now received us had enemies in Athens. He had been educated at Heidelberg and, since he spoke German, had been used by the Greeks as a negotiator with the Germans. He was a small man with a chubby face and a sultry look in limpid brown eyes. There was a whiff of scent about him. Before the war he had occupied a position of dignity and even of splendour. His manners and his wit were delightful, and I cared not a jot what his politics were or had been. Despite the inconvenience of our late arrival, he made us feel completely at ease, even when he pointed out to Isabel and me, as strangers, that he was not accustomed to entertaining in so small a house or in what he described as so limited a manner. Our lunch was an almost uproarious success. Yet for all his urbanity and the material comforts which he enjoyed, it was not difficult to discern that the chubby intellectual was a very unhappy man. I wondered if it were the unhappiness in him that constituted a bond between him and X. Our host at first declined to accompany us to the house where we were expected for tea.

"I'm going to the cinema," he said. "I go to one cinema, and I sit right through the programme, then I move on to another cinema. When I've seen the second programme, I dine."

"Why do you go to the cinema?"

"I consume films feverishly, and the more banal and vulgar the better. The cinema's my favourite pastime. When I've dined I'll go to the Argentina; the new singer there is said to be a fine performer. Will you join me there?"

X., who could be very persuasive and very obstinate in an inoffensive manner, insisted that the chubby man accompany us to the other house. Henry's wife had gone, but the place was crowded with young people, Greek, American, and British. We stood for a time in a somewhat poetical room with a bed in it, long twigs in a vase, an engraving, and a smouldering aromatic fire. The chubby man was not at his ease there. He began to spin a protective cocoon of words around himself, talking to me in French, discussing the peculiar quality of the scene from the window, the hills which, as he said, curved and blended, but never ended. While he talked he chanced to turn from the window to the darker interior of the room, and I saw his eye rest for an instant on a correct young couple squatting on the bed. As he turned back to the window and to his well-phrased reflections he shot a look into my eye. In that instant the shutter which separated him from my perception was momentarily lifted, and I looked straight into a soul in torment. A few minutes later he had driven away to the cinemas of Athens.

As X. had assured us, this second house also belonged to exceptionally charming people, but X. himself spent all but a few minutes of his long visit in the nursery, drooling over two young children, one of them still in the repulsive napkin stage. When it was time to leave he came downstairs from the nursery, the dazed look of pleasure still lingering on his red face beneath the tuft of hair, his muscular hand swelling as it gripped the stick which supported his weak leg.

After that we had an engagement of a different character. Once more we waited in the bar of "The G.B.", this time for an English schoolmaster. He took us to dine in a British club where the menu was:

Soupe à la boîte

—

Macaroni
Sauce Tomate Synthétique

—

Prunes and Custard

—

Whisky

349

The other guest was a British naval commander who had come from his post on one of the outer islands to receive a couple of decorations from the hands of the British Ambassador. He was a real product of the sea. His voice boomed and his breathing was as audible as a compressor. He won our undying regard when the energetic schoolmaster said to him: "I know that you're longing to see Millar's yacht; let's drive them down to the harbour."

The commander breathed for a second or two and then boomed: "Yacht! I don't care if I never see another boat so long as I live, for I have to see too many of the damned things every blasted day of my life. No, the inside of my bed, that's what I want to see . . ."

So we all went happily to bed, but when we rowed ourselves out to *Truant* we found that the wind had changed from the north to the south, and *Truant* was bumping into the eight-metre moored at her port side. I was obliged to put out a kedge from the starboard bow and another from the starboard quarter, and this took me a long time, for I worked slowly, happy to be in the dark, salty air, and wondering whether X., whom I had inclined otherwise to admire, was not making a mistake in staying in Greece; I think heroes are well advised to leave when the hot work is done.

* * * *

We found Mrs. Keeper-Wells in the hall. She was arranging food for a picnic in two baskets.

"Keeper's tinkering in his den," she said. "We're going off to the mountains for the day, since its Sunday."

"What is there to eat, Mummy?" Keeper asked as he appeared in the French windows. "Hullo, good people."

"Salmon sandwiches, salad, biscuits, cake."

"Cigarettes?"

"Yes."

"Gin-and-lime?"

"Lemon squash. No gin-and-lime."

"Put in some gin-and-lime at once, there's a good girl." He looked at me and murmured through his teeth: "Can't bear dry picnics, can you?"

I thought that I heard Mrs. Keeper-Wells say: "Gin-and-lime indeed!" when she returned, but she carried the bottle out to the car and they set off for the hills.

* * * *

The bottom of Turco Limano harbour was the foulest that we sampled with our anchors; the chain came up covered with a black slime so viscous and so vile that it had to be scrubbed off, inch by inch. As I worked I strove to think of good smells, of apples resting in a loft, of one's own skin in the sun, of the Paris streets in the first arrondissement at seven o'clock on a spring morning, of Covent Garden Opera from the forward rows of the stalls on an opening night. But I could not get away from the slime, and from the thought, pleasant and unpleasant, that that harbour had been serving ships for more than two thousand years; from before the hey-day of the Athenian triremes, beaked ships with twenty marines and one hundred and sixty men of the oar, to *Truant*, men had been flinging or pumping their quota of dirt into the dark water, and the land around had been crumbling to narrow the harbour space.

As we struggled with the chain we saw Keeper-Wells watching us through a telescope. We motored out of Turco Limano to the next harbour, Zea, where we were to take petrol. Zea as a harbour leaves a good deal to be desired, but it is a pretty place, and it was full of caiques, most of them spongers. We hauled our stern in as near the quay as the shallow water would allow, and sat down on deck to rest in the sun. On either side the Greek sailors, very handsome in their rough, characterful way, were polite with us, but not over-interested. I have heard that the modern Greek is of Slav origin, and again that he is a mixture of the Greek, Wallachian, and Illyrian (or Albanian) bloods. However he may be bred, we found that his first characteristic—I am not writing of the fat merchants or of expatriate Greeks—is his natural dignity. In this he seems to resemble the Spaniard, perhaps because there is more than a dash of Islam in both bloods. Keeper-Wells appeared on the quay.

"Anything I can do for you?" he shouted.

"No thank you."

"You told me you had a warrant to fly the Blue Ensign?"

"Yes."

"Then why are you flying the Red?"

"The warrant only holds good for British territorial waters."

"You should fly the Blue here."

"Are you sure?" I had flown the Blue Ensign in French waters, knowing no better, until one morning Douglas Hawkes, supported by Gwenda, and both delightfully nervous that I might be offended by having my own ignorance of nautical etiquette exposed even by friends—how agonising our incompetence must have been to them,—explained to me that I ought to fly the Red Ensign in foreign waters "in case you run into the Royal Navy, who are capable of being very exact about such things".

"I'll let you know the exact drill about the Ensigns," Keeper-Wells called.

"Don't bother, please," Isabel answered. "It doesn't really matter."

"My good lady! It certainly does matter. I'm sure your husband agrees with me in that."

I said nothing. The tanker arrived and began to fuel us through a long, thin pipe. While the petrol was trickling into our tanks, a smartly dressed young woman appeared on the quay, accompanied by a professional muleteer of drunken appearance, and two superb mules. It was Grace, who wanted to know what we had thought of the man to whom she had introduced us, the former British agent, X. She had also come to the Piræus to bring us a gift of olives from the island where her mother had an estate, and to ship off to the island the two mules, which had just arrived from the Argentine. The mules shone with sweat, and glared angrily at the water, although you would have supposed that they would have become inured to it after their long voyage. One of the most charming things about life in Greece is the large part that the sea plays in it, because there are few roads on the mainland, and because many people, like Grace's family, live on islands.

A messenger from Keeper-Wells brought us two letters. The first, from Keeper-Wells himself, contended that the Blue Ensign would be correct on *Truant* in Greek waters, since this was a means of differentiating "bona fide yachtsmen" from people attempting to smuggle Jews out of Europe to Palestine. The second letter was an invitation to dine that evening in Athens. The messenger was obviously a Boy Scout, and he had too much of that scrubbed good-deed-a-day look to trust with a white lie. I did, however, suggest that he might tell his master that *Truant* had left harbour before he arrived with the letters.

"But, Mister," he answered reproachfully, "Master would see that the letters had been read."

"Not if you put them in a clean envelope with 'O.H.M.S.' on it and write out the same address with the typewriter."

"!"

Unable to bear the trouble in his dark eyes, I wrote to Keeper-Wells, asking him to make our excuses to the distinguished persons who had invited us to dine, and to explain that we had urgent reasons for sailing to Poros. As the scout trotted across the wide square that has one side open to the quays of Zea harbour, we took up our anchor and hurried away.

It was both exhilarating and exhausting to get to sea again. We had only been in Athens for six days, but I found my work on deck much

352

heavier than usual, for my muscles had already softened, and rich food had made me sluggish. A freshening westerly breeze soon turned to a head-wind from the south. We had learned that the mine-fields had been cleared from the east side of Ægina, so we sailed her far out from that island, and then in again, working for the northern mouth of Poros harbour. We ate only fruit at midday. Beyond Ægina the swell dropped and the wind fiercened, so that we made good speed, completing the thirty sea miles in less than five hours.

Poros harbour looked like heaven; Isabel steered into its great expanse of glassy water while I took down the sails. Darkness was beginning to fall. We turned to starboard to examine a small inlet in the western part of the harbour. The inlet proved to be treeless, so we swept round in a semi-circle until the straight line of our wake lay before us, and motored down the centre of the harbour, past the wide cove holding the Russian Store—where Keeper-Wells had advised us to anchor,—past the bungalow which we knew belonged to the admiral who lived alone, past a white house set on thickly-treed terraces, and so to the cove that Isabel had noticed on our previous visit to Poros. The townspeople of Poros—I suppose it must be called a town, for although of no great size it has some sixteen churches, a market, a bank, a naval college, and a tall clock tower with a purple half-dome on it and a four-faced clock which is illuminated in the hours of darkness—had switched on their lights. The white houses sparkled into the night, turning the ordinary electric light into something supernatural. We dropped anchor in the middle of the dark cove. We smelled the pines. The anchor chain rumbled a little, occasionally, as though the boat were a great black hog lazily sniffing at the place where he must sleep.

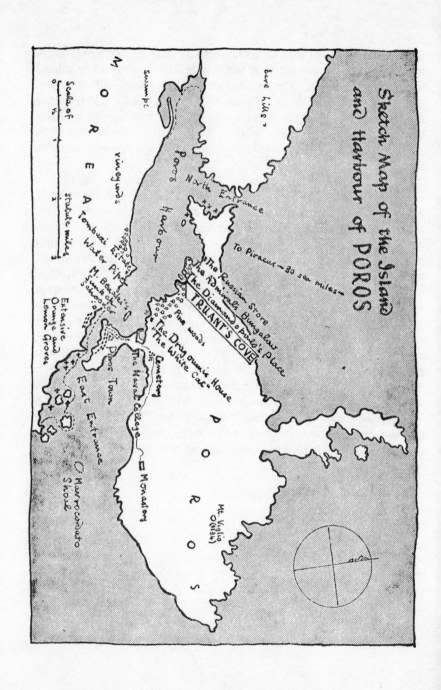

28

WHEN daylight came we were both convinced that the cove was the most beautiful anchorage in the world, and I set about mooring *Truant* there with chains. From the starboard quarter one length of chain went to a stout pine tree; the other end of the same chain would not quite reach the shore from the port quarter, but I shackled it to our heaviest kedge, which I dropped from the dinghy in water so shallow that the upper fluke appeared above the calm surface. *Truant* was thus held sufficiently inside the small cove to be invisible from the town of Poros. The only house in the vicinity, the grounds of which included the wood on our starboard hand, was hidden by the trees. Behind the sandy beach astern of us was another rampart of pines and high hills rising beyond. Ahead were two rocky points, and between them we looked across a mile of water to the mainland, to the fruit groves of the Tombazi estate and the green swamp in which malarial mosquitoes bred, backed by the mountains of the Morea, a wild, almost a terrifying scene.

The sea bottom, plainly visible beneath the boat, was of pale, greenish-grey sand freely dotted with spiky dark sea-urchins and with the great slothful worms called bêches-de-mer. Around us floated thousands of small jelly-fishes, mysterious creatures. The weather was perfect, rather warmer than an English summer's day, yet barely warm enough to call for the awnings.

It is the Middle Ages when Isabel is ill, so fortunately illness with her is a rare occurrence. Scientific aids to recovery are taboo. Doctors are eschewed. She had never recovered from the effects of the water she had swallowed after we had rounded Cape Matapan. As usual she argued that sickness must be patiently borne until the sufferer either recovers or expires. I left her in bed while I went to doctor, after my own fashion, a much simpler invalid, the one-horse-power internal-combustion engine, which we now required to charge our batteries. It had not been used since the early days at Corbeil, on the Seine, when we first met Douglas and Gwenda Hawkes, and I had learned from Douglas how to take it to pieces. When I had cleaned most parts of the engine I managed to persuade it to go, but not fast enough to charge our batteries at any substantial rate. Deciding—if so positive a verb may be used when describing the mental reactions of an engineer of my type—that Douglas had over-reduced the main jet, I borrowed one of Isabel's sewing needles, and increased the aperture. "There," I said to the engine. "That ought to fix you." I restarted it, and although it must have known that I was only bluffing over the jet, and clumsily at that, it ran perfectly. Mechanics can be most gratifying. I had not recovered from my astonishment when I heard a man's voice.

"George Millar? George Millar!"

A tall youth sat in *Truant's* shadow, leaning on the azure-painted oars of a rowing-boat. He was John Craxton, a painter from London, and he pretended that he had been on his way to visit the Diamantopoulos, our nearest neighbours. After a few not-so-shy protests that he did not care to disturb us, he came aboard. Isabel rose from her bed. We saw a lanky youth in a faded blue shirt, the wool singlet worn beneath appearing in the neck opening, khaki drill trousers touched here and there with oil paint, Athenian sandals worn over white socks with yellow stripes. Brown hair grew on his small face like bushes that seek to encroach on and smother a herb garden, and this effect was underlined by a wispy moustache growing outwards from the division of his upper lip, as though the besiegers had managed to land a feeble airborne force. He drank two glasses of iced oyzo carelessly, with the speed of a rooster's seduction, and spoke entertainingly of Poros and our mutual acquaintances in London, Paris and Hampshire. His vocabulary—only temporarily, we hoped—was pervaded by the adjective "delicious". When he had rowed himself away I fed Isabel, who was hungry, on purée of potatoes and poached eggs. After eating she slept all that afternoon and all the succeeding night. In the morning she insisted on walking to Poros. I sculled to the sandy beach and hauled the dinghy from the water, hiding the oar in the undergrowth.

The track leading on the one hand to Poros, on the other past the Diamantopoulos' house and Admiral Leondopoulo's bungalow to the place called the Russian Store, was not adequate for any motor-car, and was only used, and then but seldom, by donkeys, pack horses, mules, dogs, and pedestrians. Each house had a stone jetty poking into the sea, and the occupants were more inclined to provision themselves by water than by land. It was a two-and-a-half-mile walk to Poros with the hill always on your left, the water on your right. We walked through a good many farm-yards thickly populated with scraggy chickens and turkeys; from every building curs dragged themselves to snap at our heels and bark. The water's edge was befouled with rusting tins, proof of the help sent to a hungry people from another kind of world. We passed the house occupied

356

by Georges Seferiades, a poet usually mentioned with some awe, esteem, and affection by members of the Anglo-Saxon community in Athens, and with the words: "The T. S. Eliot of Greece, you know." The house was excruciatingly ugly, with a Victorian twist to it. It leered down an ornate flight of steps flanked by balustrading made from terra-cotta painted to imitate stone. I wondered that a poet should elect to live in so respectable a place. Beyond the ugly house we walked past a few fishermen's hovels, a family that lived in and on a twenty-foot boat, a tavern called The White Cat, and the naval college, a shapely building, which contrives with the help of a belfry to look like a cross between a palace and the stables of a great establishment. Refreshingly uncommercial boys, who clearly expected no reward, led us to our first objective in the town. The last guide—they acted in relays—left us at an iron gate leading to a yard where some lean chickens, one of them tail-less, scrabbled in the dust between the trunks of orange and tangerine trees. Craxton thundered down an exterior wooden staircase which trembled to his weight, and Lucian Freud followed him diffidently, a heavily-built young man with a habit of carrying his head forward and glancing up through his eyebrows. He wore a football jersey marked with one thick maroon horizontal stripe on an off-white ground, and, below that awesome garment, khaki-drill trousers. They lived as paying-guests with a Greek family. When they had just paid the rent they ate extraordinarily well, but when they were in arrears owing to the difficulty of getting money from England to Greece, the food fell off accordingly. Not that their landlady was mean; on the contrary, she was charming, but when she had spent their rent she had not enough money to buy food. Craxton and Freud worked in two small bedrooms, and these were naturally crowded with the signs and implements of their work. Craxton's was the more untidy of the two rooms. It enjoyed a superb view down the harbour and over the mountain called, from its remarkable outline, The Sleeping Woman. Beside Craxton's bed there hung an unusual set of photographs: one of the strangest showed Freud wearing the football jersey, seated in an armchair and holding in his arms the head of a stuffed zebra; another seemed to represent an actor declaiming, and two more were of young women in expensive and modish clothes. Freud's room, like his painting, was neater, harder, and more self-conscious than Craxton's. I found their work very good, although it was perhaps impudence on my part to judge it at all, and it seemed to me that either might by his work justify his existence. Freud was working on a self-portrait. Only the curly chestnut hair, one enraged eye, a long nose, had been minutely and exquisitely painted.

357

Down in a corner of the canvas the outline of a tall Greek thistle had been pencilled in.

They appeared to be delighted to see us, eager to drown us in impetuous descriptions of Poros and of Greece. Freud (who is indeed a grandson of Sigmund) talked fluently, with a larger vocabulary than the average young Englishman, with more tendency to exclaim and to reiterate, and with only a hint of throat guttural in the r's. Craxton, pleasingly unselfish, was often prepared to listen to his companion. Both of them darted out with us, moving with the impulsive spring of youth, to help Isabel with her shopping. We entered a spice-merchant's shop where there was honey in an earthenware pot; small flies floated in the warm liquid that we turned, tasted, and smelled with the help of a wooden spoon. We descended to the village proper, where she bought white cabbage for salads, tomatoes, leeks, beans, and bread. There seemed to be no white bread for sale—despite the proximity of the naval college, which had British rations,—but the brown bread was good, and the baker, because it was the first time that we had entered his shop, gave each of our party two slices of heavy cake-bread. The shop was lined with old iron ovens, and smelled almost suffocatingly of new bread. I invited the pair to eat with us in a tavern, and managed to override their objections, which were mainly financial. It seemed that this was one of the times when food was a little scarce in their lodgings, and they would have liked to have paid for the meal in the tavern because we were new arrivals. I hoped that they felt inwardly that it was better for me to accept the privilege of paying for the meal, since too often the non-artistic drones of society meanly seek to impede and make uncomfortable the life of any artist, instead of helping—as is no more than their duty—to support the being who contains the creative flame. It was airless in the tavern, where there was a smell of last week's fish and last year's olive oil. We ate in the garden: oyzo, a cannibal fish that had a fore-end like that of a pike and an after-end like that of a mackerel, kidneys, kail and fried potatoes, two carafes of resina. We went to a café to eat chocolate and cakes and drink Turkish coffee made on a primus stove by a man who looked hard and strong enough to have heated the coffee by holding it in his palm and placing the back of his hand over the blue, roaring flame. Isabel, who had eaten no lunch, nibbled at a piece of chocolate. The sweet that they insisted I *must* eat, a small cake covered with ultra-white, powdery sugar, had so revolting a taste and so powerful a reek of rancid goat's milk that I only managed to swallow it out of politeness to Craxton and Freud, who had wolfed theirs with every appearance of great hunger and enjoyment. Having spent most of the morning explaining to us how

358

remarkably satisfying it was for them to be out of England, both began to discuss, on the full bellies of the early afternoon, how best they might return to that country. Craxton thought that he might be able to prevail on some friend in Athens to send him back by air, while Freud had been given the idea that he might return to England by reporting himself to a British consulate as a "Distressed British Subject". I wondered how many of the people who profess to despise artists would have the courage to travel thus, and to live cheerfully, or at least philosophically, in an uncomfortable and precarious manner when it was necessary for their work. Freud had been on board the *Corinthia* when she passed us in the Straits of Messina.´ He had had enough money to pay his outward passage, but none for such luxuries as cabin accommodation and food. His favourite adjective at that time was *won*derful, and while we talked with them we reeled under enfilades of *won*derfuls and deliciouses. Freud had seen *Truant* when we passed from Hydra to Athens, for we had anchored for one night below the windows of their house. "I didn't dare to approach," he said. "For although it was absolutely *won*derful, and didn't look silly like most British yachts, I feared that some purple-faced yachting cap, or some frightful lawyer from London would leap out at me."

A boatman agreed to take us all to *Truant* for 5,000 drachmae. Craxton rowed and then, finding the work exhausting, allowed the boatman to take over. When I went to fill the kettle for tea I found that our fresh water supply was finished. Craxton said that we could get water from his friends the Diamantopoulos. He and I went off in the dinghy with a couple of water-cans. Freud borrowed my swimming trunks and dived into the sea, puffed, swam, and dived again. He was the type of young man who is highly strung, yet who flings himself impetuously at certain types of physica´ discomfort and even danger.

John Craxton and I left the dinghy at a well-built jetty and climbed up a path to the house. Craxton went in past tubs of gardenia plants, and called out: "Mina ! . . Christo ! . . Mina ! . . Christo ! . ."

"Je viens."

An old man, of striking, almost stagey, appearance, came slowly down the polished wooden staircase. Although the evening was warm he clutched a shawl around a pair of shoulders that had once been powerful but that now were bent like those seen in Dürer engravings and in pictures of the Old Man of the Sea. A skull-cap of grey wool sat on his head, and a face that in youth must, I thought, have been dreamy, fiery, mystic, and commanding, now wore an expression of humility and godliness that was set off by a long white beard, which the hand not holding the shawl played with in a constant, fluffing movement.

"Mon ami, Christo Diamantopoulo . . . Mon ami, Georges Millar," Craxton said.

The old man replied in a gentle, sighing voice. He spoke exquisite French, a lavender-scented language, carefully learned from governesses, from good books, and from conversations with persons of education and manners; he had never been to France. He told us that his wife, Mina, was confined to her bed with a carbuncle on the right leg, and at once invited us to her room. Madame Diamantopoulo appeared to be younger than her husband, and plainly she was not used to sitting in bed during the day-time, for she showed by a dozen brusque movements that the position irked her. She spoke equally good English and French, and so talked English to Craxton, whose French was not fluent, but French to me so that her husband might join in part at least of the conversation. All that I noticed of Madame Diamantopoulo on that first brief visit was that she had a dark, almost Turkish face, and I already knew that she came of the great Tombazi family, one of the families that had led the fight from Hydra against the Turks. The old man did not care to leave his wife's bed-side for long; he handed us over to "the domestic", a peasant girl whom he addressed as Nicolette, and Nicolette showed us how to work the semi-rotary pump that drew stored rain-water from the cistern behind the white house.

It was an inspiring sight to see the two artists attacking their tea. All that we could offer them to eat was bread with butter and syrup, but they both weighed in like hungry bull-terriers. They borrowed some books before I put them ashore on the beach. For a long time we heard their voices as they walked to Poros through the black stillness.

* * * *

In the early morning, while the dew still lay white on deck and the black-birds were singing at the end of the cove, I buoyed our stern chains, and we crossed the shining water to the Tombazi estate. The fresh water pipe was supported by jagged steel uprights, and had *Truant* drawn three inches more water we should not have been able to get her alongside it. Two boys helped us; one of them went into the bushes to turn on the water. We managed to wedge the metal endpiece of our canvas hose into the wide mouth of the water pipe. The water rushed below at great speed, and the boys could not understand where all of it was going. One of them carried a large trident or *fouine* for spearing fish, and we allowed him to borrow the dinghy, while we went ashore with his friend. Small farms clustered round the stone Tombazi house, which was empty because the owner, a cousin of

Madame Diamantopoulo, worked in the London office of a Greek firm. The grey house stands down by the water, really in the water, for the waves lap at the walls themselves, and people say that when the family are in residence you will often see a fishing-rod or two sticking out of the windows.

"Grapefruit!" Isabel called.

I hurried round the house. The boy had found a large basket and he and Isabel were filling it with grapefruit, oranges and green and red peppers. Two men appeared and invited us to visit the olive oil press. The Tombazi oil is renowned and on the door of the stone building were French certificates of médailles d'or won in Lyons and Paris. A motor chugged somewhere in the background, stone wheels turned on each other, stirring and grinding to powder a mess of black skins. In another corner of the "factory" two men turned the lever of a press, grunting with the effort they put into squeezing the warm oil through a giant concertina of dark felt. We sailed about the harbour a little when we left the water-pipe, but Isabel was becoming so attached to our cove that she had a quite illogical fear that some other boat would anchor there in our absence. Whenever we were anchored and had swung round our stern to the land I saw her eating a grapefruit.

"You shouldn't eat grapefruit."

"It will cure me."

"How do you know?"

"I just have a feeling."

"Well, don't overdo it. They're very acid things. Perhaps they'll make you worse."

She ate another and another, and another.

"Wonderful," she said. "We must pick some more to-morrow."

"Do you feel all right?"

"Better already. How could they do me any harm when I like them so much?"

The following day she was glad to announce herself thoroughly cured. Madame Diamantopoulo did not stay long in bed, and when she was able to get up they insisted that we should visit their house. They were amazingly polite.

"I do hope," Madame Diamantopoulo said, "that our house does not annoy you too much, for I fear that it disturbs the detachment of your anchorage."

"We must apologise for putting our boat there, since we see from the way that you have placed your house and surrounded it with trees that you deliberately chose seclusion."

"We chose seclusion to avoid persons whom we did not care to meet, and to enjoy in peace the company of persons like yourself and your husband." We took tea in their library, a room lined with tomes in five languages, and enjoying a splendid view down the lake to the town (it must be remembered that Poros, unlike most towns, would be a welcome adjunct to any view). There were home-made doughnuts for tea. Christo was dressed as when I had first seen him. He chatted amiably about one thing or another; how had we come to Greece in "that cockleshell"? God had undoubtedly protected us, for our arrival was almost a miracle; everything in life was amazing: his cat, his jasmine flowers, his cypress and pine trees, the hens, the bay, his son, the blackbirds that they fed on bread inside the library—and sought to protect from the hawks—and now our arrival must be entered as the most wonderful surprise of them all. He took me into the tiled hall where his wife sometimes wove cloth on a large and severely decorative hand-loom, and showed me pictures and china. I judged from his manner of showing them that he did not care for the pictures, although there were some very fine ones, but that he cared passionately for china, with its glazed surface, its usefulness, its geometric patterns and glistening colours. He showed me a book of his own sonnets, beautifully printed in Athens, and to me of course entirely incomprehensible.

"One of these days, when I shall know you a little better, I shall essay a translation in French," he said. "I could not translate to you yet, for they are poems that come from the heart."

He soon asked me if I believed in God. He was greatly put out by my reply, cast down his large eyes, and agreed sadly that belief could not come to a man who sought it through reason; belief in God must come through the heart, and not the brain. He told me, in the cool hall with all the shutters closed and rattan blinds drawn so that we stood in a crepuscular glow, that he was subject to visions, and that there was some writer in London with whom he would correspond in order to have his visions tabulated. It was very difficult, I would appreciate, for him to speak of his visions, but he would give me an instance of a "minor occurrence": he was passing on foot through a great, empty square in Athens during the German-Italian occupation of Greece and when all was going badly for the Anglo-Saxons; on his right stood a great, pale building with three flag-poles angled out from the façade; as he looked at the bare poles he saw flags grow on them and wave splendidly in the breeze and the sunshine, the Union Jack on one, the Stars and Stripes on another, and the Greek flag on the third; he forgot the purchases that he had come out to make, and hurried home to tell Mina what he had seen.

For all that Christo dominated the conversation that first day, it was plain to us that the household revolved around Mina, a no less saintly but a more practical character. Both of them had seen a good deal of the world before Christo retired at the age of forty to build the white house on Poros. Mina had been much abroad before she married, particularly in Russia, when her father was Greek Ambassador at the court of the Czar.

"It was a serious thing for me to retire," Christo said. "For I had the responsibility of carrying on a business founded by my great-grandfather, a house which still flourished, which had always been honourable, and which was a part of the life of Athens and of Greece. But it was only when I had sold it and withdrawn from commerce to a life of contemplation here that I began to live." Their only son was studying psychology and had been called to Oxford University. He wrote home that Oxford was cold, damp, and grey.

As we were leaving the old man filled Isabel's cupped hands with white, spiky jasmine flowers scented so hauntingly that the next morning when I thrust my head out into the pure air of the cove I still smelled them.

*   *   *   *

Until we reached Poros we had found the dinghy larger than was necessary, and too much of a handful to lift and stow on board. But it came into its own at Poros, for we sailed in it a great deal, since there is usually some wind in that magnificent harbour. Were it situated in England, America, or Sweden, the harbour would be covered with small boats of racing design, and surrounded by the bungalows, houses, and clubs of yachting enthusiasts: then the Diamantopoulos would not have settled there, and nor would we.

We sailed to Poros one day to lunch with the two artists. Craxton gave us Canadian whisky in his bedroom. He had been writing a letter to a friend in England, and it was difficult to avoid reading it for it was written in characters one inch high on a blood-coloured piece of paper measuring three feet by two. One sentence dealt with us, and pronounced us "charming" but "very English". We felt flattered and surprised that such praise and opprobrium—for "very English" in Craxton's vocabulary denoted sharp criticism should be piled on us. We wondered whether he had a huge, blood-coloured envelope, or whether he would make a parcel of his letter. The Greek family sat with us around the table, but they were like moving waxworks, only eating and smiling, while we jabbered in our own language. The food was excellent: aubergines, peppers, and vine leaves stuffed with rice and mysterious but satisfying elements; fried octopus and

363

fishes, tangerines, and coffee. It was a fine evening when we left Craxton and Freud on the quay and sailed back to *Truant*, the dinghy swishing across the smooth water. But the barograph had registered a sudden drop.

A terrible night followed. A sirocco entered our cove from the southeast and shook *Truant* until the whole boat trembled and groaned. With but one anchor out ahead we were inclined to swing dangerously, and the kedge aft dragged into deeper water before it took hold in clay, but in the darkness I could not tell that it was holding, and I was worried by the slack in the chain. When morning came at last, the wind veered to the southwest and if anything strengthened, although the point of the Diamantopoulo property gave us a little shelter. Isabel and I took a line from the starboard bow to the Diamantopoulos' jetty, which was fitted with iron mooring rings; we used a coil of one-and-a-half-inch rope which had only been once used before (by Douglas Hawkes when the mistral caught us in Monte Carlo harbour).

We had invited Freud to lunch, thinking that he would be lonely that day because Craxton was supposed to travel by caique to Athens for an exhibition of his work. The bad weather had prevented Craxton from leaving, but he remained in Poros making sketches in court of a youth who was defending himself against charges of stealing sixty-three pumpkins from a blind man. After lunch Freud went ashore in the dinghy to sketch *Truant*. The dinghy reeled beneath him, not because he was excessively clumsy, but because all his movements seemed to be conceived in such a violent hurry that one began before its predecessor had properly stopped. He explained that for a time during the war he had been a seaman in the merchant navy; when he joined his ship the mate assured him: "This trip will be the making of you, my lad. You can't tie a clove hitch yet, but when you get back to England you will be a *man*." Freud said that when he returned to England he still could not tie a clove hitch, and if he had been made into a man, they did not remember to mention the fact. He had a habit of carrying his drawing materials in the bosom of his shirt, so that he was often thrusting in a hand to claw about his paps or navel, twisting and grimacing in the effort to find a pen, a small bottle of Indian ink, or a drawing block. He had another, equally disconcerting habit of glaring at you, and then looking swiftly down in sudden shyness. There were signs of greatness in him, and I wish that I had been as brave as he at the age of twenty-three.

The Diamantopoulos came to tea, Christo well wrapped up against the wind. He was beginning to address me as "cher ami" and "cher collègue". Tea ran into drinks and it was dark when I set them ashore at their jetty.

Christo had borrowed two books from our library; Georges Bernanos's *Journal d'un Curé de Campagne* and Baudelaire's *Les Paradis Artificiels de Vin et du Haschisch*. I was a little worried about the second choice, believing, rightly, that Christo would both admire and detest it, since he was not likely to appreciate dissertations on the delights of hashish and opium, but was sensible enough to relish the exquisite prose in which they were written. Then Freud had to be landed at the head of the cove, where he spent some time hunting for his drawing materials, which, for some obscure reason, he had hidden in the bushes.

The wind blew hard all that night and the next day, but the day after was calm and hot, the blackbirds sang at the end of the cove, and our white ropes looked puerile stretched out to the land. I hastily took them in and started the engines. We attached a line to the stern chains and threw them overboard. We hauled in the forward chain until the anchor was underfoot. It had bitten so firmly that we had difficulty in getting it clear. We moved across the cove, turning to starboard, dropped the original anchor, then back to port and dropped the other. We hauled astern until we picked up the stern chains, and so rode securely to a V of chain forward and a V aft. That day we sailed to Poros in the dinghy, anchoring the small boat with the tiny bronze C.Q.R. on a length of heaving line, so that it would not bump against the quay. We were attending to this when we were interrupted by a whistle from *Poppy*, a yacht-like steamer, black-hulled with a tall, yellow funnel, a straight stem and a waspish counter, the whole giving the impression that *Poppy* was a ship that leaned back comfortably on the sea, like an elderly gentleman relaxing in a leather armchair. On this occasion, though, *Poppy* was put out because we had moored our dinghy opposite that part of the quay where she always makes fast. Nothing would satisfy her but that we move, which we made haste to do, for she seemed to be in some danger of turning over as her passengers, incensed by the delay, ran from one side to the other, listing her with their combined weight. I bought a slab of chocolate for the equivalent of eight shillings to give to Isabel the following day, her Saint's Day; I had a fierce argument with Freud over a modern house which he liked, but which, by reason of its clumsy fenestration, looked to me like a cleft palate; and I went to the barber, who spoke French.

He sat me in the single rush-bottomed chair before a cracked wall mirror, and offered me a Greek cigarette before he began to explore the forests of my hair, wondering at which avenue to begin felling. A few tattered pictures pinned to the walls depicted either Alexandria or Algiers, I could not make up my mind which, and scowling at me from behind the door was the same ferocious portrait of Mr. Attlee that we had seen in the Hydra office for fostering Anglo-Greek relations. The barber brought out his sad story as he clipped. He had been sous-directeur in a hairdressing establishment in Alexandria, where he had been earning finally £80 to £90 each month.

I complimented him on his hair-cutting. He had a deft and expensive touch.

"Ah! I can cut, I can cut," he answered. "I was the King's barber in Egypt, and I knew Alexandria when it was but a village. I grew up with Alexandria, so to speak, and now my heart is sore for Alexandria. Cursed whim that entered our heads in 1938 when my wife and I decided that we had earned a long holiday! Most of our family was gathered around us in Alexandria, but we had a son, married, with one child, who remained in Athens. We travelled from Alexandria—there was a crowd on the dock to wave us good-bye—and came to Athens. We heard rumours of war, but we were happy in Athens and we paid no attention to them. The war came, and I went to the Egyptian Consul. He said that there was no hope of visas to return to Alexandria. 'But, Monsieur le Consul,' I said, 'wait until you hear the circumstances. I cut the King's hair in Egypt.' And he answered: 'You lie, for it is an Italian who cuts the hair of His Majesty.' That was no time to get angry. 'I speak the truth,' I told him. 'An Italian cut the hair of the King's father, everyone knows that. But I have cut the hair of King Farouk since he was a whipper-snapper.' 'His Majesty was never a whipper-snapper, there is no such word where kings are concerned.' 'Oh, Monsieur le Consul, I know that my French is poor, but please let me return to my family and my business. There in Alexandria I am a wealthy man with scores of friends. Here, I am nobody, I have no background, there are millions like me. My money is running out, and my son is not rich since he has heavy expenses . . .' All to no avail. That consul would do nothing for me. I had to suffer the war, the occupation, the liberation, and then the trouble between the Communists and the others. Now I shall never go back to Alexandria. I am finished; it is the will of God. Now I cannot even afford to live in some Athenian slum. Then, I used to rather look down on le Caire. I used to go there once a week to cut the King. I would take a morning train there, and an afternoon train back to Alexandria. The King was a real gentleman. I can say no fairer than that, can I? I never seemed to care for le Caire. Alexandria was originally a Greek settlement, as you doubtless know, monsieur, and it is a town of European settlements and European culture. Le Caire is full of Arabs; I have nothing against the Arab, mind you; he is foreign to me, that is all.

366

His quick-wittedness is something to bargain with. And now I hear that things are not going so well in Egypt. The Arab is beginning to catch xenophobia, a very stupid disease. Nothing does more for a country than great settlements of foreigners, provided, of course, that the settlements do not rule the country . . ."

I often returned to his squalid shop, seeking excuses to drink at the fountain of his nostalgia for Egypt. He was a small man, very erect, with a bad cough and signs of under-nourishment on neck and chin.

*　　*　　*　　*

A white boat was rowed out from the Diamantopoulo jetty early in the morning. A hired boatman was at the oars. In the easier days before the war Christo had owned a boat and had employed his own batelier, who had also looked after the hens and done some of the heavier work around the house, and who had occupied with his wife the small cottage in the upper corner of the garden. Now only a rich man could afford to feed himself and his wife, let alone a family of servants. It was better when a boat was needed to hire one from Poros. Mina sat in the stern beside Christo. She was a somewhat sombre figure, all in black, and hatless in the hot sunlight, for although she had been in bed when I first met her, she is as hardy as a mountain goat, and relishes the sun and the wind, and even, if she can get enough to eat, the snow. Christo was a stiffly poetical figure. I would like to have had Seurat include him in *Un dimanche d'Été à la Grande Jatte*. He wore a floppy tweed hat and his beard was bent over the frogged velvet collar of a magnificent blue cloak which flowed from his shoulders to somewhere below his knees. All that was visible of the rest of the poet was dressed in white linen trousers, white socks and blue espadrilles. He raised one long hand in courtly greeting as they approached; his other hand carefully gripped the handle of a small round basket. In the bows sat a strange and dismal figure, the face wrapped up like that of a Berber woman and the eyes large with fear. This was Nicolette, the maid. Occasionally a lusty sigh would escape from behind the veil or wrapping. The old man handed me the basket. He had prepared a foundation of green leaves, jasmine, and other flowers, and had laid thereon two eggs, the first that their chickens had laid for some weeks, and a tumbler containing home-made quince jam. Madame Diamantopoulo told us that Nicolette was going to the dentist in Poros. The night before, Christo had held aside his beard, and peering into the girl's mouth had announced that one of her teeth must be removed. Nicolette had cried out: "I won't go to the tooth-doctor; I won't go, unless Madame Mina goes." And Mina said sooth-

367

ingly: "Of course I will accompany you, dear Nicolette, so long as you don't expect me to have a tooth out too." At the end of the morning when they returned, Nicolette was laughing and talking to the boatman. They brought us gifts of fruit; unfortunately Isabel, who dislikes hoarding, had been looking at the vast store of tins that we still carried and had put out an assortment to give to the Diamantopoulos. Christo became pink with vexation, and told us that we had no right to return a gift with a gift. Isabel began to throw tins into their boat, but the poet rejected them with passionate gestures, and several fell to the bottom of the sea. I had to dive in and recover them while Christo exclaimed over and over again: "You will do yourself an injury, mon pauvre ami, I shall never forgive myself for this, never, never. It was my lack of generosity of spirit that was responsible for this. Ah, God! Let there be an end to this insensate swimming! It is the 21st of November and the water is cold . . ." For all that, the thermometer in the wheelhouse registered seventy-five (F.). We ate on deck, and afterwards I settled to work there, but was distracted by the carnage plainly visible in the water. Millions of whitebait swam in clouds around us, and it seemed that the clouds were controlled by electricity, for at any hint of danger or perhaps of some food invisible to me, each unit in the cloud, like a magnetised iron filing, would turn almost quicker than the eye could follow to face in the same direction as all other units. Hunting in packs around and among the clouds of whitebait were prominent-eyed fishes, stoutly-built brutes some three to four inches long. The eyes stared from pointed heads, and they had shapely tails which flickered as they swam. The hunting packs always sought to cut off a single whitebait or a small group from a cloud. But this seldom happened, and often they would merely dart in arrowhead formation straight into the middle of a cloud, each attacker swinging round in a semi-circle with slashing teeth, but apparently blinded by his own speed. It was seldom that they had any victim, for the whitebait reacted with marvellous speed and were able to jump clean out of the water as the enemy's jaws were about to close around them, but if one poor little wounded whitebait jerked near the surface, the ugly fish would quickly tear it to pieces. Much less gruesome were fishes which lived normally in the lower strata near the sand, rose-coloured, square-shaped fishes each with an easily distinguishable brown dot where the body narrowed before the tail. They neither feared nor were feared by the whitebait or the prominent-eyed assassins. And the dot-tails seemed to have a great liking for any cabbage salad that Isabel threw overboard.

*   *   *   *

"Georges!"

"Ah, bonjour Christo."

"Bonjour cher ami . . . Venez, venez . . . Nous avons des oeufs et d'autres choses pour vous . . ." His voice came slowly across the water. He stood, both hands forming a mouth trumpet, at the corner of their property in a small rectangular structure with walls some three feet high that jutted from a leafy edge of the cove. "You must not walk barefoot," he reproved me as we landed. "If I were to walk like that I should have grippe in five minutes. Mina is on the terrace, and she has made coffee for you. Come." Mina was preparing a speech that she was to deliver that evening to the young women of Poros.

"What are you telling them?"

"I'm going to say that the young women of to-day have less sense of modesty and of responsibility than their mothers had at that age . . ."

"That's exactly what they'll expect you to say. You should put it the other way round. Tell them that they're better than their mothers. Then they'll strive for a little to be well-behaved."

Mina looked at me patiently. "That wouldn't be the truth," she said. "I must tell them the truth."

"As it appears to you."

"The actual truth."

Both Mina and Christo, I learned, were people who were apt to shy at evil like mettlesome horses which, on encountering a steam-roller, are upset no matter how wide the road. But while Christo was saddened by any glimpse of sin, Mina, who really disapproved of it more fiercely, was apt to have a fit of the giggles before she took offensive measures against it. They loaded us with gifts, as usual, and took us to the place from which Christo had hailed me. "It is my chapel," he said. "But we had only got the walls to window-level when the war came, and now it is difficult to see when we shall be able to finish it. I shall be greatly comforted when I can come here morning and evening to pray. My one sorrow in withdrawing myself to this house has been that, with my poor health, I am unable to visit places of worship."

Freud hailed us from the shore as we were finishing lunch. I rowed off to him in the dinghy, and as I ran the boat on to the sand he produced a live chicken from behind his back. He was holding the bird upside down and I saw that its legs were tied with yellow ribbon. He had heard Isabel say that she liked to eat roast chicken. (We learned later, though not from Freud, that he had sold a pair of his trousers to pay for the fowl.) I told him that if she saw the chicken alive she would not consent to eat it.

369

"How does one kill the things?"

"People wring their necks."

He instantly pulled at the fowl's neck so hard that the head came off in his hand. I sat on the shore and plucked and cleaned the bird while he, after the usual wriggles and grimaces, drew drawing materials from his bosom and set to work.

The following day he came back to help us to eat his splendid gift, and in the evening he said that he would like to introduce us to the poet, Georges Seferiades. We walked along the shore to the ugly house, opposite which a few rusty old tugs and launches were moored. These belonged to the gang of enthusiastic, wild, and noisy tramps who were striving to raise the remains of Antoine Benaki's magnificent yacht, a three-masted schooner built in England by Camper and Nicholson, which had been sunk there by German dive-bombers. The local story had it that Benaki, with a typically munificent gesture, had given to his cook the legal rights to the remains of the yacht, and the cook, having been advised that the lead keel would be well worth salving, had commissioned the tramps on the rusty tugs to do the work. They worked with occasional rowdy relapses which disturbed the contemplative surroundings of the poet Seferiades. All of their equipment was in wretched condition, and as fast as they pumped air into the steel caissons designed to lift the wreck, the air bubbled out of leaks in the caissons.

Freud banged on all the doors and windows while we stood shyly before the house, which might have been one of a row placed in Colwyn Bay or Eastbourne. At length, in response to the thunderous knocking, the poet thrust a tousled head over the edge of a balcony. He gave the appearance of being ready to be very outspoken with Freud until he saw both of us, and his natural and celebrated good manners asserted themselves. He admitted that he had been having a siesta.

We sat down in a room with a fireplace of fumed wood, the overmantel holding an aquatint of Greek nymphs, Victorian style, 180-pounders. Seferiades was a stoutish man rather awkwardly built, a good talker. He was inclined to feel his way politely with us, and he was shocked that we howled with laughter when he informed us that he had always called the wartime "B.L.O.'s" (British liaison officers) in Greece "Byrons". Isabel suggested that had they all been Byrons it might have been the worse for Greece and the better for Britain. He came down to the shore with us when we left, and Isabel showed him the kingfisher, perched as usual on a rock beside the pathway and within a few yards of the hulks occupied by the salvage crew. Seferiades broke into a run, skipping grotesquely over the uneven ground ahead of us. The bird watched him approach and then darted out over the water in a blue flash, swinging round to land behind us.

The following evening Seferiades and his wife came to our cove. They stayed for a long time on board, Georges drinking whisky and his decorative wife Cinzano. He speaks good English as well as French, and he has translated Eliot into Greek. He lay back on the settee, smoking insatiably, talking sensitively, and I wondered that good poetry could issue from a man with such fleshy hams and thighs.

The next day we lunched with the Seferiades and with the part-owner of the house where they were staying on holiday, an artist called Dragoumis. Dragoumis had rather a military air about him. He spoke utterly perfect English in a restrained voice. During the rest of our stay at Poros we were frequently to see him either walking by the edge of the sea, a haversack slung over one shoulder and a heavy stick in one hand, or standing staring fixedly across the water at some aspect of the hills that had caught his fancy. He was either a very happy or a very unhappy man, but although we both liked him he was so politely aloof that we had no means of ascertaining whether or not we might be of use to him. When we left the red Victorian house we sailed to Poros, where I arranged with a little man whom we called Punch because of his head, shaped in profile like a Turkish crescent, for a mechanic to visit *Truant*. Punch had been to America, had lived there for more than twenty years, and had brought back to Greece an all-embracing good humour, a few words of English and, it seemed, little else. He sold vegetables and some fruit, tinned salmon, and tinned milk. Punch was an elderly man, but he had taken a great fancy to Isabel. Frequently when I saw him he would say: "You'll prahsper, mister; your woman's got lucky eyes."

We had been long enough in Greece to know that most people there charge too much for most things, and I was inclined to think that the mechanic's demands might be high even for Greece when I saw him arrive the following morning in a white boat driven by a very old outboard motor with two cylinders trembling from the casing like hanging warts. The mechanic managed to convey to me by repeating a few words of Greek, Italian, French, and English, that he had worked on Benaki's yacht, and had been a friend of Spiro, the steward. He was a thin man in pale-blue overalls. He brought no equipment with him, and had to return to Poros to make a tool to dismount the dynamo; but he was a good mechanic. I spent most of the morning with him, as our batteries were desperately low, and the dynamo was assuming a role of crucial importance since our

371

auxiliary oil lighting scarcely gave us enough light to read in the long evenings. We found a roughness on the shaft of the dynamo which was responsible for the grating noise that had worried me. I was pleased with the mechanic, and made up my mind that 20,000 drachmae would be a most liberal payment for his work. While he worked, his son had been trolling up and down the harbour, using the outboard engine, and had caught four extremely large fish of the pike-cum-mackerel variety; the mechanic was delighted, since such fish fetched high prices. I looked forward to increasing his pleasure with my generous payment, but when I foolishly inquired how much he wanted, he asked for 30,000 drachmae. I paid him sourly, and both of us were angry at his extortion. Freud came aboard in time to hear some of our remarks. He told us, sensibly, that our anger was ridiculous; it was the habit in Greece for a workman to ask for double the payment that he expected to receive; instead of paying what was asked and bearing a grudge, we should beat down the price and then pay cheerfully. But for some reason we were both incapable of such behaviour.

Christo had been ca-ca-calling us all afternoon across the water, so we took Freud there for tea. Freud and Christo jarred on each other.

"Mon cher ami, the mechanic must have liked you or he would have charged you double the amount," Christo said soothingly.

"Nonsense," Freud said. "He thought George a fool for paying and a clod for paying with evil grace."

"I assure you that what I say is the truth," Christo snapped at him, and his left hand, instead of fluffing the beard, gave it an angry tug.

There was a tremendous spread for tea, with white bread, doughnuts, and real butter made from the milk of the only cow within a radius of twenty miles, a precious animal that ate from a square of artificially inseminated and stimulated grass on one of the Tombazi farms. Freud, I was glad to see, allowed his appetite free rein. We were discussing Paris, when I made a most unfortunate remark: Freud had then only once visited Paris (on his way to Greece) but he had naturally been deeply impressed by the place, and he was talking of a small square across the river from Nôtre Dame. "You mean the square with the English tea-room in it?" I asked, and he replied with a long, sardonic smile which said plainly: "English tea-room!" I saw Isabel pick up the smile and store it away. We boarded our dinghy in the dark. Freud would have liked to have come with us for the company and the comfort on the boat, but when he said: "Perhaps you are tired, and want to go to bed," Isabel answered: "Well, yes," and he went off alone through the trees, crashing into them in the darkness.

For two nights and three days I fought for the life of the batteries, getting the most loyal support from the charging motor, which phutted steadily on, pumping its steady seven amps into them. At the end of that time the hydrometer told me that all was well, but we used so much light at Poros that I was obliged to run the engine every second day, or every time that we left the boat. Isabel never liked the charging motor, but I became extremely attached to it; I lost all my original fear of it, and came to gauge its little popping exhaust note so well that I knew exactly how it was feeling, and whether its feed was too poor, too dirty or too rich. I tried to remember to run the two big engines once a week to keep them supple, and to see that they were ready in case of emergency.

*　　*　　*　　*

Two men and two scrawny dogs walked slowly along the path that circled our cove. There was a report and a bird fell from a tree. We watched them pick it up. It was a blackbird. I would have liked to have shot the men. That was the last day of November. From that day on we had no more singing round the cove. Mina Diamantopoulo had heard the shot. She ran down to the chapel to ask us what it meant. We had heard that a guerilla band was operating in the mountains behind the Tombazi estate, and although we were in small danger even if they thought *Truant* worth attacking, because they were unlikely to come to an island which had so strong a force on it as that represented by the staff of the naval college plus the police in Poros, they could have sent a few riflemen down to the shore near Tombazi whence, without danger to themselves, they could have had some nice target practise on *Truant*, which would probably have given them the satisfaction of exploding. To be exactly truthful, this idea worried the Diamantopoulos much more (on our account) than it did us. When I told Mina about the murder of the blackbird she ran angrily out of the gate and along the path, but after a time she came back, accompanied by a younger woman, a robust peasant with bare feet, a wide skirt, and a towering neck; Mina told us that she had not been able to trace the hunters. "This is your washerwoman," she said, "and you must be very gentle with her." We bundled our dirty linen into the dinghy and went ashore. The peasant woman was padding about under the trees collecting wood to light a fire beneath the cauldron in which she would boil the linen. "She is a sad young woman," Mina said. "Her husband discovered that he was a leper when they had only been married seven months. She was still in love with him, and also she was terrified that she would develop the disease. They took him away to a leper colony. The woman nearly lost her reason. She could live no longer in her own village. She moved up to a lonely house in the hills. I asked her to do your laundry because I wanted to help her to make a little money. She said she would do it, but she never came. This morning I met her on the road. She'd brought tangerines to sell to the lower farm. 'Why haven't you come to wash the English couple's linen?' I asked. 'Couple?' she answered. 'I didn't know there was a wife. You only said British people and I thought you meant soldiers, men. I never want to have anything to do with men.' "

"Will she be allowed to marry again?"

"If her husband dies. But I don't think she'll ever marry." The woman came past carrying a cleverly-tied faggot of small and large branches. She smiled at Isabel, but did not look at me. Christo hailed us from the window of his bathroom. "I am washing some underclothing," he called. "The things that we have to do nowadays! and yet somehow I get pleasure from doing them. Do you know, last winter, before we got Nicolette, Mina was kept busy with her good works at the Poros orphanage, and I cooked for myself. I cooked soup, and beans, once or twice a stew, and once a risotto—risotto à la Milanaise. But wait there, I must come down and show you our hens." He had housed the hens in a building with large windows and a southern exposure for he believed that given plenty of shade and sunlight and a pleasant outlook they would lay well. Great affection was lavished upon the fowls, and they were fed with grain from a sack bought at enormous expense. It must be admitted that they repaid these attentions but grudgingly with eggs, and almost all such payments were given to us, despite our protests. There was one hen, "la Blonde", to which Christo was greatly attached. She was the leader of the hen-house. "Do you know what hens do when one of their number is sick?" he asked me.

"They turn on the sick comrade and persecute it."

"Correct. Just as all men would do, if there were no God." He glanced at me slyly, to see if I would accept the challenge. He was looking pale and fragile, and his lovely grey beard hung loose in the damp morning air, but I could not humour him, for we had to hurry away to Poros.

Among the four or five persons who worked at that time in the Poros Post Office was a man of high intelligence whom we called Long Nose for the obvious reason that his nose would have made three of any of the other noses in the office, which all tended more to the classical shape. None of the staff, including Long Nose, could speak any language but Greek, and if he was not there when Isabel arrived to despatch our heavy mail—we were posting off Christmas cards at the time—one of the other men would go in

374

search of him. Somehow, with gesture and careful pronunciation in English and Spanish of the more complicated names, Isabel always managed to explain to him the rough location of San Sebastian, Transjordan, British Somaliland, Eire, and other places. Postage from Greece was expensive, and generally the week's mail cost us far more than food, but to make up for the expense the stamps were phenomenally attractive and varied, and it was possible to buy very pretty air-mail envelopes, white, picked out in blue, and made of fragile, smoky paper and indifferent glue. The post office was a dull place for me, since the customer's aspect of it was only a dusty, whitewashed corridor with a guichet at one end of it and a shelf to write telegrams. This was evidence of poor psychology in the Greek postal service, for how can the employees take an interest in their work if they only see the customers' mouths and their mail? Of course, the public services in Greece are hampered by the climate. In England the weather forces most people to hook themselves on to security through employment, and it is pleasant for the girl employees to enter a well-heated post office on a November morning; in Poros in November the men employees sat in their shirt sleeves eating nougat which they could not afford on their salaries; and they liked to wander out on to the balcony to gaze sleepily into the sunlit street. They looked over the waterfront of Poros. The entrance to the post office was from a lane behind, only six feet in width, where hens and turkeys pecked for invisible scraps of food. Those birds were emaciated to the point of death, especially the turkeys, which often stood, as though petrified, on single legs, a position which allowed a bird to rest one weary foot. There is no sign over the door of the post office, but a pale-blue letter-box is fixed to the wall beside the door, and that is sign enough. On the door there is a dulled-brass knocker in the shape of a human hand, a common shape in Greece, and I could never make up my mind whether I liked it or found it obscene. Why was there a knocker? If the post office happened to be shut you knocked. Sooner or later a neighbour would poke his or her head from a window opening to the lane and would tell you that the post office would be open at three o'clock.

That day we began the practice of buying white bread from Sophia, who has a small shop opposite the naval college. The shop was full of sick cats, and an ill-tempered old dog growled each time that you spoke to his mistress. Madame Diamantopoulo had told Sophia to sell us white bread, but before she would do so there had to be elaborate explanations on our side, for Sophia, who appeared to be a little deaf, had not understood Madame Diamantopoulo, but had been too shy at the time to say so. She wanted to know where we lived and whence we came. Isabel drew the Diamantopoulo house, the cove, and a small ship, representing *Truant*. Sophia shook her head helplessly and offered us the fish that she was frying over a primus stove. Isabel drew a fish, scratched it out vigorously, and drew a loaf of bread. In the end reason prevailed, and Sophia produced from behind the counter a white loaf that she had bought from a sailor and for which she charged the then reasonable price of 2,800 drachmae (approximately two shillings and tenpence). We also bought a large tin of fine Italian marmalade, which came from the same source. The sailors exchanged such rations whenever possible for olive oil and rice.

That night the rain came and the following day *Truant* was battered by wind coming in tremendous gusts from the north, astern, and hurling sheets of water with rain-drops that rattled like dried beans. The atmosphere was damp below decks, but there were no important leaks. Georges Seferiades rowed himself to us during a lull in the bad weather. He had come to say good-bye. He and his wife were leaving for Athens the following day. His holiday in Poros was over, and he was desperately sad. "Not that I dislike Athens," he said. "But I love this place, and every now and then I must get away from Athens to some quiet place, here or Ægina for example, and rest two months. In those quiet periods, which are all too few, for I must work to support my family, I clean myself. The rest and contemplation wash away the bad things that have clogged my mind in the city." He drank plain gin, a habit that he had picked up from our Royal Navy. No sooner had his ill-propelled boat disappeared round one of our sheltering points than Isabel, looking from a porthole, gave warning of a boat approaching from the opposite direction. I began to work my typewriter noisily but soon we heard oars and the familiar soft bump, and for the first time we met Admiral N. Leondopoulo (retd.) of the Royal Hellenic Navy. A small, wrinkled man, he wore a round waterproof cap of Chinese aspect, a British battledress blouse with a white scarf at the throat, trousers of pale khaki linen, and black shoes. He presented a very clean and compact appearance, and he was quickly at home with us. I gave him a glass of French brandy, knowing, from the talk of mutual acquaintances, that good brandy was his favourite drink. It would be impossible to guess the age of so active and so methodical a man, but we supposed that the Admiral must be advanced in years for we got the impression that he had retired from the navy twenty years previously, when he had built the bungalow on the point beyond that occupied by the Diamantopoulo property. He told us that he had lived the last ten years entirely in the

376

bungalow. "And I'll finish it out there. I had an old sailor servant who knew my ways, but he died during the war and I found it easy to carry on alone. I've plenty to do, and it suits me to be alone. I walk into Poros for the single loaf that lasts me one week. The fishermen sell me fish when I need it. For the rest, my favourite food is the white cabbage cut in strips with number-one-quality olive oil on it, pepper and salt, and a little lemon. I have relations in Athens who are most helpful. My brother sends me anything I need. I'm better off than any king. I'm interested in the weather and in the marine life at the bottom of the sea; I read; I keep my health; and I see everything that happens in Poros harbour. This brandy is delightful. I appreciate it because I was trained in France—as a constructional engineer—and later I spent three years superintending the building of Greek submarines at Chalon-sur-Saône." He had worked in London, and had been to New York, as well as travelling in ships all over the world. "Did you ever see a place to equal this?" he asked.

"No."

"You must come to my house, and you will understand how perfect life can be alone. I'll give you a bottle of number-one-quality olive oil when you come." The only sign that he lived away from people was his habit of casting down his eyes while he spoke. His hands were freckled, and were strongly padded with living muscle. He moved off the boat with the agility of a boy.

The rain stopped on December 4th, and I came up for breath after prolonged spells of work and interludes of reading the works of François Mauriac, all of which I had been fortunate enough to acquire at the best bookshop I had seen in post-war Europe, Kauffman's in Athens. We walked to Poros. The shops were shut because some religious festival was being celebrated, and a long black procession led by bearded priests, boy scouts, and the brass band of the naval college, was winding through the streets, stopping at certain points to allow the priests to perform rites the significance of which we could not even guess at. Sophia let us into her little shop, and sold us two loaves of white bread, some leeks, and a bottle of oyzo. I packed the goods in my big rucksack, which at Poros was again proving its usefulness. All the people were in Sunday clothes. The hotel at Poros is reputed to be very superior. Gold letters on a black marble plaque beside the entrance claim that English is spoken. We went in, thinking that we might eat there, but I recoiled before the basket chairs in the hall, which were of such a sinister "modern" design that I could go no farther. My friend King Farouk's ex-barber set chairs for us in the sunshine at the door of his shop, and brought us cups of coffee. The

377

procession halted before us, and the priests intoned beside the memorial to a former war while one third of their followers turned dreamy eyes on us. Dragoumis stood a little distance away from the crowd, his haversack over one shoulder, his heavy walking-stick in one hand, a felt hat on the back of his head. He had his back turned to the ceremony and he stared across the water to the hills of the Morea. His face looked as empty as the pale sky, a sky that had been soaked and then wrung out and hung up to dry.

Poppy, the black steamer with the yellow funnel, came in, heeling spectacularly as the passengers rushed to one side of the deck. The procession moved away to fizzle out in a church, as though that building were a giant emotion-snuffer. All the taverns and a few of the shops opened and the men began to discard hats and ties.

Poros's meat-and-fish market is a space some forty feet by twenty, surrounded by a plain, low arcade and with an entrance in the middle of each of the long sides. The fishes and octopuses for sale are displayed on stone slabs set in the rectangle, and the butchers' booths are dark lairs below the arches, while carcasses hang on hooks around, offering their poor, mangled viscera to the air, as though obeying the law of the East, flies first. A morbid allure, which had something, no doubt, to do with the shortage of meat in our diet, drew me to the arcaded courtyard on most of our visits to the town. This was to be the last time that we set foot in there. We were puzzled by the carcasses which hung around the place, white and small. Had these been lambs? or dogs? or cats? the skin was pulled up from the white backs to form brown, hairy ruffs round the necks so that the small heads were quite hidden. In one of the dark lairs pork chops were being sold. We were greatly tempted by the pork chops. But as we approached them a man entered the market, carrying two kids. He held the innocent creatures by the hind legs. Their tender nostrils brushed the bloody paving. They bleated piteously, but he stopped to speak with the man selling the pork chops. Both of the men's coarse faces seemed to bloat purple until I expected them to gush fountains of blood. He carried the kids to a room in the corner of the market. We could buy no meat. We bolted from the market and never passed either of its entrances again without shuddering, nor saw kids skipping down the quays without hating the man who followed them, and feeling kinship with the animals. But man *is* vile; and a few moments in the keen sea air outside those gory walls so calmed our disgust that we went to a small restaurant which we had not before patronised, and ordered pork chops, tomatoes, potatoes, and salad. The baskets and the rucksack were heavy as we walked back to the cove, and the sun was hot. When we had had tea on deck the evening chill came down, and we went below, where I worked for a long time while Isabel lay sleeping beside me on the settee, a blue blanket over her body, and her head and shoulders supported on a pillow. Many caiques, able to travel again after several days of bad weather, were entering the harbour, and occasionally we rocked gently in a wash.

But the sirocco returned during that night, and early in the morning I was putting out a rope from the port bow to a tree to prevent *Truant* from sawing at her anchors when a wild figure burst through the foliage above me and slithered rashly down the bank. It was Freud, wearing the striped jersey in which I had first seen him. He had travelled to Athens for the opening of Craxton's exhibition and had arrived during the night with Craxton, Lady Norton, wife of the British Ambassador in Athens, and some other people, on the *Sunbury,* a British motor launch belonging to the Commander-in-Chief in Greece.

"We shot across from Athens," Freud said. "It was *won*derful! We only took one hour and five minutes to get here and spray was breaking like mad all over the thing . . ."

"It would have to do thirty knots to get here from Athens in one hour, and there was a head wind last night."

"But it's a terrific thing, with two engines."

"How many horsepower?"

"Oh, I don't know, hundreds or thousands or something. But I came here to warn you, they will all be on top of you shortly, Lady Norton and the whole crowd. I came down to get clean—you don't mind if I borrow your swimming trunks do you—then I must rush back to breakfast. We put them all in the Poros hotel last night after we had had dinner in a restaurant and gone to a tavern to watch the men dancing. Drenning— he's the captain of the *Sunbury*—bought a rug and a dog. He'll probably rush us round here in the *Sunbury* . . ."

"Better tell him not to come if his ship draws more than five feet . . ."

"We nearly visited you last night; we shone the searchlight on you, and you rolled like mad in our wash." He dashed off at nine o'clock, for he and Craxton had invited the party in the hotel to have breakfast in their house at that hour. There were numerous jobs to be done to make *Truant* orderly and tidy, most of them in the engine-room and the after cabin. Conditions worsened; the swell slapped against *Truant*, rolling her sharply, and I noticed that a strange shudder was coming from the mast. When I went forward to investigate I found that two of the chain-plates holding the main shrouds to the hull on the port side had worked themselves loose, and one on the starboard side; this constituted an extremely dangerous

379

structural weakness, and I once more remembered the commander's remark soon after I had bought the boat: "Chain-plates a bit flimsy, aren't they?" Even I could see, however, that it would probably be possible to make them sound by bolting the bottom ends (the upper ends were still firm) through the frames outside which they were screwed, but this would be a job for a shipwright. I went carefully round the deck, and soon found another, and yet more serious weakness: the rudder blade was working loose from the rudder post, despite the iron frame that had been put on to hold it after the accident near Marseilles. Douglas Hawkes, another expert, had warned me when he saw the frame: "They've made a sound job of it, but you should have those rivets tightened up in a month or two or it'll work loose, and then you might as well have nothing there at all."

As I had expected, the captain of the *Sunbury* chose to keep his ship at Poros, where there was some shelter from the sirocco, and the visitors appeared on foot, having made the long walk to our cove. I had difficulty in getting them on board dry. Lady Norton was accompanied by two women, the wife of a Canadian diplomat, and a journalist working for a British newspaper. Craxton, blooming after his change of air and diet in Athens, and fortified by the success of his exhibition there, was positively effervescent. He told us that he planned to return to Athens with Lady Norton's party, and from there he wished to go to Crete, and then to London. We walked back with them all to Poros. Drenning, a captain in the Royal Army Service Corps (the *Sunbury* was an Army vessel and was therefore crewed by soldiers), gave us gin and passion-fruit juice in his wardroom, the bulkhead, of which were decorated (?) with drawings of American women, their flesh coloured with a tinge of the salmon to tone with the underclothing that seemed to be their normal apparel when answering the telephone or discussing men with their cats. The new dog lay dismally on the upper bridge, tied with a rope to the engine-room telegraph. Drenning had bought it because he saw it being kicked by its former owner, the proprietor of a tavern. A smooth-faced man, powerfully built with his torso leaning back from his hips and more than a hint of swagger in his shoulders, Drenning was not going to let any dog be kicked by anybody, but he was prepared, good-hearted fellow, to pay a heavy price in drachmae and cigarettes for the animal rather than resort to the force in his own arms and shoulders and knock down the owner. "In any case," he said, "if I'd tapped him he would only have taken it out on the hound when he came to."

Drenning told me that if we returned to the Piræus we should be welcomed in his own private harbour, a small place near the mouth of the main Piræus harbour, and I was very glad of his hospitable offer, for Keeper-Wells had recently written to me that the bad weather was emptying Turco Limano and that he had sent the *Myrtle* and his other boat to Eleusis "to ride out the blows".

It was suggested by several of the party, and most forcefully by the woman journalist, that the weather was unsuitable for the proposed return to the Piræus that afternoon, but Drenning would have none of such talk. "I put to sea in *all* weathers," he insisted, "and if the General heard that I'd stopped in Poros because of a bit of a blow I'd never hear the last of it." Most unenthusiastically, then—with the exception of Lady Norton, who seemed to adopt the same type of attitude as Drenning, and who was probably as good a sailor—they climbed to the *Sunbury's* high deck. There they disposed themselves, grey-faced in a bitter wind, around Lady Norton, for whom a kind of basket throne had been set on the quarter deck. None of them, it appeared, cared to face the journey in the stuffy wardroom with the salmon-coloured ladies who told their cats so many strange things about men. Isabel, Freud and I stood shivering in the centre of the crowd on the quay. Each of the two powerful aero engines started with a whine and a roar. Then Drenning suddenly burst out of the bridge doorway, leaped to the quay and raced away, followed by two or three members of his crew, with a Greek interpreter in the rear. Soon Drenning reappeared leading the beige dog—it was something of the stamp of a yellow Labrador —which had chewed through the rope attached to its collar and had run back to the former owner who kicked dogs for amusement and starved them on principle. The engines raced astern, *Sunbury* swung out into the wind and then hurried away. We all felt a little depressed, particularly Freud, who talked, as he accompanied us to *Truant*, of the impermanence of life and the probability of early, sudden, violent, and tragic death.

* * * *

We walked to the Admiral's bungalow to ask him if he would help us to have *Truant* repaired. His house was built to cope with the summer's great heat as well as the winter's gales. More than half of the floor area seemed to be given to the veranda which shaded three sides of the low building. The place was cunningly set on a point so that it enjoyed magnificent views, yet back into the hillside to obtain some degree of shelter from most of the prevailing winds. His living room was fifteen feet square, and the walls and all objects not in regular use were blackened by the smoke that was inclined to drift from the wide chimney. The Admiral's firewood, or such of it as he judged necessary to have at hand, was stacked more neatly than books on a library shelf, and was classified in its different types of wood, quick- and slow-burning, aromatic and non-aromatic. The room was furnished with two tables of smooth but unpolished wood, a dresser and three chairs of the same material, an aneroid barometer, a thermometer, a fine selection of tools, carefully set out in order on the smaller of the tables, and, on the mantelpiece, two conch shells and three hurricane lanterns of a patent type. The floor was bare, and of good cement, polished by constant sweeping. The house was the barest, and the neatest that I have seen. The Admiral had no truck with comfort as comfort is conceived by dwellers in cities. The front door always stood wide open, held in that position by a heavy brass ring taken from some ship, and he only lit his fire for cooking, or for warmth on the coldest of days. The chairs were all hard and upright as the Admiral himself.

He said that he would carry out an inspection of the damage on *Truant* the next day, and he entertained us with meticulously cut slices—every knife-blade in that place was sharper than ordinary men's razors—of a rich cake which had been sent to him by an admirer in Athens, and with glasses of a Greek brandy, coloured like cold tea and possessing a most pleasing, clean, and un-brandyish taste.

He arrived at 10 o'clock in the morning, bringing a large packet of mail which he had found waiting for us in Poros the previous evening. One letter was from the Hawkes, and as we were anxious to know what had happened to them and to *Elpis*, we asked the Admiral's pardon, and Isabel read Gwenda's precise English aloud while the Admiral rolled drops of our French brandy round his tongue.

As we had feared, the Hawkes had had a rough time of it after leaving us at Capri. They had sailed some thirty miles on the first day, and were in an exposed anchorage when the storm, which so incommoded us in Marina Grande di Capri, struck them. They rode for a while to three anchors, one of which they were obliged to abandon when they ran for Salerno, where they were still lying when we sailed past unseen, far out to sea. After further passages as uncomfortable as our own they had reached Vibo Valentia Marina two days after we left that harbour. Then they sailed to Messina, where the Moscatelli Bros., armed with an introductory note which I had left with them, descended on this new prey and were "even more expensive than they were helpful". Douglas contracted blood poisoning in one hand, and was extremely ill. Somehow they managed to sail round Sicily, and to reach Malta on the day that we arrived in Athens.

They hated Malta harbour, which they found busy and dirty. *Elpis* was hauled out of the water there, and all her gear stored for the winter. Gwenda and Douglas had posted their letter in Palestine. We were sadly disappointed at their news, for we had still hoped to see them in Greek waters that winter. The Admiral examined the chain-plates, which he said could easily be repaired and strengthened, and the rudder, which would have to be removed, examined for rot in the wood, and then have its metal casing strengthened and tightened.

"The person to do this work will be the old man who has bought the Russian Store. Let us go and talk with him immediately, for the men here are apt to deliberate over the question of work."

All three of us dropped into the dinghy. There was no wind, so I was obliged to row them past the Diamantopoulo house, across the little bay separating it from the Admiral's bungalow, and round that point to the Russian Store. The Admiral looked firmly to his front as we passed the big white house, and I saw Christo's face at one of the upper windows, but it was swiftly withdrawn. We knew that those two men, near neighbours and the only men in the immediate neighbourhood who were in some manner suited to each other's company by reason of breeding and education, were not on speaking terms, but we never knew why, for when we mentioned the Diamantopoulos the Admiral would merely constrict his lips a little tighter and ignore the name, and if we mentioned Admiral Leondopoulo to the Diamantopoulos there would ensue the kind of long, embarrassed silence that was to be avoided in the company of such good friends.

The Russian Store had been, as its name implied, a warehouse for the Navy of Czarist Russia, which had kept a squadron for a time in Greek waters, a practice that had ended when Madame Diamantopoulo's father, on behalf of the Greek Government, made representations to the last of the Czars. It is to-day a long, sandy-looking building, well situated at the inner end of its cove. The strip of grass before it is strewn with rusted chains and anchors. Behind it there is an orange grove and a field, and beyond the bare hillsides rise to the spine of the island. When we penetrated to the field behind the half-derelict building we found that ploughing had been in progress. The two best animals for the plough which were available to those islanders who could afford to pay the hiring fees, a slender white pony and a somewhat more rugged black mule, stood in the shadow of a wall, looking at us curiously over the straw edges of their nose-bags. The owner of the place, the shipwright, sat beyond the field with the man and the boy who were engaged on the ploughing. Ploughing? All that the ploughshare effected was to turn a compact stony surface into a loose stony surface.

"What will he plant here?" I asked the Admiral.

"Wheat. But first he must pick up several million stones, and then he must see what earth is left."

The shipwright resembled my conception of Father Noah, though possibly only in appearance, for we had been privately informed that he was a crafty fellow. He had a jovial, healthy, blunt face with shaggy white hair and a venerable beard which spread all over his chest. He looked everybody up and down through steel-rimmed glasses perched on the bulbous end of his large nose, and said that he would inspect the damage when the ploughing was over, and not before.

"Are they in a hurry?" he asked.

"Yes," the Admiral said.

"Then tell them that no work is well done which is done in haste."

We left the dinghy in our own cove, and walked along the shore to Poros. Half-way there we overtook Dragoumis, who, haversack over one shoulder, stick in hand and soft hat on the back of his head, was slowly strolling our way. He picked up speed and accompanied us, making a sinister remark to the effect that he never remembered such a mild winter in Poros. At the bottom of his steps, when we had passed the kingfisher and the salvage hulks, he said that he had found a most interesting English article on anchors which he would like to have "explained by an expert"; might he bring it along some time? But he never came.

We walked out of Poros, past the Naval College, and on, towards the monastery. It was the first time that we had taken that road. A few houses circled the bay before the road climbed, zigzagging. A boy sat on the step of the iron gate to a house with more pretensions than the others. He read aloud from an English text-book, and as we approached he raised his voice. "We enter the cathedral," he read. "We sit down on a peewee. There are roh-wees of peewees in the cathedral . . ." We climbed the hill, passing small houses set among thorny scrub, and a chapel, pure white, square and looking like an iced walnut cake without the nuts on top. We were tired when we came to the point whence the monastery was visible, a white building set among trees. You can eat there and stay there and buy the water, which is supposed to have some remarkable power over human intestines. But local friends had warned us that the monastery was "very expensive". The sea was flat beneath us, and then grew fiercer as the wind raised it towards Hydra. The water on the horizon showed a serrated edge. On our way back from Poros we were hailed from a boat. Noah rested on his oars, and the Admiral shouted: "He will send his sons to do the work."

"When?"

He talked for a while to the bearded man, then turned to us shrugging his shoulders. "As soon as you would like them to come."

"To-morrow."

"All right." But although we had no means of knowing it at the time, the men would not come for sixteen days.

Wednesday, December 11th, was the real beginning of winter. For two weeks we had suffered a great deal of rain and wind with short fine interludes, but on that day the cold clamped down and the rain fell as never before. To all the usual noises of a boat at anchor was added a constant drip as water penetrated below decks. The worst leaks were forward. Water entered through the hawse-holes and was siphoned in by one edge of the galley hatch. The galley linoleum was awash. The saloon hatch was siphoning, and to prevent that I had to open it a little, when water came through the opening and broke in fine spray on the companion steps. There were a few leaks in the wheelhouse, and as these could not be remedied until we had dry weather I arranged chamois leathers and cloths to gather the water. Some of the loose water in the wheelhouse came through to our cabin, half of it going on the bunk and the remainder into the clothing cupboard. Plainly the time had come to light our heating stove. I put on oilskins and went to the after cabin to get the chimney and some wood to start a fire. The only jettisonable wood was in the form of tongued and grooved boards which some knowledgeable writer had advised as "part of any yacht's necessary stores: most useful for temporarily patching smashed skylights". I had to remove the bicycles and a great deal of paint and other gear to get out the boards and the chimney; but nothing will drive a man like his comfort, and soon the stove was lit, and its all-pervading warmth began a long battle against the damp. The weather worsened all that day and the next with prolonged flashes of lightning and heavy thunder-claps. It was so dark that I had to have the lights on to work at midday; the hills around us were hidden by swirling curtains of rain. The wind pushed at *Truant's* starboard quarter as though it intended to roll her over.

"Where have I brought you?" I asked Isabel.

The stove was wonderful. It soon dried all our wet things, and it burned a fantastically small quantity of anthracite daily. When we left England we had not even bothered to fill the anthracite locker to capacity, because in those days I had believed the winter climate of Greece to be mild and even warm. On the third day the rain stopped, but the cold weather persisted. Every morning, whether wet or dry, we would see a figure in a hooded, blue nurse's cape striding along the path to Poros. That was Mina Diamantopoulo, who, as Christmas Day approached, was as busy with her different village charities as any lady of Wiltshire or Dorset; busier indeed, for there was more to be done, and there were not so many willing to do it. Every child was to be given a present; we were able to provide a good deal of clothing by thinning the contents of our overstocked cupboards and drawers, and a great deal of tinned food from the store we had brought from England. Mina often talked of the difficulty she had in feeding the children. Her committee issued tins of condensed milk to each child, but when the children returned home with their tins the mothers were inclined to sell the milk to the grocers to get money to buy the types of food to which they were more accustomed. They refused to believe that "so much milk could be good for a weaned child". Accordingly, Mina had arranged to puncture each tin before handing it to the child, and then the tin was sucked dry before the child reached its mother. But the mothers fiercely resented such treatment (although the milk was a free gift to their children), and they had registered a strong protest against behaviour so "fascist". Mina had also opened a restaurant designed to give the schoolchildren free meals of a more nourishing character than those that they were likely to enjoy at home, but again the mothers were not favourably impressed, saying that such a thing was against the scriptures since a child's place was in the home, that the children learned bad manners in the restaurant, and that they were taught there to despise their homes. Mina had the wild Tombazi blood in her, and she gave herself unsparingly to what she regarded as a battle for the children's health. She had had a more difficult war than most people, for she was a qualified nurse, a racking qualification in Poros when the inhabitants had been dying off from starvation so fast that just before the liberation they were economising on funerals and priests' fees to such an extent that, following on the tail of any funeral cortège, there would be mourners from other families carrying their own, uncoffined dead, and sometimes the bodies of dead babies and starved infants would be carried to the graveyard near the power station on ordinary household trays. During the war, there had been little to eat but a few drops of olive oil (which also had to serve for light, burning in old-fashioned Biblical lamps) and such vegetables or weeds as they could scrape together, yet Mina had been called to Poros by night and by day, and often she passed nights on end without sleep. She walked at a rate exceeding four miles per hour, for she always covered the two-and-a-half miles from her house to Poros in thirty-five minutes. She had been fat at the beginning of the war, she told us, but she had lost sixty-six pounds in weight, and she had not regained it when we met her, for she carried no more spare flesh than a racing camel. Although so good a Christian, and a woman filled with a genuine, unsparing, and undemanding charity, she was a strong hater, much stronger than her husband, but I cannot list her hates, for I did not agree with most of them, and therefore felt them to be unworthy of her.

The cold weather had driven Christo upstairs to his winter quarters. He slept in a large room looking out over the lake, and he used Mina's adjoining bedroom as a sitting-room. Nicolette was warm enough, for she had her bed in the kitchen beside the cooking range. In the mornings she would carry up a great brass urn filled with greyish-white wood ash to act—inefficiently enough—as a radiator in Mina's room, and Christo would work at his poetry there, would caress his cat, Spitha, would read the books of the sages and the stylists lying on a divan under a corner of the walls hung with Persian rugs, and would carefully attend to the demands of a petulant flicker of fire set on a raised contraption of his own invention. This room, and indeed any room that we entered in the neighbourhood, seemed almost unbearably frigid after our extremely warm quarters on the boat. Christo wrapped his bowed shoulders round with many thicknesses of wool, and always toward us he was gentle, delicate, and hospitable, eager to entertain us, making us varied gifts upon which ever more thought and oriental generosity had been lavished. I never knew so kind a man. When our anthracite was finished I had to get wood to burn, and the Diamantopoulo wood store was opened to us, despite all our remonstrances. The timber was stacked in the small house once occupied by their batelier, and many a morning I spent there, sawing and chopping in the low rooms while the rain dripped outside, and then perhaps pumping water for *Truant* from the cistern behind the house. One winter during the war, they told me, the cistern had developed a leak and Christo had been obliged to lower himself down through the inspection trap into the damp vault to cement the interior and make it watertight; their water supply for the hot months from April to November depended on the rain-water that was collected in the winter. Christo had been a great man with his hands. I was assured that he had built most of their house himself, and none of the work looked in any way amateur. When my chores were done Christo would call me from the back window of Mina's bedroom.

"Montez, montez, cher Georges. J'ai fait mon café spécial."

I would find him crouched over the flame, his beard nearly singeing, stirring a hot mixture in a Turkish pot. His *café spécial* was a mixture of coffee and cocoa which I drank for his sake, and for its nutritious warmth. Then we would talk much of the morning away. Christo ruminated with horror, compassion, and a certain ghoulish fascination on the sufferings of the war so lately ended. He liked to make me talk of some of the brutalities that I had seen and heard of in Europe, but admonished me for my belief that it would be better if man could bring himself to forgo the dubious pleasure of punishing evil that is past.

The weather worsened. Blizzards entered our great harbour, and moved around and about it like polar bears pacing their pen in some zoological garden. We saw snow on the protuberances of the mountain to the west known as the Sleeping Woman. We watched the whiteness creep down from her raised knees, the points of her breasts, her chin, and her nose until one day the lower hills in front of us were also powdered. I made up my mind to work until the end of December, and then to leave Poros, and Greece. When the rain stopped, the fishermen would come out from Poros, standing in their boats and rowing for dear life. Some of them would stretch nets around the coves, two men working each net, and others would troll energetically for big fish, rowing up and down the harbour, keeping to whichever shore offered the most shelter. We saw a good deal of the Admiral, for we were anxious to have *Truant* made ready for sea, and we called upon him most days that he did not visit us, to ask him why the workmen never came. Sometimes we found him on his veranda feeding bread and scraps to the local curs, who now knew us so well that they did not heed us, and sometimes he would be sawing wood, an operation that he performed seated in a chair, with the wood held level with his chest on one of the parapets of his bungalow, and using a very sharp little one-handed saw. The answer to our complaints about the non-appearance of the workmen was always: "The weather is too bad."

"Do Greeks never work in the rain then?"

'Why should they, when soon there will be a dry day?'

"What would happen in other countries, in Alaska, in Nottingham, in Chalon-sur-Saône, if the workmen would not stir from the taverns when a few drops of rain were falling?"

"I agree with you, but we are not in those places, and the men are not dressed to work in the rain."

Sunday, December 22nd, was clear and warm; for the first time in weeks the sea was transparent around us again, and small piles of ash that I had thrown overboard were visible below the boat. But the weather had chosen a day of fête on which to better itself; there was to be a big parade at the naval college for the cadets to celebrate their passing out and to take

388

the oath, so the shipwrights would not arrive that day. Isabel sailed me away in the dinghy. The wind deserted us near a small island off the bay containing the Russian Store. We landed there and waited, hoping for the wind to return. The island was about three times the size of *Truant* and was covered with a profusion of small flowers. A white chapel stood in the centre. The ikons inside were set in stamped tin and were all of most inferior quality. The smell of the place was interesting, being musty, earthy, and partly scented by the flowers growing round the windows, with a faint suggestion of incense. A Greek destroyer swept past with several senior officers on the bridge, among them Prince Paul, then heir to the throne, and the Admiral commanding the Royal Hellenic Navy, who was a brother of our friend, Admiral Leondopoulo. The destroyer turned its bows inshore, aiming them at the bungalow, and trumpeted wildly. But the retired Admiral had hurried away from his home an hour earlier, eager to be at the naval college in good time to greet the royal party there. We had been invited to the ceremony, but had excused ourselves.

The following day was again cold and wet, and although the fishermen were around us we knew that the workmen would not bother to come. We marched into Poros in the rain, Isabel wearing her yellow oilskin and sou'wester, a costume that drew screams of joy and envy from the children of the town. We had run out of money; Isabel had a heavy mail to send off, and it was nearly the hour when the post office closed for the three-hour midday break. I hurried to the bank and knocked on the manager's door. He was a tubby gentleman, very agreeable, and eager to spout his few words of English. We got on famously, but since he was in no way obliged to cash my letter of credit, his bank being one of the few unaffiliated with my own bank in London, I realised that the situation could not be rushed. For a long time we conversed agreeably. Sparsely furnished, the office had the stamp of all bank managers' lairs. The mahogany desk, the patent reading lamp, the swivel chair, the stove, the mahogany-framed sofa with a horse-hair seat, the small safe, and on the walls large photographs—I suppose they would want to be called portraits —of former managers, the bodies partly photographed and partly drawn in with a few bold, arty strokes of the photographers' charcoal. At long last we came to the point, and the manager left his office to régler l'affaire with the cashier, leaving me, for entertainment during his absence, with an English publication entitled *Pitman's Business Training*. I was not sorry when he returned, for when I turned over the pages of the admirable book I was transported to Cheapside during the noonday rush, I heard the buses following each other in Fleet Street, and I smelled the warrens of the

Central London Railway. After an energetic handshake we parted, he to take down his hat from the tall stand inside the door and potter off to his villa on the hill, and I to hurry down the quays to the post office. I found that Isabel had had no difficulty at all in holding that establishment open. Long Nose had invited her into the inner sanctum, and a visiting postal inspector from Athens was there who spoke French and who explained courteously that since we were the best customers for whom Poros Post Office had catered within living memory the place would open for us from then on at any hour of the day or night within reason.

"But we've made you forty minutes late in closing," I said.

"That's of no importance. Please don't worry about it at all. We'll just open forty minutes later than usual this afternoon. That's only logic."

Christmas Day was another day of summer sandwiched into the winter. We might have bathed had we not determined to work all day. Soon after first light we were both over the side in the dinghy, smoothing *Truant's* black topsides with scrapers and sandpaper. Mina Diamantopoulo came to wish us a Merry Christmas, calling it over the water from the half-built chapel. She was annoyed about her children's Nativity play in the village, a play for which she had designed and made most of the costumes, painted the scenery, and acted as producer. As the curtain was about to rise the town was plunged in darkness. The electric light could not be revived, and every shop in Poros was scoured for candles. "The curtain went up two hours late, and you could see absolutely nothing but candle-smoke. But the children acted beautifully and the audience was most patient . . ." Communist sabotage was suspected! We worked all day. By the evening the whole hull was scraped, rubbed down, and puttied, ready for painting. It chanced that I was alone in the dinghy, and hard at work with a putty knife when the launch from the naval college squealed up (it had some strange noise in its engine). The Admiral was in it, and he introduced me to the officer commanding the college, his wife, and his daughter. I knew that any interruption would mean that I could not finish the puttying that day, and some of my disappointment may have shown in my reception, but Isabel ran up on deck and invited them aboard; the lady had strained a muscle, and could not risk climbing up from the launch, so I was soon able to continue with my work. There was a further interruption when a band of young men and girls arrived; they had walked out from Poros to make us ceremonial Christmas presents of round loaves of bread each marked with a large cross botonnée.

Dressing for dinner, I realised that I had grown fat during the quiet days at Poros. With the cold weather we had been eating more heavily and taking less exercise. I had not bothered to look at my reflection for some weeks; it seemed to me that my eyes were closing between fatty pads, and the sight of the face in the looking-glass was enough to make me feel as liverish as a Strasbourg goose.

In honour of the occasion Christo had decided to come downstairs, and a great fire had been made in the library. Freud also had been invited. There was so tremendous a feast that none of us could do it justice. The meal ended with a giant Christmas pudding made by Mina. She had found a recipe in a German cookery book written in 1821 and, thinking that the author-chef was possibly inclined to be mean, she had doubled all the quantities. We returned to *Truant* after midnight. Bloated with food and quite unaccustomed to taking alcohol in the evening, I could not sleep at all.

I was early ashore in the morning for I had occasion to borrow Voltaire's *Zadig* and La Fontaine's *Fables*. Mina came into the library while I was hunting for the books, and although the shutters were drawn I could see that she was worried. Christo had suffered two heart attacks during the night, but now he was insisting that he was well enough to get up. She dared not go to Poros while he was like that, and there was so much to be done there. Christo heard our voices below.

"C'est vous, mon cher Georges? Je déscends . . ."

"Restes tranquil!" Mina shouted.

"C'était le pouding," he went on. "Une petite crise. Rien . . . Rien . . ."

"Attends," Mina cried, and excusing herself, she darted upstairs. I hurried back to *Truant*, for the painting was to begin as soon as the morning dew had dried from the topsides. We covered the dinghy with old canvas and Isabel and I dropped into it with two big and two small paint brushes and a vast pot of black paint. We began at the bows, and were working steadily down the starboard side when I heard the Admiral's usual signal, a shrill whistle on his bo'sun's pipe, and he appeared in a rowing-boat which, with two men at the four oars, fairly leaped towards us. The shipwrights, after delaying for sixteen days, had arrived when their presence would most inconvenience us. But the Admiral allowed us to go on painting while he supervised all operations. It was decided that two bolts would have to be made for the chain-plates. The galley was turned into chaos with all the china displaced and white shelves and boarding ripped out. They lifted off the rudder and balanced it over the stern of their own boat to be carried away to their workshop in Poros. By midday they were ready to go. We all drank gin (the French brandy was finished) and discussed the rival attractions of Port Said and Alexandria.

When they had gone Isabel and I each ate an orange in place of lunch and then returned to our paint-pot and brushes. By 4 o'clock the topsides were painted and gleaming, but the weather threatened change, with a grey wedge across the harbour to the south-west and a black line of high clouds above the grey. At one o'clock in the morning we were wakened by a great wind bringing with it torrents of rain. Before midday the wind dropped and the rain, which had not greatly damaged our paintwork, showed signs of easing. We ate a salad, and feeling in need of exercise, put on seaboots and oilskins and climbed the hills behind our cove. The country was so steep and stony that the rain was able to make but little mud. Blue flowers were sprouting from every crack in the rock. The hinterland of Poros is wild, and we walked most of the day with scarcely a view of human habitation. As we approached one farm, visible more than a mile away across a ravine, we heard a deep, booming bark, and saw, standing looking at us from a fold in the hills near the building, a dog, a brown-and-white animal as big as a calf. In a country where animals are often mistreated, so large and fierce-looking a dog might be more dangerous than a lion, and I made Isabel take a detour to avoid him. Returning to the boat, we heard a strange crackling from the steep valley at the mouth of which was the Russian Store. It seemed at the first frightening glance that a whole section of the hillside was moving jerkily upward in our direction. The illusion was caused by a herd of goats, the main herd of the island. They ate their way steadily uphill, champing with so catholic a disregard for what lay before their jaws that we felt that if we did not remove ourselves from their direct path they might well fail to discriminate between our limbs and those of the spiked shrubs which they attacked so freely. High above them on a spur stood a young man, the goat-herd. He held a white kid in the crook of one arm, and sent occasional raucous cries to the older goats below. *Truant* looked homely in her little cove, with a tendril of blue smoke rising from the H-shaped chimney of the stove, and another spurting from the exhaust of the small charging motor, low on the starboard side. A kingfisher, cross between clown and angel, had perched himself on the rail, only three or four feet from the engine, and would dive now and then, touching the surface with the most minute of splashes, and return to the boat.

We dined with the Diamantopoulos, a most excellent dinner: local hot hors d'œuvres, sucking-pig and salad, bonbons from Athens set in a round basket covered with blood-red cellophane, and fruits from the Tombazi estate.

The shipwrights brought our rudder the next morning. The oak had proved to be quite sound, and they had tightened up the metal strengthening put there in Marseilles by adding three bolts and two small plates to it. I would not let them fit the rudder until it had been painted with anti-fouling; so they laid it across a rock, and while I painted it they mended the chain-plates. The Admiral had them put him ashore beside the rock where I was working, and we saw that the anti-fouling was drying so quickly that it would be possible to fit the rudder that same afternoon. I asked him how much the work was to cost. He called out to them; they answered as the boat was pulling away from us and he said: "Two hundred and fifty thousand drachmae. Will that be all right?"

"Yes, I suppose so," I answered, thinking that £12 10s. was a fair charge for the work.

"How many drachmae do you get for the pound sterling to-day?" he asked.

"Twenty thousand."

"Oh," he replied. "I thought it was only ten thousand."

We painted and varnished the day away, and when the men and the Admiral arrived in the evening *Truant* was probably looking better than she had ever done under our ownership. The rudder was soon fitted. The Admiral expressed some annoyance with the men. "But it is really my own fault," he said. "I must be growing deaf."

"What's the matter?"

"I told you that the men said 250,000 drachmae this morning?"

"Yes."

"I could have sworn that they said 250,000, but they claim that I must have misheard, and that the figure was 350,000 drachmae . . ."

"Oh, I see!"

"In Greek there is a certain similarity between the spoken words for two and three . . ." There followed a long exhibition of this similarity. All three went about the boat saying: "Two . . . Three . . . Two . . . Three . . . Three-two . . . Two-three . . ." We all had a drink and were very amiable. I still felt that I had not been overcharged at £17. 10s.

The rain came again at three in the morning, and never stopped until we left Poros.

* * * *

There were a great many good-byes to be said. Dragoumis was out walking; neither Sophia at the shop by the naval college nor Long Nose at the post office fully understood what we were trying to say; Punch, the greengrocer, seemed to have had rather a lot to drink; King Farouk's barber was so sad that we feared tears, and hurried away; Freud was in his small, cold room, concentrating on an exquisite painting of a lemon, and anyway, we knew that we should meet him again. The Admiral was sharpening the blade of a plane when he heard my step on his veranda. He had lit no lamp (though to my eyes it was getting dark), and there was no fire in the grate (though I was not over-warm in two jerseys and an oilskin). He gave me a Greek cigarette and a glass of his fine tea-coloured brandy. He wished to return some books that he had borrowed, and went to a cupboard for string. He selected a piece with judgment, for there were scores of pieces of string there, each length meticulously rolled and stored away as carefully as a museum exhibit. In the same cupboard were ranged perhaps a dozen hurricane lamps of all sizes, from the smallest to the largest, and each one with its glass shining and its wick damp and trimmed. I noticed that evening for the first time that when the Admiral returned to his house he took off his outdoor shoes and put on a pair of fawn-coloured pantouffles each of which was decorated with an embroidered design, including a crown and resembling the badge on a naval officer's cap. He gave me a letter to his brother in Athens. His writing materials were set as precisely on the table as though the surface were a case fitted to take each article, the pen, the ink-bottle, the note-paper, the paper knife, the blotter. His handwriting was invincibly meticulous.

I hastened back to *Truant* to collect Isabel. She sat on the transom of the dinghy with her feet on a thwart to avoid the water which slopped over the floorboards; when incessant rain fell there came a time when I had no more energy to bail or pump out the dinghy. Nicolette received us in the dark kitchen. She was a quiet, ugly girl who came from the hills on the mainland. She was always kind to us, but we never knew what she was thinking behind her spectacles. Mina and Christo were upstairs. Their cat, Spitha, a Titian flibberty-gibbet, was asleep on the bed for she had been out all night for three nights running. Spitha must have been the fattest animal on that island for Christo spoiled her outrageously, and loved to caress her with one long finger, turning her over, teasing her, and repeating endlessly: "Speeeetha . . . Speeeetha. . . ."

Isabel did not feel inclined to eat, but Christo insisted. He said that it was rather late for tea and rather early for dinner. "Alors, nous prendrons un thé copieux." It was the command of an emperor. Mina was already making doughnuts, dropping small morsels of yellow dough into boiling olive oil, morsels that expanded and browned like bursts of flak. We had come to know them both so well that we scarcely needed to say good-bye. It was said that we would probably return quite soon to Poros, but they knew as well as we did that this was only a pleasant convention, and that we were unlikely to meet again. As we left Christo gave us a chicken which he had himself roasted. A sudden fear crossed my mind; could it be that he had made a needlessly supreme sacrifice?

"Ce n'est pas la Blonde?" I asked.

"La Blonde! Pardi, non! Je ne la tuerai jamais, ma Blonde."

We kissed them and walked through the darkness down the steps to our dinghy. Rain spat into the water as I sculled out to *Truant*.

The morning was bitterly cold, but dry. The kedge which I had dropped in the shallows had been dragged considerably nearer the boat, and had finally dug itself into a bank of clay in about five feet of water. After slacking the chain, I went off in the dinghy, dropped a bight over the upper fluke, and heaved; I might as well have tugged at Table Mountain for all the response that was obtained. There seemed to be nothing for it but to go into the water. No solution could have been more distasteful to me. Shuddering, I stripped off my clothes. I undid the shackle attaching the stock to the chain, and managed, without much difficulty, to move the stock nearly to the perpendicular, and to work the anchor to and fro until I judged it loose enough to be lifted from the dinghy. I climbed out into the boat. Peals of laughter came from *Truant*, as Isabel caught sight of my glistening body against the dark background of the trees. I still could not move the anchor, and was gloomily nerving myself to take another bath, when Isabel shouted that a fishing-boat with two men in it was about to enter the cove. I hastily put on my clothes over the wet skin. (Incidentally, I had a slight cold in the head that morning, but this immersion completely cured it.) The two fishermen had a heavy boat, and they were powerful, though unintelligent, men. Even so, it took all three of us half an hour of maximum physical effort to dislodge the anchor, which was held by the suction of the wet clay. I thanked the Providence that sometimes watches over mariners for the fishermen's timely arrival, and we rewarded them most lavishly with tins of beef and lamb. It was ten o'clock when we had finally stowed all the chain, lashed the anchors and lifted the dinghy to the deck. Mina and Christo stood waving to us from their terrace, Christo wearing a skull-cap and the magnificent bluc cloak. One long hand fluffed at his fine beard, while the other was raised to us in a dramatic farewell. While Mina called to us Christo merely nodded his head gently, accepting our departure with the other sadnesses of life. The Admiral's head and shoulders appeared on his terrace, and he kept his telescope focused on us until we were in the northern pass leading from Poros harbour, and out of sight.

29

MINA had called to us that the weather outside the harbour would be fine, but her prophecy was false, and we found ourselves plunging into a head sea. Isabel had to steer for a long time, since I had a great deal of work to do on deck. It was so cold that I wore gloves to handle the sails. As I looked at the rain sweeping toward us over the wave crests and around the pinnacles on the barren eastern side of Ægina I thought with longing of the English countryside in the winter, of the houses clinging to the ground under the strong dark arms of the trees. Isabel lay stretched on the chart table, a pillow supporting her head, and one delicate hand on the wheel. We watched the rainstorms come and go, and the light playing uneasily on Poros astern, Ægina to port, and the mainland far away to starboard. A British ship passed us, the *Clan Lamont*. Her decks were lined with men of the Royal Air Force, the collars of their blue coats turned up to blue-pink chins. Inside the harbour of the Piræus we soon saw on the starboard hand the Ensigns, blue with crossed swords, of Drenning's detachment. As we prepared to enter the small basin we saw Keeper-Wells run from the *Sunbury*, followed by the uniformed Drenning. A wreck pushed funnel and masts above the surface just inside the entrance, and there was little room to manœuvre. I was slow in putting down the anchor, missed my opportunity, and had to ask Isabel to go about in that constricted place, buffeted by a cross wind, and watched by at least thirty pairs of critical eyes. The move was at length accomplished in outward calm, which is the main object to bear in mind during such operations with a small and inexperienced crew. We dropped the C.Q.R. far out and went astern, making fast two stern lines to the quay. To port, and parallel with *Truant*, were three boats under Drenning's command, a diesel-engined boat of the drifter stamp which was used for carrying stores to army detachments, the *Sunbury*, and another launch of the same class. We visited the *Sunbury*, but found it chilly in their wardroom, since they only had radiators for heating. We were glad to return to *Truant*, where the stove glowed and crackled, and Isabel cooked dinner.

We had arrived on New Year's Eve. Drenning soon passed along the quay "going to a party" followed by his dog, the one bought at Poros which, in a few weeks, had doubled in size, had grown a golden coat, and was generally most healthy and contented. The men of the detachment judged it expedient to be merry according to the date, and became increasingly rowdy until at midnight all the ships in the harbour sounded sirens, whistles and horns, while some let off distress flares. We expected to have peace after that outburst, but unfortunately there were several Lowland Scots in the detachment, and these stained the air with their windy sentimentality. We were not spared "Auld Lang Syne" and the rest of their hackneyed melodies.

It seemed wiser on New Year's Day to lie low and let the celebrations take their course unimpeded by us. The weather blew in very hard from the west, so hard that at times waves were climbing over the top of the breakwater astern. The following day we called on Keeper-Wells, who was in something of a welter, for he and his wife were about to go to London on leave.

"You want to sell your boat?" he said. "Good gracious! And go back to England in the winter-time? You say you like England in the winter? The man is bats! Well, yes, I suppose there are a couple of people who might buy *Truant*, Englishmen, I mean, and you'd also find a buyer easily enough at the American Embassy. Of course what will put them off are those petrol engines: dangerous, you know. Wouldn't have them as a gift on my own boat."

"I used to feel that way myself."

"Of course if I wanted another yacht here I'd have it built locally and get a good solid diesel engine sent out from England."

"Judging by our difficulty in getting minor repairs done I wouldn't care to build locally."

"You've been unlucky, my dear chap. You've been unlucky."

One of the two possible purchasers came aboard the following day. He was a British general, a round-faced man with a sturdy body, a well-curled moustache, and tweed clothes of sporting cut. He did not advertise the fact, but it was plain to me that he knew a great deal more than I did about boats.

"Well, Millar," he said. "For years it's been my ambition to do the trip you've just completed, and I'll never get another chance like this. My job in Greece will fold up in a few months, and then I want to return to England by the route you followed. I shall have my wife on board, and some friends, and one hand or possibly two. I've been searching for a boat, but I haven't seen one to touch this. I'll be glad to pay what you're asking, subject to survey, of course. I'll get in touch with Lloyd's agent here, and ask him to appoint a surveyor. It'll mean hauling her out of the water.

But Keeper-Wells says he knows of a slip near-by where we should manage for £10 to haul her out, have the survey, slap a coat of anti-fouling on her bottom, and put her back in the water in twenty-four hours . . ."

We locked *Truant's* hatches, left her jumping in a head wind—the wind had changed abruptly from west to east—and went ashore to spend a sociable week-end.

*　　　*　　　*　　　*

I awoke at dawn and drew the curtains. The bedroom had windows fifteen feet high giving a view over part of Athens and the hills. As the light came up the view constantly changed, forming slowly fading patterns of pale brown, blue-grey, and white. The town looked scraggy and desolate by comparison with the fluid country beyond. The dome and towers of a Byzantine church set on the perimeter stood up like three adjacent temples. Tramcars, most disconcerting to our ears, hurried past the house, which itself was very silent. I dialled "2" on the telephone and asked the maître d'hôtel to send us breakfast.

We drove out of Athens through bare, exciting hills to the sea inside Salamis and then along a mad coast, tortured that day by wind, to Eleusis, at the end of the Sacred Road. At that place mysteries had been presented to enable or encourage the initiates to believe in the possibility of life after death. The antiquities are now surrounded by a wire-mesh fence. A female guardian unlocked the gate, and broadmindedly permitted Jock, the mad fox-terrier, to enter with us. What would happen, I wondered, if Jock, who liked digging, and who evidently was excited by certain smells in that place, should unearth something sacred. It was bitterly cold. We inspected the massive ruins. At a place where a gateway used to stand, the original surface of the narrow Sacred Road is well preserved. Two worn quarter-circles show where the heavy gates swung back. At that point there is a slight hump in the roadway, and the chariots, rushing through, wore two parallel grooves in the stone. The twin grooves evoke a picture of life and clattering movement, of wagers and lust, wealth, power, and horse dung.

We stopped the car at a tavern facing the shore near Eleusis. Fawn-coloured casks of resinated wine, each cask five feet in diameter, lay in a row under the white wall. The bar-counter, freshly painted in brown and pale-blue, leaned crazily forward, yet was the stand for many bottles, a cash register that refused to register although it would still ring its bell, and a gramophone with a long horn also painted in brown picked out with blue. A drunk man behind us nodded over his table, on which he had a glass and a jug filled with amber wine. He had been shooting, and perhaps was consoling himself after a poor morning's sport. His gun and empty game-bag lay by his loose feet on the floor. Greek taverns are very beautiful, a million times more beautiful at first sight than French cafés, where beauty is usually to be found in an interesting composition of strange and often ugly units. The beauty of a Greek tavern is positive, but the beauty of a French café is of the two-negatives kind; I don't say that I prefer the former.

The following day, Monday, January 6, was the day on which the waters were to be blessed by Archbishop Damaskinos, head of the Church, and a figure to be reckoned with in politics. We drove to the Piræus through streets lined with policemen. The Greek policeman is an un-prepossessing figure. His face is sour and his expression black. On this occasion the policemen, instead of facing the roadway, faced the pave-ments, watching for any sign of weapon or bomb, so that we did not see their dark faces, but only their caps and the tailored backs of their long greatcoats. Down at the harbour there were parades of soldiers, sailors, airmen, boy scouts, girl guides, veterans, nurses, brass bands. We climbed to the balcony of the harbour-master's office. I was stifled by my suit, tie, and town shoes. I made conversation in French with a woman and her young son. The boy spoke easily, but was inclined to exploit a dull subject, *le football*. The band below us presented a circus-like appearance with contorted silver instruments, frogged coats and tight, magenta trousers. Once, when a naval band across the square interrupted our magenta-trousered band, our conductor stopped the music abruptly, and walked stiffly across to the leader of the naval band; but though both men carried long, silver-shod staffs, they only engaged in verbal argument; our con-ductor returned to his men, and then both bands played simultaneously, each a different tune. At 11 a.m. the Archbishop, a giant, emerged stooping from a near-by church, and with a throng of holy men surrounding him as young oaks surround a monster of the forest, stalked down to the water's edge where the diplomats and the Cabinet, looking silly by comparison with professional performers like the priests and the military, stood on a dais. At 11.10 King George arrived in a grey Rolls Royce. The football enthusiast told me that the car had been a gift from the King of England. He thought that King George was a very brave man to travel in so handsome a vehicle, since there was no other like it in all Athens. "If I were the King," he said, with remarkable good sense for his years, "I'd sell the car on the black market, and drive about in a tank." Chocolates, cigarettes, and sweet liqueurs were handed round our balcony. The boy helped himself to all three, but he pushed the handful of cigarettes that he had grabbed into the breast pocket of his striped suit. The Archbishop's robes were very cumbersome, and he advanced a little gingerly to the edge of the quay, where he threw his jewelled cross into the dirty water. "Watch him now," the boy said. "See that? He's hauling the cross up with a piece of ribbon. I wish the ribbon would break, don't you? In the old days there was no ribbon, and people used to dive in for the cross. . . . Much better."

"Why have they changed the custom?"

"That cross is worth a hundred gold pounds. Who's going to admit that he found it at the bottom of the sea. The old boy would never see it again."

"Scoundrel!" said his mother. "The horrible ideas that you are picking up at that new school."

"Now that I'm twelve, Mama, you can't keep me in a glass case."

"Silence!"

The Archbishop had thrown in the cross for the third time, and there was a tumult of noise as every drummer in every band rolled out a salute and all the ships made all possible noises. The ceremony had been so brief and so noisy that it was voted an immense success by everybody.

We drove to the Yacht Club, where there was a big luncheon. The club looked most unfamiliar, its car park full of shining vehicles, and its terraces and rooms seething with stiffly-dressed people. Madame Annapolis from Hydra was there, and she enveloped us for a time in her warm friendliness. I was on the point of asking about the shotgun on her chaise-longue when Monsieur Benaki, very smart in narrow trousers and a reefer coat with black buttons that were an admirable foil to his moustache, led us off to meet Prince Paul, commodore of the club. Spiro was running about with trays of oyzo and cocktails; Isabel managed to ask him, as she passed along the balcony to do her curtsey, if he would send to *Truant* for our laundry.

That evening on our way back to the boat we made a detour in order to say good-bye to the Keeper-Wells, who were flying the following morning to London. Mrs. Keeper-Wells's luggage was conservative, but her husband, being of an exceptionally kindly disposition, had decided to entertain his friends in London, and hearing that spirits were in short supply there, had jettisoned a suitcase, and carried instead Italian Army packs holding Italian waterbottles, "remarkable what they hold; you get five bottles of whisky into two waterbottles, though you'd never think it to look at the darned things."

"It is very unfeeling of you to leave Greece," I told him. "We were relying on your help with the slipping of *Truant*."

"Is that all?" he answered. "Easiest business imaginable, my dear

400

fellow. Just pick up your hook and toddle along to Perama. What? Don't know where Perama is? Mummy, give us a scrap of paper and a pencil, and I'll do him a little drawing. It's a whole village of slipways; starboard outside the Piræus harbour—you can't miss it. Just go along there and mention my name . . ."

"How much should slipping cost?"

"Eh? Oh, not more than a tenner."

"Will they really do it for £10?"

"Mention my name, and *don't give them what they ask.*"

* * * *

After being unoccupied for three days *Truant* had become so damp below-decks that we were obliged to light a big fire in the stove and to go to bed in winter dressing-gowns. But we slept more easily than we had done in the centrally-heated house.

Drenning was very occupied at that time with inspections, and other routine matters, but he allowed me to make use of his engineers and of one of his Greek interpreters, a squat, black-visaged man whose services were invaluable. He took me to the office of the Greek colonel who was in charge of an enclosure where the relief organisations serving Greece appeared to dump everything from dynamos and three-ton lorries to powdered soups and aspirin tablets. The colonel occupied a miserable office, heated by a stove that had been fashioned out of small tins. He sent for some coffee, and listened sympathetically to my request for an empty packing-case, large enough to hold such of our personal belongings as we should not be allowed to carry in an aeroplane. The colonel himself came down to *Truant*, leading six men who carried a heavy case. That afternoon we began to pack our books. There was snow on the decks, and the clerks in the travel office told us that all Europe north of Rome was ice-bound. When I tried to light the stove the following morning I discovered that the coal, obtained for me by the Greek interpreter in exchange for cigarettes, would not burn. We could not wait to find other fuel, for it was time to cast off. The large crews of the Army vessels watched our antics with some surprise; when *they* got under way each man had only one task to perform. The anchor gave no trouble, and within an hour, following Keeper-Wells's directions, we dropped it in seven fathoms, off the straggling village of Perama.

The first man whom I met—doubtless he had watched our arrival and lay in wait for me—spoke excellent English. He was a thin creature dressed in a dark overcoat that billowed in the wind. His was the face of a man who was sensitive, courteous, educated, and intensely depressed. He took me to a drab room which served as a tavern inside the enclosure of the yard. We drank an oyzo, and discussed the possibilities of getting *Truant* out of the water. My own wish was to fix a price and get on with the work immediately. But he preferred to learn all that he could about me, my boat, and my intentions, and for a time that seemed interminable to me, we sat in that squalid place, politely engaged in verbal fencing, while a young man shredded white cabbage on the bar.

I learned that the man with whom I drank had a small engineering establishment in the yard. He had no slipping facilities himself, but would engage to help me with those men who had, all of whom, he warned me, were avaricious. He was entirely on my side in any negotiations that might take place. Did I know that the Greek name for a boat like mine was a *lord-boat*? I might take it for granted that they would demand far too much money, but whatever they asked I would know that I had him behind me, and if I thought any charge was exorbitant he hoped that I would have confidence in him, and tell him so frankly. He said that he was a refugee from Russia, although of Greek origin, and that he had learned English from his governess. I was inclined to believe him, although mistrust seemed to be in the very air of that long, seedy village and the dirty water-front that might come to life beneath the burning rays of the sun, but that now lay sullen and dead. How much was I prepared to pay, he asked. Ten pounds, 200,000 drachmae. But the boat must be ashore, I told him, before two in the afternoon because the surveyors were coming then.

"We've no time to waste," he exclaimed, with all the urgency of a man who had just wasted an hour. "Come, let me pay for the drinks, and then we must find the foreman . . ."

"Allow me to pay."

"I should be mortally offended. You're my guest."

Providentially, the foreman was hanging about outside the tavern. My interpreter soon explained what was wanted, and I took both of them out to *Truant*. The foreman measured and gauged the shape of the hull. He said that we must move eight hundred yards along the waterfront, where a suitable slip was about to be vacated. Isabel, who was still packing, came up to the wheelhouse, and we moved. I anchored according to his directions, very near the shore, and the three of us landed with the dinghy beside a slip from which a smart caique, freshly painted in grey and orange, was just entering the water. The vessel close by on another slip was an Italian coaster which had been salvaged and which was encrusted with every kind of growth and indignity that the sea can put on a sunken

402

ship; the great fissures in her belly which had caused her sinking, and which now offered grave problems to the Greeks who hoped to further resurrect her, still showed round their ugly lips the corpses of jelly fishes and molluscs. On the other side a big caique was building. Her frames were nearing completion, and whatever any casual visitor might make of the men of Perama he would have to acknowledge that they could build stout vessels in the old way. The five or six men of Perama who stood by the greased slip, waiting for our party of three, looked first at me in my blue jersey, cord trousers and sea-boots, and then at my lord-boat gleaming on the water. The man from Russia appeared to question them.

"They say that they will make a safe job of slipping the yacht for 800,000" he said.

"Out of the question, it is four times more than Major Keeper-Wells advised me to pay."

"Six hundred thousand?"

I had been taught as a boy that good manners demanded that you should do everything to preserve the self-respect of any man with whom you had dealings. And as I had been brought up in Lowland Scotland, where self-respect was largely reckoned in terms of cash or credit, financial dealings were the ones in which courtesy was most expected. I had not been trained to cope with men who reduced their demands by £10 every time that they opened their mouths. "Tell them that if they continue to ask for extortionate sums we won't slip here at all," I told the man from Russia.

"But these men are putting you in a most difficult situation! You're obliged to slip here because the surveyors are coming. Wait, I'll try to convince the director of the iniquity of their demands." He whispered for some time to the director, a man who was distinguished from the others only by an added sourness of expression. "Four hundred thousand," he exclaimed, whirling round on me. "Now that's more like it."

"It's half their original price, but it's still double my price."

"Four hundred thousand," he repeated gently, trying to mesmerise me with the words. "Four hundred thousand."

"I've decided not to slip the boat here," I told him. "I must telephone to Athens immediately."

"There's no telephone."

"Not in all Perama?"

"No, the nearest's at the Shell factory, half-way between here and the Piræus."

"How can I get there?"

"The tramway passes on the main road. I'll come with you."

"I really don't feel that I've the right to inconvenience you further."

"It's no inconvenience at all."

The tramway station was a small concrete platform, some five yards in length, rising from the dust beside the rails. Would I not consider paying 400,000, he asked. And hearing my firm negative, he mentioned at once a lower figure, 350,000.

"I am empowered to offer that sum," he said. "Shall we go back and see the director?"

"No thank you. I must telephone to the general in Athens."

"But 350,000 drachmae is only £17."

"Seven pounds more than I am willing to pay."

He raised his clenched fist and beat at the wooden sign above us, PERAMA. He looked so sad, so disillusioned, that I wanted to please him. His overcoat fell in dusty folds around his emaciated body. "But it's a *reasonable* figure," he cried, his voice petulant for the first time. "You've no idea how high wages are to-day in the yards. Living's dear and we're all taxed to death. In this place all the men are paid piece-work rates, and when there is not enough work to keep them all busy all the time then the wages automatically go up and the slipping costs go up too."

"They should drive them down again. For who is going to slip his boat for 350,000 here when he can do it for 200,000 in the islands?"

"This is a refugee settlement," he said. "When the million and more Greeks were resettled from Smyrna and Turkey this was one of the settlements. Look at the places where they live. You couldn't call those houses. The people are poor and unhappy. Just look at that hill-face," he said, waving a dusty arm at the blue-grey sweep of bare hill behind the few hovels that had been built above the tramway line. "Before this last war that hill was covered with trees, beautiful trees; but the Italians cut them all down."

I told him that they were going the right way to become poorer still.

"You mustn't think hardly of them because they asked for 800,000 to begin with. They thought that you must be a millionaire when they saw you with a yacht. Ah! here's the tram. Let us turn back. It will be an unpleasant ride."

"No," I said. "I must telephone."

"Just as you say. No, it's better not to sit down. We'll stand here, close to the doors." Despite my protests, he bought the tickets. He also paid for the telephone call. I felt that each debt was silently chalked up against the profits he intended to make from any work done on *Truant*, but I was

404

helpless in his gentle hands. The general had to leave a conference to answer the telephone.

"Accept that figure," he said. "Seventeen pounds is reasonable as prices go." I laid down the receiver and turned to the man from Russia.

"The general accepts 350,000," I said. His thin face registered utter dejection. His first reaction on clinching the deal was: "We might have done better. The general might have paid four, or even five hundred thousand." We walked back to the yard, and the men there, although they gave me glasses of oyzo and small, stiffly-fried fish, held by the tails and passed from hand to hand, and hand to mouth, reacted as the man from Russia had done. "We're doing this work for nothing," the director complained. "We'll barely cover the expenses. Why, the caique that has just left the slip paid nearly as much."

"The caique was bigger than my boat," I said to the man from Russia.

"Yes, but her owner is a poor working man."

"Are you sure? I've been told that with the scarcity of caiques some of the owners are becoming very rich."

"That particular owner drinks all his profits, and he has a son who gambles."

I found Isabel shivering in the saloon. She had opened our two best tins for lunch, an American one containing a whole spring chicken, already roasted, and a British one containing a plum pudding. The supplies of food that we had brought from Southampton were barely half-finished, although we had given away a great deal more than we had eaten in the seven months from the day we left the Hamble River.

Greek workmen are apt to be rough, and the methods of the gang that hauled *Truant* up the slipway made my hair stand on end, but their systems for circumventing the apparent shortages and weaknesses of the tools they use are proved systems that go back one thousand years and more.

The surveyor was waiting by the water's edge. He was a small, bitter-looking man in a soft black hat and a cloth overcoat, and he had brought a helper with him, a man in a flat cap and a tweed overcoat, who swung an adze in his right hand, and a heavy hammer in his left. I drew Isabel's attention to the adze. We were gratified to see when we were able to climb to the ground that *Truant's* bottom was as clean and as clear of weed as it had been when we painted her at Antibes. I approached the surveyor and his assistant in my most ingratiating manner, but they scarcely bothered to acknowledge my salutes. The surveyor borrowed the hammer and ran at the hull, striking it here and there, while the man in the cap worked with his adze, shaving away the paintwork and also the outer surface of the wood. When he tired of that he took long nails, hammered them into seams, and tore out caulking in straggling ribbons. We were utterly scandalised by these operations. "Please, please tell them to stop," Isabel kept saying to me. The surveyor climbed on deck. He called down to me that he must have all the cabin floors lifted. I obeyed swiftly, fearing that if there was any delay they would attack the floors with their adze. A little later the man from Russia tugged my sleeve. "A man is approaching in a very beautiful car, driven by a chauffeur," he said. "Could this man be the general?" I hurried to the gate of the yard. The general, healthy and smiling, bustled through the gate and paused to look at *Truant*, bow-on, slightly below us, and with the sea behind her.

"What a lovely shape!" he said. I remembered that our first comment when we saw *Truant* on dry land had been: "It looks like a barge."

For all their ferocity, the surveyor and his assistant could only find certain small things that would have to be done. The propeller shafts required re-bushing, they suggested a certain amount of caulking below the waterline, the rivets of one rudder-pintle had worked a little loose. *Truant* was sold.

I exchanged some tins of meat for two sacks of wood, and lit a big fire in the saloon. When you have become accustomed to living in a boat on the sea it is a penance to live in it on dry land; everything is at a strange angle, and the absence of the normal movements and sounds gives a lugubrious impression. You are ashamed to use the boat for shelter, feeling like the arctic hunter who slashes open the body of a walrus, and sleeps inside the hulk that its dispersing warmth may protect him against the blizzard. Again, many of such comforts and conveniences as a boat offers depend on the water which is its element, and which can be pumped in or out. I was up before dawn to dump our rubbish, and I lit the heating stove while Isabel was preparing our breakfast. There was a fine view of the sea, with well-lit naval ships passing the bay. Closer inshore many caiques were anchored, most of them with riding lights. An old woman on the Italian hulk beside us begged for clothing. She stood on the rusty deck plates, a lantern held level with her head, and cried out odd words of Italian. "Later," I told her. "Later."

"No. Now! Now!"

"We have no clothes to spare, but we can give you some food."

"Just a few clothes. Some shirts and woollen things . . ." she pleaded, stretching out her free hand towards us. When it got light I went on deck and she was still standing there. She had extinguished the lantern and set it on the deck at her feet. Isabel had given me several tins of food for her.

"Can you catch the tins," I asked her. "Otherwise I must negotiate two ladders, and I am already pressed for time." She did not answer, so I threw them across to her, singly. She caught them remarkably neatly.

"More!" she said.

"We have no more, I'm sorry."

"Now the clothes."

"We have no clothes to spare."

She did not move, except that when one of the small boys who scuffled about the deck came near her to look at the tins which lay at her feet, she would hit out savagely. The packing-case had become so heavy that I could think of no safe means of lowering it from the deck to the ground, some eighteen feet below, except to unpack the contents, lower the case empty, and repack on the ground. The old woman saw what I was about. The first articles that I took out did not interest her. A typewriter, some large books, a shotgun. But when I lifted out the sheets and blankets and towels I had to shut my ears to her moans. I lowered the empty packing-case on the port side, so that it was hidden from the deck of the Italian hulk. But while I was repacking it on the ground the old woman came creeping round *Truant's* stern and approached, stopping within about ten feet and keeping up a continuous, dribbling moan. She accepted cigarettes and a bar of chocolate from me, stuffing them into the bosom of her dress. She wore an Army blanket round her shoulders as a shawl, and her feet were bare. I looked at her, from time to time, wondering what kind of women she had been, but I could see no relics of beauty or of youth or middle age on her seamed face. Her moans and her dribbling mouth made me feel guilty. I hurried with the packing and closing of the case.

Isabel appeared on deck, an unfamiliar figure in town clothes and high shoes. "The truck should be here any minute," she said. "I've laid out your clothes and the packing's all done." I was still in the cabin when she called: "Here's the truck." The general had sent his butler to look after the boat until a yacht hand could arrive to take over. The butler was a little bewildered by it all. I showed him how to operate the stove, the cookers, the refrigerator, the fresh-water pump, and how to open and lock the hatches and the wheelhouse doors. He asked me to show him how the fire-extinguishers worked.

Isabel climbed in beside the driver but I chose to sit beside our luggage in the back of the hooded truck, to forestall the thieves who are ready in Athens to board any vehicle which may be slowed or halted in the traffic.

So as we negotiated the rough ground between the slipways I sat looking backwards as though out of the opening of a tent during an earthquake. That was the last I saw of *Truant*. The butler stood on deck, yawning, and glancing without enthusiasm at his immediate surroundings.

THE END